1-19-5c

Wayne
CR4529
Stevens
Chivalry and knighthood in
Scotland, 1424-1513
62344766

Chivalry and Knighthood in Scotland, 1424–1513

For decades, the study of Scotland in the fifteenth century has focused on the complex relationships between crown and magnates. However, the importance of the chivalric ideal to the Scottish knightly class has never been explored and the use of chivalry as a political tool by the Stewart kings has been overlooked by scholars. This is the first work to address these themes. The book considers how chivalry was interpreted in fifteenth-century Scotland and how it compared with European ideas of chivalry; the responsibilities of knighthood in this period and the impact that this had on Scottish political life; the chivalric literature of the fifteenth century; the relevance of the Christian components of chivalric culture; and the use of chivalry by the increasingly powerful Scottish crown. The book also uncovers and investigates a variety of tournaments held in Scotland by the Stewart kings. This is a crucial work for those interested in the manifestations of chivalric culture at the close of the Middle Ages, in a kingdom beginning to make its mark amongst the prominent and fashionable European courts.

KATIE STEVENSON is a teaching fellow in the Department of Scottish History, University of St Andrews

Chivalry and Knighthood in Scotland, 1424–1513

Katie Stevenson

THE BOYDELL PRESS

© Katie Stevenson 2006

All Rights Reserved. Except as permitted under current legislation no part of this work may be photocopied, stored in a retrieval system, published, performed in public, adapted, broadcast, transmitted, recorded or reproduced in any form or by any means, without the prior permission of the copyright owner

The right of Katie Stevenson to be identified as the author of this work has been asserted in accordance with sections 77 and 78 of the Copyright, Designs and Patents Act 1988

First published 2006
The Boydell Press, Woodbridge

ISBN 1 84383 192 9

The Boydell Press is an imprint of Boydell & Brewer Ltd
PO Box 9, Woodbridge, Suffolk IP12 3DF, UK
and of Boydell & Brewer Inc.
668 Mt Hope Avenue, Rochester, NY 14620, USA
website: www.boydellandbrewer.com

A CIP catalogue record for this book is available
from the British Library

Printed in Great Britain by
Cambridge University Press, England

CONTENTS

Acknowledgements		vii
Abbreviations		viii
1	Introduction: Chivalry in Scotland	1
2	Knighthood in Scotland	13
3	The Bestowal of Knighthood and the Dubbing Ceremony	41
4	Scottish Tournaments	63
5	Scottish Knights and the Display of Piety	103
6	Chivalry in Scottish Literature	131
7	The Crown's Use of Chivalry	170
Bibliography		193
Index		213

ACKNOWLEDGEMENTS

Many people have contributed to this book, both in its current form and when it was a bulky and unburnished doctoral thesis. Some contributed to the ideas contained within, others more personally.

Dr Steve Boardman, Dr Julian Goodare and, more recently, Dr Roger Mason deserve my greatest thanks, for tirelessly commenting upon this work. The community researching Scottish history at the University of Edinburgh provided a forum for discussion of many of my ideas, and although I cannot thank each member of that affinity individually, this book owes a lot to the productive and encouraging environment they provided.

Of course, my friends and family scattered across the world have also played their roles – some through proof-reading drafts, others by making sure I was keeping a balance between work and play. Special thanks should go to my sister Dr Larissa Stevenson and my partner Dr Gordon Pentland.

No work of this nature can be produced without significant financial assistance and I would like to acknowledge the Scouloudi Foundation, through the Institute of Historical Research, University of London, for their contribution to the costs of the research for this book. My deepest gratitude, however, goes to my parents, Dr James and Mrs Jennifer Stevenson, whose financial contribution to this project from its inception as a doctoral thesis has been considerable. I hope that this book demonstrates my appreciation.

Of course, none of the above share any responsibility for the views, or the possible errors, contained herein.

ABBREVIATIONS

A.B. Ill.	*Illustrations of the Topography and Antiquities of the Shires of Aberdeen and Banff*, Spalding Club (Aberdeen, 1847–69)
Abdn. Counc.	*Extracts from the Council Register of the Burgh of Aberdeen, 1398–1570*, Spalding Club (Aberdeen, 1844)
Abdn. Reg.	*Registrum Episcopatus Aberdonensis*, Maitland Club (Edinburgh, 1845)
ADA	Thomas Thomson (ed.), *The Acts of the Lords of Auditors of Causes and Complaints* (Edinburgh, 1839)
ADC	Thomas Thomson (ed.), *The Acts of the Lords of Council in Civil Causes* (Edinburgh, 1839)
APS	Thomas Thomson and C. Innes (eds), *The Acts of the Parliaments of Scotland* (Edinburgh, 1814–75)
Bannatyne Misc.	*The Bannatyne Miscellany, Bannatyne Club* (Edinburgh, 1827–55)
Barbour, Bruce	John Barbour, *The Bruce*, A.A.M. Duncan (ed.) (Edinburgh, 1997)
BL	British Library
Black Book of Taymouth	*The Black Book of Taymouth with Other Papers from the Breadalbane Charter Room* (Edinburgh, 1855)
Blind Harry, Wallace	*The Actis and Deidis of the Illustere and Vailyeand Campioun Schir William Wallace, Knicht of Ellerslie*, STS (Edinburgh & London, 1889)
Buchanan, History	George Buchanan, *The History of Scotland*, J. Aikman (trans) (Glasgow & Edinburgh, 1827–29)
Cal. Scot. Supp., I.	E.R. Lindsay and A. I. Cameron (eds), *Calendar of Scottish Supplications to Rome 1418–1422*, SHS (Edinburgh, 1934)
Calendar of State Papers (Milan)	Allen B. Hinds (ed.), *Calendar of Papers and Manuscripts, existing in the Archives and Collections of Milan* (London, 1912)
Cawdor Bk.	C. Innes (ed.), *The Book of the Thanes of Cawdor: A Series of Papers Selected from the Charter Rooms at Cawdor, 1236–1742* (Edinburgh, 1869)
CDS	J. Bain (ed.), *Calendar of Documents relating to Scotland A.D. 1108–1526* (Edinburgh, 1881–88)
Chron. Auchinleck	Thomas Thomson (ed.), *The Auchinleck Chronicle, ane Schort Memoriale of the Scottis Corniklis for Addicioun* (Edinburgh, 1819/1877)

ABBREVIATIONS

Chron. Bower	Walter Bower, *Scotichronicon*, D.E.R. Watt (ed.) (Aberdeen, 1993–98)
Chron. Extracta	W. Barclay and D.D. Turnbull (eds), *Extracta e Variis Cronicis Scocie: From the Ancient Manuscript in the Advocates Library at Edinburgh*, Abbotsford Club (Edinburgh, 1842)
Chron. Fordun	W.F. Skene (ed.), *Johannis de Fordun, Chronica Gentis Scotorum* (Edinburgh, 1871–72)
Chron. Pluscarden	F.J.H. Skene (ed.), *Liber Pluscardensis* (Edinburgh, 1877–80)
Chron. Wyntoun	Andrew Wyntoun, *The Original Chronicle of Andrew of Wyntoun, Printed on Parallel Pages from the Cottonian and Wemyss MS*, F.J. Amours (ed.), STS (Edinburgh & London, 1903–14)
CPL	W.H. Bliss *et al.* (eds), *Calendar of Entries in the Papal Registers relating to Great Britain and Ireland: Papal Letters* (London, 1921)
Edin. Chrs.	*Charters and other Documents relating to the City of Edinburgh AD 1143–1540*, SBRS (Edinburgh, 1871)
Edin. Recs.	*Extracts from the Records of the Burgh of Edinburgh AD 1403–1528*, SBRS (Edinburgh, 1869)
ER	J. Stuart *et al.* (eds), *The Exchequer Rolls of Scotland* (Edinburgh, 1878–1908)
Foedera	Thomas Rymer (ed.), *Foedera, Conventiones, Litterae etc. Cuiuscunque Generis Acta Publica* (London, 1816–69)
Fraser, *Caerlaverock*	William Fraser, *The Book of Caerlaverock* (Edinburgh, 1873)
Fraser, *Douglas*	William Fraser, *The Douglas Book* (Edinburgh, 1885)
Fraser, *Lennox*	William Fraser, *The Lennox* (Edinburgh, 1874)
Fraser, *Maxwells*	William Fraser, *Memoirs of the Maxwells of Pollock* (Edinburgh, 1863)
Fraser, *Melville*	William Fraser, *The Melvilles Earls of Melville and Leslies Earls of Leven* (Edinburgh, 1890)
Fraser, *Menteith*	William Fraser, *The Red Book of Menteith* (Edinburgh, 1880)
Froissart, *Chronicles*	Jean Froissart, *Chronicles*, Geoffrey Brereton (ed.) (London, 1978)
HBC	E.B. Fryde, D.E. Greenway, S. Porter, I. Roy (eds), *Handbook of British Chronology*, third edition (London, 1986)
Highland Papers	J.R.N. Macphail (ed.), *Highland Papers*, SHS (Edinburgh, 1914–34)
HMC	*Reports of the Royal Commission on Historical Manuscripts* (London, 1870–)
Inchcolm Chrs.	D.E. Easson and Angus MacDonald (eds), *Charters of the Abbey of Inchcolm*, SHS (Edinburgh, 1938)
IR	*Innes Review*
James IV Letters	R.L. Mackie (ed.), *The Letters of James the Fourth 1505–13*, SHS (Edinburgh, 1953)

ABBREVIATIONS

JR	Juridical Review
Lesley, De Origine	John Lesley, De Origine, Moribus et Rebus Gestis Scotorum Libri Decem (Rome, 1578)
Lesley, History	John Lesley, The History of Scotland from the Death of King James I in the Year 1436 to the Year 1561, Bannatyne Club (Edinburgh, 1830)
Letters and Papers of Henry VIII	R.H. Brodie (ed.), Letters and Papers, Foreign and Domestic of the Reign of Henry VIII, Preserved in the Public Record Office, the British Museum and Elsewhere (London, 1920)
Midl. Chrs.	Charters of the Hospital of Soltre, of Trinity College, Edinburgh, and Other Collegiate Churches in Mid-Lothian, Bannatyne Club (Edinburgh, 1861)
Mort. Reg.	Registrum Honoris de Morton, Bannatyne Club (Edinburgh, 1853)
NA	National Archives, London
NAS	National Archives of Scotland
NLS	National Library of Scotland
Orkney Recs.	Joseph Storer Clouston (ed.), Records of the Earldom of Orkney, SHS (Edinburgh, 1914)
Orkney-Shetland Recs.	Alfred W. Johnston and Amy Johnston (eds), Orkney and Shetland Records (London, 1907–13)
Pinkerton, History	John Pinkerton, The History of Scotland from the Accession of the House of Stuart to that of Mary, with Appendixes of Original Papers (London, 1797)
Pitcairn, Trials	Robert Pitcairn (ed.), Ancient Criminal Trials in Scotland from 1488 to 1624 (Edinburgh, 1833)
Pitscottie, Historie	Robert Lindsay of Pitscottie, The Historie and Cronicles of Scotland from the Slauchter of King James the First to the Ane Thousande Fyve Hundreith Thrie Scoir Fiftein Zeir, STS (Edinburgh & London, 1899–1911)
Prot. Bk. Foular	W.Macleod and M. Wood (eds), Protocol Book of John Fouglas 1501–28, SRS (Edinburgh, 1930–53)
Prot. Bk. Young	Gordon Donaldson (ed.), Protocol Book of James Young 1485–1515, SRS (Edinburgh, 1952)
PSAS	Proceedings of the Society of Antiquaries of Scotland
RMS	J.M. Thomson et al. (eds), Registrum Magni Sigili Regum Scotorum (Edinburgh, 1882–1914)
Rot. Scot.	D. Macpherson et al. (eds), Rotuli Scotiae in Turri Londinensi et in Domo Capitulari Westmonasteriensi Asservati (London, 1814–19)
RSS	M. Livingstone et al. (eds), Registrum Secreti Sigili Regum Scotorum (Edinburgh, 1908–)
SBRS	Scottish Burgh Records Society
SHR	Scottish Historical Review

ABBREVIATIONS

SHS	Scottish History Society
SHS Misc.	*The Miscellany of the Scottish History Society* (SHS, 1893).
SP	J. Balfour Paul (ed.), *The Scots Peerage* (Edinburgh, 1904–14)
Spalding Misc.	*Miscellany of the Spalding Club*, Spalding Club (Aberdeen, 1841–52)
SRS	Scottish Record Society
St A Cop.	James Houston Baxter (ed.), *Copiale Prioratus Sanctiandree: The Letter-Book of James Haldenstone, Prior of St Andrews (1418–1443)* (Oxford, 1930)
St Giles Reg	*Registrum Cartarum Ecclesie Sancti Egidii de Edinburgh*, Bannatyne Club (Edinburgh, 1859)
STS	Scottish Text Society
TA	T. Dickson and J. Balfour Paul (eds), *Accounts of the Lord High Treasurer of Scotland* (Edinburgh, 1877–1916)

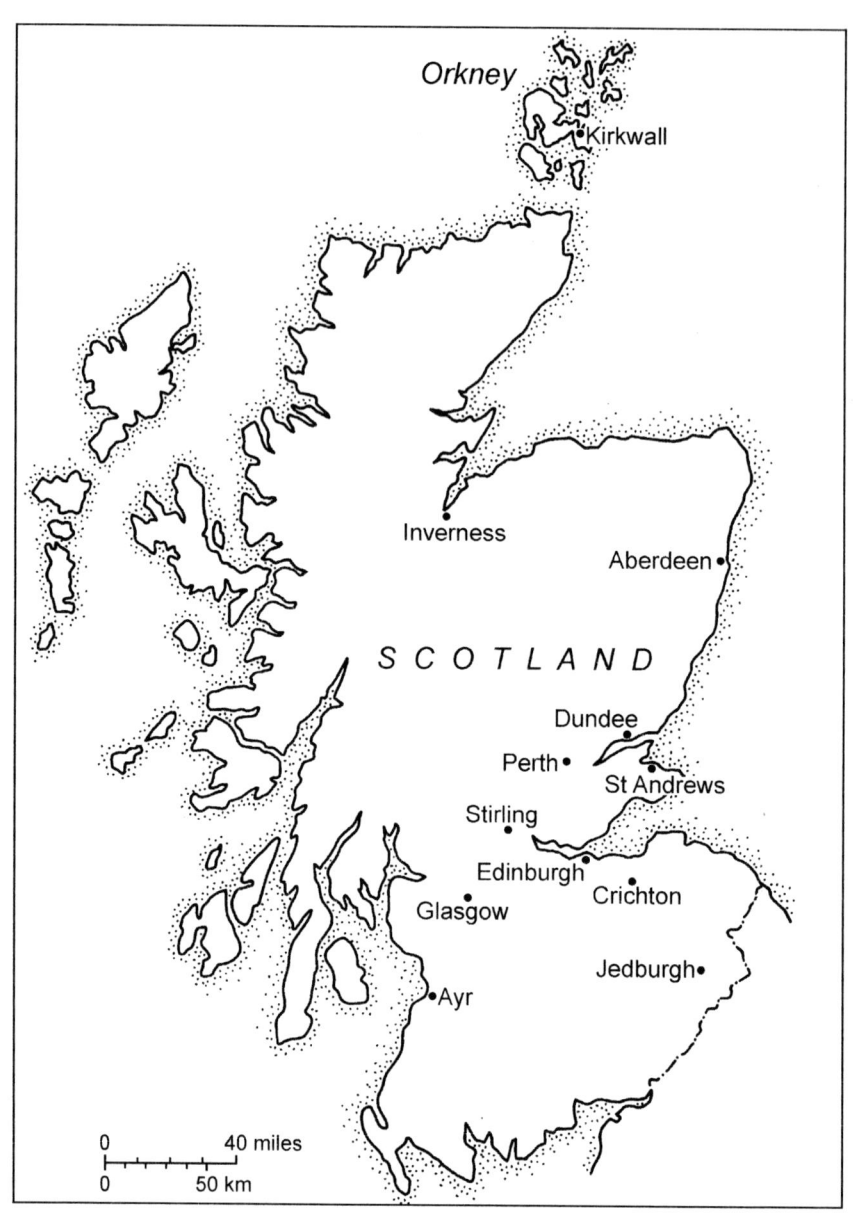

Scotland, showing places of significance in the period

CHAPTER ONE

Introduction: Chivalry in Scotland

Chivalry and knighthood have been popular areas of study amongst scholars for decades, but in Scotland little attention has been paid to these themes. With the notoriously difficult records which Scottish history has to offer, at first glance it appeared that Scottish nobles may not have engaged with the chivalric world we are familiar with in France or England. Yet some indicators, such as Scottish translations of chivalric literature, suggest that Scottish knights did participate fully in chivalric culture. Indeed, they engaged in a wide variety of displays of chivalry and subscribed to the ethos of knighthood held within the chivalric codes of conduct. Chivalry was a prominent ideology influencing social and political relationships, and knighthood was a crucial component of Scottish noble society, both in terms of war-making and public duty. This book redresses the gap in knowledge and explores the features of knighthood and chivalry in Scotland. As such, it proves that the Scottish nobility were not at the fringes of the chivalric world, but promoted and participated fully in chivalry in Scotland and in Europe.

Some of these themes have been tackled in recent work by Michael Penman. Penman's focus on David II's reign (1329–71) makes it clear that in the fourteenth century the chivalric ideal was alive and well, both at the royal court and amongst the nobility. David II's chivalry was noted by contemporary commentators, and he clearly enjoyed the outward display of status and grandeur it encouraged.[1] Penman suggests that the king was seriously influenced by Edward III when he was held in English captivity.[2] David II's reign influenced the history and tradition passed down to the knights of fifteenth-century Scotland. Whereas Robert I had simply embodied the qualities of the heroic, knightly king, David II used the chivalric ideal in such a way that he could patronise his knights and ensure their service and loyalty to the crown.[3] Respites in Anglo-Scottish warfare enabled large contingents to focus their military desires on fighting against Islam and defending the Christian faith. Crusading enjoyed a renaissance in popularity, ensuring that it became entrenched in the traditions of Scottish chivalry. David's successors Robert II and Robert III did not patronise these ideals in the same way: although they

---

[1] See for example *Chron. Wyntoun*, VI, pp. 168, 244.
[2] Michael Penman, *David II, 1329–71* (East Linton, 2004), pp. 150–1, 434.
[3] *Ibid.*, p. 201.

were part of the chivalric community, they did not influence the practice of chivalry. It was not until James I had spent a considerable portion of his life in English captivity under the influence of Henry IV and Henry V that a chivalric ethos that was directed by the crown returned to Scotland with any force.

Scotland in the fifteenth century has been the subject of much attention over the past few decades as historians have unravelled the tensions and developments during this period. It was a century characterised by close and fluctuating crown-magnate relations and long periods of royal minorities and guardianships. Nobles, whose first loyalty was ideally to the king, often demonstrated an allegiance to their kin that transcended crown bonds. Yet the power which derived from a prominent position at court was immense. Status was an important part of fifteenth-century society and much time was devoted to ensuring that station and place were maintained and emphasised, through dress, style of living, marriage, property, and proximity to the royal court. The chivalric ideal was also part of the desire for social exclusivity, and nobles sought to subscribe to chivalric values in order to keep knighthood in their possession. Tensions, of course, existed between the nobility and newly wealthy, upwardly mobile merchants who sought the privilege the nobility enjoyed. Yet the fifteenth century was still very much a 'medieval' period – kingship was executed along medieval lines, with patronage and service central to the functioning of government. The king was not a figurehead, but the leader of his kingdom with real power and authority over decisions ranging from the distribution of land among his nobility to the waging of warfare. Yet this was an exciting period in Scotland, where these medieval ideas were gradually fused with the new Renaissance ideas being imported from European courts.

The relevance of chivalry to fifteenth-century society has long been questioned by scholars who view this time as a key period of change. For many historians, post-crusading knightly society was only paying tribute to ideals that were no longer relevant and the nobility was desperately seeking a new ethos to which to subscribe. This has traditionally been viewed as the period that allowed for the significant changes influenced by humanists. The Huizinga school of thought put forward the idea that 'traditional' chivalry, that is, chivalry based on romantic notions of the mythical court of King Arthur, declined across the fifteenth century and was replaced by more prosaic ideals for contemporary knights. Huizinga argued that the ideals of chivalry were furthest removed from the realities of knighthood in the fifteenth century and does not consider that these questions may have been raised and addressed by contemporaries.[4] Nevertheless, Malcolm Vale suggests that it is doubtful whether

---

[4] Johan Huizinga, *The Waning of the Middle Ages: A Study of the Forms of Life, Thought, and Art in France and the Netherlands in the Fourteenth and Fifteenth Centuries*, Fritz Hopman (trans) (Harmondsworth, 1972), esp. p. 65. Although Huizinga personally authorised Hopman's English translation, and collaborated with him to produce this new variant version of the book, a recent translation from his original Dutch has been published, claiming to be more

knighthood ever conformed to chivalry as a guide to social behaviour and an ethical code, thereby suggesting that it was always just an ideal for knights to aspire towards.[5] Maurice Keen, on the other hand, disagrees with Vale's stance and argues that chivalry 'was at once a cultural and a social phenomenon, which retained its vigour because it remained relevant to the social and political realities of the time.'[6] Here Keen recognised the possibilities for development of the chivalric ideal and, as such, allowed for a different 'chivalry' to emerge in the fifteenth century. Yet the questions remain, what did chivalry mean in fifteenth-century Scotland, how was it practised and how did it affect knightly society? Moreover, given that Scotland's knightly community was led by the king, what was the crown's relationship with chivalry?

Still, chivalry remains an elusive concept. No entirely adequate or precise definition has yet been achieved, as it is an ideal with moving boundaries and difficult abstractions.[7] Maurice Keen's work, however, provides the most useful model, proposing a flexible definition of chivalry.

> While recognising that a word so tonal and imprecise can never be pinned down within precise limits of meaning, we are now a great deal nearer to being able to suggest lines of definition that will do for working purposes [...] chivalry may be described as an ethos in which martial, aristocratic and Christian elements were fused together. I say fused, partly because the compound seems to be something new and whole in its own right, partly because it is clearly so difficult to completely separate the elements in it.[8]

Keen argues that whilst one component may be more prominent in any given situation, the others were never completely absent, and that chivalry was 'a way of life in which we can discern these three essential facets, the military, the noble, and the religious; but a way of life is a complex thing, like a living organism; we have only the beginnings of a definition, and there is plenty left to explore.'[9] Keen certainly intended his work to be a launching pad for other studies on chivalry and knighthood, but his work is so thorough and convincing that historians are no longer searching for an alternative or more accurate

---

accurate in reproducing Huizinga's original text. See John Huizinga, *The Autumn of the Middle Ages*, Rodney J. Payton and Ulrich Mammitzsch (trans) (Chicago, 1996). See also Raymond Lincoln Kilgour, *The Decline of Chivalry As Shown in the French Literature of the Late Middle Ages* (Harvard, 1937), and Arthur B. Ferguson, *The Indian Summer of English Chivalry: Studies in the Decline and Transformation of Chivalric Idealism* (London, 1960), works which enlarged on Huizinga's thesis.

[5] Malcolm Vale, *War and Chivalry: Warfare and Aristocratic Culture in England, France and Burgundy at the End of the Middle Ages* (London, 1981), p. 5.
[6] Maurice Keen, *Chivalry* (New Haven & London, 1984), p. 219.
[7] See J. du Quesnay Adams, 'Modern Views of Chivalry, 1884–1984', in H. Chickering and T.H. Seiler (eds), *The Study of Chivalry* (Kalamazoo, 1988), pp. 41–89, for an example of the difficulties in pinning down a precise definition of chivalry.
[8] Keen, *Chivalry*, p. 16.
[9] *Ibid.*, p. 17.

definition of chivalry. Generally scholars have been satisfied with applying Keen's definition to their own areas of study. For example, Richard Kaeuper's recent work defined chivalry in very similar terms, adding only that courtly love was an essential element.[10] Indeed, Keen's definition is highly useful and this book will not proffer a significant alternative to it. Instead it will examine the three elements of chivalry he emphasises within the context of late-medieval Scottish society.

Research on chivalry and knighthood by Scottish historians has made limited use of Keen's ideas. Alan Macquarrie's *Scotland and the Crusades*, for instance, looks at a particular type of knightly culture that had a diminished relevance in the fifteenth and sixteenth centuries.[11] However, contributions on the wider impact of chivalric ideals in Scotland have been more forthcoming. In 1992 Roger Mason pointed out that

> although chivalric ideas constituted the dominant secular value system throughout later medieval Europe, their importance in shaping the outlook and aspirations of contemporary Scots has never been explored. Scottish historians have tended simply to dismiss chivalry as so much rarefied idealism with no purchase on social reality.[12]

Mason laments that a poor regard for the impact of chivalry on Scottish society has meant that no work has been undertaken to determine how the chivalric code operated in the kin-based and localised society of Scotland. He also sees a crucial distinction between the relationship of an individual to local powers and their relationship to the crown, although 'in both such contexts, the martial values of the chivalric code had a lot to offer a highly militarised and honour conscious society.'[13] This book encompasses this distinction and thus embarks on the first stage in understanding how chivalry functioned in Scotland, by giving definition to the role of the knight under royal patronage, the relationship between king and chivalry, and between knighthood and royal authority.

Roger Mason also addressed aspects of the chivalric code in Scotland in relation to its impact on national identity. He argued that national identity in the fifteenth century was defined and sustained through the manipulation of a usable past, that is the development of a Scottish '*mythomoteur*' which was 'capable of explaining the community to itself (and others) by lending meaning and purpose to the particular complex of myths, memories, values

---

[10] Richard W. Kaeuper, *Chivalry and Violence in Medieval Europe* (Oxford, 1999), p. 302.
[11] Alan Macquarrie, *Scotland and the Crusades, 1095–1560* (Edinburgh, 1985), esp. chapter 5, 'The Long Decline, 1410–1472', and chapter 6, 'Castles in the Air, 1472–c.1560'.
[12] Roger Mason, 'Chivalry and Citizenship: Aspects of National Identity in Renaissance Scotland', in Roger Mason and Norman Macdougall (eds), *People and Power in Scotland: Essays in Honour of T.C. Smout* (Edinburgh, 1992), p. 58, particularly at note 37, where Mason points out that Ranald Nicholson treated chivalry dismissively and that Alexander Grant barely mentioned it at all. See Ranald Nicholson, *Scotland: The Later Middle Ages* (Edinburgh, 1974) and Alexander Grant, *Independence and Nationhood: Scotland 1306–1469* (London, 1984).
[13] Mason, 'Chivalry and Citizenship', p. 58.

INTRODUCTION: CHIVALRY IN SCOTLAND

and symbols from which it derives its individuality'.[14] Mason sees this national identity as 'essentially martial and chivalric in character' and argues that it is worth viewing the 'Scottish *mythomoteur* as a domestic equivalent of the great historical mythologies of chivalry [. . .] which exemplified the values of Europe's militarised élites more generally.'[15] In his view, John Barbour's fourteenth-century epic poem, *The Bruce*, is the prime example of the creation of a Scottish national identity at work. Mason considers that Barbour (c.1330–95), archdeacon of Aberdeen, combined the codes of chivalry with the cause of freedom, brought together to instruct and inspire the knights of Scotland.[16] However, Carol Edington warns that

> the fusion of chivalric and national – not to say nationalistic – ideas was not as straightforward as has sometimes been assumed, and any examination of chivalric heroes raises important questions concerning the layered nature of perceived loyalties in medieval society.[17]

Mason's conclusion that Scottish versions of chivalric literature, such as *The Buik of the Most Noble and Valiant Conqueror Alexander the Grit* and *Lancelot of the Laik*, indicated that 'the Scots participated fully in this cosmopolitan chivalric culture' is certainly a pertinent point and one which will be further explored in this book.[18]

Recently, Carol Edington also related national identity to the chivalric ideal, suggesting that centuries of war with England had 'not only coloured accounts of the distant past, [but] they also provided an important corpus of material which reinforced the links between traditionally knightly ideals and Scotland's national history.'[19] Edington suggests that these wars conflated nationalistic and chivalric ideologies, but traditional chivalric assumptions still existed alongside this and often overrode patriotic considerations. Alastair J. MacDonald, on the other hand, hints that it was the pursuit of territorial and political power, particularly in the Scottish borders in the late fourteenth century, that proved a more important ambition in making war than nationalistic or chivalric motivations. However, he emphasised that chivalry played a major contributory role in motivating border wars, as did patriotism. MacDonald also addressed the problems of defining chivalry in Scotland, to a lesser extent. He suggests that

---

[14] *Ibid.*, p. 51.
[15] *Ibid.*, p. 57.
[16] *Ibid.*, p. 58.
[17] Carol Edington, 'Paragons and Patriots: National Identity and the Chivalric Ideal in Late-Medieval Scotland', in Dauvit Broun, R.J. Finlay and Michael Lynch (eds), *Image and Identity: The Making and Re-making of Scotland Through the Ages* (Edinburgh, 1998), p. 70.
[18] Mason, 'Chivalry and Citizenship', p. 57; Graeme Ritchie (ed.), *The Buik of the Most Noble and Valiant Conquerour Alexander the Grit by John Barbour, Archdeacon of Aberdeen*, 4 vols, STS (Edinburgh, 1925); Margaret Muriel Gray (ed.), *Lancelot of the Laik from Cambridge University Library MS*, STS (Edinburgh, 1912).
[19] Carol Edington, 'Paragons and Patriots', p. 72.

two aspects of this are the apparent exclusivity of 'chivalry' as an influence on the knightly and upper classes and the nature of the chivalric code, which seems to have had a powerful influence, yet was little practised in all its rigour.[20]

He defines the Scottish chivalric ethos as predominantly 'the desire to attain glory and renown through military feats and the enjoyment of martial endeavour for its own sake.'[21] However, MacDonald's definition is restricted by his material, and a wider survey indicates that Scottish chivalry was not solely focused on martial pursuits.

Over the past few years, work by Alasdair A. MacDonald has considered in more detail the influence of chivalry on fifteenth-century Scottish society. MacDonald believes, quite rightly, that there was a rich chivalric culture in Scotland at this time. He argues that, amongst other key developments, a chivalric order of knighthood was founded by James III (1460–88), but this idea has recently been refuted.[22] In his latest study MacDonald discusses chivalry as a catalyst of cultural change, suggesting that the return to Scotland of James I in 1424, after eighteen years of exposure to both the English and French courts, entailed 'a high level of cultural awareness. Innovations were to be expected, and [. . .] the cultivation of chivalry was one such new departure.'[23] James I (1424–37) brought new ideas of the crown's responsibilities in the promotion of chivalric knighthood and MacDonald's argument highlights a turning point in Scottish kingship and crown administration. One of MacDonald's main suggestions is that the cultural influence upon Scotland did not stem exclusively from England and France as has been widely assumed, but was much derived from Burgundy, especially in the 'matter of chivalry'.[24] This is a critical point and MacDonald's thesis is compelling, especially given Scotland's economic and political ties with Bruges and Gelderland during the fifteenth century.[25] By pointing out that in the fifteenth century the royal court

---

[20] Alastair J. MacDonald, *Border Bloodshed: Scotland and England at War, 1369–1403* (East Linton, 2000), pp. 170, 178, 190.

[21] *Ibid.*, p. 178.

[22] Alasdair A. MacDonald, 'The Chapel of Restalrig: Royal Folly or Venerable Shrine?', in L.A.J.R. Houwen, A.A. MacDonald and S.L. Mapstone (eds), *A Palace in the Wild: Essays on Vernacular Culture and Humanism in Late-Medieval and Renaissance Scotland* (Peeters, 2000), p. 34; Alasdair A. MacDonald, 'Chivalry as a Catalyst of Cultural Change in Late-Medieval Scotland' in Rudolf Suntrup and Jan R. Veenstra (eds), *Tradition and Innovation in an Era of Change* (Frankfurt am Main & Oxford, 2001), p. 161; Katie Stevenson, 'The Unicorn, St Andrew and the Thistle: Was There an Order of Chivalry in Late Medieval Scotland?', *SHR* 83 (2004), pp. 3–22; K.C. Stevenson, 'Knighthood, Chivalry and the Crown in Fifteenth-Century Scotland, 1424–1513', (Ph.D., University of Edinburgh, 2003), ch. 6.

[23] MacDonald, 'Chivalry as a Catalyst of Cultural Change in Late-Medieval Scotland', p. 153.

[24] *Ibid.*, pp. 154, 157.

[25] For more on this see Alexander Stevenson, 'Medieval Scottish Associations with Bruges', in Terry Brotherstone and David Ditchburn (eds), *Freedom and Authority, Scotland c.1050–c.1650: Historical and Historiographical Essays Presented to Grant G. Simpson* (East Linton, 2000).

was not always the chivalric centre of Scottish society, MacDonald's work demonstrates that questions need to be asked about each individual king's relationship with chivalry.[26]

MacDonald also attempts to bring more coherence to the definition of Scottish chivalry. He regards late medieval chivalry as involving 'at least such key features of knightly conduct as respect for a generally shared code of honour, and prowess in deeds of arms.'[27] He argues that the development in the princely culture of fifteenth-century Burgundy meant that during these years 'chivalry came to be regarded much more as an inspiration, generation and expression of true nobility. Central to this notion is that the essence of true nobility was seen as stemming from virtue rather than any accident of birth, rank or fortune.'[28] Whilst not rejecting outright the religious component that Keen distinguished, MacDonald implies that it was the martial and noble aspects of chivalry which were most relevant to fifteenth-century Scottish knights. Indeed, it could be suggested that this interpretation of chivalry is much more appropriate to Scotland than Keen's general portrayal.

Nevertheless, Keen's definition does warrant further examination and evaluation in a Scottish context. The martial component he describes naturally relates to the knight's function as a warrior. Throughout the fifteenth century, Scottish knights were still engaged in warfare: in battles, sieges, military campaigns and the staged warfare of the tournament. All knights were expected to fulfil a martial function and there is no suggestion that any were exempt from fighting, except the elderly and infirm. Richard Kaeuper claims that, in the past, scholars have tended to over-emphasise the romantic and courtly aspects of chivalry:

> chivalry was not simply a code integrating generic individual society, not simply an ideal for relations between the sexes or a means of knocking off the rough warrior edges in preparation for the European gentleman to come. The bloody-minded side of the code [. . .] was the essence of chivalry. The knight was a warrior.[29]

Chroniclers like Walter Bower, abbot of Inchcolm (d. 1449), and poets like Blind Harry (c.1440–c.1493) took delight in recording and describing Scottish knights' activities in warfare. The prevalent theme is that the individual knight and his martial function were never far removed from each other. It was in their capacity as warriors that most knights upheld the ideals of chivalry and in warfare that the ideals of chivalry could most readily be applied.

---

[26] MacDonald, 'Chivalry as a Catalyst', p. 159. MacDonald's thesis builds on work by Sally Mapstone, who argued that the Scottish royal court was not the main centre for literary production and that non-royal patronage was common. See Sally Mapstone, 'Was There a Court Literature in Fifteenth-Century Scotland?', *Studies in Scottish Literature* 26 (1991), pp. 410–22.
[27] MacDonald, 'Chivalry as a Catalyst', p. 158.
[28] *Ibid.*, pp. 158–9.
[29] Kaeuper, *Chivalry and Violence*, p. 8.

Nobility was also an essential part of Scottish chivalry. On the Continent and in England during the twelfth century, warriors of low social status who held no land and who had no political power were called knights; the title of knight referred to their function as a fighter rather than to their social status.[30] In the first half of the thirteenth century, Frederick II ordained that a man who did not have men of knightly status in his ancestry should not be considered to be eligible for knighthood, and his chancellor, Peter de Vinea, stated that nobility was hereditary. Thus knighthood officially became a matter of blood, lineage and birth.[31] By the end of the thirteenth century, knighthood had come to signify warriors of high social status. Similarly, by this time squires had also acquired social rank, and the entitlement to hold such status was principally dependent upon a proven noble lineage.[32] Part of this development stemmed from higher demands upon men-at-arms, due to ever-increasing internal and international conflicts, which meant that a larger section of the general population became involved in warfare as armoured warriors. Thus, a clear-cut distinction between ordinary soldiers and knights became more crucial. Pressure applied by young men from newly wealthy families, who sought the social status that came with knighthood, also provoked a response from the nobility and as the desire to enter into knighthood became more widespread, the criteria for eligibility and acceptance became more stringent (therefore making knighthood even more attractive and desirable).[33] To a degree, this further fused nobility and knighthood, predominantly evident in a knight's public duties that he held as both a man of noble status and as a man of knightly status.[34] This trend not only occurred throughout the Continent and England, but also in Scotland, where it was well established by the fifteenth century that knighthood should only be granted to men of noble status.

By this time it was also generally accepted that knightly virtues were intrinsically inherited and acquired from the men with whom a boy was in direct contact, from his father to his wider community. A knight from an elevated background was expected to embody the qualities of his lineage and a nobleman was obliged to display proper knightly behaviour and honour his inheri-

---

[30] *Ibid.*, p. 189.
[31] Keen, *Chivalry*, p. 143.
[32] Richard Mortimer, 'Knights and Knighthood in Germany in the Central Middle Ages', in Christopher Harper-Bill and Ruth Harvey (eds), *The Ideals and Practice of Medieval Knighthood: Papers from the First and Second Strawberry Hill Conferences* (Woodbridge, 1986), pp. 96–8; Matthew Bennett, 'The Status of the Squire: the Northern Evidence', in Christopher Harper-Bill and Ruth Harvey (eds), *The Ideals and Practice of Medieval Knighthood: Papers from the First and Second Strawberry Hill Conferences* (Woodbridge, 1986), pp. 10–11; Keen, *Chivalry*, p. 143; Kaeuper, *Chivalry and Violence*, pp. 189–90.
[33] Grant, *Independence and Nationhood*, p. 121.
[34] Martin Aurell, 'The Western Nobility in the Late Middle Ages: A Survey of the Historiography and Some Prospects for New Research', in Anne J. Duggan (ed.), *Nobles and Nobility in Medieval Europe: Concepts, Origins, Transformations* (Woodbridge, 2000), p. 272.

tance.[35] As noble birth and knighthood were so closely linked, Elspeth Kennedy poses the question of how far the position and reputation achieved by a knight was dependent upon personal effort and vocation, as exemplified by his qualities and acquired skills, or simply by merit of his noble ancestry. Indeed it was generally accepted throughout works of chivalric literature that chivalric qualities were rooted in hereditary inheritance.[36] For example, the good Sir James Douglas (d. 1330) had an appropriate lineage, being born into a family of middle baronial rank, hence enabling his outstanding knightly career. *The Buke of the Ordre of Knychthede* endorsed this idea, stating that a knight should come of good lineage and must have sufficient wealth to support his rank.[37] Being born into a noble family was considered to be essential to a knight. However, there were notable exceptions and whilst distinguishing nobility based on measures of wealth was an essential part of its social construction, in reality the poorer noble or the wealthier burgess blurred the distinction which noble wealth was meant to make visible. Indeed, in some instances, proof of nobility became accepted through the family's style of living and its general reputation.[38] In Scotland, the Forresters of Corstorphine (near Edinburgh) proved this to be the case and rose from burgess status to knightly status very quickly by royal patronage.

Nobles' relationships with the crown were the essential foundation of the late medieval court. Many Scottish nobles held administrative positions within the royal household or government and those who had been dubbed by the king held most of these posts. Knights such as Sir Walter Ogilvy of Lintrathen, James I's treasurer, were welcomed into roles of high prestige, although positions such as Chancellor, Treasurer and Secretary were held almost exclusively by clerics until the second half of the fifteenth century.[39] The degree to which nobility and knighthood can be separated in these instances is, of course, problematic, as they were essential to each other.

---

[35] Matthew Bennett, 'Military Masculinity in England and Northern France, c.1050–c.1225', in D.M. Hadley (ed.), *Masculinity in Medieval Europe* (London & New York, 1999), p. 76.

[36] Elspeth Kennedy, 'The Quest for Identity and the Importance of Lineage in Thirteenth-Century French Prose Romance', in Christopher Harper-Bill and Ruth Harvey (eds), *The Ideals and Practice of Medieval Knighthood II: Papers from the Third Strawberry Hill Conference* (Woodbridge, 1988), p. 72; Kaeuper, *Chivalry and Violence*, p. 190.

[37] Sonja Väthjunker, 'A Study in the Career of Sir James Douglas' (Ph.D., University of Aberdeen, 1992), p. 27; Jonathan A. Glenn (ed.), *The Prose Works of Sir Gilbert Hay Volume III: 'The Buke of the Ordre of Knychthede' and 'The Buke of the Governaunce of Princis'*, STS (Edinburgh, 1993), p. 9.

[38] Richard Barber, *The Knight and Chivalry* (Woodbridge, 1995), p. 43.

[39] *HBC*, pp. 182–3, 187–8, 193; Athol L. Murray, 'The Procedure of the Scottish Exchequer in the early Sixteenth Century', *SHR* 40 (1961), pp. 89–117; Athol L. Murray, 'The Comptroller, 1425–1488', *SHR* 52 (1973), pp. 1–29; Peter J. Murray, 'The Lay Administrators of Church Lands in the 15th and 16th Centuries', *SHR* 74 (1995), pp. 26–44. For more on the positions held by lay nobles from James III's reign see A.L. Brown, 'The Scottish "Establishment" in the Later 15th Century', *JR* 23 (1978), pp. 89–105; Trevor M. Chalmers, 'The King's Council, Patronage, and the Governance of Scotland, 1460–1513' (Ph.D., University of Aberdeen, 1982), esp. pp. 127–31, 151, 333–4.

Indeed, the Scottish nobility was a small group and with social status being a requirement for granting of knighthood, consequently it could only be from amongst these men that a king chose his public officers. In his translation of key chivalric works in the mid-1450s, Sir Gilbert Hay stressed the idea of a knight's public responsibilities more than his original French sources had done. He made it perfectly clear that knights were public figures with public duties to perform. It was within the terms of a knight's responsibilities to his wider community that Hay attempted to reinterpret the values of the chivalric code. He suggested that knighthood was not meant solely to elevate an individual, but that knights were intended to serve the crown for the 'commoun prouffit'.[40] Other chivalric writers made similar emphases and in his fourteenth-century *Livre de chevalerie*, Geoffrey de Charny, a French knight, stressed the propriety of a king choosing his officers from amongst the knighthood.[41]

The relationship between knighted nobles and central authority has emerged as a theme in the works of some Scottish historians. Revisionists such as Jenny Wormald and Alexander Grant argue that the traditional interpretation of a weak crown made weaker by the irresponsible antics of anarchic feudal barons is a naïve view, and that Scotland's allegedly over mighty magnates were, in fact, engaged in a constructive and positive relationship with the crown. By the same token, the early Stewart kings were astute realists who recognised that a powerful nobility was an essential component of effective governance.[42] Roger Mason agrees with the Revisionists and argues that crown-magnate relations in fifteenth-century Scotland were, on the whole, co-operative rather than confrontational.[43] However, more recently Mason pointed out that 'post-Revisionists' see the Stewart monarchy 'as much more self-confident, aggressive and predatory than revisionist historians have generally allowed'.[44] Nobles were a crucial and dominant force in society through the variety of roles they undertook as masters, employers, householders, patrons, purveyors of justice, and holders of royal or public offices. They com-

---

[40] Glenn (ed.), *Buke of the Ordre of Knychthede*, pp. 18, 21; Mason, 'Chivalry and Citizenship', p. 58.
[41] Geoffrey de Charny, *'Livre de chevalerie'*, in K. de Lettenhove (ed.), *Oeuvres de Froissart* (Brussels, 1873), tome I, part III, discussed in Keen, *Chivalry*, p. 14.
[42] Mason, 'Chivalry and Citizenship', p. 70, n. 41; Jenny Wormald, *Lords and Men in Scotland: Bonds of Manrent, 1442–1603* (Edinburgh, 1985), p. 5; Jenny Wormald, 'Taming the Magnates?', in K.J. Stringer (ed.), *Essays on the Nobility of Medieval Scotland* (Edinburgh, 1985), pp. 270–1; Grant, *Independence and Nationhood*, esp. chs 6 and 7.
[43] Roger Mason, 'Kingship, Tyranny and the Right to Resist in Fifteenth Century Scotland', *SHR* 66 (1987), pp. 125–51; reprinted in Roger Mason, *Kingship and the Commonweal: Political Thought in Renaissance and Reformation Scotland* (East Linton, 1998), p. 8; see also Michael Hicks, *Bastard Feudalism* (London, 1995), p. 2.
[44] Roger A. Mason, 'This Realm of Scotland is an Empire? Imperial Ideas and Iconography in Early Renaissance Scotland', in Barbara E. Crawford (ed.), *Church, Chronicle and Learning in Medieval and Renaissance Scotland: Essays Presented to Donald Watt on the Occasion of the Completion of the Publication of Bower's* Scotichronicon (Edinburgh, 1999), pp. 73–4.

manded in war, took the lead in national politics and directed local government through the power they derived from the control of their men. The manpower at their disposal was secured through a range of different mechanisms and relationships: through service in their households, tenancy of their estates, and employment and payment for services.[45] Within most of these roles a nobleman's behaviour was theoretically regulated by his status as a knight.

The role of noblemen within crown politics has been the focus of much work by Scottish historians. Scholars including Roger Mason, Norman Macdougall and Alexander Grant have engaged in debate over whether the Scottish political community was held together by a cohesive force preventing it from disintegrating.[46] It is certainly an attractive view that there was a common ideology which encouraged aristocratic unity. Grant suggests the nobility were bound together by the 'fundamental principle that royal authority must not be flouted. If it was, that was ultimately treason.'[47] He asks:

> Can it be argued that the development of the principle of royal authority, when taken to its logical conclusion, threatened a counter-productive effect of the cohesiveness of the political community? I am not sure; but I do have a sense of two sets of political principles, the Crown's and the community's, running in parallel through the fifteenth century, and at times tending to collide.[48]

One cohesive factor may well have been chivalry, or its practical application through knighthood; binding knights and nobles to a common philosophy and a goal which, with its enshrined codes of conduct on and off the battlefield, provided a type of social (if not political) order.

Whilst the exploration so far suggests that Scottish chivalry broadly follows Keen's model, the Christian element was, in fact, far less apparent than the noble and martial aspects. In a differing model of chivalry, Huizinga suggested that the Christian element could never have been an integral aspect of chivalry:

> medieval thought did not permit ideal forms of noble life, independent of religion. For this reason piety and virtue have to be the essence of a knight's

---

[45] Hicks, *Bastard Feudalism*, pp. 2–3. For a discussion and definition of the nobility in fifteenth-century Scotland see Alexander Grant, 'The development of the Scottish peerage', *SHR* 57 (1978), pp. 1–27, where he describes a change, around 1450, in definition of levels of nobility, from earls, 'provincial lords', 'greater barons' and freeholders, to lords of parliament and lairds. See also Jenny Wormald, 'Lords and Lairds in Fifteenth-Century Scotland: Nobles and Gentry?' in Michael Jones (ed.), *Gentry and Lesser Nobility in Late Medieval Europe* (Gloucester & New York, 1986).
[46] Mason, *Kingship and the Commonweal*, p. 26; Alexander Grant, 'To the Medieval Foundations', *SHR* 73 (1994), p. 6; Norman Macdougall, 'Response: At the Medieval Bedrock', *SHR* 73 (1994), pp. 25–6. See also Michael H. Brown, 'Scotland Tamed? Kings and Magnates in Late Medieval Scotland: A Review of Recent Work', *IR* 45 (1994), pp. 120–46.
[47] Grant, 'To the Medieval Foundations', pp. 9–10.
[48] *Ibid.*, p. 11.

life. Chivalry, however, will always fall short of this ethical function. Its earthly origin draws it down.[49]

However, there was clearly an expectation that religion should play a central role in Scottish chivalry, with Sir Gilbert Hay's translated prose highlighting the proximity of knighthood to the defence of Christianity. Hay wrote in 1456:

> And as all thir proprieteis beforesaid pertenis till a knycht as to the nabilnes of his corps – Rycht sa is thare othir proprieteis pertenand to the saule [...] And forthy quhen a knycht has all strenthis and habiliteis yat appertenis to the corps – and has nocht thame yat appertentis to the saule – he is nocht verray knycht – bot is contrarious to the ordre and inymy of knychthede [...] ffor the principale caus of the ordre is to the manetenaunce of the cristyn faith.[50]

Whether Hay's motives were to encourage knights to behave in a more pious fashion, or to attempt to elevate knighthood beyond the aggressive and violent characteristics it naturally held, is difficult to ascertain. Hay's opinions may stand alone, but as he was a knight and not a cleric, his writings and thoughts remain significantly pertinent. Although pious crusading ideals had waned by this time and the Church played a lesser role in secular institutions such as knighthood (for example, within the dubbing ceremonies of which detail survives, the clergy and the Church were barely involved), religious aspects, which were inherent in society as a whole, cannot be divorced from chivalry.[51]

Keen's model, therefore, is generally a reasonable pattern to be applied to late-medieval Scottish knighthood. Chivalry was a set of ideals in which knights fundamentally believed and aspired towards. Scottish chivalry not only suggested appropriate codes of conduct, but also supported its martial function, promoted its elitism through emphasis on nobility and encouraged piety and model Christianity. However, this must be tested to establish how these chivalric ideals operated in practice, both in the field and under royal patronage. More importantly, what must be considered is whether chivalry regulated the way in which knights were recruited and behaved.

---

[49] Huizinga, *The Waning of the Middle Ages*, p. 67.
[50] Glenn (ed.), *Buke of the Ordre of Knychthede*, p. 17.
[51] See Keen, *Chivalry*, pp. 65, 76, for descriptions of thirteenth- and fourteenth-century examples of the Church's role in the dubbing ceremony.

CHAPTER TWO

Knighthood in Scotland

Knight was a title that indicated a precise function and social position in late-medieval society. By being dubbed, knights took on martial and other service obligations and agreed to uphold the codes of conduct implied by chivalric ideology. In his description of the development of knighthood, Richard Barber stated that 'the "knight" is a mounted warrior who enjoys a specific social status and a distinct ethos, *ésprit de corps*, mentality – call it what we will – which eventually blossoms into the wider culture of chivalry, and draws on literary and spiritual ideals.'[1] Being dubbed admitted a man to the fraternity of knighthood, but the exclusivity of knighthood and the associated prestige ensured its popularity for centuries. Across Europe knights held the same set of values, were dubbed in the same way, and organised themselves along similar lines. It is clear that they were part of an international 'club' and there is no question that in a meeting on an international battlefield, the opposing knights had more in common with each other than with the men-at-arms in their retinues. Extensive explorations of medieval knighthood have been undertaken, particularly focusing on England, France and Germany. Nevertheless, Scottish sources also reveal a great deal of information about knighthood and provide some interesting findings about the extent that knighthood and chivalry were embraced by the Scottish nobility. Indeed, we find that Scottish knights were very much part of the international society of knighthood, but they had their own set of peculiarities and obligations to the society in which they lived.

Eligibility for Knighthood

Although a great number of people from all social levels operated within knightly society, eligibility for knighthood was an entirely different matter. First and foremost a knight was expected to have a noble lineage and prove that he was directly descended from a line of knights. Contemporary Scottish commentators often reveal just how crucial this was. A papal supplication of 1420 claims that Alexander Lauder, who was 'alleged to be of knightly race', was exposed as a fraud because 'although he is a kinsman of sundry knights

[1] Barber, *Knight and Chivalry*, p. 4.

in the second and third degrees, [. . .] neither his grandfather nor his great-grandfather was a knight'.[2] Alexander had been given mandate of provision of the parish church of Ratho, near Edinburgh, and two ecclesiastical benefices from Benedict XIII before he was deposed. This was called into question, not only because he neglected to mention the value of the archdeaconry which he held, but also because his knightly heritage was falsely reported. Although the original enquiry doubted whether his claim was valid, Alexander was ultimately successful in his suit and the issue of his knightly background was not raised again.[3]

In the 1440s, the chronicler Walter Bower, abbot of Inchcolm, discussed the Scottish hero William Wallace's descent from a noble family. Bower attributed to him the qualities that a heroic knight should possess:

> he came from a distinguished family, with relatives who shone with knightly honour. His older brother called Andrew was a belted knight who held a patrimony of lands in keeping with his status, which he bequeathed to be held by his descendants.[4]

Bower's late fourteenth-century source, the *Gesta Annalia*, attached to John of Fordun's chronicle *Chronica Gentis Scotorum*, described a very different picture of Wallace's lineage. The *Gesta Annalia* wrote that amongst the earls and lords of the kingdom Wallace was looked upon as low-born, even though both his father and his elder brother were knights, and his brother's landed estate was large enough for his social station.[5] The chronicler gives no indication as to why the earls and lords thought that William was low-born, but he may have been hinting that Wallace was thought to be illegitimate.

In the 1420s, Andrew Wyntoun (d. 1426) had asserted that Wallace had a noble lineage, arguing that his father was a manly knight and his mother was a lady. Wyntoun thus sought to place emphasis on his birth within wedlock and the chronicler stressed that his elder brother was also a knight.[6] Later in the century, furthermore, any hint of illegitimacy had been carefully veiled. The anonymous chronicler of the *Book of Pluscarden*, who abridged Walter Bower's *Scotichronicon*, claimed that Wallace was the son of a noble knight and that his brother was a 'very distinguished and gallant knight'.[7] In the 1470s, Wallace's biographer, Blind Harry, wrote that Wallace was of worthy blood, his whole lineage was a true Scottish line, and that his father, Sir Malcolm

---

[2] *Cal. Scot. Supp.*, I, pp. 235–6.
[3] *Ibid.*, p. 290.
[4] *Chron. Bower*, book XI, 28.
[5] *Chron. Fordun*, vol. IV, p. 321. The emphasis that both Fordun and Bower place on Andrew Wallace's estates demonstrate how necessary land was to support the knightly status. See James E. Fraser, ' "A Swan from a Raven": William Wallace, Brucean Propaganda, and *Gesta Annalia* II', *SHR* 81 (2002), pp. 5–6, 19, for a discussion of English chroniclers' comments on Wallace's low-born status.
[6] *Chron. Wyntoun*, V, p. 299.
[7] *Chron. Pluscarden*, II, p. 72.

Wallace, was a 'full gentill knycht'.[8] These chroniclers make no mention of maternal lineage, either wishing to avoid the issue or indicating that only paternal inheritance was considered important by this time. Nevertheless, the descriptions of Wallace's lineage show that heredity was a prime concern with regard to eligibility for knighthood in the early fifteenth century.

Whilst it was generally accepted that only men of noble status could be knighted, there are some notable exceptions to this, such as the Forresters of Corstorphine and Thomas Todd. In cases like this, proof of nobility through the family's style of living and its general reputation could be enough to enter into lower-level noble society.[9] Landownership also increased social standing and brought with it the privileges of lower-status nobility. Certainly, entry into noble society via this route was not unheard of in the late Middle Ages. In England the Paston family rose via legal avenues from yeomen to knighthood in a few generations. In France, also, Jean Boutard did much the same in 1475, when he produced witnesses to swear that his family had always lived in a noble fashion and had served in the king's armies.[10] In Scotland these social moves had become possible during the fourteenth century. For example, burgesses could rise in social rank: William Chalmers went on a diplomatic mission in 1394 as a squire and Andrew Mercer was knighted some time prior to 1385. Chalmers and Mercer both held extensive landed possessions and thus their entry into the noble classes was assured, but it was through royal service that they had their final legitimisation for entry into knighthood. By the fifteenth century, descendants of wealthy burgesses could achieve high social positions. Sir John Forrester of Corstorphine, a prominent knight in James I's service, was a descendant of a wealthy burgess, and the family had managed over the course of a few generations to secure a privileged position in royal favour.[11] The Forresters' tombs at the Collegiate Church of Corstorphine in Edinburgh show effigies of three Forrester men, all dressed in full knightly armour and weaponry. Most Scottish secular effigies of this type show knights who achieved fame for themselves on the battlefield and who attained distinction in governmental duties, such as the Douglas effigies in Douglas, South Lanarkshire, or Sir Alexander Irvine of Drum in Aberdeen, and there is no doubt that the Forresters' self-promotion through the effigies served to further reinforce their relatively new knightly status.[12] This further

---

[8] Blind Harry, *Wallace*, I, 36. For more on this see R. James Goldstein, 'Blind Harry's Myth of Blood: The Ideological Closure of *The Wallace*', *Studies in Scottish Literature* 25 (1990), p. 74.
[9] Barber, *Knight and Chivalry*, p. 43.
[10] See Richard Barber (ed.), *The Pastons: A Family in the Wars of the Roses* (Harmondsworth, 1981); Barber, *Knight and Chivalry*, p. 43.
[11] *ER*, III, p. 119; Elizabeth Ewan, *Townlife in Fourteenth-Century Scotland* (Edinburgh, 1990), p. 134. By the fifteenth century the Forresters' reputation had made them suitable to enter into knighthood and Adam Forrester, John's father, was knighted in or before 1403, and John was knighted before 1404. *ER*, III, pp. 564, 622.
[12] Robert Brydell, 'The Monumental Effigies of Scotland from the Thirteenth to the Fifteenth Century', *PSAS* 29 (1894–95), pp. 334, 382; David Laing, 'The Forrester Monuments

secured their social position and ensured their family's place in knightly society for generations to come.

Whereas the Forresters' status may have derived from the large amount of land they acquired in the fourteenth century, this was not the case for all non-nobles who were knighted. For example, Thomas Todd held no land and had been a burgess of Edinburgh during James III's reign and from 1488 to 1489 he acted as Comptroller for James IV.[13] James IV (1488-1513) must have held Todd in considerable esteem, as from 1490 he was being styled as knight. At this point Todd entered James's service as a royal messenger, a role which he held for at least seven years.[14] Todd's dubbing indicates that new routes to knighthood had opened up by James IV's reign, possibly due to a burgeoning royal government and thus more areas in which a burgess could impress the king. Todd's status, nevertheless, was an individual privilege and honour rather than a permanent elevation for his family. Todd's increase in social position was not passed on to his son, also Thomas, who was recorded as simply an Edinburgh burgess in late 1506.[15] Nor did his other descendants benefit from a rise in status, although perhaps they did receive royal patronage: in 1527 William Todd, burgess of Edinburgh, was made Master Waxmaker to the King.[16] Sir Thomas Todd never completely abandoned his burghal interests and seems to have been involved in mercantile enterprise up until his death, owning a tenement in which other burgesses rented booths.[17] It would seem that Todd was part of a significant development in Scottish knighthood and his role in what would appear to be purely administrative duties indicates that the martial emphasis of the status was shifting. Indeed, Sir Thomas did not carry out the other duties of knighthood and was not involved in military service or even the knightly games of tournaments. Therefore, he must have been knighted as an individual honour for his administrative service to the crown or for his commercial and financial expertise.

The rise of the mercantile class certainly had an effect on knighthood and the nobility, as merchants competed with noble courtiers for administrative positions. A large number of burgesses managed to elevate their position to that of squire, although they most often remained unknighted.[18] The rank of

in the Church of Corstorphine', *PSAS* 11 (1876), pp. 353-62; Margaret Cochrane Scott, 'Dress in Scotland 1406-1460' (Ph.D., University of London, 1987), pp. 104, 108-11, 143-50.
[13] *ER*, IX, p. 511, X, pp. 21, 40, 58, 102; *Prot. Bk. Young*, no. 50; Murray, 'The Comptroller', p. 29.
[14] Norman Macdougall, *James IV* (East Linton, 1997), p. 88; *CDS*, IV, 1571, 1614; *TA*, I, p. 314.
[15] NAS GD430/186 28 November 1506. A Sir John Todd is recorded as part of James IV's household in 1508 but his knightly status is not supported by any other source. Andrea Thomas, 'Renaissance Culture at the Court of James V, 1528-1542' (Ph.D., University of Edinburgh, 1997), Appendix B, pp. 376-83; *RMS*, II, 2114, III, 605.
[16] *RSS*, I, 3621.
[17] *Prot. Bk. Young*, no. 1717.
[18] Aldo Scaglione, *Knights at Court: Courtliness, Chivalry and Courtesy from Ottonian Germany to the Italian Renaissance* (Berkeley, Los Angeles & Oxford, 1991), p. 21.

squire was not bestowed in any formal sense, but it did indicate an element of service, membership and adherence to the values of knightly society. In the 1450s, Alexander Hepburn, Archibald Hepburn, Thomas Hepburn and Robert Airth were all designated as squires, but they were also burgesses of Haddington (East Lothian). Around the same time, John Dalrymple, a burgess of Edinburgh, also appeared styled as a squire.[19] The mid-fifteenth-century effigy of Gilbert Menzies of Pitfoddels shows him dressed in full body armour, although he was never knighted and was simply a successful merchant. In her doctoral thesis, Margaret Scott argues that Menzies' armour reflected the parliamentary act of 1430 stating the amount of armour required for different levels of society, but Menzies' outfit is far more an indication that he adhered to the codes of conduct of knightly society without being a formal member of it.[20] As far as the records show, these burghal squires were never knighted but they were clearly elevated to something close to knightly status. Perhaps these particular men had been involved in the military activities, both foreign and domestic, that played such a large part in the reign of James II.[21] Thus their status might have been achieved either through military or administrative duties, or a shared military training and subscription to the knightly code and way of life.

Military Training and Service

The knighting ceremony was the defining moment in a knight's career but there was neither a set age nor circumstance under which this occurred. Dubbing could act as a coming of age, as a recognition or conferral of status, as an acknowledgement of or incentive to martial prowess, or as an appreciation of service.[22] In his excellent general work on chivalry, Maurice Keen suggested that men were commonly knighted around the age of eighteen, the age at which the famous knight William the Marshal (1147–1219) had been knighted.[23] English records further support this and suggest that the late teens and early twenties were the common ages at which men 'came of age' and took up arms. In other instances, knighthood was bestowed at a much younger age. Towards the end of the fourteenth century, witnesses for dis-

---

[19] *RMS*, II, 737, 1477.
[20] Scott, 'Dress in Scotland', pp. 65, 111–13.
[21] See Barbour, *Bruce*, Book XVI, 79–81, and Wormald, *Lords and Men*, ch. 8. 'Uncertain Allies: Burghs and Politicians', pp. 137–56, for examples of burgesses engaged in armed conflicts. For more on James II's warmaking see Stevenson, 'Knighthood, Chivalry and the Crown', chapter 3; Christine McGladdery, *James II* (Edinburgh, 1990), pp. 93–115.
[22] Fionn Pilbrow, 'The Knights of the Bath: Dubbing to Knighthood in Lancastrian and Yorkist England', in Peter Coss and Maurice Keen (eds), *Heraldry, Pageantry and Social Display in Medieval England* (Woodbridge, 2002), p. 197.
[23] Keen, *Chivalry*, pp. 19–20. William the Marshal, thanks to the *Histoire de Guillaume le Maréchal*, was one of the most famous knights of the late Middle Ages. His career was exceptional and provided an exemplar to which knights could aspire.

putes in the English court of chivalry told the court how long they had been bearing arms. In the case of Scrope *v.* Grosvenor in 1386, of the ninety-four witnesses for Sir John Scrope, the youngest claim was from Sir John Bromwich, saying he had borne arms from the age of eleven. Many others claimed to have been knighted in their mid-teens, but the largest group by far claimed to have been bearing arms from around twenty.[24] In Scotland this was also the case: in 1398, David Stewart, the duke of Rothesay, was knighted around his twentieth birthday, at a tournament held specifically for the conferment of the honour.[25] Other Scottish nobles were dubbed around this age and George Seton, first Lord Seton, was knighted between the age of eighteen and twenty, and James, ninth earl of Douglas (c.1427–88), would have been at the most twenty-two when he was knighted.[26] John Ross of Hawkhead (1429–1501), knighted in the same ceremony as the ninth earl of Douglas, can also only have been about twenty when he received the honour.[27] Parliament legislated that sixteen was the standard age considered suitable for men to begin armed fighting, although boys as young as twelve could be called upon in time of war, and this was obviously reflected by the age at which many males became knights.[28]

However, it is impossible to know what proportion of knightly society was knighted at this age and it is clear that, in Scotland, nobles were often knighted once their careers were already well established. John Red Stewart of Dundonald (d. 1425) and John Stewart of Cardney, who were knighted by James I at his coronation in 1424, were both illegitimate brothers of Robert III (1390–1406) and thus must have been reasonably advanced in years when knighted. This suggests that even royal status was not a catalyst to receiving the honour at an early age. At the other end of the scale, James II (1437–60) was knighted whilst still an infant, at his baptism in 1430, and he shared the honour alongside boys of approximately five years of age.[29] Of course, these knightings were for particular occasions that had special associations and this must have had some influence over when they took place. Nevertheless, a large proportion of nobles with no familial ties to the crown were also knighted once their careers were established; an example is Sir Andrew Wood of Largo, who was knighted by James IV after around ten years of outstanding

---

[24] N. Harris Nicolas (ed.), *The Controversy between Sir Richard Scrope and Sir Robert Grosvenor in the Court of Chivalry A.D. MCCCLXXXV–MCCCXC* (London, 1832), I, p. 205; Nicholas Orme, *From Childhood to Chivalry: The Education of the English Kings and Aristocracy 1066–1530* (London & New York, 1984), p. 191.
[25] *Chron. Bower*, book XV, 4; Stephen Boardman, *The Early Stewart Kings: Robert II and Robert III, 1371–1406* (East Linton, 1996), pp. 57, 212.
[26] *RMS*, II, 206; *SP*, III, pp. 174, 175, 178, VIII, p. 575; George Chastellain, 'Historie du bon chevalier Messire Jacques de Lalain frere et compagnon de l'ordre de la Toison d'Or', in P. Hume Brown (ed.), *Early Travellers in Scotland* (Edinburgh, 1978), pp. 33–4.
[27] *Ibid.*, pp. 33–4; *SP*, VII, pp. 248–50.
[28] *APS*, II, pp. 10–11, 48.
[29] NAS GD124/1/129, GD124/1/423; *Chron. Bower*, book XVI, 16.

military service at sea.[30] Walter Haliburton of Dirleton also had a career spanning the entire reign of James I before he was knighted. John Lindsay de Byres, a noble who had acted as a hostage for James I in 1424, was not knighted until James II's reign, suggesting that he was at least in his early thirties, if not older, before receiving the honour. Alexander Hume of that Ilk must also have been around thirty when he was knighted.[31] Unfortunately, due to the difficulties in ascertaining exact birth dates, it is impossible to survey the full range of ages at which men were knighted or even suppose whether this would be especially revealing. Nevertheless, there does seem to be a significant proportion knighted in their late teens and early twenties, but knightings at much younger or much older ages were evidently not uncommon. As there was thus no standard age at which men were knighted in Scotland, this implies that knighthoods were not bestowed simply as an entry into manhood at the coming of age but for more diverse political, personal and military motivations.

In general, nobles began their training in the arts of knightly warfare when they were young squires, and preferably when they were still young children. They were taught the practical aspects of warfare, including how to ride and control horses, how to 'gouerne' armour and how to use weapons effectively.[32] Although in 1521 John Mair lamented that 'the gentry educate their children neither in letters nor morals', this was clearly untrue.[33] Parliament of 1496 had ordained that all barons and freeholders should send their eldest sons to grammar school at eight or nine, until they had perfect Latin, after which they should learn art and law for three years.[34] Nevertheless, there was no formal provision for physical education. Squires were taught by kinsmen in the household or in neighbouring households and by observing their fathers and elders, by being at the royal court and beside companions in

---

[30] *RMS*, II, 1563, 2040, 2231; Norman Macdougall, *James III: A Political Study* (East Linton, 1982), p. 146; Macdougall, *James IV*, p. 28.

[31] *RMS*, II, 12, 119, 102, 201, 203, 204. 'Of that Ilk' means 'of the same' and was used when the names of both the family and the estate were the same: Alexander Grant, 'Service and Tenure in Late Medieval Scotland, 1413–1475', in Anne Curry and Elizabeth Matthew (eds), *Concepts and Patterns of Service in the Later Middle Ages* (Woodbridge, 2000), p. 150, n. 19.

[32] Glenn (ed.), *Buke of the Ordre of Knychthede*, pp. 11–12; S.D. Church, *The Household Knights of King John* (Cambridge, 1999), p. 39; Bennett, 'Military Masculinity', p. 73; Ian Pierce, 'The Knight, his Arms and Armour in the Eleventh and Twelfth Centuries', in Christopher Harvey-Bill and Ruth Harvey (eds), *The Ideals and Practice of Medieval Knighthood: Papers from the First and Second Strawberry Hill Conferences* (Woodbridge, 1986), pp. 152–3. For a general discussion on noble education see J.H. Hexter, 'The Education of the Aristocracy in the Renaissance', in J.H. Hexter, *Reappraisals in History* (London, 1961).

[33] Archibald Constable (ed.), *A History of Greater Britain as Well England as Scotland, Compiled from Ancient Authorities by John Major, by Names Indeed a Scot, but by Profession a Theologian, 1521*, SHS (Edinburgh, 1892), p. 48; Carol Edington, *Court and Culutre in Renaissance Scotland: Sir David Lindsay of the Mount (1486–1555)* (East Linton, 1994), p. 13; John Durkan, 'Education: The Laying of Fresh Foundations', in John MacQueen (ed.), *Humanism in Renaissance Scotland* (Edinburgh, 1990), p. 124.

[34] *APS*, II, p. 238.

battle. Knightly games also assisted and Ralph Ferrers told the court of the Constable of England that tournaments were 'where the school and study of arms is'.[35] Although military training was clearly essential for members of martial society, there is no record of any formal training programme existing in Scotland.[36] Thus much of the responsibility for education was undertaken by kin and family friends. *The Buke of the Ordre of Knychthede*, translated into Scots in the mid fifteenth century, laid particular stress on the requirement of a good knight to teach his children the points and properties of chivalry, as well as the knightly codes of conduct. This chivalric manual stressed that these lessons should be taught when boys were young, so as not to disadvantage them when they became knights.[37] Maurice Keen concluded in his study of chivalry that military training was regarded as one of the social responsibilities of the nobility, which should be provided from private resources, much like the equipping of oneself as a man-at-arms.[38] There are certainly fourteenth-century instances where armour was purchased in England for use at jousts in Scotland, and it can be assumed that as the crown did not take responsibility for knightly martial training, it was done privately.

Although the crown did not fund training, it did, of course, take a necessary interest in ensuring that men were prepared to fight in wars on its behalf. In August 1456, as a response to the threat of impending war with England, James II set aside Greenside, on the road from Edinburgh to Leith, for the practice of tournaments and games of war.[39] This was, of course, for the practice of skills already gained in childhood and teenage years. At the same time, parliament legislated for the training and equipping of ordinary soldiers, men who were not knights but who made up the bulk of the king's army. New meetings, wapinschawings, were introduced, which were generally ordered by parliament and their frequency largely determined by the threat of war; they were attended by all the men of the realm who could bear arms, and their purpose was to assess the level of weaponry held by individuals that was available for warfare. Men were mustered through their lords, whom parliament had directed to attend. Julian Goodare has pointed out that wapinschawings served four primary functions: they impressed military values on the men who were in attendance, they defined who was obliged to perform military service, they established the obligations of weapon posses-

---

[35] Nicolas, *Scrope v. Grosvenor*, I, p. 155; Keen, *Chivalry*, p. 99.
[36] Keith M. Brown, *Noble Society in Scotland: Wealth, Family and Culture from Reformation to Revolution* (Edinburgh, 2000), p. 181.
[37] Glenn (ed.), *Buke of the Ordre of Knychthede*, pp. 11–12.
[38] Keen, *Chivalry*, p. 226; *APS*, II, pp. 10, 45, 226. Ian Pierce argues that in the eleventh and twelfth centuries a squire graduated to knightly status only when his military skills were perfected. This was not true in the fifteenth century, when squires often stayed at that status and could command armies without having been knighted. Pierce, 'The Knight, his Arms and Armour', pp. 152–3.
[39] *Edin. Chrs.*, no. 36.

sion, and in some cases they offered military training.[40] In October 1456 the estates declared renewed regulations for the arms to be borne at wapinschawings, which included a threat of punishment for those who did not come fully armed to the meetings once a month. In March 1457, parliament decided that quarterly wapinschawings were adequate, but at the same time criticised the Scots' interest in football and golf instead of games which would prepare them for warfare. In 1458, parliament decreed that shooting was to be practised each Sunday, from Easter to All Hallowmass, and each man was required to shoot at least six shots. Each burgh was additionally ordered to have a bowyer and fletcher, with the town supplying them with the necessary materials.[41] However, as this legislation was mainly concerned with the level of skills and preparation of ordinary soldiers, we still have very little indication of the types of preparations made by knights.

Whilst most martial training for knights clearly took place within the small community of the noble household, there were men of exceptional knightly skill who attracted a broader range of followers to their company in order to learn from their knightly wisdom and experience. The chronicler Walter Bower tells us of one such knight, Sir Alexander Ramsay of Dalhousie (d. 1342), who in the early fourteenth century

> shone with such prowess, and was so widely honoured for his outstanding military service [. . .] that virtually none of the nobility, whether adult or growing boy, thought he could gain any measure of manhood or merit unless he had experience for a while in his military school. Therefore, young squires attached themselves to him.[42]

The anonymous Pluscarden chronicler wrote around the same time as Bower that Ramsay was 'a most famous knight'. At any time he could attract a retinue of between thirty and one hundred men because he was able to offer protection and enforce obedience, an indication that he was a man of considerable personal influence.[43] Blind Harry similarly praised Alexander by saying that he was one of the best under the crown and that any gentleman who had been with Ramsay became more 'courtly', suggesting that his reputation stretched beyond straightforward military competence.[44] However, Ramsay's reputation cannot be viewed separately from his affinity to the powerful Black Douglas family and his role in real and brutal Anglo-Scottish warfare. It seems

---

[40] Julian Goodare, *State and Society in Early Modern Scotland* (Oxford, 1999), pp. 137, 151.
[41] *APS*, II, pp. 45, 48. For more on armourers and their craft see Charles Ffoulkes, *The Armourer and his Craft from the XIth to the XVIth Century* (New York, 1912 reprint 1988); Charles Ffoulkes, 'Some Aspects of the Craft of Armourer', *Archaeologia or Miscellaneous Tracts Relating to Antiquity* 79 (1929), pp. 13–28.
[42] *Chron. Bower*, book XIII, 47; see also *Chron. Wyntoun*, VI, p. 147.
[43] For more on this see Jennifer M. Brown, 'The Exercise of Power', in Jennifer M. Brown (ed.), *Scottish Society in the Fifteenth Century* (London, 1977), p. 54; *Chron. Pluscarden*, II, p. 218; Michael Brown, *The Black Douglases: War and Lordship in Late Medieval Scotland, 1300–1455* (East Linton, 1998), pp. 36–7, 39.
[44] Blind Harry, *Wallace*, VII, 904–12.

certain that his reputation was a direct result of his effective application of violence in border warfare.[45] Therefore, it does seem unlikely that there was ever a fully-developed 'school' of chivalry in Scotland, as Bower seems to suggest, as there is no evidence to corroborate its existence. It is possible, however, that Alexander Ramsay did pass on advice and assistance to knights and squires who needed to improve their martial skills.

Whilst there is no evidence that a knightly school existed, members of knightly society certainly recognised a need for a more formal training programme. Indeed, the *Buke of the Ordre of Knychthede* lamented that whilst there were schools of clerics, there were no schools of chivalry, and the author asks that kings and nobles band together to right this wrong.[46] There are records of men seeking out famous and reputable knights whom they wished to serve, much as we imagine might have been a frequent occurrence in Sir Alexander Ramsay's case. Serving a prominent and publicly renowned knight may have led to a better knightly training and an increase in reputation for the squires attached to the prominent lords they served. In June 1472, a squire, John Paston, wrote to his relation Sir John Paston asking him to recommend him to Sir Thomas Boyd, earl of Arran (d. c.1474), in order that he might enter into Boyd's service. The fact that Boyd was exiled in London after being forfeited by the Scottish king seems to have borne no ill effect on his knightly reputation. Paston's reasons for wishing to be tied to Boyd were that he was

> the most corteys, gentylest, wysest, kyndest, most compenabyll, freest, largeest, most bowntesous knyght [. . .] Hereto he is one of the lyghtest, delyverst, best spokyn, fayrest archer; devowghtest, most perfyghte, and trewst to hys lady of all knygthys that ever I was aqwentyd with.[47]

The qualities Paston described were obviously designed to curry favour with Boyd, but they also served to demonstrate that he desired to be in the company of a man who was regarded as a good knight. Whether Boyd deserved this reputation is difficult to assess as he appears in the records predominantly in association with diplomacy.[48] Needless to say, Paston's request highlights his desire to learn from a great knight, and as Boyd was not a native of England, demonstrates that the bond between knights often transcended international borders, particularly in the pursuit of martial knowledge.

By this time, the influence of humanist educationalists was being felt in Scotland. Although it did not reduce the need for military training, nobles were encouraged to demonstrate a more well-rounded education, which might include grammar, rhetoric, ethics, poetry and history.[49] Indeed, Paston remarked that the earl of Arran was the 'best spokyn' knight he had ever met,

---

[45] Brown, *Black Douglases*, pp. 36–7, 39.
[46] Glenn (ed.), *Buke of the Ordre of Knychthede*, p. 13.
[47] James Gairdner (ed.), *The Paston Letters A.D. 1422–1509* (London, 1904), V, p. 144.
[48] Buchanan, *History*, II, pp. 132–3; *SP*, V, pp. 147–8.
[49] *APS*, II, p. 238; Edington, *Court and Culture*, p. 44.

and Sir Gilbert Hay was fluent enough in French to translate chivalric manuals into Scots. Sir David Lindsay of the Mount (1486–1555) also embodied this new learning as both Lyon King of Arms and a court poet. However, Lindsay was highly critical of those who set martial skill above more learned abilities, conforming to the policies of the humanists.[50] But martial training remained essential and Lindsay himself remarked that a king should ensure to learn to: 'Ryde hors, ryn speris with gret audacitie,/Schute with hand bow, crossbow, and culueryng.'[51]

In whichever way knights learnt to do battle, their obligations to serve on the battlefield were the same. Men were expected to equip themselves for battle, and this they financed themselves or they entered into agreements where a lord would cover these costs.[52] Scottish military service in the fifteenth century was still partly conducted along feudal lines, with knights owing their lords service and the lords owing the king. Individual retinues, however, were often constructed through 'non-feudal' obligations and agreements. This effectively meant that the king called his lords (who were generally all knights) to muster for battle, and the lords brought along their retinues, containing knights, squires and men-at-arms, who owed that lord military service under a variety of terms. In 1430, for example, Alexander of Ogistoun made a bond with Sir Alexander Forbes, who was in turn a vassal of Alexander Stewart, earl of Mar, agreeing that he

> is becumyn lele man ande trew till a nobill man Sir Alexander of Forbes [. . .] for all the dayis of my lyffe agaynys all dedelyke myn alegeans tyll my lorde the Kyng anerly outane for a certane some of money and I [. . .] sall serff witht iii hors qwyll my fader leffis and effer hym witht sex.[53]

Mar and Forbes, of course, may have been most concerned with Ogistoun's service in a local context. However, it is also likely that when Forbes appeared in a royal host that Ogistoun would attend in his retinue under the terms of his bond. Don Pedro de Ayala, a Spanish ambassador who visited the court of James IV in the 1490s, confirmed that Scottish landholders were vassals to the king and that they were obliged to 'serve him forty days, at their own expense, every time he calls them out'.[54]

---

[50] 'The Complaynt of Schir Dauid Lindesay', in Douglas Hamer (ed.), *The Works of Sir David Lindsay of the Mount, 1490–1555*, STS (Edinburgh & London, 1931–36), I, pp. 44–5, lines 165–86; Edington, *Court and Culture*, pp. 80–1.
[51] 'The Testament of Papyngo', in Douglas Hamer (ed.), *The Works of Sir David Lindsay of the Mount, 1490–1555*, STS (Edinburgh & London, 1931–36), I, p. 64, lines 285–6.
[52] See for example *APS*, II, pp. 10–11, 45; Frédérique Lachaud, 'Armour and Military Dress in Thirteenth- and Early Fourteenth-Century England', in Matthew Strickland (ed.), *Armies, Chivalry and Warfare in Medieval Britain and France: Proceedings of the 1995 Harlaxton Symposium* (Stamford, 1998), p. 350.
[53] *A.B. Ill.*, IV, p. 391; Michael Brown, 'Regional Lordship in North-East Scotland: The Badenoch Stewarts. II. Alexander Stewart Earl of Mar', *Northern Scotland* 16 (1996), p. 36; Grant, 'Service and Tenure in Late Medieval Scotland', p. 164.
[54] Don Pedro de Ayala, 'Letter to Ferdinand and Isabella', pp. 47–8. Although Don Pedro

After forty days, however, the king could lose his most experienced fighters, who were there at no cost to the crown. At the siege of Dumbarton in 1489, James IV tackled the problem by using rotating call-ups. In this instance parliament drew up a timetable so that no one was in the field for longer than twenty days, allowing the king to call upon a further twenty days later in the year. Colin Campbell, earl of Argyll, the Chancellor, initially besieged Dumbarton with men from Argyll, Lennox, Menteith and Strathearn. After twenty days the lords, barons and men of Angus, Fife, Kinross, Clackmannan, Perthshire, Stormonth, Atholl and Rannoch took over, then similar intervals were to be covered by George, second earl of Huntly; William Keith, third earl of Marischal; William Hay, third earl of Errol; and Alexander, Lord Forbes; with the men of the Mearns and the country north of the Mounth.[55] However, measures such as this were not enough and James IV had to resort to paying men to stay in the field.[56] Once this precedent was set, the practice of paying for service continued throughout James IV's reign and he paid Sir Robert Kerr of Cessford (also known as of Ferniehirst) around £100 a week as Master of the King's Artillery during the 1497 border wars.[57] During the course of the century, paying for the employment of labourers to undertake specific duties during sieges became commonplace. The king would send bellmen into cities crying for workmen to take their wages: as on 13 September 1496, when bellmen went out into Edinburgh to employ men for the siege of Ellem in the Scottish borders. In July 1497 James IV was forced to pay enormous sums for skilled workers: two hundred and twenty-one men were paid for one week of work using shovels, spades and picks, and sixty-one quarriers and masons, four smiths and around thirteen gunners were required.[58] The total cost of the border sieges of 1496 and '97 was considerable: James's personal liability for the raids was underestimated and he was forced to coin his great chain and other effects, to provide victuals. He also levied a spear silver tax, and took an

---

de Ayala grossly overestimated the number which the king could assemble, he did report some points accurately. Letters of muster were sent out in February 1497 which specifically designated a maximum forty days of military service confirming this was the standard service time. *TA*, I, p. 320. In support of this, on 2 August 1513, the Aberdeen Burgh Council authorised the raising of £400 to provide for and support for forty days a small force of men to fight for James IV in his wars with England. *Abdn. Counc.*, p. 85; Macdougall, *James IV*, p. 280, n. 136. Scotland seems to have been one of the few remaining countries where military service was still carried out like this: in England the last time an army was called out by the feudal levy of forty days was in 1385, although it remained a technical obligation into the fifteenth century. A system of taxation based on landed wealth, which raised the revenue to pay an army, replaced the forty day service. See Barber, *Knight and Chivalry*, p. 42.

[55] *APS*, II, p. 124; *TA*, I, p. xc. By staggering the armies like this, James IV ensured that he could call these men out again in that year. It also meant that he exhausted the service of those situated closest to the castle in the early stages of the siege, then mobilised those further away.

[56] *TA*, I, pp. 123–6; Macdougall, *James IV*, p. 75.

[57] *TA*, I, pp. 329, 339, 340, 346, 348, 350.

[58] *Ibid.*, pp. 295, 346–7, 350.

[59] *ER*, XI, p. 120; *TA*, I, pp. cliv, clv, 82, 312–14.

additional contribution of £670 from the abbot of Arbroath and £100 from Sir David Hume of Wedderburn.[59] Given the expense to the crown of the 1497 raids and sieges, it is apparent that skilled workers had become increasingly useful and essential in the field. The crown depended upon these men to undertake tasks which knights and men-at-arms could not or would not perform.

Knights, however, were still the core of Scottish royal armies and, in order to keep noble affinities in the field, the crown offered additional incentives to knights and squires for military service. These rewards included land grants, individual one-off payments and increased positions of responsibility and honour. For instance, Sir William Forbes received lands after the 1429 Highland campaign, and Sir Alexander Livingston of Callander was made keeper of Methven castle, near Perth, after the siege there in 1444.[60] George, second earl of Huntly, was promised one hundred marks of land from James III for his services in taking Dingwall castle (north-west of Inverness) from the forfeited John, earl of Ross, although Huntly considered this meagre remuneration offensive.[61] Sir Alexander Bruce of Earlshall was well rewarded by both James III and Henry VII for his services during Henry's invasion of England in 1485. James granted Bruce, his *familiari armiger*, some of Albany's forfeited Berwickshire lands, and Henry VII gave an annuity of £20 to Bruce 'in gracious remuneration of his good, faithful, and approved services, and his great labours in various ways heretofore'.[62] Bruce had led a contingent of Scots who were serving in Henry's army at the battle of Bosworth and Henry must have granted the pension as a direct result of this. The reasons for James's favouring of Bruce are less obvious, as in the period prior to Bosworth, Bruce had been in France, but it may suggest that Henry VII's triumph was pleasing to the Scottish king.[63] Given that these rewards indicate that the crown was keen to keep knights and their retinues in the field, then the nobility clearly remained crucial to the waging of warfare throughout the fifteenth century.

The Obligations of Knighthood

Knights, particularly those in royal service, had a number of civic responsibilities including governmental, judicial and diplomatic duties, in addition to any post which they may have held in the royal household and their assumed primary duty of bearing arms on the battlefield. Naturally some of their duties were more relevant to their noble status, but as nobility and knighthood were

---

[60] *RMS*, II, 127; *ER*, V, p. 219.
[61] *Spalding Misc.*, IV, Papers from the Charter Chest at Gordon Castle, nos. V, VI, pp. 133–5.
[62] *RMS*, II, 1638; *CDS*, IV, 1518.
[63] For Bruce's involvement in Bosworth see Michael Bennett, *The Battle of Bosworth* (Gloucester, 1985), pp. 9, 83, 162. It is possible that James III had encouraged Scottish participation at Bosworth to undermine the duke of Albany.

so closely related, ideal knightly careers included all duties expected of men of noble status. However, subsequent to their knighting the duties they undertook were not uniform. They had vastly varied roles within the royal court, some holding significant positions, others barely appearing except to witness charters. The very nature of historical records, of course, means that most careers that are traceable belong to knights who were engaged in royal service. Knights had two distinct obligations and were required to take on both martial and administrative duties for the crown. Different kings, naturally, placed different emphases on these obligations, dependent upon their own political and military needs, but knights were still expected to function within both roles. Nevertheless, there were knights who operated entirely within one sphere, and often this was linked to the reason that they were dubbed.

Martial Careers

The knight's primary duty was to bear arms on the battlefield. He was a trained warrior and, even though the way in which warfare was executed changed over the fifteenth century, the knight was still expected to fulfil his martial function. Indeed Alastair J. MacDonald noted the importance of the martial obligation in Scotland and wrote that 'the desire to attain glory and renown through military feats and the enjoyment of martial endeavour for its own sake' was central to Scottish ideas of chivalry.[64]

The chivalric ideal of the pursuit of individual glory was never far removed from the Scottish knight's actions in war. Even James IV was criticised by contemporaries for following knightly, rather than kingly, desires. Don Pedro de Ayala, who arrived in Scotland around June 1496 and immediately joined James IV on his border campaigns, remarked that the king 'is not a good captain, because he begins to fight before he has given his orders'.[65] Charles Blyth has pointed out that this is clearly a description of the king acting as a knight, 'more concerned with his own private encounters in battle than he is with the over-all success of his army'.[66] In John Barbour's epic poem, the *Bruce*, it is not Robert Bruce who is the central chivalric character, but his brother Edward.[67] Indeed Barbour portrayed Edward as, above all else, interested in attaining individual glory, particularly on the Irish campaigns.[68] So, although by definition knights were obliged to take on a martial role, it was

[64] MacDonald, *Border Bloodshed*, p. 178.
[65] Brown, *Early Travellers in Scotland*, p. 40; G.A. Bergenroth (ed.), *Calendar of Letters, Despatches, and State Papers, Relating to the Negotiations between England and Spain, Preserved in the Archives at Simancas and Elsewhere* (London, 1862–1954), I, no. 211, p. 179; *TA*, I, p. cxxx; Macdougall, *James IV*, p. 133.
[66] Charles R. Blyth, *'The Knychtlyke Stile': A Study of Gavin Douglas's Aeneid* (New York & London, 1987), pp. 241–2.
[67] Väthjunker, 'A Study in the Career of Sir James Douglas', p. 178; Bernice W. Kliman, 'The Idea of Chivalry in John Barbour's *Bruce*', *Mediaeval Studies* 35 (1973), pp. 479, 507.
[68] Barbour, *Bruce*, IX, lines 588–9; Liam O. Purdon and Julian N. Wasserman, 'Chivalry and Feudal Obligation in Barbour's "Bruce" ', in Liam O. Purdon and Cindy L. Vitto (eds), *The Rusted Hauberk: Feudal Ideals of Order and their Decline* (Gainsville, 1994), p. 81.

the influence of the chivalric ideal which encouraged them to prove themselves worthy on the battlefield. Perhaps even being given the chance to prove themselves, encouraged knights to wholly commit themselves to campaign and war.

Indeed, Scottish kings, utilising the forty-day obligations for military service, never seemed to have trouble in persuading knights to campaign with them, although it often proved more difficult to raise an army. For example, a number of the men James I had knighted at his coronation were keen to campaign with him against Alexander, Lord of the Isles, in the highlands in 1428 and 1429. At the 1428 campaign prominent nobles and knights led retinues including the earl of Mar; Sir James Douglas of Balvenie; Sir Patrick Ogilvy of Auchterhouse; and Sir John Forrester of Corstorphine; and in 1429 he managed to muster Archibald, fifth earl of Douglas; Alexander Lindsay, earl of Crawford; Sir Walter Haliburton of Dirleton; Sir Alexander Seton of Gordon; Sir William Crichton of that Ilk; Sir Adam Hepburn of Hailes; and Sir Walter Ogilvy of Lintrathen. James struggled, however, to raise a full army for these campaigns and in parliament in 1429, the king promised to pay his lieges for their service in going to the highlands.[69]

The decline of Anglo-Scottish warfare must have had an effect on the type of military careers which a nobleman could expect. No reputations on the same scale as those held by the Black Douglases were built up in the fifteenth century, and commentators only seem to have been comfortable with praising men in the context of the 'international' conflicts. Indeed, the number of Scots serving French kings during the fifteenth century suggests that those knights who wished to pursue a career in full-scale campaigning and warfare really had to look to the Continent. Whilst Richard McCoy has argued that in fifteenth- and sixteenth-century Europe, few knights truly sought glory outside their own country, in Scotland we find this to be far from the truth.[70]

The Stewarts of Darnley, for example, upheld a long tradition of entering French service. John Stewart, first Lord Darnley (d. 1495), a descendant of a line of renowned military knights, built on their reputations in the mid fifteenth century. Both his father, Sir Alan (d. 1439), and his grandfather, Sir John (d. 1429) had been in French military service and in 1428 his grandfather had been permitted to quarter the royal arms of France with his paternal coat.[71] When, on 12 October 1463, John, Lord Darnley attempted to reach agreement with James III over his claim to the earldom of Lennox, Darnley offered to provide one hundred spears and one hundred bows for a year at his own expense, 'in quhat part of the realme that ze [James III] will charge me, in

---

[69] *RMS*, II, 109–15, 127; *APS*, II, p. 20.
[70] Richard C. McCoy, *The Rites of Knighthood: The Literature and Politics of Elizabethan Chivalry* (Berkeley, Los Angeles & London, 1989), p. 27.
[71] *SP*, V, pp. 346–8; William Forbes-Leith (ed.), *The Scots Men-at-Arms and Life-Guards in France From Their Formation until their Final Dissolution* (Edinburgh, 1882), I, pp. 15, 16, 20, 22, 32, 33, 34, 36, 50.

resisting of zoure rebellis and ennemyis quhatsumeuir thai be'.[72] James III may well have taken up this offer by making Darnley governor of Rothesay castle in February 1465.[73] Problems with the Lordship of the Isles in the 1460s effectively made this a 'front-line' commission, but this also demonstrates that the Stewarts of Darnley were a family of 'military' knights.

Other Scottish knights also sought military prestige through French service. Sir Bernard Stewart, third Seigneur d'Aubigny (1447–1508) was a commander of the Scots guard in France. He had successfully served Louis XI, Charles VIII and Louis XII, and excelled in the Italian wars.[74] Indeed, Geoffrey de Charny in his *Livre de chevalerie* claimed that those who had served with distinction in wars in their own lands were to be honoured, but more to be honoured were those who had seen service in distant and strange countries. He even wrote a treatise on the art of warfare in French, which shows he was influenced by the teachings of humanism.[75] In 1508 Stewart was invited by James IV to return to Scotland and preside over the tournament of the Wild Knight and the Black Lady. Stewart's reputation by this time was well established and his arrival was eagerly anticipated. It prompted William Dunbar (c.1460–c.1513), James IV's court poet, to write 'The Ballade of Barnard Stewart', where Stewart was described as 'the prince of knightheyd and flour of chevalry'.[76]

Although these examples show knights who sought chivalric glory through their martial function, knights were also made in Scotland for purely military purposes. For instance, at James III's coronation in 1460 at Kelso in the Scottish borders, one hundred knights were dubbed.[77] Norman Macdougall has suggested that these hundred men were knighted primarily for the purpose of immediately increasing military might and that they were

---

[72] Fraser, *Lennox*, II, pp. 76–7.
[73] *Ibid.*, pp. 78–9; *SP*, V, p. 348.
[74] Douglas Gray, 'A Scottish "Flower of Chivalry" and his Book', *Words: Wai-Te-Ata Studies in Literature* 4 (1974), pp. 22–34; MacDonald, 'Chivalry as a Catalyst', pp. 163–4; Forbes-Leith, *Scots Men-at-Arms*, I, pp. 72, 76, 78–9, 80, 82–3.
[75] Keen, *Chivalry*, p. 13; Élie de Comminges (ed.), *Traité dur L'Art de la Guerre de Bérault Stuart Seigneur D'Aubigny* (The Hague, 1976); P. Contamine, 'The War Literature of the Late Middle Ages: The Treatises of Robert de Balsac and Béraud Stuart, Lord of Aubigny', in C.T. Allmand (ed.), *War, Literature and Politics in the Late Middle Ages* (Liverpool, 1976).
[76] William Dunbar, 'The Ballade of Bernard Stewart' in Bawcutt (ed.), *William Dunbar*, pp. 222–7, line 18; Louise Olga Fradenburg, *City, Marriage, Tournament: Arts of Rule in Late Medieval Scotland* (Wisconsin, 1991), p. 174. Dunbar wrote 'The Ballade of Barnard Stewart' on his arrival in Edinburgh in 1508, and it was published on 9 May 1508 by Chepman and Myllar. See William Beattie (ed.), *The Chepman and Myllar Prints: Nine Tracts from the First Scottish Press, Edinburgh 1508 Followed By the Two Other Tracts in the Same Volume in the National Library of Scotland* (Edinburgh, 1950). Printed when the taste for chivalric spectacular was strong in James's court, the nine prints, including John Lydgate's 'Complaint of the Black Knight' and 'Golagrus and Gawain', are especially relevant to the courtly and chivalric tradition in the early sixteenth century. Fradenburg, *City, Marriage, Tournament*, pp. 177–8, 181–2.
[77] *Chron. Auchinleck*, p. 21, Macdougall, *James III*, p. 51. See also 'The Short Chronicle of 1482' in MacDougall, *James III*, Appendix A, pp. 311–13.

used to assist in the taking of the castle of Wark, which was seized and demolished shortly afterwards.[78] There is no indication given by the chroniclers as to whom the hundred men were, but the sheer number of men raised to knightly status suggests that the king was indeed providing himself with a force for instant military support. The very fact that James III was crowned in the borders, which were being aggressively defended at the time, adds weight to the suggestion that military force was at the forefront of royal concerns. Large-scale knightings were not unusual in the late Middle Ages and other instances occur throughout the fourteenth and fifteenth centuries, especially when military strength and support was required with some urgency. Indeed, the *Buke of the Ordre of Knychthede* advised that 'quhare grete multitude of honourable and worthy men suld assemble for honourable actis tobe done And thare suld the king mak mony new knychtis'.[79] This also seems to have been a common practice in England and in 1306 Edward I knighted his son and two hundred and eighty-two other squires for the purpose of bolstering his knights and men-at-arms for a renewed war with Scotland.[80]

What further suggests that these were purely martial knights, created on this military campaign, is that James III's court did not benefit from an influx of these hundred new knights undertaking administrative duties. Unlike the beginnings of James I and James II's reigns where new knights frequently witnessed charters and held positions at court, at the commencement of James III's administration this was not the case. In general, the royal records do show that fewer men around the royal court were styling themselves as knight than was previously so, but it still might be expected that a number of the hundred men would appear on royal witness lists as they acquired places in the royal household. Instead, there are less witnesses of knightly status to James III's early acts, or at least less denoting their knightly status, than had previously been the case in the fifteenth century.[81] This may, of course, be an indication

---

[78] *Chron. Auckinleck*, pp. 21, 58; *ER*, VII, pp. 7, 33; *TA*, I, p. 74; Macdougall, *James III*, p. 51. There has been some issue as to whether James III remained in the borders after his coronation. The Auchinleck chronicler does not report whether James stayed there, but according to Buchanan, the seven-year-old James III had returned to Edinburgh castle after his coronation, but 'the nobles thought nothing should divert their attention from the war', so they remained in the field. Buchanan, *History*, II, p. 107. However, John Lesley reported that James and his 'haill nobillis' did not return to Edinburgh until after the 'victories' at Wark. Lesley, *History*, p. 33. It would seem very unlikely that the young king would have taken over the military command of the army, but given his mother's reported attitude, the royal party may well have stayed until the Wark siege was over. Buchanan, *History*, II, p. 105; Pitscottie, *Historie*, pp. 144–5.
[79] Glenn (ed.), *Buke of the Ordre of Knychthede*, p. 5.
[80] Peter Coss, 'Knighthood, Heraldry and Social Exclusion in Edwardian England', in Peter Coss and Maurice Keen (eds), *Heraldry, Pageantry and Social Display in Medieval England* (Woodbridge, 2002), pp. 60–1. Barber counts 276 knights dubbed at this ceremony: Barber, *The Knight and Chivalry*, p. 34.
[81] See the witness lists of the Great Seal charters which demonstrate this trend, *RMS*, II, pp. 47–8, 158–60, 365–7, 848–50. In general, from James III's reign onwards, regular royal witnesses tend to be styled by the office that they held, rather than by their knightly status.

that the role of the knight at the Scottish court changed under the rule of James III's minority regime. Some of the hundred men did, of course, continue to serve the crown in a military role and we find James Crichton of Carnis appointed keeper of Doune Castle, Stirlingshire, in 1464 and 1467.[82] However, it is most likely that the knights made at James III's coronation were intended only for military support and were not necessarily bound in service to the king in a civic capacity.

The career of Patrick Hume of Polwarth (d. 1503) also shows that emphasis was placed on his martial ability after he had been knighted during the border wars of 1497. Prior to his dubbing, Patrick had held considerable favour with the young James IV. After James III's death at Sauchieburn, the fifteen-year-old James IV rewarded Patrick Hume of Polwarth for his support during the events of 1488 with the office of Chamberlain of Stirlingshire.[83] In 1489 Hume was granted the position of Chamberlain of Fife and Kilmarnock. Rather fantastically, he dared an attempt to embezzle a small amount of the deceased James III's money which he had acquired by force after Sauchieburn. Generously, James IV overlooked this misdemeanour and even allowed him to keep some of the money, suggesting that Hume was indeed held in significant favour by the young king.[84] He was appointed keeper of Stirling castle in 1494.[85] After his dubbing, Hume continued in James's favour, being given the position of Chamberlain of Stirlingshire during 1497, 1499 and 1501. In 1499 Hume was granted extra pay for collecting fees during the time of plague. He was made Chamberlain of Fife and Kilmarnock a second time in 1501, and in 1499 and 1501 he was also Comptroller.[86] In 1501 Hume also held the post of keeper of Stirling Castle for the second time. At the same time he continued to be rewarded for his military prowess and in 1499, for his services in war and resisting the English, James IV confirmed on him lands within the lordship of Menteith.[87]

Sir Andrew Wood of Largo also had a distinguished career in military service and was ultimately dubbed for his excellence sometime before Febru-

---

For example, David Guthrie of that Ilk is styled '*Clericus Rotulorum et Registri*'. Of course, some did use both titles, like James Stewart of Auchterhouse, who was styled '*miles, Avunculus Regis*', but this was less usual. There was also a significant increase in the number of clerics engaged in royal service.

[82] *RMS*, II, 771,1088; *ER*, VII, pp. 253, 486.

[83] Macdougall, *James III*, p. 243.

[84] Patrick Hume and George Towers, an Edinburgh burgess who later was appointed custumar of Edinburgh, had captured John Stewart, earl of Atholl, at or just after Sauchieburn. They had forced his countess to deliver two boxes of James III's money which Atholl was holding, but before they gave it to James IV they removed 320 Harry nobles from one of the boxes. On 21 June 1488, when the boxes were examined at Edinburgh, Hume and Towers were forced to hand over the money, but James returned forty Harry nobles to Hume. *TA*, I, pp. 79–87; Macdougall, *James IV*, p. 50.

[85] *Ibid.*, pp. 135, 137–9.

[86] *ER*, XI, pp. 16, 134, 137, 212, 259, 289, 314, 357; *SP*, VI, pp. 2–3; *RSS*, I, 335.

[87] *ER*, XI, pp. 161–3; Macdougall, *James IV*, p. 152.

ary 1495.[88] Wood, a lesser noble, was active in public service under James III, and was a clear favourite of the king's, especially for his naval exploits.[89] On 18 March 1483 Wood received a feu-charter of Largo from James III for his services and losses during war on the land and the sea, and the grant makes it clear that he had inflicted extensive damage on the English at sea.[90] Prior to Sauchieburn in 1488, Wood acted as James III's personal ferryman and he also played a crucial role in the king's military campaigns in this period.[91] After Sauchieburn, Wood, who had been steadfastly loyal to James III, quickly transferred his allegiance to the new king and James IV recognised this loyalty by confirming his barony of Largo.[92] Perhaps this acceptance of Wood under the new administration was partly due to James IV's naval preoccupations: Wood commanded two ships, the *Yellow Carvel* and the *Flower*, later becoming a captain in James's navy.[93]

In spite of a three-year truce agreed with England in October 1488, the war continued at sea. The early chapters of Pitscottie show Andrew Wood cast in the role of victorious hero, winning two sea-battles against superior English forces in the summers of 1489 and 1490.[94]

> Schir Androw Wode being bot tua scheipis as forsaid, the Zallow caruall and the Floure, the king of Inglandis schipis was fyue in number witht great artaillzerie, zeit notwithstanding the Scottis sceipis prevaillit at the length and that be wosdome and manheid of thair captane quhilk tuik all the fyue Inglis scheipis and brocht them to Leyth as pressoneris [. . .] For the quhilk wictorieous and manlie act captane Schir Andrew Wode was weill revairdit witht the kingis grace and consall and haldin in great estimatioun thaireefter witht the nobilietie of Scottland.[95]

During parliament on 18 May 1491, Wood was given a royal licence confirming the approval of the king and estates for building operations which he had already undertaken within his burgh and lands of Largo in Fife. Parliament recognised Wood's services in inflicting damage on the king's enemies at sea and his losses in the process and also confirmed his feu-charter of Largo.

---

[88] *RMS*, II, 2040, 2231.
[89] Wood was in command of at least two ships, and it was in this role, for both James III and James IV, that he was the most useful.
[90] *RMS*, II, 1563; Macdougall, *James III*, p. 146; Macdougall, *James IV*, p. 28.
[91] *Ibid.*, p. 49; *TA*, I, p. lxii.
[92] *TA*, I, p. lxxv; Macdougall, *James IV*, p. 50.
[93] *Ibid.*, pp. 225, 232.
[94] *Ibid.*, p. 226.
[95] Pitscottie, *Historie*, I, p. 227. Although Wood was a 'new' type of knight, that is, he was drawn from a mercantile background rather than an aristocratic one, the adjectives used to describe him here are used commonly in literary descriptions of knights. Macdougall does warn that Pitscottie is not reliable in these sections of his chronicle and suggests that there was probably only one sea battle. There is, however, some truth in his description of the sea-battle on 10 August 1490, when Stephen Bull, an English commander, with three heavily-armed vessels, lay in wait off the Isle of May for Wood's two ships returning from Flanders. Macdougall, *James IV*, p. 226.

Macdougall interprets the treatment of Wood in the early years of James IV's reign as a deliberate plan by the minority government that was anxious to retain the services of a skilled seaman. They hastened to confirm Wood's private enterprise in Largo by licensing his fortalice long after it had been built.[96] On 9 August 1497 Andrew Wood was appointed keeper of Dunbar Castle and he was more active on land after this time until 1513, when James IV sent Wood, along with Archibald, earl of Angus, to relieve James Hamilton, Lord Hamilton, earl of Arran, of his command as admiral.[97]

But knighting a man in a martial situation did not necessarily preclude him from an administrative career. For example, during the border wars of 1497, James IV knighted Robert Lundy of Balgony.[98] In the couple of years prior to this Lundy had been royal usher. His responsibilities continued along these lines after he was knighted and as well as holding the position of treasurer, Robert Lundy held various diplomatic posts and was Comptroller in 1500.[99] However, other knights made on the battlefield did continue their careers in a military vein. John Ogilvy of Finglask, for instance, who was also knighted in the borders in 1497, was appointed constable of Inverness Castle.[100] In February 1506 he became sheriff of Inverness, at which point he was also acting as a royal messenger for James IV.[101] This clearly demonstrates that when and where a man was dubbed influenced his knightly role but did not preclude him from serving the crown in a more diverse capacity.

The border wars of 1497 also draw our attention to specific roles and positions held by knights. In 1496, Sir John Sandilands of Hillhouse was in control of James IV's arsenal, and he was placed in command of the bigger guns at the commencement of the wars in support of Perkin Warbeck's claim to the English throne.[102] In Sandilands' charge were two gunners from the Low Countries, Henric and Hans, and a French gunner, Guyane, who were paid approximately ten shillings for each week's work.[103] Sandilands' role in these

---

[96] *RMS*, II, 2040; *APS*, II, pp. 227–8; Macdougall, *James IV*, p. 227.
[97] *TA*, I, p. 350; Buchanan, *History*, II, p. 184; Macdougall, *James IV*, p. 269.
[98] *ER*, X, pp. 484, 577, 589; *RMS*, II, 2342; *ADC*, II, p. 233. From May 1498 until February 1501 Lundy was in the post of Treasurer, and although the accounts have been lost for this period, it is possible that he was a knight prior to taking on this role. However, he would still have been knighted around May or June, and as the king was in the borders at this time it is most probable Lundy was knighted on James's campaign. *ER*, XI, pp. 163, 169, 172, 217, 261, 278; *TA*, II, p. xii.
[99] *CDS*, IV, 1653; *TA*, II, p. liv; NAS GD4/24; *ER*, XI, pp. 261, 278, 264–82. In June 1499 Lundy, along with the Archbishop of Glasgow, Andrew Forman the Prothonotary and the earl of Bothwell, was sent as an ambassador to treat for James IV's marriage with Princess Margaret of England.
[100] *TA*, I, p. 211; NAS GD32/8/3; *ER*, XI, p. 356.
[101] *RSS*, I, 1214; *APS*, II, pp. 263–4; Macdougall, *James IV*, p. 188.
[102] *TA*, I, pp. 260, 269, 288–91, 294, 304.
[103] *TA*, I, p. 300. For other payments and preparations see *TA*, I, pp. 260, 297–301. Foreigners clearly had the skills required to operate the artillery as James II had similarly employed French gunners for the siege of Abercorn castle. See *ER*, V, p. 525, VI, p. 12; *Chron. Auchinleck*, p. 35.

sieges suggests that he had acquired 'new' military expertise now that guns had been introduced to the battlefield. Although Richard Barber has said that 'the knight was not interested in learning the skills of firearms', Scottish knights were clearly adapting to the use of new technologies and becoming skilled in areas beyond traditionally knightly ones.[104]

By 1497 John Sandilands of Hillhouse had been replaced by Sir Robert Kerr of Cessford (also of Ferniehirst), as Master of the King's Artillery. After an initial raid of Hume, James IV was quickly diverted by a sea attack on the east coast and took a considerable portion of his army with him.[105] James left Robert Kerr in the borders, in what we can gather was a position of considerable seniority, ensuring that Kerr regularly received payments for furnishing the artillery. Kerr also received a fee of £33 6s 4d as a Whitsunday payment, and an average fee of £100 a week, which was dramatically higher than the £100 annual pension he received for the post of Master of the King's Artillery.[106] Sandilands' and Kerr's employment, of course, is an indication that knightly nobles were adapting to the use of guns. Indeed, Warner has remarked that:

> It has often been claimed that the greater use and efficacity of artillery during the fifteenth century ruined warfare as a knightly finishing school, and that this new and destructive technology was incompatible with the chivalric ethos of the period. However, there is no evidence to support this view. Instead, the aristocratic combattants of the age readily adapted themselves to the changing nature of warfare, throwing themselves wholeheartedly into the development of this dangerous technology.[107]

Whilst Warner's studies are primarily concerned with those in command of English armies, in Scotland knights clearly embraced the possibilities provided by firearms. Sir John Ramsay, for example, appears to have also held a position of responsibility over the gunners in the border wars and may well have been Robert Kerr's second-in-command.[108] Two men of this name, however, operated in James IV's court, one John Ramsay and one Sir John Ramsay, the former Lord Bothwell (d. 1513), who had lost his title because of his support for James III.[109] In all probability the Ramsay who had responsibility for the gunners was the disgraced Lord Bothwell, as he was certainly

---

[104] Barber, *Knight and Chivalry*, p. 234.
[105] The raid of Hume was named as such in the *Treasurer's Accounts*, although it appears unlikely that it was Hume which was raided as Lord Hume was very much part of James IV's military campaigns at this time. The Scots, who must have used Hume as a base to make cross-border raids, also held jousting while they were camped there. *Calendar of State Papers (Milan)*, I, no 526, p. 317; *TA*, I, p. 329; Macdougall, *James IV*, p. 137. The seventy English ships were probably headed off by Sir Andrew Wood of Largo.
[106] *TA*, I, pp. 329, 339, 340, 346, 348, 350, IV, p. 267.
[107] M. Warner, 'Chivalry in Action: Thomas Montagu and the War in France, 1417–1428', *Nottingham Medieval Studies* 42 (1998), p. 166.
[108] *TA*, I, p. 350.
[109] Macdougall, *James III*, pp. 202–3; Macdougall, *James IV*, pp. 58–9; *SP*, II, pp. 132–4.

involved in the beginnings of the attacks in 1496. Ramsay had been in England until early 1496 and he appears to have returned to Scotland as a spy for Henry VII.[110] Yet his conspiracies against James IV and Perkin Warbeck, the pretender to the English throne, do not seem to have been drawn to the Scottish king's attention and it is entirely plausible that James, ignorant of Ramsay's true allegiance, placed him in a position of responsibility in the borders in 1497.

With the decline of Anglo-Scottish warfare and the changes in siege technology, there were fewer battlefield arenas in which knights might prove their 'chivalric' worth. The types of warfare in Scotland required coordination and discipline, not war which encouraged acts of individual prowess. Although chronicle accounts retained the idea of one-on-one combat as chivalric, war was not, at least during this period, largely influenced by the chivalric code. The only arena left exclusively available to knightly society was the tournament, a stylised battleground where chivalric qualities reigned supreme.

Administrative Careers
In the mid-1450s Sir Gilbert Hay emphasised that knights were public figures with public responsibilities. In a marked departure from earlier ideas of knighthood, Hay intimated that knighthood was not meant solely to elevate an individual, but that knights were intended to serve the crown for the 'commoun prouffit'.[111] Other chivalric writers made similar emphases and in his fourteenth-century *Livre de chevalerie*, Geoffrey de Charny stressed the propriety of a king choosing his officers from amongst the knighthood.[112] In Scotland this was an essential function of knighthood.

Knights were encouraged by the Stewart kings to hold a number of civic responsibilities. The duties which they undertook could be varied and included governmental, judicial and diplomatic roles, or a place in the royal household. It was no longer adequate for a knight to be good with a sword alone – he also had to perform other tasks and duties that required more than brute force. James I, in particular, liked his knights to hold administrative offices, especially knights whom he had personally dubbed. For instance, Patrick Ogilvy of Auchterhouse (d. 1429), who was knighted by James at his coronation in 1424, was immediately set to work as auditor of taxation for the payment of James I's ransom, along with William Erskine of Kinnoul. Ogilvy of Auchterhouse 'was very highly regarded by the king and his subjects', and 'was a man of acute mind, distinguished speech, manly spirit, small in stature,

---

[110] A.F. Pollard (ed.), *The Reign of Henry VII from Contemporary Sources* (London, 1913), I, no. 100, 101; Macdougall, *James IV*, pp. 129–30.
[111] Glenn (ed.), *Buke of the Ordre of Knychthede*, pp. 18, 21; Mason, 'Chivalry and Citizenship', p. 58.
[112] Geoffrey de Charny, '*Livre de chevalerie*', in K. de Lettenhove (ed.), *Oeuvres de Froissart* (Brussels, 1873), tome I, part III, discussed in Keen, *Chivalry*, p. 14.

but notable and trustworthy in every kind of upright behaviour'.[113] In 1425 he sat on the trial of duke of Albany and the following year he was an auditor for the crown's revenues.[114] In July 1429 he acted as a Scottish representative in France and attended the French coronation at Rheims.[115] He did, of course, have military obligations and, as justiciar north of the Forth, attended the 1428 highland campaign.[116]

William Crichton of that Ilk (d. 1454) stands out as a particular favourite of James I and, after he was knighted by him at his coronation, Crichton became his close counsellor. Later in that same year he was made Gentleman of the Bedchamber and by 14 April 1435 he was appointed Master of the King's Household. Crichton was involved in diplomatic duties for James I and on 8 May 1426 he was appointed to treat with Eric, king of Norway and Denmark, for firm and lasting peace between the kingdoms. In this case, Crichton's diplomatic services demonstrate that there was a measure of real royal trust from the king. Crichton also undertook his martial duties and served on the 1429 highland campaign. Around this time he also began to appear as a witness to royal charters.[117] In 1434 he was appointed captain of Edinburgh Castle and sheriff of Edinburgh in 1435.[118] After James II's accession he was appointed Chancellor, then keeper of Edinburgh Castle in 1438 and in the same year again became sheriff of Edinburgh.[119] In 1448 he under-

---

[113] *APS*, II, p. 5; *Chron. Bower*, book XVI, 26. In the early years of the fifteenth century many knights had achieved chivalric reputations through bold and valiant deeds on the battlefield, including Archibald Douglas, fourth earl of Douglas, Alexander Stewart, earl of Mar, and Sir John Swinton.

[114] *ER*, IV, p. 400; *Chron. Bower*, book XVI, 10. Archibald Douglas, fifth earl of Douglas, William Douglas, earl of Angus, George Dunbar, earl of March, William Hay of Errol, constable of Scotland, Herbert Herries of Terregles and Patrick Ogilvy of Auchterhouse also sat on the trial of the duke of Albany in 1425.

[115] *Chron. Bower*, book XVI, 26. Bower says nine men were knighted, although he only names eight: Alexander Barclay, Laurence Vernon, Walter Leckie, John Turnbull, William Rossy, Thomas Lovell, Gilbert Hay and Nicholas King. The Corpus MS version, which was annotated by Sir Gilbert Hay personally, records a different story. Hay's marginalia instructed that chapter twenty-six should be revised because it was ill-informed. Hay's corrections included that Christian Chalmers (Cristin de Camera), Laurence Vernon and Hay himself were taken from Charles VII's household and knighted by him. Ogilvy, then, only knighted Barclay, Rossy, Turnbull, Lovell and King. The Harleian MS version of the *Scotichronicon*, copied around 1483–84, accommodated these changes. See Sally Mapstone, 'The *Scotichronicon*'s First Readers', in Barbara E. Crawford (ed.), *Church, Chronicle and Learning in Medieval and Early Renaissance Scotland: Essays Presented to Donald Watt on the Occasion of the Completion of the Publication of Bower's* Scotichronicon (Edinburgh, 1999), pp. 32–3, *Chron. Bower*, book XVI, 26, notes. See also Forbes-Leith, *Scots Men-at-Arms*, I, p. 158. Forbes-Leith claimed that Walter Leckie was already a knight and in the service of Charles VII by 1424, I, p. 43.

[116] *RMS*, II, 108, NAS GD137/3694; Roland J. Tanner, 'The Political Role of the Three Estates in Parliament and General Council in Scotland, 1424–1488' (Ph.D., University of St Andrews, 1999), Appendix B, p. 389.

[117] *CDS*, IV, 941, 942; *RMS*, II, 127, 134, 142.

[118] Michael Brown, *James I* (Edinburgh, 1994), p. 132; *Chron. Bower*, book XVI, 10, 33; *RMS*, II, 127, 134, 142; *ER*, IV, pp. 573, 602, 607; *SP*, III, pp. 57–8.

[119] *HMC, 6th Rep, Manuscripts of Sir Robert Menzies*, p. 691, no. 18; *SP*, III, pp. 57–61.

took further diplomatic duties, travelling to France to ratify the ancient league and to seek out a bride for James II.[120] Crichton then travelled to Burgundy where the party secured Mary of Gueldres and on his return he founded the Collegiate Church of Crichton.[121] Following this he resumed his martial duties and took a leading role at the siege of Dundas in January 1450.[122] It is clear that throughout his career Crichton was heavily involved in household, diplomatic and military duties for the Scottish crown and thus is an example of an 'ideal' Scottish knight who embodied all of the qualities required of him to meet these varied tasks.

During the same period, Andrew Gray of Foulis (1390–1469) also demonstrated considerable career 'flexibility'. He was part of the diplomatic party who accompanied Margaret of Scotland to France on her marriage to the dauphin in 1436. Under James II, Andrew Gray was created a Lord of Parliament in 1445 and he was an ambassador and guarantor of the truces with England in 1449 and 1451. On 22 January 1452 he was issued with a safe conduct to go on pilgrimage to Canterbury, demonstrating his knightly piety.[123] In 1452 Gray was appointed Master of the Household of James II, around the time that he was involved in the king's killing of the eighth earl of Douglas, and in 1459 he fulfilled his military function by being appointed Warden of the Marches.[124]

Other knights demonstrated their diplomatic skills on missions such as at Hawdenstank, where Walter Haliburton, lord of Dirleton, redressed English complaints, or throughout England where Sir Thomas Cranston of that Ilk and his son, Sir William Cranston, were employed by James II as ambassadors for negotiating a truce.[125] William Cranston also fulfilled his Christian duty by accompanying the eighth earl of Douglas to Rome for the papal jubilee in 1450, and in 1452 he was made a coroner in Roxburgh.[126] Advisory roles were

---

[120] *SP*, III, pp. 57–61.
[121] *Midl. Chrs.*, pp. 305–12; *SP*, III, pp. 57–61. Margaret Scott argues that founding churches was an assertion of nobility, usually to prove wealth and benevolence. Scott, 'Dress in Scotland', p. 65.
[122] *ER*, V, p. 345.
[123] *APS*, II, p. 60; *Foedera*, X, pp. 235, 243, 244, 245, 294, 300, 306; *SP*, IV, pp. 273–4.
[124] *ER*, V, 491; *Chron. Auchinleck*, p. 47; *SP*, IV, pp. 273–4.
[125] *Chron. Bower*, book XVI, 16; *RMS*, II, 127, 531; *CDS*, IV, 1032; *APS*, II, pp. 28, 46, 47, 48, 54, 55, 56, 57, 61; *Foedera*, X, pp. 446–7; McGladdery, *James II*, p. 67.
[126] *Chron. Auckinleck*, pp. 46–7; McGladdery, *James II*, p. 67, 69, 122. McGladdery also points out that the rewards received by the Cranstons in the wake of the earl of Douglas's death were considerable. Whilst the *Auchinleck Chronicle* names Sir Alexander Boyd, Sir Andrew Stewart, Sir William Cranston, Sir Simon of Glendenning, and the lord Gray, the *Extracta* names only William Cranston and Patrick, master of Gray as being involved in the murder. *Chron. Extracta*, p. 242. Cranston had been part of the Douglas party to the papal jubilee in Rome in 1450, and probably took part in tournaying at Chalon. *CDS*, IV, 1229; *Rot. Scot.*, II, p. 343; Fraser, *Douglas*, I, p. 466; Brown, *Black Douglases*, p. 287; Otto Cartellieri, *The Court of Burgundy: Studies in the History of Civilisation* (London & New York, 1929), pp. 121–2; Richard Barber and Juliet Barker, *Tournaments: Jousts, Chivalry and Pageants in the Middle Ages* (Woodbridge, 1989), pp. 118–19.

also maximised, as shown by Walter Ogilvy of Lintrathen, who was consulted by James I in 1426 as an advisor in the north over the Mar issue. Ogilvy was already the king's treasurer and auditor and became Master of the Household in 1431.[127]

James II's difficult relationship with the Douglases led to extremely close ties to certain nobles. This is evident in his relationship with Alexander Boyd of Drumcoll (d. 1469), who was a close familiar of the king and had been knighted by him at his marriage celebrations in 1449.[128] Alongside the king, Boyd played a part in the death of William, eighth earl of Douglas, ultimately proving his loyalty to the crown. Alexander also held some position of military superiority, as in 1456 he was appointed Warden of Threave Castle (Dumfriesshire).[129] In the same year he became custodian of Dumbarton castle, near Glasgow, and in 1464 he was a custodian of Edinburgh castle.[130] However, Boyd witnessed no charters during the reign of James II and he does not seem to have been involved in public life or James II's politics or administration. Boyd rose to prominence at court only under James III and he appears as a royal witness initially on 15 October 1463, after which he regularly witnessed royal charters and sat in parliament in 1463 and 1464.[131] On 11 April 1464 he was appointed as one of the envoys to treat with English ambassadors over issues of the truce, and in January 1465 he witnessed the agreement of a fifteen-year truce at York.[132] On 4 December 1465, following the success of the York truce, Boyd was again appointed as an envoy to meet an English ambassador at Newcastle.[133] Alexander twice acted as an auditor of the exchequer and by March 1466 he was chamberlain of the royal household.[134]

Sir Alexander Boyd of Drumcoll was, reportedly, personally close to the young king James III. In his introduction to the exchequer rolls, George Burnett claims that Boyd was appointed to instruct the knightly exercises of the young James III in 1466.[135] However, there is no evidence whatsoever to support this assertion. In fact, it seems that Burnett's suggestion may be based

---

[127] *RMS*, II, 54, 55, 56, 57; *A.B. Ill.*, IV, p. 389; HMC, *7th Report*, II, p. 707a; Brown, *James I*, pp. 82, 92, 195. However, in April 1431, Ogilvy's knightly status was not used in a charter witness list, where he was styled as Master of the King's Household. HMC, *Home*, p. 19, no. 4.

[128] *ER*, V, 329, 356. Other events occur in this time period, such as the tournament held at Stirling in February 1449 between three Burgundian knights and three Scottish knights. However, there is no indication that Boyd was present in Stirling, whereas as a noble close to the king, he would have been present at the marriage.

[129] *Chron. Auchinleck*, p. 47; *ER*, VI, pp. 208–9.

[130] *Ibid.*, VI, p. 209, VII, pp. 284, 362, 422.

[131] *RMS*, II, 760, 776–9, 788, 811, 828, 834–5, 847–9, 853–9, 861, 863–5, 868, 870, 871, 871n, 874, 876, 877, 881–4, 1327, 1385; *APS*, II, p. 84, Supplement, p. 28.

[132] *CDS*, IV, 1341; *APS*, Supplement, p. 30.

[133] *CDS*, IV, 1362.

[134] *ER*, VII, lvii–lviii, as auditor, 302, 380, as custodian of Edinburgh castle, 284, 362, 422, as chamberlain of royal household, *RMS*, II, 867. See also Macdougall, *James III*, pp. 70–4.

[135] *ER*, VII, p. lvii. The editor gives no contemporary evidence for this assertion. Nicholson, *Scotland*, p. 409.

on an entry in George Buchanan's late-sixteenth-century history that claimed that Alexander Boyd of Drumcoll was:

> eminently skilled in all the showy accomplishments of a gentleman, who was introduced to the king by the other royal guardians; and particularly at the desire of John Kennedy, his relation, now, on account of age, unfit for youthful exercises, to instruct his majesty in the rudiments of military tactics, in which he was acknowledged to excel. Trusting to these advantages, the Boyds were neither content with the honourable situation they held, nor the authority they possessed at court, but determined to transfer all public power into their own family; to accomplish which, Alexander was employed to bias the mind of the king. Having found him a pliable youth, he so won upon him by his politeness and flattery, that he gained his entire confidence. Being admitted into the most intimate familiarity, he would frequently hint to the young prince:– That he was now capable of reigning himself; that it was time that he should emancipate himself from the slavery of old men; that he ought to have the military about him, and begin in earnest, those exercises in which, whether he chose or not, he must spend the vigour of his age.[136]

There are clear questions about the accuracy of this passage. Buchanan was writing for a late-sixteenth-century audience and was distrustful of the influence of the great aristocracy on government. In addition to this, the Kennedys and the Boyds were opposed to each other in the struggle for possession of James III, so it is unlikely that John Kennedy would have actively encouraged Alexander Boyd to take any such position with the young king.[137] On 9 July 1466 the Boyds did seize possession of James and whilst the young king initially pardoned them for this, three years later at the parliament of 1469 they were accused of treason. Sir Alexander was found guilty and beheaded on the castle hill of Edinburgh immediately after the trial on 22 November 1469.[138] There is no direct evidence that Alexander was commissioned to teach the young king in chivalric exercises and it is more likely that this suggested role has been confused with his role as chamberlain of the royal household. However, what can be implied by Buchanan's entry is that Boyd had a well-known chivalric reputation. More importantly, Boyd's relationship with the crown implies that royal favour brought knighthood and that knighthood brought social and political standing.

---

[136] Buchanan, *History*, pp. 125–6.
[137] See Macdougall, *James III*, pp. 70–4. However, two bonds of friendship survive, one from 20 January 1466 between Robert, Lord Boyd and Gilbert, Lord Kennedy, and the second from 10 February 1466 between Sir Alexander Boyd and Gilbert, Lord Kennedy on the one side, and Robert, Lord Fleming on the other, which could be considered to support Burnett's assertion that 1466 was when Alexander took up the position as James's tutor in knightly exercises. The 10 February bond agreed that Robert, Lord Fleming would be 'of special service, and of cunsail to the Kyng' as long as Kennedy and Boyd were the same and that he promised not to remove the young king out of the keeping of Kennedy and Boyd.
[138] *APS*, II, pp. 185–7; Macdougall, *James III*, pp. 81–2.

Boyd's career may also demonstrate the typical career of a royal knight. However, whether knights' careers were notable because of their knighthoods, or because they were noble, is difficult to discern. Certainly those men who stayed at the status of squire – nobles who did not take knighthood but shared in the martial training and philosophy of knighthood – could also enjoy prominent public careers, such as Patrick Crichton of Cranstonriddel.[139] He does not appear to have been particularly active in public life during James III's administration, but from 1495 he took on many public duties.[140] In 1495 he became keeper of Edinburgh Castle, a position which he held again later in 1499 and 1501.[141] In 1498 and 1499, Crichton was the ranger of the ward of Tweed and in 1513 he sat in parliament.[142] Although only a squire, Patrick Crichton performed the same types of public functions as knights, holding a number of royal offices. This suggests that it was not always necessary to be a knight for a prominent public career, although public service remained an obligation of knighthood in Scotland.

The Emergence of the 'Renaissance' Knight

From the middle of the fifteenth century a new model of ideal knighthood was beginning to emerge. This placed less emphasis on the knight as a 'warrior', and instead placed equal weight on both military and administrative roles. As knights became more 'courtly' and the influence of humanist teachings became more apparent, knights demonstrated their worth in increasingly diverse ways. Sir Gilbert Hay translated chivalric texts, and half a century later, Sir Bernard Stewart d'Aubigny, wrote a treatise on the art of war. Sir John Ross of Montgrennan, demonstrating the influence of humanism, had a distinguished career as a lawyer and an administrator in royal service.[143] Many other knights attempted to embody the new values being embraced by the nobility.

Of course the armed nature of knighthood did not wane and no amount of 'new' education could destroy the glory of martial achievements. Indeed, prominent chivalric families such as the Douglases and the Hamiltons continued to be revered for their physical prowess in war and tournaments, although they also had high-powered positions in the royal court. As late as the mid sixteenth century the Hamilton's recourse to violence was still felt

---

[139] Hicks, *Bastard Feudalism*, p. 7.
[140] *RMS*, II, 956, 1975.
[141] *ER*, X, p. 505, XI, pp. 203, 321. Although the index to volume XI refers to him as Sir Patrick, no entries in the records confirm this status.
[142] *ER*, XI, pp. 101, 201; *APS*, II, p. 281.
[143] Brown, 'The Scottish "Establishment"', p. 99; Mason, *Kingship and Commonweal*, p. 115; John Finlay, *Men of Law in Pre-Reformation Scotland* (East Linton, 2000), ch. 7. 'The Office of the King's Advocate', esp. pp. 170, 208.

throughout Scottish society and in addition to the Cleansing of the Causeway in 1520, Sir James Hamilton of Finnart (d. 1540) had a reputation as being the most 'bluddie bouchour ewer thristand for blude'.[144] His physical dominance and use of violence, promoted by the knightly code, were both respected and feared by James V's courtiers. What did change in the early sixteenth century was the way in which this violence was perceived – from the admiration of glossy, chivalric violence to a firm disapproval of unrestrained physical prowess.

---

[144] Pitscottie, *Historie*, I, pp. 282–3.

CHAPTER THREE

The Bestowal of Knighthood and the Dubbing Ceremony

In his study of chivalry, Maurice Keen concluded that there were three normal occasions on which knighthood was bestowed. The first was at solemn court events or coronations, the second to signify a pilgrimage to the Holy Sepulchre (either before, during or after the pilgrimage), and the third on the eve of a battle or the storming of a city, when men sought knighthood 'in order that their strength and virtue may be the greater'.[1] It should be noted that these three occasions also correlate broadly to Keen's three-fold model of chivalry: the noble aspects of chivalry are encompassed within court events; the martial element is demonstrated by dubbings on the eve of a battle; and the religious component linked to the pilgrimages to the Holy Land. Many questions arise from Keen's conclusions: not least, were these three occasions the same ones upon which men were knighted in Scotland and did Scottish kings have any other occasions upon which they usually dubbed knights? It is also important to establish whether there was any direct link between where and when a man was knighted, and whether dubbing had any effect on his subsequent activities. In addition, we must ask why Scottish kings knighted particular men and whether this new status brought with it new responsibilities. In Scotland, most records of dubbings are of those bestowed by the kings, but there were instances where knights received the honour from other knights and the issue of whether or not there was a royal monopoly on dubbing will also be addressed.

Dubbing at Solemn Court Events: Coronations

Bestowal of knighthood at royal and state events was a necessary display of power by the king. The anonymous writer of the *Book of Pluscarden* highlighted the fact that wearing a crown on such occasions further emphasised the symbolism and authority of royal power. The chronicler wrote that the king should wear a crown at:

[1] Keen, *Chivalry*, p. 79, who directs his readers towards P. Contamine, 'Points du vue sur la chevalerie en France à la fin du moyen âge', *Francia* 4 (1976), p. 272ff.

Christmas, the Epiphany, Easter, Whitsunday, Ascension Day, the Assumption of Our Lady, the raising of the Holy Cross, All Saints; also on all days on which he holds general judicial sittings in parliament, and on days on which he confers knighthood in state,[2]

clearly demonstrating the close link between knighthood and the crown. Ritual ceremonies played a crucial role in the way men recognised their social obligations towards one another and thus the coronation ceremony was a vital expression of the king's relationship to his nobles and their own interrelationships.[3] It was quite common and indeed expected for knightings to be included in the coronation ceremony: *The Buke of the Ordre of Knychthede* opens with a young squire wanting to be knighted at the king's coronation, which suggests that royal dubbings provided more prestige than receiving knighthood from other lords or knights.[4] That the most important ceremony in the king's reign was marked by the creation of knights indicates a great deal about the relationship between monarchy and chivalry and the exercise of chivalrous kingship. Perhaps just as significant was that the chivalric importance of the occasion also affected the worth of the knighting that took place.[5]

In a retrospective section of his late-eighteenth-century *History*, covering the mid fifteenth century, John Pinkerton describes how 'knights were generally created with a great solemnity by the king himself.' He also draws attention to a section of a book published in Edinburgh in 1594 entitled *Certaine Matters Composed Together*, which included a knightly oath. This 'ancient oath administered in Scotland' gives further insight into the type of oaths which knights took at the end of the sixteenth century and is 'a curious relique of the spirit of chivalry'.[6] Of course we need to bear in mind that these oaths were published in post-Reformation Scotland and may have been adjusted accordingly. Indeed Frances Gies remarked that 'the chivalric mystique was rebuffed not only by Renaissance humanism but by Protestantism'.[7] *Certaine Matters* records that the knightly oath was as follows:

1. I shall fortifie and defend the Christian Religion, & Christes holy Evangell, presently preached in this Realme, to the vttermost of my power.
2. I shalbe leille and true to my soverane Lord the Kings Majestie, To all orders of Chieualry, and to the noble office of Armes.
3. I shall fortifie and defend Iustice at my power, and that without favour or feed.
4. I shall never flie from my soverane Lord, the Kinges Majestie, nor from his Hienes Lieutenants in time of mellay, and battell.

---

[2] *Chron. Pluscarden*, II, p. 62.
[3] Keen, *Chivalry*, p. 216.
[4] Glenn (ed.), *Buke of the Ordre of Knychthede*, pp. 4–5.
[5] Pilbrow, 'The Knights of the Bath', p. 201.
[6] Pinkerton, *History*, I, pp. 426–7.
[7] Frances Gies, *The Knight in History* (New York, 1984), p. 203.

5. I shall defende my natiue Realme, from all allieners and strangers.
6. I shall defend the just action and quarrell of al Ladies of Honour, of all true and friendles Widdowes, of Orphelings, and of Maidens of good fame.
7. I shall do diligence, where soever I heare there is any Murthers, Traytours, or masterfull Reavers, that oppresseth the Kings Lieges, and pure people, to bring them to the Lawe at my power.
8. I shall maintaine and vphold the noble estate of Chevalrie, with horse, harnes, and other Knightly abillzements: And shall help and succour them of the same order at my power, if they haue neede.
9. I shall enquyre and seeke to haue the knowledge and vnderstanding of al the Articles and points contained in the book of Chievallry.

All these premisses to obserue, keepe, and fulfill: I oblesse me, so helpe me God, by my owine hand, so helpe me God.[8]

Whilst it is difficult to know whether similar oaths were sworn in the fifteenth century, as Pinkerton inferred, it is certainly not improbable. The fact that such a strong emphasis was placed on chivalric duty in these oaths indicates that although a 'curious relique' at the end of the sixteenth century, these ideals were still at the heart of the knightly ethos in earlier periods.

As knights undoubtedly pledged themselves in this way to their king, it was considered necessary for a king to be dubbed prior to bestowing the honour himself. As the leader of knightly and military society, it was essential for the king to be a knight. As described by Walter Bower in his *Scotichronicon*, while the preparations were being made for Alexander III's inauguration in 1249, the assembly broke into an argument about whether or not a king should be knighted before he was crowned. Sir Alan Durward, justiciar of the kingdom and 'regarded as the flower of the knightly order', wanted to invest the king into knighthood immediately.[9] However, Sir Walter Comyn, earl of Menteith,

> roundly asserted that he had seen a king consecrated even though he was not yet a knight, and he had often heard, and knew for a fact, that kings had been consecrated who were never invested ceremonially with the order of knighthood. He added this also, that inasmuch as a crowned king is adorned with golden knightly insignia (which crown and sceptre are said to signify) – comparing the position to that stated in the *Decrees* that the son of a king ought to be called a king even though he may not possess a kingdom – so all the more a king should be considered a knight.[10]

---

[8] *Certaine Matters Composed Together* (Edinburgh, 1594), Folio F, pp. 2–3, bound under the title of *Description of Scotland*. This also prints a list of the knights of Scotland in 1594. The knightly oath is also quoted in Pinkerton, *History*, I, p. 427, where he standardised the spelling.
[9] *Chron. Bower*, book X, 1.
[10] *Ibid*.

Bower recorded that Comyn managed to persuade each side that Alexander should be first knighted and then crowned, suggesting that the chronicler, in the retelling of this story, thought a king should be officially dubbed a knight before he accepted the crown. So as the bishop of St Andrews 'girded the king with the belt of knighthood in the presence of the magnates of the land, and set out the rights and promises which pertain to a king [...] and readily underwent and permitted his blessing and ordination', the correct order of proceedings, in Bower's mind, took place.[11] However, Bower's version of events has caused much debate amongst scholars, as both Fordun and Wyntoun described the proceedings differently, claiming Alexander III was not knighted at his coronation but at a later date by Henry III.[12] M.D. Legge has argued that Fordun's account is probably more accurate than Bower's and she suggests that although Bower may have been using sources which have since disappeared, it is more likely that he invented this version based on the English coronation ceremony, where a king was always knighted prior to his crowning.[13]

The association between the solemn court ceremonial of the coronation and the bestowal of knighthood is apparent, and of the Stewart kings it was James I who most frequently used court events like these to bestow knighthood on his nobles. On his return to Scotland after a long period in English captivity, James dubbed *en masse* at his coronation at Scone on 21 May 1424. According to Walter Bower, sir Henry Wardlaw, bishop of St Andrews, conducted James's coronation and he was installed upon the royal throne by Sir Murdac Stewart, duke of Albany, by the right of his privilege as earl of Fife. The *Pluscarden* chronicler described the ceremony in much the same way as Bower and wrote that 'many aspirants were girded and decorated with the belt of knighthood by the king.' Bower recorded that James knighted twenty-seven men, although he actually only named twenty-five.[14] By accepting knighthood from James I in this way, these noblemen pledged themselves to exemplify the virtues of the order of knighthood. When receiving the honour in a communal ceremony like this, they were bonded not only to the wider community of knights but also, in an immediate sense, to the group that had been unified through that particular collective experience.[15]

---

[11] *Ibid.* Whilst in the fifteenth century there are no surviving Scottish examples of bishops or priests making knights, it was not an uncommon practice in earlier centuries throughout Europe. An early fourteenth-century Roman pontifical describes a liturgical order for the making of a knight in St Peter's. For more on this and other examples see Keen, *Chivalry*, pp. 65, 71–7.
[12] *Chron. Fordun*, II, pp. 289–91; *Chron. Wyntoun*, V, p. 115.
[13] M.D. Legge, 'The Inauguration of Alexander III', *PSAS* 80 (1948), p. 81.
[14] *Chron. Bower*, book XVI, 2, 10; *Chron. Pluscarden*, II, p. 279; and *Chron. Extracta*, p. 227, which excludes Walter Ogilvy and Andrew Gray of Fowlis. For an extensive discussion of the knightings at James I's coronation see Stevenson, 'Knighthood, Chivalry and the Crown', pp. 22–35.
[15] Georges Duby, *The Three Orders: Feudal Society Imagined* (Chicago & London, 1980), pp. 300–1.

Whilst the chroniclers' list of those who received knighthood at James's coronation is an impressive collection of some of the most prominent nobles in Scotland at the time, it is not possible that all of these men were knighted on this day. In particular, three of the noblemen, Robert Cunningham of Kilmaurs, Herbert Maxwell of Caerlaverock and Alexander Irvine of Drum, had already been knighted well before May 1424.[16] However, this does not necessarily mean that these men were not knighted on a second occasion, by having their status raised to the higher status of 'knight banneret'. In other countries, particularly England, knights could be dubbed a second time and raised to the status of banneret. Bannerets were generally men of an extremely high social status with an impressive level of wealth, although these factors did not contribute solely to the superior knightly status they held.[17] Maurice Keen argues that the title of 'knight banneret' had strong military implications, usually indicating that the banneret could raise a considerable retinue to serve him. The association between bannerets and warfare were strong, stemming from the square banner displaying personal arms that the knight could use on all martial occasions, at war or tournament.[18] Indeed, in his *History*, John Pinkerton says that bannerets were 'an intermediate order, between the peers and the lairds; possessing estates of such extent, and of so many knights fees, that they could lead a great number of followers to the field, whence they had a title to display a banner.' He records that they were also distinguished by their 'peculary enseigny or *cri de guerre* and by supporters to their armourial bearings.'[19] However, there were no Scottish knights who actually styled themselves as 'knight banneret', nor do we find them being made on the battlefield. Indeed, when the duke of Gloucester made thirty-two English knights banneret and fourteen new knights whilst on campaign in Scotland in July 1482, the duke of Albany only dubbed new knights.[20] There is one example which could be proffered tentatively as an instance where bannerets were made on the battlefield: the knighting of Sir James Douglas at Bannockburn in 1314. There has been much debate amongst historians surrounding Douglas's dubbing prior to the battle. Many scholars have argued that Douglas's career was so advanced by 1314 that he must have been raised to banneret at this time, not simply knighted;[21] but, John Barbour, Robert Bruce's

---

[16] NAS GD16/3/8; *RMS*, II, 48; Fraser, *Maxwells*, I, no. 29, pp. 155–7, no. 30, pp. 157–9; *Abdn. Reg.*, I, pp. 220–1.
[17] Coss, 'Knighthood, Heraldry and Social Exclusion', pp. 66–7.
[18] This differed from the pennon which all knights could bear. Keen, *Chivalry*, p. 168.
[19] Pinkerton, *History*, I, pp. 365–6.
[20] William A. Shaw (ed.), *The Knights of England: A Complete Record from the Earliest Times to the Present Day of the Knights of All the Orders of Chivalry in England, Scotland and Ireland, and of Knights Bachelors* (London, 1906), II, pp. 18–19.
[21] See Anne McKim, 'James Douglas and Barbour's Ideal of Knighthood', *Forum for Modern Language Studies* 17 (1981), pp. 168–9; also printed in W.H. Jackson (ed.), *Knighthood in Medieval Literature* (Woodbridge, 1981); and G.W.S. Barrow, *Robert Bruce and the Community of the Realm of Scotland* (3rd edn, Edinburgh, 1988), where Barrow remarks that it is 'strange' that Douglas only received his knighthood on the eve of Bannockburn. Barrow then cites a

biographer, gives no indication that Douglas was made banneret and refers to him consistently as without knightly status in the years prior to Bannockburn.[22] In addition to this, many other Scottish knights had outstanding martial careers or were of high social status a long time prior to being dubbed. Of course, this does not prove conclusively that knights banneret were never made on Scottish military campaigns but if the status of knight banneret was mainly a military accolade, then it seems improbable that James I raised knights to that status at his coronation, where they were not being honoured for military achievements.

There are, however, a number of instances in Scotland at which the rank of banneret was specifically referred, mainly in parliaments held during James I's reign. In 1426, the parliamentary acts were reported to have been made by certain lords of parliament, bannerets, barons, freeholders and wisemen.[23] Moreover, in 1428, bannerets were directly mentioned as part of a parliamentary reform in line with English patterns. Parliament stated that 'all bischoppis abbotis prioris dukis erlis lordis of parliament and banrentis' should attend parliament if the king desired.[24] If James I did attempt to introduce this new status, just below the rank of earl, then it is possible that he might have raised Robert Cunningham of Kilmaurs, Herbert Maxwell of Caerlaverock and Alexander Irvine of Drum to knight banneret at his coronation, although they were never styled as such, nor do they appear to have been heavily involved in parliamentary proceedings. Moreover, if these men were raised to the status of knights banneret, they do not appear to have been significantly involved in James I's administration.[25] If we assume that Alexander Grant is right in concluding that James I was attempting to emulate an English parliamentary model, then the king might well have sought to elevate knights to bannerets at his coronation, but the evidence is inconclusive. The rank was seemingly only of temporary attraction to the crown and it never became a permanent feature of the aristocratic hierarchy in fifteenth-century Scotland.

French account which claims that Sir John [sic] Douglas was knighted, implying that he was raised to banneret, although Barrow himself warns the account is 'characterized by a mixture of gross error and accurate detail', p. 367, n.42.
[22] Barbour, *Bruce*, XII, 417–18.
[23] *APS*, II, p. 13. This occurred again in 1431, *Ibid*., II, p. 20.
[24] *Ibid*., I, p. 15. For more on James I's use of English terminology and concepts, with direct reference to this act, see Grant, 'Development of the Scottish Peerage', pp. 18–21. Although Grant argues that from 1437 banneret became synonymous with lord of parliament, he heavily emphasises the parliamentary implications of the status of banneret during James I's reign. Grant, 'Development of the Scottish Peerage', p. 20. Grant argues that in 1476, when John of the Isles was made *'baron banrentum et dominum parliamenti'* that these were the same title. However, it is quite clear that they are not, although *'baron banrentum'* does not appear to be a knightly styling either. Sir James Ogilvy of Airlie, knight, was similarly made *'barone et banret et lordis of this parliament'* in 1491. *APS*, II, pp. 113, 228.
[25] *Chron. Bower*, book XVI, 10, 11, 21; *APS*, II, p. 57; *Rot. Scot*., II, pp. 341, 353, 367; *SP*, IV, pp. 231–2, VI, p. 475; Brown, *James I*, p. 50.

Dubbing at Solemn Court Events: Baptisms and Parliament

As Maurice Keen argued, coronations were clearly a time when knighthoods were normally bestowed. Royal baptisms also provided excellent opportunities to demonstrate political authority and create personal alliances through knighting, and it is no surprise to find an example of this in Scotland. When a prince was knighted at the same time as his peers, taking the same pledge through accepting the honour that the others also took, it bonded him in equal measure to his king and to his fellow knights. The prince, then, undertook the same rite of passage as the others, and was only distinguishable from them outside the knightly code, as Georges Duby comments 'for the moment [he was] asking no more than to be first among equals'.[26]

James I carefully planned that his twin sons would be granted the belt of knighthood alongside some of their peers. At their baptism in 1430 James knighted them both, along with the son of Stephen Porcari, a Roman prince who was in attendance; William Douglas, the son and heir of Archibald, fifth earl of Douglas; William Douglas, later eighth earl of Douglas and son of Sir James Douglas of Balvenie; John, son and heir of Simon Logan of Restalrig; the son of James Edmonstone of that Ilk; James Crichton, the eldest son and heir of Sir William Crichton; and William Borthwick, the son and heir of Sir William Borthwick. James I was keen to tie the sons of his close local allies to the princes through knighthood, as the immediate political value of the boys' birth had made James's dynasty seem more secure.[27] However, by binding their sons with his own, James also reasserted his own bonds with these magnates and as a result further reinforced his power base in the Lothians.

The boys whom James I knighted alongside his sons were all around five years of age and this is unusual given that they had not yet been fully versed in knightly obligations. The *Buke of the Ordre of Knychthede* warned that 'quhen a childe is maid knycht he thinkis nocht on the poyntis of the ordre yat he sueris to kepe', so the dubbing at the baptism must have been a long-term investment.[28] These boys were clearly knighted because of their lineage and inherent social status, and not because they had earned a strong military reputation or had performed duties worthy of the honour. This, then, indicates that there were alternative pathways to a knightly career, dependant upon many factors including lineage. However, these knighthoods were not simply honorific, as the boys reportedly did perform knightly duties later in their careers and thus took seriously their responsibilities as knights. The chronicler Walter Bower reported in the 1440s that 'all of these [...] are now fellow-soldiers with

---

[26] Duby, *Three Orders*, pp. 300–1.
[27] *Chron. Bower*, book XVI, 16, and notes p. 365; Brown, *James I*, pp. 117, 132.
[28] Glenn (ed.), *Buke of the Ordre of Knychthede*, p. 27.

our reigning king', indicating that they did take up their martial role as knights.[29]

Another one of the solemn court ceremonies that Keen regarded as appropriate for the granting of knighthood was parliament. Although it was not usual to knight men in parliament, it did occur at least once in the fifteenth century. On 29 January 1488, James III created four new lords of parliament, raised the Marquis of Ormond to the dukedom of Ross, confirmed William Douglas of Cavers, sheriff of Roxburgh, in his regality of Cavers and created three new knights. The new knights were David Kennedy, son and heir of John, second Lord Kennedy; William Carlyle, grandson and heir of John, first Lord of Carlyle; and Robert Cunningham of Polmaise.[30] In the face of the political problems around this parliament and much dissent from his nobility, James III publicly rewarded those whom he believed were loyal to the crown and thus attempted to ensure that he retained their loyalty.[31] Above all, what can be drawn from an analysis of dubbings at solemn court events in Scotland is that the men knighted at these ceremonies did have one common feature, that is that they appear to have been taken predominantly from the upper nobility.[32]

Dubbing on Pilgrimage to the Holy Sepulchre

According to Maurice Keen, the second occasion on which knighthoods were normally bestowed was as part of a pilgrimage to the Holy Sepulchre, with the ceremony usually performed in Jerusalem itself.[33] Whilst there were men who went on pilgrimages from Scotland to the Holy Land in the fifteenth century, there is very little evidence to suggest that any received knighthoods while they were there. Around 1455, Alexander Preston, canon of Glasgow, 'went lately with a notable company to the Holy Land to fight against the infidels, and whose father and many others of his kinsmen have fought against the infidels in the lands of the infidels and been made knights.'[34] The implica-

---

[29] *Chron. Bower*, book XVI, 16. Bower may be referring to the siege of Methven which took place around 29 November 1444, which James II led and in which many of his knights participated. It seems probable that this is what prompted Bower to call them 'fellow-soldiers'. See McGladdery, *James II*, p. 32; *RMS*, II, p. 283.

[30] *APS*, II, 181; Macdougall, *James III*, p. 237.

[31] Roland Tanner suggested that the dispensing of peerages and knighthoods in this parliament simply served to further deepen the already existing division amongst the nobility. Tanner, 'The Political Role of the Three Estates', p. 307.

[32] Using Alexander Grant's definitions, the upper nobility consisted of earls, provincial lords and greater barons, whereas the lesser nobility were barons and freeholders. From the mid fifteenth century they were divided between lords and lairds. Grant, 'Development of the Scottish Peerage', p. 2.

[33] Keen, *Chivalry*, pp. 78–9.

[34] *CPL*, XI, pp. 158–9. Later in December 1458 it was said that Alexander Preston had been fighting for a year with twelve archers and more fighting men against the Infidel. *CPL*, XI, p. 519; Macquarrie, *Scotland and the Crusades*, p. 95.

tion here may be that the Prestons were made knights in the Holy Land but none of the records indicate who were the members of Preston's party, nor if any Prestons returned as knights. Indeed, the records are almost silent on this point. William Preston might potentially have returned with this group, but he does not seem to have been knighted at any time.[35]

Although pilgrimage knightings at the Holy Sepulchre have no direct royal associations, a Scottish example suggests that in one instance a king took a direct interest in knighting a man who was preparing to undertake such a pilgrimage. Anselm Adornes was a Brugeois merchant who had become a close familiar of James III when he had attended his court on diplomatic missions in 1468 and 1469. James III bestowed knighthood upon him on 15 January 1469 and, at the Scottish king's behest, Anselm undertook a pilgrimage to the Holy Land, beginning his journey on 19 February 1470.[36] On his return he dictated to his son John the events of his travels, speaking at length of how he had felt ill-equipped to undertake the pilgrimage before being invested as a knight.[37] Writing to James III, John related his father's experience, claiming that

> from day to day his eagerness was all the greater to view the holy places, when by your benign favour he had received the knightly insignia from your most illustrious majesty, and his resolution grew that he, decorated as a knight of the chivalric order, would set forth on this renowned and noble pilgrimage, than which nothing more distinguished or more holy might be imagined, advancing from the status of novice to that of true knight, and thence to that of one out of a thousand.[38]

From his account it would seem that Anselm may have sought knighthood from James III solely for the purpose of undertaking this journey, and this certainly suggests that receiving knighthood before going on pilgrimage was

---

[35] *St Giles Reg.*, no. 77, pp. 106–7; *RMS*, II, 705, 12 July 1459 where William Preston is not styled as knight; David McRoberts, 'Scottish Pilgrims to the Holy Land', *IR* 20 (1969), p. 83. This may be William Preston of the Craigmillar branch of Prestons. In 1421 his father, John Preston, died, leaving him in the tutory of his cousin Archibald Preston. *RMS*, II, 87n; *SP*, III, p. 118.

[36] Bruges, Stadsarchief, Fonds de Limburg Stirum, 15 January 1469, transcribed in Alan Denis Macquarrie, 'The Impact of the Crusading Movement in Scotland, 1095–c.1560' (Ph.D., Edinburgh, 1982), Appendix I, no. 3; Lille, Bibliothèque Municipale, MS 330, 43, transcribed in Macquarrie, 'The Impact of the Crusading Movement', Appendix I, no. 4; Bruges, Stadsarchief, Cartulaire Rodenboek, f. 270r–v, transcribed in Macquarrie, 'The Impact of the Crusading Movement', Appendix I, no. 6. See also C.A.J. Armstrong (ed.), 'A Letter of James III to the Duke of Burgundy', *SHS Misc. VIII* (Edinburgh, 1951), pp. 21–2; Alan Macquarrie, 'Anselm Adornes of Bruges: Traveller in the East and Friend of James III', *IR* 33 (1982), p. 15; John Malden, 'Anselm Adornes and the Two Collars', *The Double Tressure: Journal of the Heraldic Society of Scotland* 10 (1988), p. 7; Macquarrie, *Scotland and the Crusades*, p. 97.

[37] *Ibid.*, p. 97.

[38] Taken from Jacques Heers and Georgette de Groer (eds), *Itinéraire d'Anselme Adorno en Terre Sainte (1470–1471)* (Paris, 1978), p. 30, translated in MacDonald, 'Chapel of Restalrig', pp. 46–7, n. 68. The only surviving manuscript of Adornes' *Itinéraire* is in Lille, Bibliothèque Municipale, MS 330. The phrase 'one out of a thousand' probably refers to being made a knight, i.e. one knight out of a thousand men, not one knight out of a thousand knights who had been to the Holy Land, although both interpretations are valid and illuminating.

important, at least to the Brugeois merchant. However, Adornes' knighting is more problematic than John Adornes' account indicates and is more likely to have been granted for diplomatic services, an idea which has been extensively explored in recent research.[39]

Dubbing for Military Service

Returning to Keen's model, it is certain that Scottish kings did knight men at battles and at sieges, ostensibly to encourage greater valour from their men.[40] Indeed, the *Buke of the Ordre of Knychthede* advised that 'quhare grete multitude of honourable and worthy men suld assemble for honourable actis tobe done And thare suld the king mak mony new knychtis'.[41] Scottish literary accounts abound with reports of men being knighted prior to battle or for their achievements, most famously when Robert Bruce knighted James Douglas, Walter Stewart and 'other als of gret bounté' prior to the battle of Bannockburn in 1314.[42] Similarly, on the eve of the 1402 battle of Humbleton (or Homildon) Hill, Sir Thomas Erskine knighted John Mowbray, lord of Drummany, and Sir John Swinton dubbed Adam Gordon of that Ilk during the battle itself. New knights were also created at the battle of Sauchieburn in June 1488, and Dominic Lovell, Thomas Brochton and Roger Hartilton all first appeared styled as knight just over a week after the battle.[43] Whereas in the fourteenth and earlier in the fifteenth centuries it was often high status noblemen who were dubbed on the battlefield (presumably due to the associated chivalric prestige), what is notable from these dubbings is that none of these men were of a high social status. This perhaps indicates a trend that may have developed during the fifteenth century as the increasing cost of being dubbed precluded lesser nobles from being dubbed at a formal court ceremony.

Courtesy of the richer variety of sources available for James IV's reign, it is evident that James IV often chose the option of knighting his men during or after military campaigns. Patrick Hume of Polwarth's dubbing is just one example of James's bestowal of knighthood in this situation. The Hume family were heavily involved in the defence of the borders in the late 1490s

---

[39] Stevenson, 'The Unicorn, St Andrew and the Thistle', pp. 3–22; Stevenson, 'Knighthood, Chivalry and the Crown', pp. 253–60.

[40] This was a widespread practice: before the battle of Verneuil in 1424 many knights were created, including James Douglas, the younger son of Archibald, fourth earl of Douglas. Fraser, *Douglas*, I, pp. 393, 399. On 16 October 1449 the Comte de Dunois knighted the Scottish knight William Monypenny at the siege of Rouen. McGladdery, *James II*, p. 98; Forbes-Leith, *Scots Men-at-Arms*, p. 58. (Neither McGladdery or Forbes-Leith give evidence for this assertion and there is an indication that Monypenny was a knight before 15 June 1434 which may suggest that he was raised to banneret, especially as it was a French knighting, *RMS*, II, 228.)

[41] Glenn (ed.), *Buke of the Ordre of Knychthede*, p. 5.

[42] Barbour, *Bruce*, XII, lines 415–20.

[43] *Chron. Bower*, book XV, 14; *RMS*, II, 1738.

and they took leading roles at Hume in February 1497, at Duns, Melrose and Lauder in June, and Norham in July and August 1497.[44] Patrick Hume seems to have excelled in these raids and on 8 June he was involved in a skirmish at Duns when the English attacked the East March. Ten days later, James rewarded Patrick for his services in Duns by granting him lands in Rednach. On 5 August 1497 at Upsettlington, two miles north of Norham, Northumberland, James again bestowed favour upon Patrick, giving him five merks of the lands of Unschenach, £5 worth of the lands of Rednach, and other grants.[45] James also knighted Patrick at this time, presumably as a reward for his military service, and he appeared not long afterwards styled as knight.[46] During the summer campaigns of 1497, James IV knighted a number of other men for military service, including Robert Lundy of Balgony and John Ogilvy of Finglask.[47]

James IV also knighted his nobles for general military service, though not necessarily in association with a particular battle or campaign. Sir Andrew Wood of Largo, for example, was knighted sometime before February 1495, after a distinguished career as a naval commander for James III and James IV.[48] Wood's dubbing suggests two important points: firstly, that it was not a requirement of outstanding military leadership to be a knight, and secondly, that knighthood was probably offered rather than sought, as Wood would have been eligible to take it much earlier in his career and might have done so from James III had it been appropriate to request this.

Of course, knighthood was not always accepted when it was offered and there are some recorded cases of men who refused to be dubbed, for financial or personal reasons. The fourteenth-century French chronicler, Jean Froissart, recounts the story of a squire refusing knighthood at the battle of Otterburn in 1388. Froissart introduces 'the gallant squire' David 'Colleime' when he was already dead, lying beside the wounded earl of Douglas, bearing Douglas's banner beside him. The chronicler wrote that David had that day refused to become a knight, even though the earl of Douglas had wanted to dub him, because 'wherever he fought he had been an outstandingly good squire'.[49] Given the chivalric ethos of developing a well-known reputation, it is possible the squire may have been concerned that he was not renowned as a knight. Consequently, he may have felt he could not perform as well on the battlefield with a new status. Presumably, in a battlefield context, David could not expect that Douglas would provide him with lands and goods to support his potentially raised status and this may also have been a deterrent if he did not have

---

44 Macdougall, *James IV*, pp. 135, 137–9.
45 *RMS*, II, 2365; Macdougall, *James IV*, pp. 137, 139.
46 *Prot. Bk. Young*, no. 980.
47 *ER*, X, pp. 484, 577, 589; *TA*, I, p. 211; NAS GD 32/8/3.
48 *RMS*, II, 2040, 2231.
49 Froissart, *Chronicles*, pp. 344–5.

the means to support it himself. Of course, Froissart's general point may simply have been that it was better to die a famous squire than an unknown knight.

Dubbing at Public Royal Events: Weddings and Tournaments

Military campaigns and solemn court ceremonies were not the only times dubbings took place and there were, of course, other occasions upon which knighthoods were granted by Scottish kings. These were more festive, public royal events, such as weddings and tournaments, which do not fall into the categories that Maurice Keen established but where knightings occur as frequently, in Scotland, as they do at other types of occasions. James II, for example, often raised the status of his nobles to honour them at public celebrations such as tournaments.

The associations between the bestowal of knighthood and tournaments are obvious: tournaments were an occasion at which knights were engaged in the stylised and ritualised performance of their function as warriors and they were therefore tied to the acceptance of new members to the rank of knighthood. Indeed, in 1398 a tournament was held with the specific purpose of celebrating David, duke of Rothesay's investiture into knighthood.[50] James II seems to have been very keen to promote tournaments, and it is not surprising that this led to the bestowal of more knighthoods. For example, in February 1449 Jacques and Simon de Lalain and Hervey de Meriadet, three noble knights from Burgundy, came to Stirling to engage in single combats presided over by James II, with James Douglas, the brother of the eighth earl of Douglas, and later ninth earl, John Ross of Hawkhead and another James Douglas, the brother of Sir Henry de Douglas of Loch Leven.[51] On the appointed day, after the Burgundians had arrived, James Douglas and his party entered the lists and were attended by a great company that included the eighth earl of Douglas.

> Then the three champions, all armed, and clad in their coats of mail, dismounted at their pavilion, and afterwards all three went to do reverence to the King of Scotland, and all three prayed that he would confer on them the

---

[50] *Chron. Bower*, book XV, 4; Boardman, *Early Stewart Kings*, pp. 57, 212.
[51] *Chron. Bower*, Harleian MS Additions, Ch. 9, p. 141; *Chron. Auchinleck*, p. 40; *Chron. Extracta*, p. 238; Francisque Michel, *Les Écossais en France, les Français en Écosse* (London, 1862), p. 207. A long-standing tradition of Shrovetide tournaments throughout Europe existed, and Tuesday was the traditional day to commence a tournament. In the High Middle Ages, the traditional day to commence was Monday. See Joachim Bumke, *Courtly Culture: Literature and Society in the High Middle Ages* (Berkeley, 1991), p. 253. A series of Shrovetide tournaments was held by James IV in the early sixteenth century which will be discussed later.

order of knighthood, which he freely granted to them. So he descended from his throne, and made all three knights.[52]

Some issues surround the knightly status of these men prior to the tournament. Chastellian recorded that all six men 'were renowned as valiant knights, powerful in body and limbs' before they were knighted by the king.[53] None of the other chronicles refer to any of the Scottish men as knights before the tournament, with the exception of the Harleian addition to Bower's *Scotichronicon*. As this was compiled in 1473, a quarter of a century after the tournament, it is understandable how an error might have been made. Chastellain's assertion that they were valiant knights was probably just a general comment designed to highlight his subject's martial prowess, and cannot provide an accurate description of the Douglases' or John Ross's knightly status.[54] Therefore, James II probably did knight these men before they entered the lists, in all likelihood so that they were evenly matched in terms of status against the Burgundian knights. Moreover, the honour of having received knighthoods from the king in a public ceremony would encourage them to fight gallantly during the tournament, thus honouring the king and the kingdom.

Like James II, James IV also knighted men before they entered the lists. In May 1508 James put on a lavish tournament of the Wild Knight and the Black Lady, after which, according to the sixteenth-century historian Pitscottie, he rewarded all of his nobles and made thirty new knights.[55] James IV was particularly keen on such public display of his wealth and power, and a few years previously had staged an ostentatious and extravagant wedding ceremony to celebrate his union with the English princess Margaret Tudor. On the third day of his wedding celebrations in August 1503, James IV knighted forty-one men, after which began a three-day joust in the courtyard of Holyrood Palace in Edinburgh.

> After the Othe sworne and taken, the Erle Bothwell [gave] them the gylt spourneys, and the Kynge gaffe them the Stroke of his Swerde, wich was born before hym. This doon, he sayed to the Qwene, the Lady – these are your knyghts.[56]

The courtly love overtones of this declaration – that the knights were bound in service to the queen – are unusual in a Scottish context. Indeed, a component

---

[52] Chastellain, 'Historie du bon chevalier Messire Jacques de Lalain', pp. 33–4.
[53] *Ibid.*, p. 33.
[54] John Ross of Hawkhead certainly was not a knight before the tournament. *RMS*, II, 383, 411.
[55] Pitscottie, *Historie*, I, p. 244.
[56] John Younge, Somerset Herald, 'The Fyancells of Margaret, Eldest Daughter of King Henry VIIth to James King of Scotland: Together with her Departure from England, Journey into Scotland, her Reception and Marriage There, and the Great Feasts Held on that Account', in Thomas Hearne (ed.), *Joannis Leland Antiquarii de Rebus Britannicis Collectanea* (London, 1770), p. 298. Bothwell was given prominence at this tournament because he had been crucial in securing the marriage treaty.

distinctly absent from the Scottish chivalric tradition is courtly love. Whilst courtly romance was popular in Scotland, there is no indication from Scottish sources that these themes were ever ritually expressed at the Scottish court. What cannot be overlooked in this instance is that the report came from an English herald familiar with the processes and tributes of courtly love. In fact, there is no indication that the men knighted by James IV at this time were ever bound in service to the queen, although this may be a problem with the sources which have survived rather than an true indication of the reality.[57]

It is therefore clear that the three occasions, according to Keen, upon which knighthood was normally bestowed, were not the only occasions upon which dubbings occurred in fifteenth-century Scotland. Royal knightings did take place at solemn court ceremonies, such as coronations and baptisms, and also during military campaigns and around the time of battles, not just specifically on the eve of battles as Keen suggested. However, the most popular occasions upon which Scottish kings might knight their subjects seems to have been at public royal events, such as weddings and tournaments, which had a festive and celebratory atmosphere and were an ideal time to assert and display royal authority.

Dubbing In Absentia

The question of whether there could be dubbing *in absentia* is raised by a number of Scottish cases. For instance, Alexander Lindsay, earl of Crawford (d. 1439), was allegedly knighted at James I's coronation in 1424 and was recorded by Walter Bower, inaccurately, as having been dubbed at this time. Crawford was a hostage for James's release and had been exchanged at Durham some months earlier and thus was not present at the coronation ceremony. He remained in English captivity until 1427 when he was exchanged for Malise Graham, earl of Menteith.[58] The earl of Crawford took part in public affairs almost immediately on his return, but he witnessed only one charter for James, on 27 July 1429 at Inverness, styled earl of Crawford, not as a knight.[59] He was present only a few months later at parliament on 10 March 1430, was an ambassador to England in January 1431, and on 31 March 1438 he

[57] *RMS*, II, 3007, sees John Hay of Belltown (de Snaid) and *RMS*, II, 3339, sees John Melville of Raith, witnessing charters for James IV.
[58] In his work on the Lindsays, Lord Lindsay argues that Alexander was present at the coronation and then immediately went to England to take his place as a hostage. Lord Lindsay, *Lives of the Lindsays, or A Memoir of the Houses of Crawford and Balcarres* (London, 1849), I, p. 120. However, Lindsay took the oath of an hostage on 28 March 1424, two months before the coronation and it would seem unlikely that he returned to Scotland for the coronation, only to go back England again, *CDS*, IV, 942, 953. Malise Graham had been disinherited from the earldom of Strathearn in 1427, but was granted the earldom of Menteith six weeks later, which suggests that James granted Graham the earldom to raise his rank so that he could be sent south to London to replace the earl of Crawford. See Brown, *James I*, p. 86.
[59] *RMS*, II, 127.

was appointed by James II as a commissioner for the truce with England.[60] Although it is generally held that, as an earl, he was automatically of knightly status, D.E.R. Watt suggests that he may never have received the honour and there is no evidence of him ever being knighted.[61] Crawford's case might point to the bestowal of knighthood *in absentia*; yet, if this were true, we would expect that Crawford would have designated his knightly status. Moreover, from English evidence it would appear that a knight had to be physically present at the ceremony in order to be dubbed.[62]

Nevertheless, by the sixteenth century knighting *in absentia* could be employed in exceptional circumstances by the Scottish crown. On 16 February 1534, James V knighted Adam Otterburn of Redhall by letter, as at this time Otterburn was in England. James stated that it became kings and princes to reward and honour men of eminent merit and in the letter the king dispensed with Otterburn's physical absence and directed that he be immediately entitled 'of Redhall, knight'. James charged everyone to honour Sir Adam as a knight and do nothing to the contrary of this writ on the appropriate pain of contravention.[63] That James qualified that he was dispensing with his absence obviously indicates that dubbing by letter was extraordinary, but the king blatantly wanted to secure Otterburn's service. Since 1528 Otterburn had been acting as king's advocate and in May 1534 he was a Scottish representative at the signing of a peace treaty in London. James clearly felt Adam should be knighted during the negotiations for this treaty and he wanted to ensure Otterburn's allegiance to the Scottish crown.[64]

Non-Royal Dubbings

Royal occasions and crown-led battles or sieges were, of course, not the only circumstances in which knighthood could be bestowed. The sheer number of knights in Scotland indicates that at various times new knighthoods were granted without being associated with special occasions. Of the knights in royal service, a large proportion cannot have received their knighthoods at any of these events. For example, Walter Stewart of Strathavon, was knighted during a time when no major royal 'events' are recorded (September 1438 to June 1439), and John Montgomery of Corscrag received the honour at a time

---

[60] *APS*, II, p. 28, *Foedera*, X, pp. 446–7.
[61] *Chron. Bower*, book XVI, 10, notes p. 353.
[62] The statutes of the Order of the Garter indicate that when a companion was elected he was notified but he had to be installed in person within a year before he was a member. D'Arcy Jonathan Dacre Boulton, *The Knights of the Crown: The Monarchical Orders of Knighthood in Later Medieval Europe, 1325–1520* (Woodbridge, 1987), p. 135.
[63] Denys Hay (ed.), *The Letters of James V: Collected and Calendared by the late Robert Kerr Hannay* (Edinburgh, 1954), p. 253.
[64] Jamie Cameron, *James V: The Personal Rule 1528–1542* (Edinburgh, 1994), pp. 14, 27, 63, 117.

when James IV was not engaged in wars, tournaments, or public displays of any note (June 1498 to March 1501).[65] This suggests either that kings were bestowing knighthoods at other times, perhaps when they were attempting to retain the service of a specific individual, or, more crucially, that the crown did not have a monopoly on dubbing and that ordinary knights were granting new knighthoods.

In fact, it is certain that the crown did not have absolute control over the granting of knighthood and there are indications that lord-knight and lord-squire relationships in non-royal retinues were strong. Late in the fourteenth century there was ample evidence of a tradition of lords knighting men in their retinues. Alexander Lindsay, the second surviving son of David, lord of Crawford, began his knightly career as a squire in the service of his cousin, Thomas Stewart, earl of Angus (d. c.1362).[66] Lindsay was promised the sum of forty merks of land 'in the qwilkes the forsaid erle of Angors was obligit be his lettres to gyve me heritably, eftir I had tane the ordre of Knycht', presumably at the hands of Angus himself.[67] This forty merks of land served as a mark of prestige and a reward for his services as a squire, but it functioned as a bond for his services yet to come as a knight and guaranteed his exclusive personal loyalty to Angus. The sum of forty merks of land must also have been enough to put him on the threshold of the landed wealth necessary to support the status of knighthood.

In March 1415, Archibald, fourth earl of Douglas, rewarded his beloved squire, David Hume, with the lands of Bayherdlands, for services rendered and to be rendered.[68] After the earl of Douglas's death in 1424, Hume appears to have sought out the lordship of William Douglas, earl of Angus, and in July 1436 Angus gave Hume, styled 'his beloved squire', the lands of Lee, Wollee and Wolhoplee and their pertinents for his services done and to be done.[69] This was clearly a relationship based on knightly ties and presumably Hume would have wished to be knighted by the earl of Angus. In January 1439, Sir Thomas Erskine promised on oath to his cousin and his squire, Patrick Galbraith, that he would be a good and faithful lord and master to him during his life and defend him against all persons in his righteous causes in return for

---

[65] NAS GD124/1/141, GD124/1/145, GD3/2/1/12, GD3/2/1/16; *RMS*, II, 2626.
[66] It was quite usual for young noblemen to be sent to members of their kin-group to be trained as squires. For example, in his youth William the Marshal had been sent by his father, John Fitzgilbert, an English baron, to the household of John's cousin, the count of Tankarville. Keen, *Chivalry*, p. 20. We also find that the young Walter Stewart, in John Barbour's epic poem the *Bruce*, was entrusted to the care of his cousin, Sir James Douglas, in the lead-up to the battle of Bannockburn. Barbour, *Bruce*, II, 333. See also Orme, *From Childhood to Chivalry*, especially chapter two, 'Away from the family', pp. 44–80.
[67] See the release by Sir Alexander Lindsay to the heirs of Thomas Stewart, earl of Angus, of the obligation to give him forty merks of land on becoming a knight. Fraser, *Douglas*, III, p. 28; *SP*, III, p. 12.
[68] HMC, *Home*, p. 18. See also Brown, *Black Douglases*, pp. 113, 177; *SP*, IV, pp. 444–5. Hume also received lands in Wedderburn from Douglas, HMC, *Home*, p. 19, no. 4; *ER*, IV, p. 379.
[69] HMC, *Home*, p. 20.

his services.[70] Whilst these bonds can only indicate for certain that there were clearly defined lord-squire relationships working in Scotland, the implication behind the terminology used is that the lord would eventually knight his squire.

Although aspiring knights often wanted to receive knighthood from a man of particular social distinction, such as the king, it was of similiar honour to receive knighthood from the hands of one who had established a reputation of chivalric prowess and outstanding knightly deeds.[71] There are certainly fifteenth-century instances of this. At the battle of Humbleton (Homilden) Hill in 1402, Walter Bower tells us that as the English advanced, showering the Scots with arrows,

> a brave knight called Sir John Swinton shouted out in a harsh voice as if he were a crier saying: 'Illustrious comrades! Who had bewitched you today that you do not behave in your usual worthy manner? Why do you not join in hand-to-hand battle nor as men take heart to attack enemies who are in a hurry to destroy you with their flying arrows as if you were little fallow-deer or young mules in pens? Those who are willing should go down with me and we shall move among our enemies in the Lord's name, either to save our lives in so doing at least to fall as knights with honour.' On hearing this the most famous and valiant Adam de Gordon of that Ilk who indeed for a long time had cultivated mortal enmity against the said lord of Swinton following the death of stalwart men-at-arms from both sides in various fights, knelt down before him to ask pardon from him in particular (as the most worthy knight in arms in the whole of Britain, as he claimed) so that he might be girded as a knight by the hands of the same Sir John. This was done, and a band of a hundred respected knights followed these leaders who had thus been reconciled.[72]

John Swinton certainly had a fine chivalric reputation, having taken service under John of Gaunt in his earlier years, but in Bower's estimation it was Swinton's overtly chivalric rhetoric at the battle which encouraged Adam Gordon to be dubbed by a man who was the embodiment of knightliness.[73] Adam Gordon's demonstration of kneeling before Swinton and asking him to dub him also acted as a form of dispute settlement, where previously feuding

---

[70] HMC, *Mar and Kellie*, I, p. 17. See also McGladdery, *James II*, pp. 20–1, for information on the events of the Erskine claim to the earldom of Mar which was the background to this bond, and pp. 21–2, for Galbraith's involvement with the Erskines and Dumbarton Castle. We can assume that if Galbraith was knighted, it would have been by Erskine, as there is no record of him having been knighted by the crown.

[71] Keen, *Chivalry*, p. 77.

[72] *Chron. Bower*, book XV, 14. D.E.R. Watt has pointed out that although the battle is customarily called 'Homildon Hill', the hill it is most likely to have occurred beside is Humbleton Hill. See notes p. 169.

[73] George S.C. Swinton, 'John of Swinton: A Border Fighter in the Middle Ages', *SHR* 16 (1919), p. 262. This article outlines Swinton's career as a young knight in England and in France, his return to Scotland in later life and his death at Humbleton Hill. He also includes some discussion on Sir Walter Scott's 'Halidon Hill'.

men agreed to be bound together through the lord-man obligations of knighthood. Similarly, in 1460, Alexander Gordon, earl of Huntly, used this act of bestowing knighthood in a similar way and dubbed James, Lord Forbes, with whom he had a long-standing history of enmity.[74] Certainly in 1402 there was no royal monopoly on the bestowal of knighthoods, as the eve of the Battle of Humbleton Hill saw other knights granting knighthoods. Sir Thomas Erskine, for example, gave John Mowbray, lord of Drummany, 'the ordre of knychthed' before the battle and granted him ten merks worth of land.[75]

In 1406, Alexander Stewart, earl of Mar, took a retinue to England comprising sixty men including three Aberdeenshire lords, Alexander of Forbes, Walter Lindsay of Kinneff and Sir William Hay, lord of Nauchton.[76] The following year, in September 1407, Mar took this company of 'knychttis and squyeris, and gret gentyll men [. . .] men of cousaile and of wertu' to France. Whilst there, Mar made acquaintance with the duke of Burgundy and pledged his services to the king of France, agreeing to provide a contingent for the Burgundian army against Liège.[77] On their arrival in Liège, Mar knighted five of his men, clearly attempting to establish ties of loyalty to and amongst them. These new knights were John of Sutherland, Mar's nephew, who was a 'lord appearande of wertu'; Alexander of Keith; Alexander of Irvine; Andrew Stewart, Mar's brother; and John of Menteith.[78] Granting of knighthoods was not even limited to earls, implying that any knight could dub another knight, and on the same campaign, Sir William Hay, lord of Nauchton, knighted his kinsman Gilbert Hay.[79]

[74] NAS GD52/412.
[75] HMC, *Mar and Kellie*, I, p. 15. Although it is not specified that this knighthood was granted before the battle, Sir Thomas Erskine was captured during the battle, so the obvious conclusion is that he bestowed knighthood on John Mowbray beforehand. See Boardman, *Early Stewart Kings*, pp. 246, 262; HMC, *Rep X*, App VI, pp. 77–8. On 18 October 1408, John Mowbray gave up the ten merks of land and all other conditions to Sir Robert Erskine, the heir of Sir Thomas, and presumably renounced his allegiance to Sir Thomas's heir at the same time. This may have been because the lord-knight bond between Thomas Erskine and Mowbray was a personal one, and Thomas had died four years earlier. Thomas Erskine had received his own knighthood at the hands of his father, Sir Robert Erskine, in 1367. David Sellar, 'Courtesy, Battle and the Brieve of Right, 1368– A Story Continued', in David Sellar (ed.), *The Stair Society Miscellany II* (Edinburgh, 1984); Fraser, *Douglas*, I, pp. 253–4; George Neilson, *Trial by Combat* (Glasgow, 1890), pp. 216–17; *SP*, V, p. 596.
[76] *Rot. Scot.*, II, p. 179; Brown, 'Regional Lordship in North-East Scotland', p. 32. On 20 September 1406 Sir Walter Lindsay and William Hay esquire, along with the earl of Mar, appeared as witnesses for Archibald, fourth earl of Douglas. NLS Adv. MSS 80.4.15, Dundas of Dundas, Mac.XXVI, Dunberny, no. 1. According to Wyntoun, this 'honest company' contained ten or more knights, and clerks, other of 'gret wertu' and sixty horses. *Chron. Wyntoun*, VI, p. 420.
[77] *Chron. Wyntoun*, VI, pp. 422, 423, 429; Richard Vaughan, *John the Fearless: The Growth of Burgundian Power* (London & New York, 1979), p. 55. The Burgundians retained eighty of Mar's company but they were still led by the north-eastern lords. Brown, 'Regional Lordship in North-East Scotland', p. 32.
[78] *Chron. Wyntoun*, VI, pp. 431–2; *Chron. Pluscarden*, II, p. 263; Brown, 'Regional Lordship in North-East Scotland', p. 33; Michel, *Les Écossais en France*, I, p. 112.
[79] *Chron. Wyntoun*, VI, p. 432; Michel, *Les Écossais en France*, I, p. 112.

It could be suggested, especially of the early years of the fifteenth century when James I was absent from the throne, that knights were bestowing knighthoods themselves as there was no king in place to do so. However, even after James I returned in 1424, this practice continued. Walter Bower reports that in July 1429 at Senlis, returning to Paris from the coronation at Rheims, Sir Patrick Ogilvy of Auchterhouse knighted Alexander Barclay, Laurence Vernon, Walter Leckie, John Turnbull, William Rossy, Thomas Lovell, Gilbert Hay, and Nicholas King.[80] Even though Alasdair A. MacDonald implies that James I attempted to impose a monopoly on knightings on his return, this was clearly ineffectual as Ogilvy was Constable of the Scots in France and might well have seen dubbing in his remit as military leader.[81]

In the mid fifteenth century, William, sixth earl of Douglas (1425–1440), was also alleged to have knighted members of his own retinue, but by this time attitudes towards such an act had changed. A sixteenth-century chronicle entry by George Buchanan complained that the sixth earl behaved so poorly that he imitated royal roles, something clearly regarded by Buchanan as inappropriate. For example he would always

> appear in public attended by a great train, greatly beyond the retinue of any other chieftan; to retain his ancient vassals by kindness, and to acquire new ones by gifts; to create knights and noblemen . . .[82]

Whilst it is impossible to know if Douglas's contemporaries thought that his behaviour was reprehensible, it nevertheless seems that in the sixteenth century it was felt, at least by Buchanan, that knighthoods should only be bestowed by monarchs.

Non-royal dubbing continued over the course of the fifteenth century: in the 1470s and 1480s James III's brother, Alexander Stewart, duke of Albany (1454–1485), often dubbed his retainers and supporters.[83] A steward for the duke of Albany, James Liddale of Halcerston, was one such man in receipt of Albany's favour. Liddale had been a member of James III's household as early

---

[80] *Chron. Bower*, book XVI, 26. Bower says nine men were knighted, although he only names eight. The Corpus MS version, which was annotated by Sir Gilbert Hay personally, records a different story. Hay's marginalia instructed that chapter twenty-six should be revised because it was ill-informed. Hay's corrections included that Christian Chalmers (Cristin de Camera), Laurence Vernon and Hay himself were taken from Charles VII's household and knighted by him. Ogilvy, then, only knighted Barclay, Rossy, Turnbull, Lovell and King. The Harleian MS version of the *Scotichronicon*, copied around 1483–84, accommodated these changes. See Mapstone, 'The *Scotichronicon*'s First Readers', pp. 32–3; *Chron. Bower*, book XVI, 26, notes. See also Forbes-Leith, *Scots Men-at-Arms*, I, p. 158. Forbes-Leith claimed that Walter Leckie was already a knight and in the service of Charles VII by 1424, I, p. 43.
[81] MacDonald, 'Chivalry as a Catalyst', p. 153.
[82] Buchanan, *History*, II, p. 61; Roland Tanner, *The Late Medieval Scottish Parliament: Politics and the Three Estates, 1424–1488* (East Linton, 2001), p. 99.
[83] For more on Alexander Stewart, duke of Albany, see Charles Adrian Kelham, 'Bases of Magnatial Power in Later Fifteenth-Century Scotland' (Ph.D., University of Edinburgh, 1986), pp. 212–93.

as 1461, when he was Master of the Queen's Avery.[84] Around July 1471 he was knighted by Albany and he later proved himself to be ultimately loyal to the duke during the political conflict between Albany and James III.[85] Although he subsequently held a number of positions in Albany's household, Liddale never received any material reward from the duke for his loyalty,[86] and seems to be an example of a knight who remained loyal to the man who dubbed him to the point of being forfeited alongside him in 1483. Yet it is difficult to determine just how significant the bond of knighthood truly was and it may have just been a small contributing factor in dictating Liddale's behaviour.

The duke of Albany had embarked on a campaign for the throne in the early 1480s, and near Edinburgh on 24 July 1482 he continued the practice of knighting his retainers. Albany had recently returned to England from France and started negotiations with Edward IV to enter into the English king's service as the self-declared king of Scotland.[87] With English support, Albany returned to Scotland and drew up a treaty with the duke of Gloucester, whilst an enormous English force invaded Scotland.[88] To commemorate the signing of the treaty, the duke of Gloucester made thirty-two English knights banneret and fourteen new knights, the earl of Northumberland knighted some of his men, and Lord Stanley, Steward of the King's House, made fifteen new knights. Alexander, duke of Albany, knighted Adam Murray, Thomas Lindsay, John Cunningham and John Rutherford.[89] These knightings, however, are problematic if we are trying to determine the extent of royal monopoly on dubbing as Albany would have believed himself entitled to do so as self-declared king and this cannot be divorced from their bestowal.

There was never an absolute royal monopoly on the bestowal of knighthoods in the fifteenth century, but instead a growing emphasis on the prestige associated with receiving knighthood at the hands of the king. Whilst clearly there were Scottish knights created in the service of lords and earls and other knights, the most prominent knights of the kingdom were in royal service and received their knighthood from the king. These royal knights, who had usually been dubbed at a solemn court ceremony such as a coronation, were of high noble status and held various powerful positions at court and in royal administration. Indeed, such men as Archibald Douglas, earl of Wigtown, William Douglas, earl of Angus, Alexander Lindsay, earl of Crawford, and George Dunbar, earl of March, all appear to have waited until they could be knighted by the king, a clear indication that they sought the prestige and

---

[84] *ER*, VII, p. 84; Macdougall, *James III*, p. 118.
[85] *ER*, VIII, p. 100; *ADA*, I, 23; Macdougall, *James III*, pp. 167, 270; *CDS*, IV, 1489; *Foedera*, XII, p. 173; Kelham, 'Bases of Magnatial Power', p. 240.
[86] *Foedera*, XII, pp. 172–3; *APS*, II, pp. 151–2; Macdougall, *James III*, pp. 180, 188–9; Kelham, 'Bases of Magnatial Power', p. 265.
[87] Macdougall, *James III*, pp. 152–3.
[88] Shaw (ed.), *Knights of England*, II, p. 17; Macdougall, *James III*, pp. 154–5.
[89] Shaw (ed.), *Knights of England*, II, pp. 18–19. This took place in the Englishmen's camp.

benefits associated with this.[90] Part of the development of an emphasis on royal knighting was due to the cost of maintaining a large body of knights. Gradually the crown took on the responsibility of providing for the men who in turn served the kingdom. With the collapse of the major regional lordships, for example the Albanys and especially the Douglases, this focus on the crown to provide knights was even more crucial. There was no vast retinue of knights which could be called upon, nor could lesser lords afford to maintain larger retinues. Potential knights, therefore, naturally sought out crown sponsorship and the crown encouraged them to do so with various social, political, and economic incentives.

Gifts of land were one such incentive. Land grants were common in association with receiving knighthood, as the lord agreed to ensure that the knight could maintain a standard of living befitting this status. *The Buke of the Ordre of Knychthede* supported this idea, claiming that 'the ordre of knychthede is sa hye yat quhen a king makis a knycht he sulde mak him lord and gouernour of grete landis and contreis efter his worthines.'[91] John Barbour reported that when Thomas Randolph, earl of Moray, paid homage to Robert Bruce, Bruce

> knew his worthy vassalage, his great knowledge and judgement, his trusty heart and loyal service, and, for that, trusted him, and made him rich in lands and beasts, as was indeed the right thing.[92]

Conversely, this implied that men who had the required amount of land to support knightly status were expected to become knights. In England, Henry VIII insisted that those who were wealthy enough to support knightly status and the knightly lifestyle had to take up knighthood or they would suffer financial penalties. This was partly an attempt to raise revenue and partly an attempt to raise armed warriors.[93] There was no similar dictum from the Scottish crown and many squires remained at that status throughout their lives.

Scottish knights were no strangers to receiving financial inducements alongside their knighthoods. In 1412 Sir Gavin Dunbar received a payment of £40 for his services on the Marches during the time of war and Sir Patrick Hume of Polwarth received the lands of Rednach around the time that he was dubbed for his services in the border wars in 1497.[94] In the fourteenth century, Thomas Stewart gave Alexander Lindsay forty merks worth of land when he

---

[90] *Chron. Bower*, book XVI, 10.
[91] Glenn (ed.), *Buke of the Ordre of Knychthede*, p. 15.
[92] Barbour, *Bruce*, Book X, 270–5.
[93] Bennett, 'The Status of a Squire', p. 8; Francis Morgan Nichols, 'On Feudal and Obligatory Knighthood', *Archaeologia: Or, Miscellaneous Tracts Relating to Antiquity* 39 (1863), pp. 213–4, 228. It was extremely costly to provide arms, body armour, horses and equipment for warfare. See Pierce, 'The Knight, his Arms and Armour', p. 152. The knight's fee had been widely used by English kings. However, by 1641 this had changed and the members of the Long Parliament voted that no one should be fined or compelled to become a knight. H.H. Leonard, 'Distraint of Knighthood: The Last Phase, 1625–41', *History* 63 (1978), p. 23; Nichols, 'On Feudal and Obligatory Knighthood', p. 189.
[94] *ER*, IV, pp. 163–4.

knighted him, and in 1402 Sir Thomas Erskine gave John Mowbray ten merks worth of land when he dubbed him knight.[95] On 17 January 1451 James II gave John Ross of Hawkhead the lands of Tarbart in Ayrshire and Auchinback in Renfrewshire two years after he had knighted him.[96] For supporting him at Blackness, James III granted James Dunbar of Cumnock, in feu farm, £44 worth of Morayshire lands on 20 May 1488.[97] Knights and squires could also receive occasional payments for knightly services. For instance, William Cranston received £6 13s 4d as a fee for his services as a squire to the duke of Rothesay.[98] Many of these types of grant were made to ensure that the knight was able to support his status. As the crown seems to have covered the shortfall in these ways, having adequate financial means must have been a crucial factor in eligibility for knighthood.

Across the fifteenth century, there was no regulated or consistent way in which knighthood could be attained. Men were knighted sometimes as a reward for their services, at other times to initiate periods of service or to increase their performance and their loyalty. Thus knighthood could be both the beginning of a prominent career, or the mark of a distinguished career. At court ceremonials, those who were dubbed came mostly from the ranks of the higher nobility, whereas at other, less formal times, lesser nobles and even non-nobles could be knighted. This distinction can particularly be drawn between court and battlefield dubbings. Where royal ceremonies were dominated by a sense of status, lineage and place within the political community, the battlefield was a space where men of lower social status could gain honour and rewards from military service alone.

---

[95] Fraser, *Douglas*, III, p. 28; *SP*, III, p. 12; HMC, *Mar and Kellie*, I, p. 15.
[96] *RMS*, II, 411.
[97] *Ibid.*, II 1727; Macdougall, *James IV*, p. 35.
[98] *ER*, V, p. 33.

CHAPTER FOUR

Scottish Tournaments

The tournament as a chivalric spectacle and as stylised warfare has been explored in most studies of chivalry. The games were intimately linked to the culture of chivalry and knighthood, which had found expression in the rise of courtly romantic literature and the development of a clear concept of knighthood in the twelfth century.[1] The tournament remained central to chivalry in the fifteenth and early sixteenth centuries because it was a 'potent ritual' that initiated knights into 'the rights and responsibilities of their traditional chivalric role'.[2] Whilst the French, Burgundian, German and English tournaments of the same period have been thoroughly explored in studies encompassing everything from the armour used to the symbolic meanings behind their pageantry, little work has been undertaken on tournaments which were held in Scotland. Indeed, until recently most of these had not been recognised as having taken place; but as Carol Edington has pointed out, 'Scottish knights were part of a cosmopolitan chivalric community with members the length and breadth of Christendom' and the evolution of Scottish tournaments followed a broadly similar pattern to the rest of Europe.[3] Louise Olga Fradenburg made some attempt to investigate Scottish tournaments in her work on late-fifteenth- and early-sixteenth-century Scottish culture, but she concentrated only on the tournaments of the Wild Knight and the Black Lady held by James IV in 1507 and 1508.[4] These were well-recorded tournaments, rich in imagery and spectacle, and have been the subject of sustained analysis. But the tournaments of 1507 and 1508 were part of a tradition of Scottish tournaments and jousts sponsored by the crown.

In late-medieval Scotland two principal types of chivalric activity have been recorded: the joust which took place between two men of similar

---

[1] For more on the rise of the tournament see Maurice Keen, *Chivalry*, chapter V, 'The Rise of the Tournament', Bumke, *Courtly Culture*, esp. pp. 247–51; Barber and Barker, *Tournaments*, esp. chapter 1, 'The Origins of the Tournament', and for a discussion of the relationship between princes and chivalric display see Alison Rosie, 'Ritual, Chivalry and Pageantry: The Courts of Anjou, Orléans and Savoy in the Later Middle Ages' (Ph.D., University of Edinburgh, 1989).
[2] McCoy, *The Rites of Knighthood*, p. 21.
[3] Carol Edington, 'The Tournament in Medieval Scotland', in Matthew Strickland (ed.), *Armies, Chivalry and Warfare in Medieval Britain and France: Proceedings of the 1995 Harlaxton Symposium* (Stamford, 1998), p. 46.
[4] Fradenburg, *City, Marriage, Tournament*, pp. 153–264.

knightly rank and the tournament which was a series of jousts and other knightly games involving a larger body of knights. The chivalric joust gave the individual the opportunity to distinguish himself and it was purely an exhibition of one knight's skill pitted against that of another, designed to test his manhood in full view of his peers. Both the chivalric joust and the tournament provided space for a knight to demonstrate to a public audience that he was motivated by the chivalric codes of conduct and a desire to be knightly.[5]

Duels were frequently staged in Scotland to decide the outcome of judicial trials, but these were not chivalric in nature. According to the *Buke of the Law of Armys*, the only time judicial duels or trials by combat could be fought were over matters of law and, even then, usually only in times of peace.[6] In most cases they were held to answer charges of treason. For example, in 1412 a duel was fought between John Hardy and Thomas Smith at Battlehaugh which was presided over by Archibald, fourth earl of Douglas and: 'Thomas Smith fell there as an accuser who falsely charged the said John with the crime of treason'. Importantly, neither Hardy nor Smith was of knightly status, suggesting that judicial duels were not fought exclusively amongst knights.[7] If this is the case then trials by combat, although influenced by the codes of chivalry, cannot be considered to be chivalric. In his chronicle, Walter Bower recorded that a judicial duel took place between Henry Knox, a man-at-arms of gentle status, and 'a certain common tailor'. This was held before the king at Edinburgh castle in 1426 and, according to Bower, the tailor laid complaint before James I that Knox had verbally abused the king. When Knox was prosecuted on this account and denied the charges, the tailor accused him of treason and the duel was held. However, as occurred in most of these duels, James I called a halt to the combat.[8] Other judicial duels were reported in chronicle sources,

---

[5] V.G. Kiernan, *The Duel in European History: Honour and the Reign of Aristocracy* (Oxford, 1988), pp. 39–40; Juliet R.V. Barker, *The Tournament in England 1100–1400* (Woodbridge, 1986), p. 145; Bumke, *Courtly Culture*, p. 266. In the early fifteenth century, Nicholas Upton claimed the joust for honour was a test of manhood, see Kiernan, *The Duel in European History*, p. 41.

[6] J.H. Stevenson (ed.), *Gilbert of Haye's Prose Manuscript (A.D. 1456), Volume I, The Buke of the Law of Armys or Buke of Bataillis* (Edinburgh, 1901), pp. xcix–ci. For more on judicial duels see: Neilson, *Trial by Combat*, esp. pp. 188–90 where he contrasts and compares duels of law, or judicial duels, and duels of chivalry or jousts, Robert Bartlett, *Trial by Fire and Water: The Medieval Judicial Ordeal* (Oxford, 1986), esp. pp. 103–26; Cynthia J. Neville, *Violence, Custom and Law: The Anglo-Scottish Border Lands in the Later Middle Ages* (Edinburgh, 1998); Robert Baldick, *The Duel: A History of Duelling* (London, 1965); and Kiernan, *The Duel in European History*, who defines the judicial duel as 'the ordeal by combat, intended to determine right or wrong, and the joust, an exhibition of courage and prowess', see pp. 1–2. For proceedings of a judicial duel, and a chivalric joust, allegedly contemporaneous with James I's reign, see 'The Order of Combats for Life in Scotland as they are anciently recorded in ane old Manuscript of the Law Arms and Offices of Scotland pertaining to James I King of Scots', *Spalding Misc.* (Aberdeen, 1842), II, pp. 383–90; also printed in Neilson, *Trial by Combat*, pp. 261–72. This makes it clear that although there was little variation between the way the judicial duel and the chivalric duel were carried out, there was nevertheless a distinction.

[7] *Chron. Bower*, book XV, 23, and notes p. 187; *Chron. Extracta*, p. 216.

[8] *Chron. Bower*, book XVI, 15; *ER*, IV, pp. xcvii, 411; see also Neilson, *Trial by Combat*, pp. 275–6.

including three that occurred in 1453, between Sir Alexander Nairn of Sandford and Sir James Logan; William Heriot and David Galford; and William Hacket and Jonathan Seton. These appear to have been held at the same time, and it is most likely that Heriot, Galford, Hacket and Seton were retainers of either Nairn or Logan. It is almost certain that these duels arose from charges of treason, possibly in connection with the Black Douglases.[9] In 1456 a duel between Alexander Cunningham and a man referred to as Dalrymple was presided over by James II at Stirling. Its outcome was decided by lot at James's discretion and honour was granted on both sides. Again, neither Cunningham nor Dalrymple had a knightly status attributed to them.[10] The practice of judicial duelling continued into the sixteenth century, when in mid-1532 Sir James Douglas of Drumlanrig and John Charteris of Amisfield fought over charges of treason at Holyrood Abbey in Edinburgh.[11] Although the participation of both Sir James Douglas of Drumlanrig and Sir Alexander Nairn of Sandford, who was Lyon King of Arms, must have brought a chivalric tone to the proceedings, what is clear is that judicial duels were not knightly affairs. They were fought over matters of law and were not primarily designed for chivalric display. Informally organised duels could also take place, often when knights were engaged in battle, although these were never sanctioned by the crown. For example the siege of Cocklaws in 1403 was resolved by a duel between the captain of the castle, John de Grymslaw, and one of the English knights in Sir Henry Percy's army.[12]

The Organisation of the Tournament

Most of the documented information about both judicial duels and chivalric jousting comes from chronicle sources or royal accounts of expenditure. Both of these sources are problematic. Chroniclers usually report only the names of the participants, the length of the tournament, and who won. Royal accounts

---

[9] *Chron. Extracta*, p. 243. Alexander Nairn was a Douglas adherent and he had been comptroller 1435–38, 1444–47, and from 1451 to 15 January 1453. He seems to have been sent to Henry VI's court in the wake of the murder of the eighth earl of Douglas. *ER*, V, p. 672; *HBC*, pp. 189–90; Murray, 'The Comptroller', pp. 4–5; *ER*, V, pp. 258, 297, 477; Fraser, *Douglas*, III Charters, pp. 373–4, no. 303, p. 424, no. 406. Nairn was also Lyon King of Arms from 1437 to 1460. George Seton, *The Law and Practice of Heraldry in Scotland* (Edinburgh, 1863), Appendix I, no. 1, pp. 477–8. Nairn was killed during his duel with James Logan.
[10] *Chron. Bower*, Harleian MS Additions, volume IX, p. 141; *Chron. Extracta*, p. 238; *Chron. Auchinleck*, p. 55; Neilson, *Trial by Combat*, pp. 276–7.
[11] Henry M. Paton (ed.), *Accounts of the Masters of Works for Building and Repairing Royal Palaces and Castles, Volume I, 1529–1615* (Edinburgh, 1957), pp. lix, lx, 102; Pitscottie, *Historie*, I, pp. 347–8.
[12] *Chron. Bower*, book XV, 15; Edington, 'Tournament in Medieval Scotland', p. 50. For a discussion examining the use of the judicial duel as a substitute for full-scale battle see Matthew Strickland, 'Provoking or Avoiding Battle? Challenge, Duel and Single Combat in Warfare in the High Middle Ages', in Matthew Strickland (ed.), *Armies, Chivalry and Warfare in Medieval Britain and France: Proceedings of the 1995 Harlaxton Symposium* (Stamford, 1998).

detail payments to armourers, bowyers and other workers, with very few other details. However, there is one Scottish source which might describe the details of jousting and structure of the tournament, although this too is enigmatic. A manuscript entitled 'The Order of Combats for Life in Scotland', apparently dating from James I's reign, was discovered in the archives of the House of Erroll in the early nineteenth century. The treatise details the role of officials during duelling and probably belonged to the Hays of Errol, who were the hereditary Constables and, as such, had an established role in the tournament.[13] Nothing is known of the author, nor when it was written, and, if it does date from James I's reign, it has certainly been edited and modernised from its original fifteenth-century form. The manuscript, printed by the Spalding Club, is the earliest version available, but it dates from the late seventeenth or early eighteenth century. This, of course, causes serious problems with authenticity and it is plausible that a later author attributed it to James I's reign to bestow antique authority and precedence upon it. Whilst this makes it difficult to come to reliable conclusions about fifteenth-century duelling, the document might still provide some insight into how a joust may have been organised.

'The Order of Combats' indicates that chivalric and judicial duels, although held in the same manner and subject to the same rules, were quite distinct from each other. A judicial duel began when the 'bill of quarrell' was brought to court before the Constable. When the truth of the matter could not be proven, a trial by arms was decreed and the Constable assigned a day for the battle within the following forty days.[14] With the king's consent, the Constable requested that lists (or rails) be set up, enclosing an area sixty paces long and forty paces wide, which was plain and dry 'without riggs, hills, or other impediments'. At either end of the lists a gate or entry was made with a strong bar across it 'to keep out the people'. Measures were also taken to ensure horses could not enter the gates. The Constable then appointed a sergeant-at-arms to guard each gate, commanding them not to let any man approach within four feet. On the day of the duel the king would sit on a high seat or scaffold, at the foot of which was another seat for the Constable. The challenger would come to the east gate of the lists 'and brought with him such armours as wer appoynted by the Constable, and wherwith he determined to fight.' The Constable approached him, asked him to state his business, then opened the visor of his headpiece 'to see his fface, and therby to know that man to be he who makes the challenge.'[15] Once the defendant had been similarly identified, the duel took place and the loser was punished. The rules for a chivalric duel were much the same, with the only real distinction being that

---

[13] 'The Order of Combats', pp. cxxi–cxxiii, 383–90; RSS, VI, 46.
[14] 'The Order of Combats', p. 383.
[15] Ibid., pp. 384–5.

the knight who lost the duel was not punished. Instead, the losing knight was deemed to have lost honour, a trait that was essential in the chivalric code.

The 'Order of Combats' suggests that during the jousting the Constable had the most prominent duties, followed by the Marischal. The Constable and the Marischal were not paid for these duties, but instead received remuneration from the jousting itself. This may explain why there are no official records of the Constable or the Marischal's involvement in tournaments or jousts. The Constable received all the armour and weapons which the loser brought with him, 'that is to say, a spear, a shield, a long sword, a square sword, and a knyfe, with the haill jewells and rings the vanquisht had about him at his entring the quarrell.' The Marischal received 'all horses, broken armour, or other ffurnitur that fell to the ground efter the combatants did enter the lists, als weill from the Challenger as from the Defender.' This differed from European tournaments, particularly those held in Spain, where the winning knight received the losing knight's armour. The Marischal also received all the bars, posts, rails and other parts of the lists as part of his fee.[16] This treatise suggests that the king's role was simply to preside over the joust, ensure that the rules were being followed, and to call a stop to it if he felt that both parties had proved themselves worthy.

Heralds and Heraldry

Heralds also played a key role in tournaments. As knighthood became more exclusive throughout Europe, heraldic devices came to be used, and heralds' interest in genealogy developed. As early as the twelfth century, heralds had appeared in connection with tournaments: in Chrétien de Troyes' *Lancelot*, in the *Historie of Guillaume le Maréchal*, and in *Fulk Fitzwarin*. This concern with heraldry was cemented towards the end of the twelfth century with the exclusion from the tournament of men who were not entitled to knighthood. By the late thirteenth century, heralds had taken on an important role in the organisation of the tournament. Prior to a tournament, heralds travelled to proclaim its place and date.[17] At the event itself they announced the combatants to the spectators, adding their own commentary on the deeds and renown of each of them: the tournament at Chauvency, according to Bretel, was 'full of heralds' who recognised the knights by their arms and called out their names as they entered the lists.[18] Their roles at tournament developed over the fourteenth century and became a more professional occupation: heralds kept score sheets, judged blows, inspected arms and crests, and verified the heredity of participants.[19] At this time they also took on a more defined role in chivalric society, acting as diplomatic messengers and journeying through their realms to record the insignia of all the noblemen and to note family connections.

[16] *Ibid.*, pp. 389–90; Barber, *Knight and Chivalry*, p. 195.
[17] *Ibid.*, pp. 43–4, 220.
[18] Keen, *Chivalry*, p. 135; Barber, *Knight and Chivalry*, pp. 44, 141.
[19] Keen, *Chivalry*, p. 137.

Indeed, Sir David Lindsay of the Mount's *Armorial* of 1542 testifies to this duty being undertaken in Scotland.[20] In addition to this, heralds used rolls to study arms, and often held them in their personal collections, such as Sir Thomas Holmes, an English herald, who held a Scottish roll of arms in the fifteenth century.[21]

Heraldry was really the 'universal labelling of chivalry' that placed the arms-bearer immediately. Whilst initially heraldic devices were used to proclaim his identity on shields and armour, later they were also employed as an ornamental device on personal property.[22] These appeared in numerous places, but most prominently throughout castles and churches where the family wished to reinforce their association with the building, such as William Sinclair did at Roslin Chapel in the 1450s. Others were interested in heraldry more generally: for example, a sixteenth-century ceiling decoration in the first storey of an old house in High St, Linlithgow (about 100 yards from the gateway of the palace), showed the armorial bearings depicted in Lindsay's *Armorial*.[23]

Heraldry quickly developed in Scotland, like elsewhere in Europe, and its practitioners became increasingly essential to chivalric culture. Indeed, by 1471 they were considered level with knights as far as sumptuary laws dictated – due to the 'gret poverte of the realme' only knights, heralds, minstrels, and those with landed rents of at least £100 a year were permitted to wear silk.[24] No mention is made of pursuivants in this legislation, but they too had an increasingly important role in knightly society. By the fifteenth century Scottish heralds were used to record chivalric prowess of those participating in tournaments.[25] Indeed, there is no question that many Scottish chroniclers based their descriptions of tournaments on heralds' accounts. The Scottish heralds certainly appear to have been the 'technical' experts of chivalry, with Sir William Cumming of Inverallochy, Marchmont Herald, commissioning a heraldic treatise to be translated from French into Scots by Adam Loutfut, Kintyre pursuivant in 1494.[26] Sir David Lindsay of the Mount made this connection more apparent. As Lyon King of Arms, Lindsay oversaw the tournaments in James V's reign. His role also informed his writings as court poet and we find not only descriptions of the tournament planned for Queen

---

[20] David Laing (ed.), *Facsimilie of an Ancient Heraldic Manuscript Emblazoned by Sir David Lyndsay of the Mount, Lyon King of Armes, 1542* (Edinburgh, 1878); Keen, *Chivalry*, p. 138; Barber, *Knight and Chivalry*, p. 44.
[21] Colin Campbell (ed.), *The Scots Roll: A Study of a Fifteenth Century Roll of Arms* (Heraldic Society of Scotland, 1995), p. 5.
[22] Annie I. Dunlop, *The Life and Times of James Kennedy, Bishop of St Andrews* (Edinburgh & London, 1950), p. 387.
[23] T. Etherington Cooke, 'Notice of the Heraldic Painted Ceilings in a House at Linlithgow, Now Destroyed', *PSAS* 7 (1867–68), pp. 409–12.
[24] *APS*, II, p. 100; Nicholson, *Scotland*, p. 433.
[25] Edington, *Court and Culture*, p. 28.
[26] L.A.J.R. Houwen (ed.), *The Deidis of Armorie: A Heraldic Treatise and Beastiary* (Edinburgh, 1994), I, p. xiii.

Madeleine's entry in Scotland in 1437 in the 'Deploratioun', but also heralds supervising the jousting in the 'Historie of Squyer Meldrum', ordering the crowd and giving the signal to commence the fight.[27]

Keen remarked that towards the end of the fifteenth century:

> in an age in which tournaments were staged with didactic intent in Arthurian dress, and when great court feasts and ceremonies sought to catch an echo of legendary occasions [. . .] true mastery of heraldic erudition had come to demand much more than a knowledge of genealogy and blazon. Ideally it required besides a command of the whole literary and historical culture of chivalry, an understanding of the laws of nobility and inheritance, and a knowledge of the mystical properties ascribed to plants, beasts, birds and colours.[28]

In Scotland this was clearly true. Scottish heralds organised and policed public events, adjudicated in disputes over precedence, genealogy and armorial bearings, made public the royal proclamations, carried royal letters and messages and accompanied foreign embassies.[29] Although the duties of heralds and pursuivants were largely ceremonial, their long-standing associations with tournaments demonstrated the Scottish crown's desire to fully comply with the ceremony and tradition of chivalry.

Scottish Tournaments

Much of the Scottish evidence places the crown as central to the tournament, but, as many crown-sponsored tournaments that we know took place were not mentioned by chroniclers at all, royal records must be used in conjunction with chronicle reports in order to obtain a broader picture of where and when tournaments and jousts were held in Scotland. As many of these records have unfortunately been lost, including the treasurer's accounts for the reigns of James I and James II, and most of James III's reign, it can be safely assumed that there were more tournaments held in Scotland than can be gleaned from the extant sources. There were no tourneying societies in Scotland, as there were in Germany and the Low Countries, and this raises the question of whether there were privately sponsored tournaments.[30] Exceptionally wealthy and powerful nobles across Europe hosted lavish and grandiose tournaments, most notably from the court of the dukes of Burgundy, but no

---

[27] Edington, *Court and Culture*, pp. 28–9.
[28] Keen, *Chivalry*, p. 141. For more on heralds and heraldry see Maurice Keen, 'Introduction', in Peter Coss and Maurice Keen (eds), *Heraldry, Pageantry and Social Display in Medieval England* (Woodbridge, 2002), pp. 1–16.
[29] Thomas, 'Renaissance Culture at the Court of James V', pp. 272–3.
[30] Keen, *Chivalry*, pp. 186–7, 209–10. For more on Germany tourneying societies see William H. Jackson, 'Tournaments and the German Chivalric *renovation*: Tournament Discipline and the Myth of Origins' in Sydney Anglo (ed.), *Chivalry in the Renaissance* (Woodbridge, 1990), esp. pp. 84–7.

chroniclers record that private tournaments were held in Scotland, and if prominent nobles, such as the Black Douglases or the Albany-Stewarts, hosted them we might expect that contemporary commentators would have made some reference to them. In the absence of private financial records it is not possible to rule out the existence of privately sponsored tournaments, but this lack of evidence means this study is restricted, perhaps artificially, to the assumption that the majority of tournaments held in Scotland were crown sponsored.

1424–1437

The requirement for kings to hold tournaments was central to the idea of late-medieval kingship. In part this was because the king was the leader of knightly society, but it also provided him with an opportunity to display to his subjects and the wider chivalric community his power, benevolence and adherence to knightly codes of conduct. James I had been keen to promote himself along these lines when he returned to Scotland in 1424. Even though Walter Bower described James as the 'best of archers and a knowledgeable jouster' there is very little indication of him having participated in activities like these. Instead, Bower may simply have been attributing standard qualities expected of a king to James and this may not be a real insight into the personal and knightly qualities of the king.[31] Although if the 'Order of Combats' does date to his reign then we can assume that he had a much keener interest in tournaments than has been recorded. In fact, there is only evidence of one tournament held in Scotland during his reign and this was not a particularly outstanding example of chivalry in practice.

James's experience of tournaments and their promotion of the chivalric ideal had been limited whilst he was held in English captivity. At the age of thirteen he had been witness to a duel held at Nottingham on 12 August 1407 between Bertrand Usana and John Bolomer. Bolomer had accused Usana of treason, but this was a judicial duel, not a chivalric joust, and whether this had an impact on James is uncertain.[32] Perhaps surprisingly, James's earlier guardian, Henry IV, does not himself appear to have supported the promotion of chivalric games. Henry IV had enjoyed a remarkable tourneying career when he was earl of Derby, but after his coronation in 1399 he gave little time to the sport, holding only two court-sponsored chivalric tournaments. Both of these were in the early years of his rule, well before James had been taken prisoner.[33] It is uncertain why Henry lost interest in the sport, but it must have had an influence on James's ideas of rulership. Henry V paid even less attention to

---

[31] *Chron. Bower*, book XVI, 28. See also Brown, *James I*, p. 2; and E.W.M. Balfour-Melville, *James I, King of Scots, 1406–1437* (London, 1936), p. 264. Bower certainly held James I in high esteem and spent the last section of his chronicle outlining his qualities and interests. See *Chron. Bower*, book XVI, 28–38.

[32] Neilson, *Trial by Combat*, p. 198; *Foedera*, VIII, pp. 538–40. It was James who suggested that Henry stop the duel between Usana and Bolomer.

[33] Barber and Barker, *Tournaments*, p. 37. See also Barker, *The Tournament in England*.

chivalric sports, presumably having inherited his father's perspective that holding tournaments had no political advantage. Once he had relaunched the war against France, Henry V's attitude was that chivalrous sports should not be pursued if there was a chance of real combat on the battlefield.[34] Henry V's ambassadors, including James I, were entertained at the French court in June 1420 by *à outrance* feats of arms between French and Portuguese knights. Henry's response to this jousting was critical, and he stated that

> I command all my own servants that tomorrow morning we all of us be ready to go and besiege Sens, where my lord the King's enemies are. There may we all tilt and joust and prove our daring and courage, for there is no finer act of courage in the world than to punish evildoers so that poor people can live.[35]

Henry V's preoccupation with the waging of serious warfare and his formidable disapproval of all forms of jousting reflected the established tradition that knightly sports, although useful in times of peace, simply distracted the knights whilst on campaign. As James I was involved in these wars between England and France, it is possible that he was influenced by the policies of Henry V and may have returned to Scotland with similar views.[36]

Given that James was not exposed to a culture that promoted jousting or tourneying as valid knightly pastimes, it is unsurprising that we only find records of one tournament staged by him. This took place in the early 1430s and an exchequer entry of 1433 to 1434 indicates that a tournament presided over by James I was held at Perth when eight spears were transported for the games from Dundee.[37] The tournament must have taken place at a General Council in October 1433, which James had called after an English knight had arrived with commissions and instructions from Henry VI. The council aimed to discuss peace with England and the advantages of entering into marriage negotiations, but even after two days of debate no conclusion was reached.[38]

---

[34] *Ibid.*, p. 37.
[35] M.L. Bellaguet (ed.), *Chronique du Religieux de Saint-Denys, Contenant Le Régne de Charles VI, De 1380 À 1422* (Paris, 1844), pp. 408–15; Janet Shirley (trans), *A Parisian Journal 1405–1449, translated from the Anonymous 'Journal d'un Bourgeois de Paris'* (Oxford, 1968), pp. 92–3, 151; Barber and Barker, *Tournaments*, p. 37.
[36] James Hamilton Wylie and William Templeton Waugh, *The Reign of Henry the Fifth* (Cambridge, 1929), pp. 327, 328.
[37] *ER*, IV, p. 561.
[38] *Chron. Bower*, book XVI, 23; *Chron. Pluscarden*, II, pp. 285–6; Tanner, 'The Political Role of the Three Estates', pp. 75–6; Tanner, *Late Medieval Scottish Parliament*, pp. 58–9. Walter Bower, who was present at the council, named the English knight as Scrope, whom D.E.R. Watt identifies as John, Lord Scrope of Masham, a regular diplomatic envoy for England. However, Michael Brown thinks it was unlikely that it was Scrope who had attended at Perth, because by this time Scrope had lost favour with the English crown and had been removed as treasurer in the summer of 1433, only a couple of months prior to the council. Brown thinks it much more probable that it was Edmund Beaufort, count of Mortain, who was sent from England, and Bower's error was with confusing Masham with Mortain. Mortain was Queen Joan's youngest brother, making his kinship with James favourable for

Bower, who was in attendance at Perth, may have witnessed this tournament, but he makes no reference to it in his account of the council, instead focusing on the discussion of diplomacy and legislation. According to Bower, all of the prelates and magnates of the realm were present at the council and the nobles who were present may well have taken part in the jousting.[39] There is no indication from the chronicler that the English party attended the council, but if present, this may have seen the continuation of a tradition, most recently seen in the 1390s, of Scottish knights jousting against English knights.[40]

1437–1460

During James II's reign there is a significant increase in the evidence for tourneying activities. James had a strong chivalric reputation which was well known in the European courts and he was described as '*un vaillant chevalier et homme de grant corage*'.[41] The most well-known tournament held and presided over by him was at Stirling in 1449. Stirling castle proved to be a popular venue for royal tournaments that may have stemmed from a belief that Stirling, or Snowdon, was linked with Arthurian legend. The association was first articulated by Jean Froissart who visited David II's court in 1365 and spent three days at Stirling castle. While he was there Froissart was told that the castle had been known as Snowdon since the days of Arthur and that it had been frequented by the knights of the Round Table. Froissart further perpetuated this by making Stirling the venue for the staging of splendid tournaments in his romance *Méliador*.[42]

On Shrove Tuesday 1449 Jacques and Simon de Lalain and Hervey de Meriadet, three noble knights from Burgundy, came to Stirling to engage in single combats with James Douglas, the brother of the eighth earl of Douglas (and later ninth earl), John Ross of Hawkhead and James Douglas of Ralstoun (often styled of Lugton and Loch Leven), the brother of Sir Henry de Douglas of Loch Leven.[43] Such a strong Douglas presence has led some historians to consider whether the Douglases, rather than the king, were the patrons and promoters of chivalric culture within Scotland at this time. Michael Brown even suggests that the tournament gave the Douglases the opportunity to

---

such discussions and indeed Mortain was dispatched in August 1433 with an embassy to go to Scotland. Michael Brown, *James I*, pp. 152–3, and n. 40. Roland Tanner does not pick up on, nor expand upon, this debate in his recent book on general councils and parliaments, Tanner, *Late Medieval Scottish Parliament*, pp. 58–9, nor in his doctoral thesis, Tanner, 'The Political Role of the Three Estates', p. 75.

[39] *Chron. Bower*, book XVI, 23.

[40] *Ibid.*, XV, 4, 6; *Chron. Wyntoun*, VI, pp. 103–15, 359–61; *Rot. Scot.*, II, pp. 87, 90, 111, 117, 119; *CDS*, IV, 425, 439, 452, 453, 711; Edington, 'Tournament in Medieval Scotland', pp. 51–2.

[41] Bibliothèque Royale de Belgique, MS 9470, fo. 15, Bibliothèque Nationale Paris N.a. Fr.6214, fo. 62v, cited in Dunlop, *Life and Times of James Kennedy*, p. 208.

[42] Edington, 'Tournament in Medieval Scotland', p. 53.

[43] *Chron. Bower*, Harleian MS Additions, ch. 9, p. 141; *Chron. Auchinleck*, p. 40; *Chron. Extracta*, p. 238; Michel, *Les Écossais en France*, p. 207.

'pose as the armed defenders of Scotland's honour'.[44] However, the Douglases had been at the forefront of diplomatic negotiations with Burgundy in 1448 and 1449, therefore it is most probable that the Burgundian party directed their challenge towards this group because they had previously been involved with them.[45] Nevertheless, James II's vigorous attack against the Douglas family over the following years may indicate that the Douglases' involvement in the tournament was not confined to a competitive level. They might well have been deliberately using the promotion of chivalric culture as part of a wider assertion of their social pre-eminence and political power – a message which James II would have been eager to quash. What is clear is that the tournament was not strictly a 'royal' tournament initiated by the crown, and although it was held at Stirling and paid for by the royal purse, Carol Edington has argued that James II was keen to patronise and exploit an essentially aristocratic competition.[46]

A lengthy account of the tournament has survived, which is so richly described that it provides a clear picture of what took place. The account was penned by George Chastellain, the biographer of Jacques de Lalain. The details are generally regarded as having been given to him directly by Jacques de Lalain, particularly as some obviously erroneous statements indicate that he was not present in person. Chastellain wrote that on the appointed day after the Burgundians had arrived, James Douglas and his party entered the lists and were attended by a great company including the eighth earl of Douglas. Amongst this party were Gilbert Corry, the son of James Corry; James, Lord Frendraught, knight; Alexander Nairn of Sandford, Lyon King of Arms; Robert Liddale, the king's steward; James Kerr; and Adam Wawane.[47] The king mounted his throne and the Burgundian knights entered the lists. They dismounted before their pavilion, entered, and did reverence to James II.

---

[44] Brown, *Black Douglases*, p. 276.
[45] *Ibid.*, p. 276.
[46] Edington, 'Tournament in Medieval Scotland', pp. 55–6.
[47] *RMS*, II, 319. On Nairn of Sandford's Douglas connections see Fraser, *Douglas*, III Charters, pp. 373–4, no. 303, p. 424, no. 406. For more on James Kerr and Robert Liddale's associations with James, ninth earl of Douglas, see Brown, *Black Douglases*, pp. 296, 300, 301. See also p. 174 for the Corry family. A fifteenth-century roll of arms may help ascertain who was also present at the tournament. However, some question has been raised as to the dating of the roll. None of the arms within it can be dated to a contemporaneous period, with the latest arms, those of Lord Herries, dating to after 7 February 1492. The editor of the roll dates it to c. 1455–58, concluding that it may be a later copy of an earlier roll with later coats added, but this dating also seems too late as the Douglas earldoms were forfeited in 1455. If this is the case, then some of the arms may well date to 1449 and may have come from a tournament roll from Stirling. This is a highly speculative argument. However, a large number of Douglas and Livingston arms are present, putting parts of the roll firmly in James II's reign. Additionally we find the earl of Douglas arms on f. 47r., and the Ross of Hawkhead and Douglas of Loch Leven arms, side by side, on f. 49r. Although the presence of the arms of the three Scottish contestants at Stirling is nowhere near conclusive evidence that this is what the roll is, it certainly warrants consideration. See Campbell (ed.), *The Scots Roll*.

Returning to their pavilion 'they armed themselves at their ease, and had abundant leisure, for they had come more than three hours before the others'.[48] Master James Douglas, John Ross of Hawkhead and James Douglas of Ralstoun arrived at the appointed time and proceeded to enter the lists. The fully armed Scots dismounted and approached James II, who may have been seated in the manner described by the anonymous author of the 'Order of Combats'. James II 'descended from his throne' and dubbed the three Scots.[49]

After these preliminary proceedings, the six knights decided amongst themselves with whom they would joust. It was agreed that Jacques de Lalain would fight James Douglas of Douglas, Meriadet 'who was renowned as the most powerful body' would fight John Ross of Hawkhead and Simon would fight James Douglas of Ralstoun.[50]

> [. . .] they were to fight with lances, axe, sword, and dagger *à outrance* [with sharp weapons, until serious injury or death], or till the king signified his will; but at the request of the above-named Scots, the throwing of the lance was forbidden, for they trusted greatly their lances. So the uncle, the nephew, and Meriadet agreed among themselves that they would neither fight with their lances nor throw them at their opponents, but that when they met them they would cast their lances behind them, and fight with their axes.[51]

According to Chastellain, Jacques de Lalain then spoke with Meriadet, as 'according to the rules of the combat, each one might carry assistance to his comrade'. Lalain requested that Meriadet should not come to his assistance if he was injured, but should allow him to 'meet such fortune, be it good or ill, as God may please to send'.[52] This rule, which probably only applied in *à outrance* jousting, indicates that if a knight was injured a member of his team could help him.

> When the six champions were apparelled and ready to issue from their tent, awaiting the proclamations, orders, and prohibitions that are wont to be made in the lists, straightaway with sound of trumpet were thrice proclaimed at the four corners of the lists the conditions appointed by the King of Scotland.[53]

The fact that the king appointed the conditions of the tournament, presided over it and provided men to attend to the Burgundians, does suggest that

---

[48] Chastellain, 'Historie du bon chevalier Messire Jacques de Lalain', p. 33.
[49] *Ibid.*, pp. 33–4.
[50] *Ibid.*, p. 34.
[51] *Ibid.*, p. 34. *À outrance* jousting was with sharp weapons, those used in normal warfare, instead of blunted jousting weapons. The joust could be fought to the death, although the tournament overseer would normally halt the duel before serious injuries were sustained. See Barber and Barker, *Tournaments*, pp. 100, 125–6, 160, 165.
[52] Chastellain, 'Historie du bon chevalier Messire Jacques de Lalain', p. 34. The brutal nature of *à outrance* jousting probably did require such a rule.
[53] *Ibid.*, p. 34.

James II had a significant role in the organising and running of this tournament. The Douglases cannot have solely promoted such activity and must have done so in co-operation with the king. If the 'Order of Combats' is accurate for a fifteenth-century tournament, the Constable, Sir William Hay of Errol, probably read the proclamations. The rules of the competition may have been much like those defined at Edward IV's command in 1466 by the earl of Worcester, the Constable of England. The rules were that whoever broke the most spears, as they should be broken, would win a prize; that whoever hit their opponent three times on his helmet would win a prize; and that whoever met twice head-to-head would win a prize. Removing an opponent from his saddle, or forcing him and his horse to the ground could also win prizes. If any man was identified as having stayed longest in the field, run the fairest course, given the greatest strokes and performed best with his spear, he could also win the overall tournament prize. There were also rules outlining how a knight could lose. If he struck a horse or a man's back or disarmed him of his spear, hit the tilt three times, or lost his helmet twice he was automatically disqualified. Additional rules described how spears could be broken and what constituted a disqualifying spear-break.[54]

After the rules and conditions of the jousting had been outlined, the Burgundians and the Scots set forth from their pavilions. As they marched towards one another their planned order deteriorated. In the end, Meriadet fought James Douglas of Ralstoun, and Simon de Lalain fought John Ross of Hawkhead. Chastellain described their jousts in much detail:

> Then the said Des Lalains and Meriadet threw their lances behind them as they had agreed. Then they seized their axes, and with much vigour began to fight and strike at the Scots who defended themselves with their lances. Messire James de Duglas fought with his lance; but it did not remain long in his hand: so he took his axe and fought for a little time with it, but not for long, for Messire Jacques soon made him lose it as he had lost his lance. And this Messire James being very wroth, and disturbed at seeing himself thus disarmed of his lance and his axe, at once with great fury seized his dagger and so tried to strike Messire Jacques in the face as he fought without his vizor and with his face uncovered. But Messire Jacques seeing him approach, with great force stuck him a blow with his left hand and made him stagger backwards. Notwithstanding this, Messire James sought with all his power to strike him in the face. Then Messire Jacques threw away his axe, and with his left hand seized Messire James by the head-piece, and held him so fast that he could not approach him, and with the right hand he drew his sword (which was a short blade), holding it near the point to use it as a dagger, for he had lost his own and did not know how (some say that he who armed him did not arm him with this). And thus he sought to make a dagger of the said sword, as had been said, and sought to strike the said James with

---

[54] BL Ashmolean MS 763, II, p. 5, Herald's College MS.M.6, cited in R. Coltman Clephan, *The Tournament: Its Periods and Phases* (London, 1919), pp. 46–7.

the hand with which he held the beaver; and in trying to strike him, the said blade fell from his hand and he was without a weapon. And when he saw himself disweaponed, very swiftly and furiously he seized the said James with both hands by the hollow of his head-piece, and by the strength of his arm made him move backwards to the throne of the king, twice lifting him off his feet with the intention of throwing him on the ground, and so putting him out of breath; and in so doing he did rightly, for Messire James fought in his basinet with closed vizor, which the said De Lalain was without his vizor and breathed freely, it being quite the contrary with Messire James, and this soon appeared, when his vizor was removed after the king had thrown down his truncheon.[55]

Chastellain's account then describes in similar detail the fights between Simon de Lalain and John Ross of Hawkhead, and Meriadet and James Douglas. In Meriadet and James Douglas's combat, Meriadet showed superior fighting skills and levelled Douglas to the ground, 'and it is the truth that if he had hastened to slay him, he could easily have done so, and without blame since the fight was *à outrance*.'[56] At the end of the tournament, the guards:

> laid hands on the six champions as they had been ordered to do; and all were brought before the King of Scotland, who said that they had all fought valiantly and well, that he held the combat at an end, and that he wished that they should be good friends. The trial of arms over, each returned to his lodging. And some days after the king feasted them very grandly, and gave them honourable gifts for which they thanked him.[57]

This passage clearly indicates that Chastellain was not present at the tournament and was recording second-hand information – a banquet taking place 'some days after' would have fallen during Lent. Instead, such a banquet would most probably have occurred immediately after the jousting on Shrove Tuesday itself.

After visiting Scotland, Jacques de Lalain went to Bruges, where he participated in a tournament held on Mary of Gueldres' bridal journey to Scotland.[58] During the tournament Lalain competed with and defeated an English squire. The duke of Burgundy, who presided over the tournament, had deemed that their weapons were not equal. The English squire's axe was declared to be superior to Lalain's, but Lalain argued that the squire should still be allowed

---

[55] Chastellain, 'Historie du bon chevalier Messire Jacques de Lalain', pp. 35–6.
[56] *Ibid.*, p. 37.
[57] *Ibid.*, p. 38.
[58] Lalain won the tournament. Van Severen (ed.), *Inventaire des Archives de la Ville de Bruges*, V, p. 498; Fradenburg, *City, Marriage, Tournament*, p. 173; Barber and Barker, *Tournaments*, p. 130. The bridal party left Sluys on 9 June 1449, so the tournament must have taken place at the end of May or the beginning of June. Mary of Gueldres was a niece of the duke of Burgundy and it is likely that the Stirling tournament and the bridal tournament in Bruges were connected. The direct connection to the court of Burgundy may also have influenced the promotion of tournaments and chivalry in Scotland.

to use it.[59] According to the chronicler Olivier de la Marche, the English squire fought with his visor closed but Lalain left his face exposed as he had done at Stirling. The squire tried to use this to his own advantage but the contest remained even until he caught the open end of Lalain's gauntlet and severely cut Lalain's arm. To avoid being accused of favouring Lalain, the duke of Burgundy allowed the combat to continue and, despite his injury, Lalain succeeded in throwing the Englishman to the ground.[60] La Marche's account of the jousting does not mention the Scottish knights who accompanied Mary of Gueldres through Bruges, nor whether they took part in the jousting, although their participation does seem likely.[61]

Scotland was often included amongst the places where heralds visited to proclaim tournaments, such as for the *pas d'armes* near Calais in 1449 held by Jean de Luxembourg, bastard of St Pol. This demonstrates that Scottish knights were well enough known amongst knights from countries like France, England, Germany and Spain, to be invited to compete in chivalric games.[62] Chivalric ideology suggested that no knight should avoid a tournament if he could get there in time but, of course, adherence to this ideal was variable. Many Continental knights, such as Jacques de Lalain, did go on extended tours in search of tournaments and the *Buke of the Ordre of Knychthede* remarked that a good knight 'auenturit his persone to pursue and manetene justis tourneymentis and weris'.[63] Whether Scottish knights also travelled extensively in pursuit of tournaments is more difficult to ascertain, but they evidently had an intermittent presence at Continental jousts.

Shortly after the Bruges tournament, Mary of Gueldres arrived in Scotland. On 3 July 1449 she married James II at Holyrood Abbey. Contrary to what might be expected of a late-medieval royal wedding, there is no clear evidence that a tournament was held in connection with the marriage celebrations.[64]

---

[59] Weapons checks were a standard part of tournaments. 'The Order of Combats', p. 386.
[60] Barber and Barker, *Tournaments*, pp. 130–2.
[61] Sir William Crichton, the Chancellor, was one of the knights who may have participated. *Chron. Auchinleck*, p. 41.
[62] Barber and Barker, *Tournaments*, pp. 117–18; Edington, 'Tournament in Medieval Scotland', p. 58; CDS, IV, 1184. For the *pas d'armes* near Calais the duke of Burgundy specifically sent heralds at his own expense to England, Germany, Spain and Scotland, although it does not seem that any Scottish knights took up the challenge. A *pas d'armes* was when an individual or team of knights proclaimed that they would defend a place against all comers. Froissart reports that heralds were sent to Scotland in 1348 to proclaim the feasting and jousting to commemorate the founding of the Order of the Garter. See Froissart, *Chronicles*, p. 66; Penman, *David II*, p. 150. In 1540 the countries that were included on the travels of tournament proclaimers were France, England, Flanders, Scotland and Spain. John Stow, *A Survey of London: Written in the Year 1598*, Henry Morley (ed.), (Stroud, 1994), p. 405.
[63] Kaeuper, *Chivalry and Violence*, p. 164; Barber and Barker, *Tournaments*, pp. 49–51, 177; Glenn (ed.), *Buke of the Ordre of Knychthede*, p. 3.
[64] Fradenburg, *City, Marriage, Tournament*, p. 173; Barber and Barker, *Tournaments*, pp. 169, 172–3. It was established by the fifteenth century that jousting commonly occurred at weddings. See, for example, William Dunbar's poem, 'Schir Thomas Norny', in Bawcutt (ed.), *William Dunbar*, p. 162.

There is, however, an indication that some tourneying activity might have taken place around the time of the marriage and we can assume that this was probably part of the wedding celebrations. Between September 1448 and July 1449, Sir William Cranston received £20 for bows, lances and armour equipment.[65] Before 21 July 1450, John Liddale, a squire, received £12 for lances and spears of different colours for what is described simply in the exchequer entry as 'the tournament'. This entry may refer back to an earlier date in summer 1449.[66] Cranston, and probably also Liddale, were known Douglas adherents at this time and again the influence of the family on chivalric displays is apparent.[67] Additionally, before 18 July 1449, James II had a suit of armour made for himself and around the same time he received lances, harnesses and other martial equipment. This suggests that he had participated in jousting at some point before these dates.[68] Unfortunately the loss of the treasurer's accounts for this period makes it difficult to draw firm conclusions, but all of these payments were made from Edinburgh accounts, further supporting the idea that jousting took place at James II's marriage celebrations.

After competing in the jousts at Bruges in 1449, Jacques de Lalain, with the consent and support of Philip the Good, duke of Burgundy, set up a *pas d'armes* near Chalon sur Saône. This tournament, called the Fountain of Tears, was held in a most unusual manner: the games were to take place on the first day of each month for an entire year. A herald, who was accompanied by a lady and an image of a unicorn, met all challengers who came. The herald's main duty was to record the names of the participants and which of the unicorn's three shields they had touched, thereby indicating the event in which they intended to compete. The pavilion was initially pitched on 1 November 1449, but no challengers came forward until 1 February 1450.[69] The popularity of *pas d'armes* on the Continent at this time serves to demonstrate that the 1449 tournament at Stirling does not fit well with developments on the Continent, although Scottish knights were clearly part of a cosmopolitan chivalric culture. Unlike elaborate *pas d'armes*, the Stirling tournament was a straightforward battle of physical strength with limited use of imagery and spectacle.[70]

Lalain had selected Chalon as the tournament's location because it was expected that many pilgrims from France, England and Spain would pass through the town on their way to Rome for the papal jubilee celebrations in

---

[65] *ER*, V, p. 345. This is the same William Cranston who was probably knighted by James II at his coronation.
[66] *Ibid.*, V, pp. 383, 385.
[67] Brown, *Black Douglases*, pp. 257, 272, 287. Cranston quickly converted to royal allegiance when James II made it clear he was attempting to subvert the power of the Black Douglases.
[68] *ER*, V, pp. 312, 315, 339, 345, 346.
[69] Barber and Barker, *Tournaments*, pp. 118–19.
[70] Edington, 'Tournament in Medieval Scotland', p. 59.

1450.[71] There is also clear evidence that a Scottish party heading to Rome, led by William, eighth earl of Douglas, attended the tournament at Chalon. The earl of Douglas sailed from Scotland directly to the Low Countries and arrived at the court of Philip of Burgundy at Lille on 12 October 1450. Here he was joined by the rest of his company who had travelled through England. These men included, amongst others, Sir James Douglas (later ninth earl), who had jousted with Jacques de Lalain at Stirling the previous year; Sir James Hamilton; Sir John Ogilvy of Lintrathen; Sir Alexander Hume; Sir William Cranston; and Sir Colin Campbell of Glenorchy.[72] Douglas's entourage then travelled to Paris to attend Charles VII's court, presumably having been reminded by the duke of Burgundy of the tournament which he was sponsoring at Chalon.[73] From Paris, the party's route would have been naturally directed through Chalon, so it is likely that the seven knights in the Douglas party would have participated in the *pas d'armes*.[74]

The Douglases' clear involvement in the promotion of chivalry through chivalric pastimes, and their use of this to advertise themselves as chivalric exemplars for the rest of the Scottish nobility, was just one factor which contributed to James II's aggressive attempt to destroy their power in the early 1450s. With the downfall of the Black Douglases, James was free to assert royal dominance over such activities. A few years after he had killed the eighth earl,

---

[71] Cartellieri, *The Court of Burgundy*, pp. 121–2; Edington, 'Tournament in Medieval Scotland', p. 58.

[72] Also part of the group were Adam Auchinleck, cleric; Jonathan Clerk, cleric; Andrew Gray; William Lauder; Thomas Cranston; Andrew Kerr; Charles Murray; George Haliburton; Jonathan Haliburton; Jonathan Dodds; Jonathan Greenlaw; George Felawe; Alan Lauder; and James Bishop. *ER*, V, p. 439; Brown, *Black Douglases*, p. 287; Fraser, *Douglas*, I, p. 466; *Rot. Scot.*, II, p. 343; *CDS*, IV, 1229; NAS GD16/46/3; Dunlop, *James Kennedy*, pp. 123–6. The eighth earl of Douglas returned to England just after 27 February 1451, when the Garter King of Arms was dispatched by Henry VI to the sea coast to await his arrival, to take him to the king's court and attend on him during his stay. *CDS*, IV, 1231.

[73] Dunlop, *James Kennedy*, p. 124.

[74] During James IV's reign, Scots were also participating in Continental tournaments. In 1494, Chevalier Bayard hosted a *pas d'armes* under the walls of the town of Aire in France, for which the prizes were diamonds, and a gold bracelet enamelled with Bayard's colours. Edward Cockburn Kindersley (ed.), *The Very Joyous, Pleasant and Refreshing History of the Feats, Exploits, Triumphs and Achievements of the Good Knight without Fear and without Reproach the Gentle Lord de Bayard* (London, 1848), pp. 33–9; Forbes-Leith, *Scots Men-at-Arms*, I, pp. 72–3. Forty-six men participated in this tournament, a large number of them from the Scots guard in France. Two judges presided, 'the good captain Louis d'Ars, and the Scotch lord Saint Quentin', Cuthbert Carr, lord of St Quentin, a Captain in the Scots Guards. Bayard's biographer described the main fighting between Bayard and Tartarin, and Bellabre and a 'Scotch gentleman, the captain David de Fougar'. He describes how they jousted two and two until they had run their courses, and then they all proceeded to the sword fight. 'And though each did right well, the best were the good Knight, Bellabre, Tartarin, the captain David, one of the company of my lord des Cordes named the Bastard of Chimay, and Tardieu.' On the second day, Tardieu and David of Scotland were set against each other, and 'did their devoir right well'. It was decided at the feast that night that Bayard had won the tournament, and he could bestow his presents where he thought fit. After some consideration, Bayard gave the prize of the first day to Bellabre, and the prize for the second day to the captain David Foggo.

at a time when he was facing war with England, James II began to place more emphasis on chivalric activities. In 1456 he declared that the space at Greenside should be used for tournaments and other warlike sports.[75] However, the Edinburgh city records do not record whether Greenside was actually used for this purpose and there are no suggestions that a tournament was ever held there. James II's intention in establishing a permanent space for jousting and tourneying is clear: he wanted to train men in skills of warfare and knighthood and planned to increase the number of trained knights and men-at-arms at his disposal. In addition, his move brought chivalric pastimes under strict royal control.

However, the decline of the Black Douglases had left a space in which other members of the nobility could patronise chivalric ideals. In particular, William Sinclair, earl of Orkney, attempted to assume this role from his castle at Roslin. Having been made Chancellor in 1454, Sinclair had been heavily involved in James's crushing of the Douglases in 1455 and 1456.[76] Sinclair had close ties to the Douglases through marriage and he shared the same social and cultural circle, but these types of ties clearly did not guarantee political unity and loyalty.[77] By 1456 Sinclair was at the peak of his personal and political power and may have decided to champion a programme of knightly reform by commissioning Sir Gilbert Hay to translate three chivalric treatises. In doing this, the earl of Orkney firmly established himself as central to the upsurge of interest in chivalry following the events of 1449. Whilst Hay's translations proved popular, Sinclair was not. He lost the Chancellorship in October of that year, and this was followed by his immediate loss of favour at court. Whilst Sinclair's sudden decline in royal favour has been attributed to his unwillingness to further the Scottish crown's aims in Danish and Norwegian politics, one cannot help but wonder whether his sudden patronage of chivalry, much like the eighth earl of Douglas's, might have contributed to his political downfall.[78]

1460–1488

Unlike James II's involvement with chivalric activities, James III appears to have entirely avoided chivalric sports. There is no surviving evidence for any tournaments or other chivalric activities held by James III. Of course, his neglect of chivalric pastimes may have been simply because he was not personally interested in them. Norman Macdougall sums up James's rule as one

---

[75] 'pro tournamentis, jocis, et justis actibus bellicis ibidem'. Taken from *Edin. Chrs.*, no. 36.
[76] Barbara E. Crawford, 'William Sinclair, earl of Orkney, and His Family: A Study in the Politics of Survival', in K.J. Stringer (ed.), *Essays in the Nobility of Medieval Scotland* (Edinburgh, 1985), p. 232; Sally Mapstone, 'The Advice to Princes Tradition in Scottish Literature, 1450–1500' (D.Phil., University of Oxford, 1987), p. 66; *HBC*, p. 182; *Chron. Auchinleck*, p. 53.
[77] See Brown, *Black Douglases*, pp. 235, 238, 247, 255, 257, 262, and Genealogical Table 4, p. 98.
[78] Crawford, 'William Sinclair', pp. 232, 235–6.

where the king did not recognise the responsibilities of kingship and he argues that James's most serious mistakes lay in not rewarding his nobles adequately and failing to provide them with an appropriate court life. Instead, he hoarded money rather than spending it on public celebrations like tournaments.[79]

In distinct contrast, James III's brother, Alexander Stewart, duke of Albany, did participate in tournaments and other chivalric activities. The duke of Albany was reputed as: 'sa expert in all faittis of armys, that he wes haldin and repute as ane fadir in chevalry'.[80] Indeed, it has been argued that the duke of Albany was the model for Blind Harry's *Wallace* – a brave, bold warrior hero. *The Wallace*, written in the late 1470s, has also been interpreted as a denunciation of James III's policy of peace with England, clearly comparing the two brothers and favouring Albany.[81] Albany had fled to France in the spring of 1479, the year he was indicted by parliament for treason.[82] He was well received at the court of Louis XI and in January 1480 he married Anne de la Tour, daughter of the Count of Auvergne and Bouillon, after which he returned to Scotland in 1482 in an attempt to claim the throne.[83] He re-entered France in 1483 after being forfeited and became a knight of the Order of St Michael.[84] His enthusiasm for jousting ultimately led to his death at the age of thirty-one, when he duelled with the duke of Orléans in Paris in 1485 and was killed by a splinter from his lance.[85]

Even though James III did not hold any tournaments, he must have paid some attention to chivalric institutions and pastimes as he, like his brother, was a knight of the Order of St Michael. James was also a knight of the Danish Order of the Elephant.[86] Until recently it was also widely held that James III founded his own Scottish chivalric order, but this has been proven to be erroneous.[87] The Order of St Michael was founded in 1469 and James III was one of its original companions. Louis XI had planned the first meeting of the order for 1471, but this was subsequently cancelled. Instead it took place under

---

[79] Macdougall, *James III*, pp. 305–6; Leslie J. Macfarlane, *William Elphinstone and the Kingdom of Scotland, 1431–1514: The Struggle for Order* (Aberdeen, 1985), pp. 182–3.
[80] Lesley, *History*, p. 51.
[81] Sir James Liddale of Halkerston was one of Blind Harry's main sources of information, and Liddale's relationship with both James III and the duke of Albany cannot be ignored. See also Kelham, 'Bases of Magnatial Power', p. 240; Macdougall, *James III*, pp. 269–70.
[82] *APS*, II, pp. 125–8; Macdougall, *James III*, pp. 128–9. Norman Macdougall suspects that Albany was abusing his position as a warden of the Marches, and that he was responsible for serious violations against the Anglo-Scottish alliance. Macdougall, *James III*, p. 129.
[83] Pitscottie, *Historie*, I, p. 189; Macdougall, *James III*, p. 130.
[84] Michel, *Les Écossais en France*, p. 264; Boulton, *Knights of the Crown*, p. 444. His son, John, also became a member of the order.
[85] Lesley, *History*, p. 51; *SP*, I, p. 152; Nicholson, *Scotland*, p. 517; Macdougall, *James III*, p. 212; *ER*, IX, p. lvi; Michel, *Les Écossais en France*, p. 264.
[86] *TA*, I, pp. 81, 86.
[87] Stevenson, 'The Unicorn, St Andrew and the Thistle', pp. 3–22; Stevenson, 'Knighthood, Chivalry and the Crown', ch. 6.

Charles VIII in 1484, at which point the order numbered thirty knights. James III did not attend the meeting, nor did the king of Denmark. They had previously been informed they did not need to attend, although there is no indication of why they were exempted from this obligation.[88] James's membership of these Orders does not indicate that he had a significant interest in chivalry, nor that he actively promoted himself as a chivalric king. Instead it speaks more of his desire to be recognised as an effective ruler by his European peers. James III was heavily criticised by his contemporaries for seeking the counsel of low-born, young and inexperienced advisors, and his lack of chivalric display may be symptomatic of the importance he placed on the advice of these men.[89]

1488–1513

In this light, James IV's extravagant expenditure on tournaments, jousts, and other public celebrations, his military and naval forces, and his general benevolence to his nobles, can all be interpreted as his attempt not to repeat the mistakes of his father. If his father had been reluctant to display or encourage chivalric activity, James IV revived and elaborated upon chivalric culture in its most extravagant forms. Maurice Keen argues that in the late Middle Ages, as men rediscovered the romance and richness of the chivalric tradition, they expressed this revelation in the rituals of chivalry: dubbing ceremonies, heroic exploits and tournaments. According to Keen these ideals were so flamboyantly asserted because men, just like James IV, sincerely intended to do justice to their class ideal which placed a premium on outward expressions of the chivalric and knightly ethos.[90] In the introduction to his English translation of the *Order of Chivalry*, William Caxton urged Richard III to hold jousts twice a year, in the hope that 'the noble order of chivalry be hereafter better used and honoured than it hath been in late days past'.[91] In the late sixteenth century Pitscottie wrote of James IV that:

> This prince was wondrous hardie and deliegent in the executioun of iustice and loweit nothing so weill as abill men and guid hors and vsed gret justing and treatit his barrouns wondrous weill that was abill thairfoir, and sundrie tymes wald gar mak proclematiouns out throw his realme to all and sindrie

---

[88] Boulton, *Knights of the Crown*, pp. 427, 436, 443–4. The original members of the order included thirteen non-royal knights and French officials of the Constable, the Admiral, both Marshals, the Grand Master of the Household, and the royal governors of four of the most important provinces in France, along with René, duke of Anjou, Christian I of Denmark, Norway and Sweden, and his son and successor Hans, and James III. Charles, duke of Burgundy, François, duke of Brittany, and Adolph, duke of Guelders, all refused membership.
[89] Macdougall, *James III*, esp. pp. 269–72.
[90] Keen, *Chivalry*, pp. 216–7.
[91] Caroline Barron, 'Chivalry, Pageantry and Merchant Culture in Medieval London', in Peter Coss and Maurice Keen (eds), *Heraldry, Pageantry and Social Display in Medieval England* (Woodbridge, 2002), pp. 240–1.

his lordis, earleis and barrouns quhilk was abill for iusting or tornament to come to Edinburgh to him and thair to exerceis them selffis for his plesour as they war best accustomit, sum to rin witht speir, sum to fight witht the battell axe and harnis, sum to feight witht the tuo handit suord, sum to schut the hand bow, corsebow and collvering. And everie man as he faught best gat his wapouns deliuerit to him be the king in this maner; he that ran the speir best, he gat ane speir witht gould deliuerit in to him witht gilt harnis thair to kepi in memorieall of his practick and ingyne thari to, and also the harrottis blasonitt him to be the best justar and rynnar of the speir in the realme amang his bretherine; and the battell axe deliuerit to him that faught best thariwitht, and in lykewyse the suord, hand bow and corse bow deliuerit be the heraldis the samin maner to them that wssit them best. Be this way and meane the king brocht his realme to great manheid and honouris, that the fame of his iusting and tornamentis sprang throw all Europe quhilk caussit money forand knychtis to come out of strange contrieris to Scottland to seik iusting because they hard the nobill fame and knychtlie game of the prince of Scottland and of his lords and barrouns and gentillmen. Money strangeris came bot few reffussit bot they war fouchin witht and wairit in singular battell be the Scottis men.[92]

Although Pitscottie was a notoriously inaccurate chronicler, his opinions about James IV appear to have been well informed. James did hold a large number of tournaments, including most famously one for the pretender to the English throne, Perkin Warbeck, in 1496 and the two called the Wild Knight and the Black Lady in 1507 and 1508. He also held many others that have hitherto been obscured by the difficulties with the Scottish sources.

During the 1490s James hosted a number of small-scale jousts and tournaments. On 25 May 1491, £3 12s was paid to a bowyer to provide jousting spears for the king, suggesting that James himself was either practising or participating in jousts at this time. Amongst the spears ordered for the raid of Hume in the Scottish borders in January 1497 was a payment for the heads for twenty-four jousting spears and a part payment for a further thirty jousting spears.[93] Jousting and small tournaments were common when armies were on campaigns and helped to fill long periods of inactivity.[94] James IV was almost certainly encouraging his men to take part in such activities by personally providing the equipment. These entries in the treasurer's accounts also distinguish between jousting spears and spears used in war – the heads on the jousting spears were clearly distinct and were probably blunted. Given that war spears were sharp, the existence of different heads for jousting spears suggests that by this time *à outrance* jousting may have lost some of its popularity. As the tournament became an imitation of war, it became orchestrated and elaborate and lost much of its practical martial function. Tournament combat

---

[92] Pitscottie, *Historie*, I, pp. 231–2.
[93] *TA*, I, p. 310. It is possible that the 'diamonds' and 'virales' often referred to in association with heads of jousting spears were types of blunted head.
[94] For another example of this see *Chron. Wyntoun*, VI, p. 129.

became increasingly stylised as competitors sought to display their skills and knightliness rather than their ability simply to overpower their opponent.[95] The tournament became a vehicle for displaying the power of violence, rather than providing an opportunity for the exercise of it. Due to the pressing need to avoid serious injury during jousting, the use of blunted weapons became common.

A year prior to the raid of Hume, in January 1496 Perkin Warbeck married James IV's cousin, Lady Catherine Gordon. James seems to have been rather taken with Warbeck and provided him with a lavish wedding ceremony, clothing him in white damask at the cost of £28.[96] As part of the wedding celebrations, James held a tournament. The king personally participated in the jousting alongside Perkin Warbeck; Sir Robert Kerr of Cessford (also known as of Ferniehirst), later Master of the King's Artillery; Patrick Hume of Polwarth; Patrick Haliburton; and William Sinclair. Both Robert Kerr and Patrick Hume went on to distinguish themselves in the military campaigns of 1496 and 1497. The four Scots were all close to James IV, but only Robert Kerr had been knighted before the tournament. The knightly status of these men was also reflected in their clothing allowances for the tournament: Kerr, as the only knight, received an extra £20 for damask clothing, whereas Hume, Haliburton and Sinclair only received an extra £8 for tartar. There is only evidence that these four men, the king and Warbeck, participated in the tournament. As they were uniformly attired, we can assume that they made up a royal team, but against whom they may have fought is not known.[97] James IV was generous in meeting the additional costs of the tournament: velvet was bought for the horses' harnesses at £50, two trumpeters were gowned in Rowan tan with red stockings at over £10, and Laurence, the tournament armourer, was clothed in Rowan tan, a velvet doublet, a brown hogtoune and black stockings at the cost of around £14.[98] No record of the proceedings or outcome of the tournament survives but the king was wounded during the jousting. It is unclear how this happened as blunt weapons were probably used, particularly as this was a tournament focused on chivalric display rather than martial glory. James's wound was only a minor hand injury, which was bandaged and worn in a sling of taffeta.[99]

---

[95] Bumke, *Courtly Culture*, pp. 257–8; Fradenburg, *City, Marriage, Tournament*, pp. 194–5; Barker, *The Tournament in England*, pp. 17–44.

[96] *TA*, I, p. 263. Warbeck also received two pairs of black stockings at 35 shillings a pair, and a velvet coat of 'new fassoune' with sleeves and lined in damask at the cost of £32. For more on Perkin Warbeck see David Dunlop, 'The "Masked Comedian": Perkin Warbeck's Adventures in Scotland and England from 1495 to 1497', *SHR* 70 (1991), pp. 97–128; Macdougall, *James IV*, pp. 117–38.

[97] *TA*, I, pp. 262, 263–4. Six hogtounes were made, close-fitting tunics worn under a hauberk, of tartar and braid ribbon at the cost of £12. Six gowns of damask were made at considerable expense, highlighting that they were dressed in a 'team uniform'.

[98] *TA*, I, pp. 262, 264.

[99] *TA*, I, p. 257; Fradenburg, *City, Marriage, Tournament*, p. 176; Macdougall, *James IV*, pp. 122–3; Edington, 'Tournament in Medieval Scotland', p. 59.

A few years after Warbeck's tournament, Scotland hosted a foreign visitor who wished to joust with a Scottish knight. John Caupance, a French squire, participated in a duel with Sir Patrick Hamilton of Kincavil, an illegitimate brother of James, second Lord Hamilton. This was presided over by James IV and took place in Edinburgh, under the castle wall, around 1500.[100] The only report that has survived of this duel was penned by Pitscottie in the late sixteenth century and must be read with the greatest caution. Pitscottie wrote that the French squire

> desyrit fighting and iusting in Scottland [. . .] bot nane was sa apt and redy to fight witht him as was Schir Patrick Hammilltoun, beand then ane zoung man strang of body and abill to all thing, bot zeit for lack of exercioun he was not so weill practissit as neid war, thocht he lackit no hardiement strength nor curage in his proceidingis [. . .] efter the sound of they trumpit [they] suchit rudlie togither and brak thair speiris on ilk syde wpoun wther; quhilk efterwart gat new speiris and recounterit freischelie againe. Bot Schir Patrickis horse wtterit witht him and wald on nowayis reconter his marrow, that it was force to the said Schir Patrick Hammelltoun to lyght on footte and gif this Dutchman [Pitscottie confuses his nationality] battell; and thairfor quhene he was lichtit doune, cryit for ane tuo handit suord and bad this Dutchman lyght frome his horse and end out the matter, schawand to him ane horse is bot ane wiak warand quhene men hes maist ado. Than quhene batht the knychtis war lyghtit on fute they junitt pairtlie togither witht right awfull contienance; ewerie on strak maliciouslie at wther and faught lang togither witht wncertane wictorie, quhill at last Schir Patrick Hammilltoun ruschit manfullie qpoun the Dutchman and strak him wpoun his kneis. In the meane tyme the Dutchman being at the eird the king cast out his hatt out of the castell wondow and caussit the iudges and men of armes to sinder and red thame. Bot the harrottis and the trumpitis blew and cryit the wictor was Schir Patrick Hammilltounis.[101]

There is no precise date for this duel but John Caupance was definitely in Scotland in 1499, when the exchequer granted him money for his expenses in Edinburgh and Stirling.[102]

John Caupance and Patrick Hamilton have sometimes been confused with another duelling pair, Sir Anthony D'Arcy de la Bastie and James, second Lord Hamilton, James IV's cousin. Hamilton and D'Arcy fought against each

---

[100] Pitscottie calls him John Clokbuis, a Dutch knight, although he probably meant German, as his tendency was to confuse the two nationalities. Pitscottie, *Historie*, I, p. 234, II, p. 373. See also Neilson, *Trial by Combat*, pp. 284–5. Patrick Hamilton of Kincavil was the son of James, first Lord Hamilton, and the brother of James, first earl of Arran and John Hamilton of Broomhill. Patrick Hamilton was a favourite of James IV and he had been knighted by him around 1496. *TA*, I, pp. 360, 379; George Hamilton, *A History of the House of Hamilton*, (Edinburgh, 1933), p. 522. On 2 February 1501 he was granted the office of the sheriff of Linlithgow and the custody of Blackness Castle. *RMS*, II, 2480.
[101] Pitscottie, *Historie*, pp. 234–5.
[102] *ER*, XI, pp. 231, 235, 258–9; 'The Errol Papers', *Spalding Misc.*, II (Aberdeen, 1842), pp. 212–13, IV. A shorter version appears in *Edin. Recs.*, p. 91.

other in Stirling in 1506.[103] John Lesley reports that the duel took place on 24 September 1506, but as James IV was not in Stirling at this time, the duel probably took place around 3 July of that year. Lesley wrote that Lord Hamilton 'faucht with him in harneis vailyeantlie, bot nether of thame leiset ther honor thairthrouch', suggesting that James IV awarded honour on both sides.[104] Duels were fought between a challenger and the knight he challenged and these examples provide evidence that French knights and squires wished to duel with Scottish knights (or the Hamiltons!) and were prepared to travel to do so. That the crown paid for their expenses whilst in Scotland demonstrates quite clearly that the king regarded it as his duty to support and promote such events.

In the early 1500s, James IV's patronage of the arts and chivalry continued and his courtly aspirations were represented in the poems of William Dunbar (c.1460–c.1513). Dunbar was not only a prominent and popular court poet but he also served in the royal household as a scribe, secretary and envoy. He is thought to have attended the University of St Andrews in the 1470s and is known to have served as a procurator at various times.[105] While he wrote poems on various knightly and chivalric topics, including 'The Ballad of Barnard Stewart' and 'Schir Thomas Norny',[106] his most interesting exploration of chivalry is contained within a larger poem entitled 'Fasternis Evin in Hell', the setting of which is Dunbar's own dream vision of the underworld. In a trance, Dunbar first envisions the dance of the Seven Deadly Sins and then, at stanza twelve, a mock tournament between a tailor and a soutar (cobbler). Both of these were diabolic entertainments provided for the celebrations of Fastern's Even (Shrove Tuesday).[107] There is considerable controversy over the date of the poem's composition. Priscilla Bawcutt dates the poem to 1505, but proceeds to suggest that the dating is symbolic rather than actual. Ian Simpson Ross dates the poem to 1507: Dunbar states that the poem was set on 15 February and Shrove Tuesday fell on that date in 1507.[108] The poem

---

[103] *TA*, III, p. 354; Fradenburg, *City, Marriage, Tournament*, p. 176; Hamilton, *House of Hamilton*, p. 522.
[104] Lesley, *History*, p. 75; *RMS*, II, 2972.
[105] Bawcutt (ed.), *William Dunbar*, pp. 2–3. Dunbar represented Sir John Wemyss of Wemyss on 15 February 1502 in a suit against members of his own family. He is known to have been in England in 1501, presumably on a diplomatic mission for James IV.
[106] Both 'The Ballad of Bernard Stewart' and 'Schir Thomas Norny' appear in Bawcutt (ed.), *William Dunbar*, pp. 161–4, 222–7.
[107] Bawcutt (ed.), *William Dunbar*, p. 178; Tom Scott, *Dunbar: A Critical Exposition of the Poems* (Edinburgh & London, 1966), pp. 234–7; Ian Simpson Ross, *William Dunbar* (Leiden, 1981), pp. 168–77; Steven R. McKenna, 'Drama and Invective: Traditions in Dunbar's "Fasternis Evin in Hell" ', *Studies in Scottish Literature* 24 (1989), p. 129; and Priscilla Bawcutt, *Dunbar the Makar* (Oxford, 1992), pp. 283–92, where Bawcutt tackles the problem of whether the three parts of the poem can be considered as one work or three. Dante Alighieri, at the end of the thirteenth century, in the same sort of dream premise, placed the tournament in his vision of hell. Dante Alighieri, *The Divine Comedy: Volume I, Inferno*, Mark Musa (ed.), (New York, 1984), Canto XXII, lines 6–9.
[108] Bawcutt (ed.), *William Dunbar*, p. 179; Ross, *William Dunbar*, p. 171.

could conceivably be dated earlier, as an actual duel took place in 1502 in which a Christopher Taylor participated, and this might have been the inspiration for Dunbar's satire.[109]

Dunbar's choice of a tailor and a cobbler was certainly deliberate as they were the most obvious professions at which a poet might poke fun. Both crafts held little social esteem and to place them at the centre of a fictitious knightly society emphasised their lower status through humorous juxtaposition. Steven McKenna has suggested that an element of the poem constantly overlooked

> is that these shrewish tradesmen are necessary for the very social order that allows Dunbar to look down on these tradesmen [. . .] The tailors and cobblers are less than ideal types, but they provide an essential service that all people want – the material with which to create an appearance that covers the reality (of unsightly physical characteristics) and which is itself a mark of social distinction.[110]

Dunbar himself made this point in his apology to the craftsmen after writing the poem. Of cobblers he wrote: 'Sowtaris, with schone weill maid and meit,/Ye mend the faltis of ill maid feit,/Quhairfor to hevin your saulis will fle:/Telyouris and sowtaris, blist be ye.' Of tailors Dunbar wrote: 'Thocht a man haif a brokin bak,/Haif he a gude telyour, quhattrak,/That can it cuver with eraftis slie:/Telyouris and sowtaris, blist be ye.'[111] Although he made a point of apologising for his portrayal of them in the 'Fasternis Evin' poem, Dunbar's usual satirical targets were those far removed from chivalric and aristocratic values.[112]

Dunbar uses the tailor and the cobbler to highlight the farcical nature of his imagined tournament, as the usual requirement for participation in a tournament was knightly status. Dunbar describes how the tailor took to the lists with his banner of cloth in front of him, much as real knights would have entered. His treatment of the tailor, however, is disdainful and he writes 'For quhill the Greik sie fillis and ebbis,/Telyouris will nevir be trew.' As the tailor enters the lists he loses all his boldness and 'he chaingit hew', at which point 'Mahoun [the Devil] him comfort and maid him knycht,/Na ferly thocht his hart wes licht/That to sic honour grew.'[113] The tailor vows before the Devil

---

[109] *TA*, II, p. 345. This duel was part of a larger tournament in which James IV also participated. *TA*, II, pp. 348, 352.
[110] McKenna, 'Drama and Invective', p. 141.
[111] William Dunbar, 'Amendis to the Telyouris and Soutaris', in Bawcutt (ed.), *William Dunbar*, p. 191, lines 13–16, p. 192, lines 29–32.
[112] Joanne S. Norman, 'William Dunbar's Rhetoric of Power', in Graham Caie, Roderick J. Lyall, Sally Mapstone and Kenneth Simpson (eds), *The European Sun: Proceedings of the Seventh International Conference on Medieval and Renaissance Scottish Language and Literature, University of Strathclyde, 1993* (East Linton, 2001).
[113] Dunbar, 'Fasternis Evin in Hell', in Bawcutt (ed.), *William Dunbar*, lines 131, 137–8, lines 141, 142–4. As at the 1449 tournament at Stirling where James II knighted the three Scots

that he will 'ding the sowtar doun' but when he faces the lists and sees the cobbler approaching his courage shrinks and he is unable to speak his words of challenge. The cobbler enters the lists as the brave defender with a banner of tanned hide, 'Full sowttarlyk he wes of laitis,/For ay betwix the narnes plaitis/The uly birstit out.'[114] When the cobbler sees the tailor, however, he also becomes fainthearted. Whilst the tailor responded to his fright with 'Ane rak of fartis lyk ony thunner/Went fra him, blast for blast', the cobbler 'In to his stommok was sic ane steir,/Of all his dennar, that cost him deir.'[115] The Devil then grants the privilege of knighthood to the cobbler as well: 'To comfort him or he raid forder,/The devill of knychtheid gaif him order,/For stynk than he did spitt,/And he about the devillis nek/Did spew agane ane quart of blek./Thus knychtly he him quitt.'[116] As the fighting begins, it becomes obvious to those watching that the tailor and the cobbler are both flustered and thus not displaying appropriate knightly qualities such as hardiness, bravery and boldness. The tailor does not fare well on his horse: as it slides over the grass, 'he left his sadill all beschittin' and as he falls to the ground his armour breaks.[117] The cobbler's horse, that 'wes rycht evill', is frightened by the noise of the rattle of the breaking armour and runs 'with the sowtar to the devill'.[118] The Devil, worried that he may again be vomited upon, moves away from the cobbler and, deciding to pay him back, 'He turned his ers and all bedret him,/Quyte our from nek till heill./He lowsit it with sic a reird,/Baith hors and man flawe to the eird,/He fart with sic ane feir,' at which point the cobbler renounces the duel.[119] The Devil puts them into a dungeon and takes away their knighthoods, a punishment which they preferred to ever having to bear arms again.

Dunbar thus emphasises the tailor and the cobbler's lack of knightly qualities, their subsequent poor behaviour and the stripping away of their new status. However, he also makes it clear that they should never have been given knighthood in the first place: they were not of the right social status, nor did they understand the true meaning of the behaviour they were imitating.[120] A prevalent idea in chivalric circles was that a man who was not of noble status should not participate in knightly activities. This was a theme picked up by Sir David Lindsay of the Mount in his 1538 'Iusting betuix Iames Watsoun and

---

nobles before they entered the lists, here the Devil, presiding over the tournament as the king would, followed the same procedure.
[114] Dunbar, 'Fasternis Evin in Hell', lines 146, 166–8.
[115] *Ibid.*, lines 155–6, 172–3. Steven McKenna has pointed out that this was a traditional way of portraying Hell. McKenna, 'Drama and Invective', pp. 132–3.
[116] Dunbar, 'Fasternis Evin in Hell', lines 175–80.
[117] *Ibid.*, line 191.
[118] *Ibid.*, lines 196–7.
[119] *Ibid.*, lines 203–7.
[120] Norman, 'William Dunbar's Rhetoric of Power', p. 200.

Ihone Barbour'.[121] Walter Bower likewise remarked, through the voice of Sir William de Dalzel, that children born of 'cooks and churls, serfs and villeins, and sometimes friars and confessors' were 'men neither suited to warfare nor efficient at fighting battles'.[122] This was an important point to be made at James IV's court as this chivalric society, encouraged by the king, reasserted its definitions and values. Tom Scott remarks that

> the object of Dunbar's laughter, however, is not merely the two tradesmen, but the code of chivalry and the custom of jousting. Not merely are the petty bourgeois tradesmen being laughed at under the guise of knights, but knights are being laughed at under the guise of tradesmen.[123]

Scott correctly points out that Dunbar's attack on the tradesmen was premised in their lack of honour, the most esteemed virtue of the chivalric code. Through this, Scott argues, the custom of tourneying is also called into question and the two lifestyles are compared and contrasted. 'The tradesmen lack the courage and daring of knights, yet they have better things to do than waste their time and blood in useless activities like jousting.'[124] Scott, however, fails to recognise Dunbar's loyalty to the courtiers surrounding him, and his sympathies which clearly lie within the world of his patrons, James IV's chivalric court. At the end of the poem social order is restored with the craftsmen stripped of their knighthoods and cast into the Devil's dungeon.

Dunbar's 'Fasternis Evin' poem also alerts us to the types of celebrations held in Scotland on Shrove Tuesday. A long-standing tradition of Shrovetide tournaments existed throughout Europe; for example at Buonconsiglio Castle, in north-east Italy, a series of frescoes on an internal wall of the castle represents the month of February as a tournament.[125] Richard Barber and Juliet Barker suggest that the association of Shrove Tuesday and tournaments may go back to the time when a group of young nobles visited St Bernard at Clairvaux just before Lent, searching for tournaments in which to participate. St Bernard persuaded them, with some difficulty, not to bear arms in the few days before the fast.[126] Throughout the fourteenth and fifteenth centuries, Shrove Tuesday tournaments were regularly held in Italy, Prague, England, Germany, Austria, France and Burgundy, and Scotland also held similar festivities.[127]

The first recorded tournament to be held on Shrove Tuesday in the fifteenth century was that in 1449 between the three Burgundian and three Douglas knights. In 1476, 1477 and 1478, James III celebrated the day by holding games

---

[121] 'The Iusting betuix Iames Watsoun and Ihone Barbour', in Hamer (ed.), *Works of Sir David Lindsay of the Mount*, I, pp. 114–16.
[122] *Chron. Bower*, book XV, 5.
[123] Scott, *Dunbar*, p. 236.
[124] *Ibid.*, p. 236.
[125] See Barber and Barker, *Tournaments*, p. 176.
[126] *Ibid.*, p. 173.
[127] *Ibid.*, pp. 58, 60–1, 69, 109, 162, 173, 176, 189; Penman, *David II*, pp. 86, 311.

within his chamber but these were probably card playing and feasting rather than chivalric and knightly games.[128] James IV took the celebrations more seriously and held a series of tournaments on Shrove Tuesday between 1503 and 1506. In 1503, Shrove Tuesday fell on 28 February and the previous day two shillings had been given by the treasurer for a helmet to be used by James IV at the 'turnaying at Fasteringis Evin'.[129] On 20 March 1503, seven shillings were paid to John Mayne, a bowyer, for three white spears and an axeshaft taken from him at 'Fasteringis Evin bipast'.[130] Later in that year James Hogg was paid 24 shillings for cleaning and repairing the swords and harnesses left at the 'tourneying of Fasteringis Evin', possibly to be prepared for similar games which were held at James IV's wedding ceremony on 8 August.[131]

No Shrove Tuesday tournament was held in 1504, but by 1505 James's interest in celebrating this festival had been renewed. On 3 February 1505, Robert Cutlar was paid £4 for four long swords for the lists and for four short swords for the 'tourneying at Fasteringis Evin' the following day.[132] Twenty-six shillings were paid for twenty-six socket heads, into which spear-heads were fixed, twenty-seven shillings was paid for twenty-four virales and diamonds for jousting spears, and £5 2s was paid for fifty-one spears intended for the Shrove Tuesday tournament of that year.[133] John Heartshead was paid five shillings for drying and handling the tournament pavilions. James Hogg was paid £3 2s for the preparation of eight swords, mending their handles, and for cleaning three steel and emery saddles, two wooden axes and two spearheads, probably similar to the work for which he had been paid in 1503.[134] The level of preparation that preceded the tournament indicates that this was a large celebration incorporating many tilts and probably involving many participants. James IV also made preparations for feasting and dancing, including a new dance designed by Peter the Moor that was performed at the banquet by twelve dancers dressed in black and white stockings.[135]

James held another Shrove Tuesday tournament the following year, in 1506, but far less information about its preparations has survived. On 22 February 1506 James IV paid £5 10s for spears for the jousting at 'Fasteringis evin', £6 to Robert Cutlar for six long swords and six short swords, twelve shillings for twelve spearheads and twelve shillings for virales and diamond heads.[136] It does seem to have been a much smaller affair than the 1505 tournament, but it may have been similar in size to the 1503 celebration. This suggests that in

---

[128] *ER*, VIII, pp. 333, 404, 512.
[129] *TA*, II, p. 202.
[130] *Ibid.*, II, p. 363.
[131] *TA*, II, p. 386; Fradenburg, *City, Marriage, Tournament*, p. 102.
[132] *TA*, II, p. 477.
[133] *Ibid.*, II, p. 477.
[134] *Ibid.*, II, p. 476.
[135] *Ibid.*, II, p. 477.
[136] *Ibid.*, III, p. 182.

1505 James attempted to build on his 1503 celebrations with a large and lavish tournament, which cost the crown a considerable sum, but he only carried on the tradition the following year on a smaller scale. The 1506 Shrove Tuesday tournament was the last of its kind held by James IV, and it would appear that his son did not continue the tradition. It may be that the king's attempt to promote himself and his court on such occasions had not been as successful as he had hoped. Foreign knights were possibly not attending because it was difficult to travel to Scotland in the winter months and there were other Shrove Tuesday tournaments throughout Europe that were easier to reach. Of course, James may also have been distracted from staging the Shrovetide events, as in February 1507 his first son was born and the queen was taken ill during her labour. However, James IV's shift in 1507 to the Wild Knight and Black Lady tournaments further suggests a change in the focus of his attempts to use chivalric sport to promote his own chivalric image both in Scotland and on the Continent.

Shrove Tuesday tournaments were not the only jousts that James sponsored in the first decade of the sixteenth century. 1503 saw not only a tournament in February, but also two tourneys associated with his marriage to Margaret Tudor. On Margaret's bridal journey to Edinburgh she travelled from Haddington through Dalkeith where she stopped to rest. She then proceeded to Greensward, half a mile south of Edinburgh (not to be confused with Greenside which James II assigned for tournaments in 1456 on the road from Edinburgh to Leith).[137] Here a pageant was staged for her entertainment, presided over by her future husband and witnessed by Sir Patrick Hepburn of Dunsyre, earl of Bothwell; James, second Lord Hamilton, the king's cousin; and 'many other Lords, Knyghts, and Gentylmen' who were in her company.[138] Two fully armed men, Sir Patrick Hamilton of Kincavil and Patrick Sinclair, squire, fought for the love of a lady.

> Halfe a Mylle ny to that, within a Medewe, was a Pavillion whereof cam owt a Knyght on Horsbak, armed at all Peces, havyng hys Lady Paramour that barre hys Horne. And by Avantur ther cam an other also armed, that cam to hym, and robbed from hym hys said Lady, and at the absenting blew the said Horne, wherby the said Knyght understude hym, and tourned after hym, and sayd to hym, wherfor hast thou this doon? He answerd hym, what will yow say therto? – I say, that I will pryve apon thee that thou hast doon Owtrage to me. The tother demaunded hyn if he was armed? He said, ye, well then, said th'other, pree the a Man and doo thy Devoir.[139]

[137] While she was in Dalkeith, the stables where the queen's horses were kept appear to have suffered from a minor fire. *Ibid.*, II, p. 385.
[138] Younge, 'Fyancells of Margaret', p. 287.
[139] *Ibid.*, p. 288; Douglas Gray , 'The Royal Entry in Sixteenth-Century Scotland', in Sally Mapstone and Juliette Wood (eds), *The Rose and the Thistle: Essays on the Culture of Late Medieval and Renaissance Scotland* (East Linton, 1998), p. 16; Edington, 'Tournament in Medieval Scotland', pp. 59–60. Two manuscripts of Somerset Herald's account exist: one is a seventeenth-century copy of the earlier MS held at the College of Arms 1M.13, fols 76–155v.

Hamilton of Kincavil and Sinclair proceeded to duel and 'maid a varey fair Torney' until James intervened to halt them and with 'the Qwene behynd him' called 'Paix' and fixed a date for the settlement of their dispute over the lady.[140] It is unlikely that this was a real dispute as it was a stylised performance directed at the princess where she was honoured as the 'lady', with James indirectly asserting that he, too, would honour her love. This is one of the few jousts held in Scotland with the overtly courtly theme of honouring the lady and it cannot be dissociated from its performance before an English princess. Gavin Douglas, in the 1501 *Palice of Honour*, wrote of tournaments that they were 'plesand pastance, and mony lustie sport' and knights entered 'in deidis of armis for thair Ladyis saikis'.[141] However, women are mostly absent from the records of Scottish tournaments and this begs the question of whether the courtly love tradition was relevant to Scottish knights at this time. Most records of tournaments are financial and carry little information about the proceedings, so it is perhaps unsurprising that we find no reference to women. As courtly literature was popular in Scotland, we can assume that some tournaments, if not all, were held with women in the audience, in the name of a lady, to win a lady's honour or other such gesture.

After James IV and Margaret Tudor's wedding ceremony on 8 August 1503, James celebrated with lavish displays and entertainment for his subjects. These wedding celebrations were grander and more spectacular than any Scotland had previously seen. They included an elaborate banquet, a large royal entry and the commissioning of Dunbar's 'The Thrissill and the Rois'.[142] On the third day of the wedding celebrations in the queen's honour, James belted forty-one knights 'for the Luffe of the present Qwene and hyr Ladyes', then after Mass and lunch he signalled the commencement of three days of jousting in Holyrood Palace courtyard.[143] The *Buke of the Ordre of Knychthede*, which had been circulated in Scotland from the 1450s, remarked that on the day of a knight being newly made 'suld thare be grete festyng justing and tourneymentis'.[144] In preparations for the jousting, James IV paid £27 for one hundred and eighty jousting spears, £12 to Robert Cutlar for twelve long swords and twelve short swords, thirty shillings for spearheads and £3 10s for one hundred and forty virales and diamonds for the spears. Twenty-four shillings were also paid to clean and repair older swords and harnesses. It took two days for seven men, headed by Lioun the tailor, to construct the lists, although the English Somerset Herald reported that the 'Place was without

---

[140] Younge, 'Fyancells of Margaret', p. 288; Mackie, *King James IV*, p. 108.
[141] Gavin Douglas, *Palice of Honour*, Bannatyne Club, (Edinburgh 1827, reprinted New York, 1971), p. 46.
[142] William Dunbar, 'The Thrissill and the Rois', in Bawcutt (ed.), *William Dunbar*, pp. 199–208; Fradenburg, *City, Marriage, Tournament*, p. 173.
[143] Younge, 'Fyancells of Margaret', p. 298; Fradenburg, *City, Marriage, Tournament*, p. 102.
[144] Glenn (ed.), *Buke of the Ordre of Knychthede*, p. 33.

Barreres, and only the Tyllt'.[145] The number of weapons and the level of preparations were much greater than James had ordered for other tournaments, indicating that the marriage tournament was significantly grander than previous affairs. Moreover the removal of the tournament from 'public' spaces into the walls of the king's palace further emphasised royal control over the spectacle and also reflected the development of accessibility as an index of social status.[146]

On the first day of jousting the defenders were James, second Lord Hamilton, who was dressed in red satin; John, Lord Ross of Hawkhead, the grandson of Sir John Ross of Hawkhead who had jousted at Stirling in 1449; Sir David Hume of Wedderburn, a cousin of Sir Patrick Hume of Polwarth; William Cockburn of Langton; Patrick Sinclair, who had jousted at Greensward a few days before; and Henry Bruce. The challengers were Cuthbert, third Lord Kilmaurs (who became second earl of Glencairn during the celebrations) and an Englishman, Lord Treyton. The assistants 'to all the comers during the Jousts' were Sir Alexander Seton, the master of Montgomery; Sir Patrick Hamilton of Kincavil; and an English knight Sir John of Treyton. Each of the competitors completed a course with spears and a course with swords 'with the Poynte broken'. The king watched the tournament from his window, along with the Archbishop of St Andrews, the Archbishop of York, the Bishop of Durham and other prelates, and the queen watched from her window accompanied by her ladies. Presiding over the tournament and seated on the scaffold were the lord of Surrey and Sir Patrick Hepburn of Dunsyre, earl of Bothwell, possibly as an honour for their crucial roles in concluding the treaties for the marriage.[147] Lord Morley, William Hay, third earl of Errol, the Constable, the Officers of Arms and trumpeters stood in the field as the events took place.[148] The second day of the tournament saw the games commence again after Mass and lunch. Six men are recorded as jousting and they broke many spears at their pleasure. Two men also fought on foot, armed with half spears and swords. Again James watched from his window, but this time with the earl of Surrey and other prelates and lords. The queen watched from her windows, along with her attendants and various Scottish ladies. On the third day the tournament was held at the same time, but only involved four men who had jousted on the previous days and presumably this acted as a competition 'final'.[149]

After the three tournaments in 1503, James did not hold a tournament at Shrovetide in 1504, but held one at midsummer instead. No information about

---

[145] *TA*, II, pp. 386, 388–9, 390; Younge, 'Fyancells of Margaret', p. 298.
[146] Roy Strong, *Art and Power: Renaissance Festivals 1450–1650* (Woodbridge, 1984), p. 43.
[147] Pinkerton, *History*, II, p. 39; *Foedera*, XII, p. 776; City Archives, Edinburgh, Protocol Book of John Foular, Volume III, June 1519–April 1528, where the earl of Bothwell stood proxy for the king at his betrothal on 25 January 1502; *SP*, II, p. 152.
[148] Younge, 'Fyancells of Maragaret', p. 298.
[149] There is no record of whom these men were. Younge, 'Fyancells of Margaret', p. 299.

this tournament has survived except an indication that the king participated in the jousting.[150] The following year, in May 1505, only three months after he had staged the large Shrovetide tournament, James held a jousting display on the boats moored at Leith.[151] Uniting James's nautical preoccupations and the promotion of his chivalric image, the jousting was part of a wider celebration to mark a crucial point in the building of the pride of his fleet, the *Margaret*. A special dock had been built in Leith in spring 1504 before work on the vessel had begun, and at each stage in the *Margaret*'s construction a celebration was held. On 25 May 1505 James IV went to Leith and dined on board his partly constructed ship: tapestries of woodland scenes were hung for the occasion and a silver platter for the dining table was carried from Edinburgh.[152] After the banquet, James and his guests were entertained with a 'mock' tournament, although whether mounted jousting took place is questionable. No such tournament had been held before and prizes were not awarded. Instead James paid each of the participants forty-two shillings, indicating that they were paid as entertainers rather than being treated as serious competitors.[153]

After the small tournament at Shrovetide 1506, James IV attempted to make his tournaments more lavish and extravagant as a way of promoting himself as a chivalric ruler and knightly king. Frances Gies has remarked that as the ideals of chivalry were resuscitated in the late fifteenth and early sixteenth centuries the actual jousting became secondary to the elaborate masques and allegories and displays of horsemanship.[154] But whilst scholars such as Hionjin Kim have argued that in the later Middle Ages 'extravagant pageants and tournaments [. . .] were very rare', in Scotland this was not the case at all.[155] The tournaments of the Wild Knight and the Black Lady held in June 1507 and May 1508 have attracted most scholarly attention, as they were the most flamboyant and expensive tournaments held by a Stewart king. Their elaborate allegorical themes drew attention to James IV's declaration and revival of chivalry and assertion of his own chivalric capabilities.[156] James went so far as to joust in keeping with the allegorical theme, dressed up and characterised as the Wild Knight, something that has generally surprised scholars.[157] However, the explicit use of symbolism in this manner was not

---

[150] *TA*, II, pp. 476–7.
[151] *Ibid.*, III, p. 141; Edington, 'Tournament in Medieval Scotland', p. 60.
[152] *TA*, III p. 143. See also Macdougall, *James IV*, p. 233.
[153] *TA*, III, p. 141.
[154] Gies, *Knight in History*, p. 202.
[155] Hyonjin Kim, *The Knight Without the Sword: A Social Landscape of Malorian Chivalry* (Cambridge, 2000), p. 13.
[156] Fradenburg, *City, Marriage, Tournament*, esp. Ch. 12. 'The Wild Knight' and Ch. 13. 'The Black Lady'. On allegory in the tournament see Ruth Huff Cline, 'The Influence of the Romances on Tournaments of the Middle Ages', *Speculum: A Journal of Medieval Studies* 20 (1945), pp. 204–11.
[157] Pitscottie, *Historie*, I, pp. 242–44; Fradenburg, *City, Marriage, Tournament*, pp. 231–4. The image of the Wild Knight was a very powerful one as he represented the anonymous,

unheard of in the Middle Ages and Edward III had appeared in the Dunstable tournament of January 1334 dressed in disguise as 'Monsiuer Lyonel', marrying the association of the leopard with the crown.[158] Extensive preparations were made in 1507 for the arming of the king in line with the colours of the Wild Knight. The wearing of costumes turned the tournament into a vibrant spectacle where the knights fighting for the king, or as brothers-in-arms, could easily be distinguished.[159] In a society that revered and honoured chivalric warrior heroes, this was the one way in which James could gain the respect of his nobles. By becoming the Wild Knight, James paid tribute to the chivalric code which promoted a king as the ultimate knight. Many Scottish nobles must have jousted at the 1507 tournament but only a few are mentioned in the accounts. Master William Ogilvie and Alexander Elphinstoun were squires to the Black Lady, John Dunlop and Alexander MacCulloch, dressed in gold, were attendants to the Wild Knight, and Thomas Boswell, Patrick Sinclair and James Stewart were squires for the lists.[160]

Such a marked departure from his other tourneying activities might indicate that James wished to commemorate a significant moment in his reign. The 1507 tournament may well have been staged as a celebration for the birth of James's first legitimate son who was born on 21 February 1507. As a result of Margaret's illness when she gave birth to the infant James, the king undertook a penitent pilgrimage to the shrine of St Ninian at Whithorn, one hundred and twenty miles from Edinburgh. On his return, Margaret had been restored to health and James took this as a sign of confirmation of his pure faith and his strength and power as king.[161] The tournament of June 1507 may have been used as an elaborate display of James IV's power, bolstered now that he had a direct heir. When we consider, however, all the various tourna-

---

liminal man of uncontrolled prowess and physical power, but his acceptance in knightly society was uncontested. Richard Bernheimer, *Wild Men in the Middle Ages: A Study in Art, Sentiment, and Demonology* (Harvard, 1952), pp. 8, 18–19.

[158] Caroline Shenton, 'Edward III and the Symbol of Leopard', in Peter Coss and Maurice Keen (eds), *Heraldry, Pageantry and Social Display in Medieval England* (Woodbridge, 2002), p. 79.

[159] It was common for kings to issue the participants in a tournament with the same coloured clothing in line with the tournament's colour theme. *TA*, III, pp. 252–61; Fradenburg, *City, Marriage, Tournament*, p. 233–4; Barker, *The Tournament in England*, pp. 99–100.

[160] *TA*, III, pp. 258–9. These squires were all members of the royal household. Thomas, 'Renaissance Culture at the Court of James V', Appendix B, pp. 376–83. Alexander MacCulloch was well known as a member of the royal household and Pitscottie names him as one who wore the king's livery. Pitscottie, *Historie*, I, p. 273; Macdougall, *James IV*, p. 300. The prizes awarded at the tournament were made out of the gold of a chain which had belonged to James. *TA*, III, p. 255.

[161] The infant died a year later, in February 1508, *TA*, III, p. 287; Macdougall, *James IV*, pp. 196–7; Fradenburg, *City, Marriage, Tournament*, p. 227. For more on James's visits to Whithorn see John Higgit, 'From Bede to Rabelais – or How St Ninian got his Chain', in Paul Binski and William Noel (eds), *New Offerings, Ancient Treasures: Studies in Medieval Art for George Henderson* (Stroud, 2001), pp. 189–90.

ments that James IV had held in the few years prior to 1507, it would appear instead that he was experimenting with different methods of promoting himself as a chivalric king. His attempts to inaugurate a regular Shrovetide celebration had failed and his midsummer tournament of 1504 went almost unrecorded. The 1507 tournament was an attempt, on an unprecedented scale, to secure an increased chivalric reputation. Edington has suggested that the development was also indicative of the change in emphasis from the celebration of physical strength and military skills to the expression of the cult of honour centred on service to the crown.[162] James repeated the tournament in the following year, a clear attempt to re-assert his personal success of 1507.

The 1508 tournament of the Wild Knight and the Black Lady was held on an even grander scale than the celebration of the previous year. It was held in honour of Sir Bernard Stewart d'Aubigny, who also presided over the games. Stewart was a commander of the Scots guard in France and he had successfully served under a number of French kings.[163] Bernard Stewart's visit to Scotland was eagerly anticipated and it prompted Dunbar's poem 'The Ballade of Barnard Stewart', where the poet described him as 'the prince of knightheyd and flour of chevalry'.[164] Pitscottie wrote that James commanded all the lords and barons of Scotland to make themselves ready for the tournament and to arm themselves in their best array with their best armour and weapons, and that many knights came from England, France and Denmark to participate. He described the tournament as taking place at Holyrood House and lasting forty days. Forty days appears to be a rather lengthy event, although John Lesley agreed that the tournament took place in May and June followed by a three-day banquet commencing at nine in the morning and finishing twelve hours later.[165] Few records of those who jousted in either 1507 or 1508 have survived, but in 1508 John Forman, Adam Cockburn and, for the

---

[162] Edington, 'Tournament in Medieval Scotland', p. 62.
[163] Pitscottie claims that James made Bernard Stewart a judge of the tournament, partly so that Stewart would have the honour of presiding, but also so that the king, disguised in his Wild Knight costume, could participate. As James had participated as the Wild Knight in the previous year it is unlikely that this is why he asked Bernard Stewart to preside over the tournament. Pitscottie, *Historie*, I, p. 243. For more on Bernard Stewart's life see Gray, 'A Scottish "Flower of Chivalry"', pp. 22–34, Contamine, 'The War Literature of the Later Middle Ages', MacDonald, 'Chivalry as a Catalyst', pp. 163–4, and Forbes-Leith, *Scots Men-at-Arms*, I, pp. 72, 76, 78–9, 80, 82–3. Geoffrey de Charny, author of the *Livre de chivalerie*, claimed that those who had served with distinction in wars in their own lands were to be honoured, but more to be honoured were those who had seen service in distant and strange countries. See Keen, *Chivalry*, p. 13.
[164] William Dunbar, 'The Ballade of Bernard Stewart' in Bawcutt (ed.), *William Dunbar*, pp. 222–7, line 18, Fradenburg, *City, Marriage, Tournament*, p. 174. Dunbar wrote 'The Ballade of Barnard Stewart' on his arrival in Edinburgh in 1508, and it was published on 9 May 1508 by Chepman and Myllar. See Beattie (ed.), *Chepman and Myllar Prints*. Printed when the taste for chivalric spectacular was strong in James's court, the nine prints, including John Lydgate's 'Complaint of the Black Knight' and 'Golagrus and Gawain', are especially relevant to the courtly and chivalric tradition in the early sixteenth century. Fradenburg, *City, Marriage, Tournament*, pp. 177–8, 181–2.
[165] Pitscottie, *Historie*, I, p. 242; Lesley, *History*, p. 78; *TA*, IV, p. 119.

second time, Alexander MacCulloch, were attendants to the Wild Knight.[166] Pitscottie reported that James, second Lord Hamilton, earl of Arran, was presented with the prize for best archer either on horseback or on foot. Cuthbert, third Lord Kilmaurs, earl of Glencairn, was given the prize for best wielder of the spear. Andrew, second Lord Gray, won the prize for best with the battleaxe, and Sir Patrick Hamilton of Kincavil was awarded the prize for best with the two handed sword, the weapon that had seen him beat John Caupance in 1501.[167] James IV as the Wild Knight won the tournament overall, as he had done in 1507, a careful articulation of the king's ability to control his nobles and country in a way which the wider chivalric community could understand.[168] Indeed, Richard Barber confirms that by the end of the fifteenth century, rulers really only used elaborate and expensive tournaments to prove themselves to be the leaders of chivalry and to impress their magnificence on their subjects and visiting foreign envoys.[169]

Thanks to the richness of the records for James IV's reign there is a clear indication that some knights were participating in tournaments regularly. During the 1490s Sir Robert Kerr of Cessford, Sir Patrick Hume of Polwarth and Sir Patrick, earl of Bothwell, Lord Hailes, all participated in tournaments. Kerr and Hume both participated in the 1496 tournament at Perkin Warbeck's marriage and all three took part in the January 1497 tourneying at Hume. These tournaments coincided with Kerr being made Master of the King's Artillery and he obviously had a strong link to the crown through his military service. The earl of Bothwell also served in military campaigns: in the wars with England in the 1480s, on the rebel side at Sauchieburn in 1488 and at the sieges of Duchal and Dumbarton in 1489. Bothwell's military career continued into the 1490s, particularly in the borders throughout 1497. In 1504 he took part in the raid of Eskdale and was at Flodden in 1513. Bothwell is not recorded as taking part in any other royal tournaments but in 1503 he observed both the joust for Princess Margaret at Greensward and the tournament at the marriage celebrations and was integral in the dubbing ceremony.[170] Whilst he clearly had a strong martial and possibly chivalric reputation, this honour at the wedding tournaments was due primarily to his assistance in the marriage negotiations. Nevertheless, links between a high military reputation and participation in tournaments clearly existed.

By the early sixteenth century James IV had created a 'royal team' of knights that regularly participated in tournaments. Its members can be identi-

---

[166] *TA*, IV, p. 63. All of these men were members of the royal household. Thomas, 'Renaissance Culture at the Court of James V', Appendix B, pp. 376–83.

[167] Pitscottie, *Historie*, I, p. 243. Both the earl of Arran, Lord Hamilton and the earl of Glencairn had participated in the tournament at James IV's wedding.

[168] Fradenburg, *City, Marriage, Tournament*, pp. 177–8.

[169] Richard Barber, *The Reign of Chivalry* (Newton Abbot & London, 1980), p. 171.

[170] Bothwell gave the new knights their spurs as the king dubbed them. Younge, 'Fyancells of Margaret', p. 298.

fied as Sir Patrick Hamilton of Kincavil; James, second Lord Hamilton; Cuthbert, third Lord Kilmaurs, earl of Glencairn; and Patrick Sinclair, squire. Irregular appearances were made by John, Lord Ross of Hawkhead, the grandson of John Ross of Hawkhead of the 1449 tournament; David Hume of Wedderburn, a cousin of Sir Patrick Hume of Polwarth; and Andrew, second Lord Gray.[171] Most of these men had served the crown on military campaigns, particularly the earl of Glencairn, Lord Gray, Lord Hamilton, Lord Ross and David Hume of Wedderburn.[172] Patrick Hamilton of Kincavil does not appear in any record as having been involved in warfare but he jousted in 1501, 1503, and 1508 and observed the other knights from this group joust at James IV's wedding. He was obviously interested in knightly pastimes, which James IV encouraged, but he does not appear to have been required to translate these skills onto the battlefield. The case of Patrick Sinclair is also interesting. He was a squire in the royal household and fought against Patrick Hamilton at the jousting at Greensward in 1503.[173] He then fought at Holyrood Palace at James IV's wedding, although Hamilton did not. He was not included amongst the men whom James IV knighted at these celebrations and, still not dubbed, Sinclair acted as a squire to the Wild Knight in the 1507 tournament of the Wild Knight and the Black Lady. Thus we find a group of men, some of very high social status, forming a team of knights who took part in jousts and tournaments. They also played prominent roles in the warfare waged by the crown, with the possible exceptions of Patrick Hamilton and Sinclair. Thus it would seem that James IV was not only reviving chivalric ideology, but also patronising a group of men skilled in the physical expression of chivalry.

The ostentatious display of James IV's tournaments sought to impress upon his magnates his martial vigour.[174] The flurry of tournaments in the 1500s was not just a reaction to the warfare and skirmishing of the late 1490s, but also a space where James's success in real warfare allowed him to pose as a martial leader in the stylised warfare of the tournament. The sole purpose of the renewal of the vitality of these tournaments was to make the king the hero and focus of the legends and romance of chivalry.[175] Throughout Europe tournaments were becoming increasingly stage-managed to ensure that the monarch was always the victor and James IV's tournaments were no exception.[176] His Shrove Tuesday tournaments and his elaborate chivalric displays were an attempt to be noticed as a leader of chivalry on a European level, and to have the crown and kingdom recognised and respected through these dis-

[171] John, Lord Ross, was sufficiently well known at court to appear named in court poetry and to have his death noted by Dunbar. See William Dunbar, 'The Dregy of Dunbar', and 'The Flyting of Dunbar and Kennedie', in Bawcutt (ed.), *William Dunbar*, pp. 110, 263.
[172] These men were all members of the royal household. Thomas, 'Renaissance Culture at the Court of James V', Appendix B, pp. 376–83.
[173] *Ibid.*, Appendix B, pp. 376–83.
[174] Macdougall, *James IV*, p. 295.
[175] Strong, *Art and Power*, p. 43.
[176] *Ibid.*, p. 50.

plays of power. To an extent, he succeeded in this wish. Sir David Lindsay of the Mount remarked that:

> [. . .] of his court, thouch Europe sprang the fame
> Off lustie Lordis and lufesaum Ladyis ying,
> Tryumphand tornayis, iustyng, & knychtly game,
> With all pastyme according for one kyng.
> He wes the glore of princelie gouernyng.[177]

Lindsay's work stressed the colourful chivalric spectacle associated with James IV's enthusiastic devotion to the cult of chivalry.[178] James IV's tournaments seem to have combined so many different elements of display, social interaction and chivalric literary references that they probably served a number of functions, many of which seem to have been unconsciously rather than overtly pursued.

James IV's legacy: James V's tourneys, 1513–1542

Although only an infant when James IV died, James V appears to have been heavily influenced by his father's delight in chivalric spectacle and he too used the events to his own gain. His reputation for prowess in jousting at an early age was brought to the attention of Henry VIII: envoys reported to the English king that the thirteen-year-old James relished his martial training and desired a full-sized adult sword to replace his child-sized version.[179] The young king clearly had an interest in knightly and chivalric activities and as early as 1527 he was evidently staging tournaments. At Holyrood in April 1527 lists were built, and in August 1529 similar structures were built at Stirling.[180] A further tournament was held at Holyrood in May 1530 and in January 1531 another tournament was held at Stirling, possibly to celebrate New Year.[181] Further preparations for jousting were made in early 1532 and by September of that year serious preparations that were underway for a tournament included the purchase of blue and black materials to line and trim the saddles of six of the king's horses, new orange velvet shoes for the king, and the repair and purchase of pavilions of red and yellow buckram.[182] Other small indications from the treasurer's accounts suggest that there was jousting of some sorts in December 1533, in Stirling in August 1534 and at Christmas in

---

[177] 'The Testament of Papyngo', in Hamer (ed.), *The Works of Sir David Lindsay of the Mount*, I, p. 71, lines 500–4.
[178] Edington, *Court and Culture*, pp. 15–16.
[179] *Ibid.*, p. 103; Thomas, 'Renaissance Culture at the Court of James V', p. 267.
[180] *TA*, V, pp. 326, 381.
[181] Paton (ed.), *Accounts of the Masters of Works*, p. 36; *TA*, V, pp. 411, 412; Thomas, 'Renaissance Culture at the Court of James V', p. 268.
[182] *TA*, VI, pp. 25, 73.

1535.[183] The early 1530s were clearly a period in which James V was engaging in the pageantry and ceremonials of a 'Renaissance' court and he gradually began to emulate the most fashionable aspects of the events staged at the French, Burgundian and English courts, as well as drawing on the tastes of his forefathers.[184]

Indeed, James's first exposure to French ceremonial display had a profound influence on the Scottish manifestations later in the 1530s. Andrea Thomas has successfully recovered the details of the major tournaments and public celebrations in which James V was involved, most notably the tournaments held to celebrate his marriage to Madeleine of France on 1 January 1537 in Paris; she records in detail the various ceremonies associated with the Paris marriage, including James V's extravagant royal entry into the city.[185] After the wedding, two weeks of jousting took place, in which James distinguished himself. The tournaments were held in specially built and decorated lists in the courtyard of the Louvre and at Tournelles and appear to have been in keeping with the grand reputation of the French court.[186] There were jousts, both on horse and on foot, artillery salutes, feasts, triumphs and plays involving elaborate special effects such as fire-breathing dragons and mock naval battles in the especially flooded streets.[187] In his 'Deploration', Sir David Lindsay of the Mount commented on the splendour of the Paris tournaments:

> I neuer did se one day more glorious,
> So mony in so riche abilyementis
> Of Silk and gold, with stonis precious,
> Sic Banketting, sic sound of Instrumentis,
> With sang, and dance, & Martiall tornamentis.[188]

A number of Scottish earls, lords and barons attended the wedding in Paris and Pitscottie suggested that the celebrations were so splendid as to recall the golden age of Charlemagne. James V spent a considerable sum on himself and his party for the celebrations and bought a red taffeta, silk and velvet sword belt. He paid for huge amounts of jousting spears and also more frivolous items such as 181 crowns for Oliver Sinclair, at that time a very close familiar

---

[183] *Ibid.*, VI, pp. 214, 225, 261.
[184] Thomas, 'Renaissance Culture at the Court of James V', p. 289.
[185] *Ibid.*, pp. 250–3.
[186] Pitscottie, *Croniclis*, I, p. 366; Thomas, 'Renaissance Culture at the Court of James V', pp. 252, 268; Alexandre Teulet, *Relations Politiques de la France et de l'Espagne avec L'Écosse au XVIe siècle: papiers d'état, pieces et documents inedits ou peu connus tires der bibliotheque et des archives de France* (Paris, 1862), I, pp. 107–8; Dana Bentley-Cranch and Rosalind K. Marshall, 'Iconography and Literature in the Service of Diplomacy: The Franco-Scottish Alliance, James V and Scotland's Two French Queens, Madeleine of France and Mary of Guise', in Janet Hadley Williams (ed.), *Stewart Style 1513–1542: Essays on the Court of James V* (East Linton, 1996), pp. 279–80.
[187] Pitscottie, *Croniclis*, I, pp. 365–6; Thomas, 'Renaissance Culture at the Court of James V', p. 252.
[188] 'The Deploration of the Deith of Quene Magdalene', in Hamer (ed.), *Works of Sir David Lindsay of the Mount*, I, p. 108, lines 85–89.

of the king, to spend on feathers to decorate the caps and caparisons of the king and his knights for the entry and tournaments. James also covered the cost of the repair of one hundred and ten iron spears that were broken during the jousting, indicating that this was indeed an elaborate celebration.[189] James had clearly enjoyed preparing for the tournament and it was remarked that the Scottish king had gone through the marriage ceremony with bruises on his face due to injuries he had sustained during one of the jousts.[190]

Sir David Lindsay also suggested in his 'Deploration' that James might have been inspired by the level of pageantry of the Paris tournaments and planned similarly extravagant celebrations for Princess Madeleine's entry into Scotland. However, these plans were never realised, as she was too unwell (probably with consumption) and died shortly afterwards.[191] James did not spend too long seeking a new bride and the following year he married Mary of Guise. A number of entries were arranged for her throughout the country, but her first entry, into St Andrews on 16 June 1538, was accompanied by forty days of festivities, including tournaments.[192] Considerable expense was provided for the jousting including, amongst other things, erection of lists and counter-lists; the importation of five hundred spears from France; the importation of horses from Denmark; and three new sets of velvet harnesses and jousting outfits for the king.[193] Much as the 1502 duel of Christopher Taylor may have inspired Dunbar's 'Fasternis Evin in Hell', Sir David Lindsay of the Mount may also have been encouraged by the celebrations for Mary of Guise's arrival in St Andrews to pen 'The Iusting betuix Iames Watsoun and Ihone Barbour'. The comical joust described by Lindsay was supposed to have taken place at St Andrews on Whit Monday and, as Mary arrived on Whit Sunday, it is not unfeasible that Lindsay was placing his fictitious joust at the heart of a real tournament. However, Carol Edington has pointed out that James V's court was habitually in St Andrews at this time of year and jousting was not uncommon and thus it cannot be assumed that the royal entry sparked the poem's creation. It could have been written at any time between 1538 and 1540 and, given Lindsay's heavy involvement in the preparations for the reception of Mary of Guise, Edington believes that a later composition date seems more

---

[189] *TA*, VII, pp. 8, 10, 11, 16, 17; Thomas, 'Renaissance Culture at the Court of James V', p. 268.
[190] Thomas, 'Renaissance Culture at the Court of James V', p. 250; Caroline Bingham, *James V King of Scots 1512–1542* (London, 1971), p. 125.
[191] 'The Deploration of Quene Magdalene', in Hamer (ed.), *Works of Sir David Lindsay*, I, p. 111, lines 169–70; *TA*, VI, pp. 303, 313; Thomas, 'Renaissance Culture at the Court of James V', pp. 253–5.
[192] *Ibid.*, p. 257; Cameron, *James V*, p. 263; Pitscottie, *Croniclis*, I, pp. 378–81. James cannot have been present for a full forty days after the entry: he arrived in St Andrews on 1 June and was in Edinburgh by 15 July. *RMS*, III, 1793, 1801.
[193] Paton (ed.), *Accounts of the Masters of Works*, pp. 221–2; *TA*, VI, pp. 387, 402, 412–13, VII, p. 48; Hay (ed.), *Letters of James V*, p. 345; Thomas, 'Renaissance Culture at the Court of James V', p. 269.

likely.[194] As was the case with Dunbar's poetry, the fact that Lindsay chose to entertain and make social commentary through the use of knightly (and non-knightly) characters shows just how central chivalry was to courtly culture.

Festivities for Mary's coronation in February 1540 were similarly extravagant. Mary had not been allowed to be crowned until she had proven she could bear children. The coronation was not planned until she was two months pregnant and she was six months pregnant when the ceremony took place.[195] No narratives of the event have survived but the preparations recorded in the treasurer's accounts indicate that it was a magnificent occasion.[196] The whole event took a total of five weeks to prepare and dismantle. More horses were sought from abroad, lists were erected, and James V had a further three jousting outfits made.[197]

Although James V saw the benefit of extravagant and costly celebrations to demonstrate his royal authority at times such as his marriages, this did not extend to lavish expenditure for the sake of it. The other jousts and tournaments that he held were much less extravagant and are barely evident in the records. James held a small tournament around May Day at Falkland in 1539, and incidental references suggest he also held jousts in July 1539, August 1541 and July 1542.[198] Whilst James V was keen on the practice and physical expression of chivalry, he did not use it in the same way as his father had done – James V's love of jousting appears to have been the motivation for many smaller jousts, rather than a desire to promote himself as a chivalric king or to bring his nobles under royal control. This is a departure from the trends evident in the fifteenth century, where the Stewart kings (particularly James II and James IV) used the tournament as a political tool and a public declaration of their patronage of chivalry.

---

[194] Edington, *Court and Culture*, p. 36; Cameron, *James V*, pp. 263–4.
[195] *TA*, VII, p. 254; Thomas, 'Renaissance Culture at the Court of James V', p. 261.
[196] *Ibid.*, p. 264.
[197] Paton (ed.), *Accounts of the Masters of Works*, pp. 288–9; *TA*, VII, 278, 287, 292–3, 295, 317; Hay (ed.), *Letters of James V*, p. 388; Thomas, 'Renaissance Culture at the Court of James V', p. 269.
[198] *TA*, VII, pp. 155, 165, 168, 176, 184, 469, VIII, p. 92; Thomas, 'Renaissance Culture at the Court of James V', p. 268, n. 102.

CHAPTER FIVE

Scottish Knights and the Display of Piety

The demonstration of commitment to Christianity and the defence of the Christian faith were integral parts of the chivalric ideal. Although the Church's role in the ceremonies and institution of knighthood had declined by the fifteenth century, religion was still an important component of chivalric values. Knightly piety was apparent in Scottish chivalric society and the *Buke of the Ordre of Knychthede*'s statement in the mid fifteenth century that 'the principale caus of the ordre is to the manetenaunce of the cristyn faith' was not an empty pronouncement.[1] Other fifteenth-century commentators also noted the bonds between knighthood and the Christian faith: for example, Walter Bower, abbot of Inchcolm, remarked in the 1440s that the sword was given to a knight 'when he was invested for the defence of the Church and its members'.[2] The demonstration of knightly piety could be carried out in a number of ways, but these were dependent upon the resources available to the knight. Other contributing factors included commitments such as service to the crown, which, for example, might have interfered with a pilgrimage trip. There was a tendency for more socially and financially established knights to patronise parish kirks or found collegiate churches, whereas the younger sons of lesser nobles might pursue a career as a 'crusader knight' or enter into a military order.[3]

Crusading

The most obvious and extreme way for a knight to act as a 'soldier of Christ' was to be involved in crusading. Crusades were akin to an armed pilgrimage and were a voluntary, rather than obligatory, element of Christian life. Both crusading and pilgrimage offered spiritual benefits and were undertaken to aid the soul as well as to prove Christian and chivalric worth.[4] Alan Macquarrie's study on the topic regards the fifteenth century as a period of

---

[1] Glenn (ed.), *Buke of the Ordre of Knychthede*, p. 17.
[2] *Chron. Bower*, book XVI, 13.
[3] The latter was more commonly seen prior to the fifteenth century when crusading was still a popular option.
[4] David Ditchburn, *Scotland and Europe: The Medieval Kingdom and its Contacts with Christendom, c.1215–1545* (East Linton, 2000), p. 65.

declining interest in crusading as a form of knightly activity and there is undoubtedly some force in this argument.[5] This decline, however, was a Europe-wide trend and even while the opportunity to take up arms against the Infidel had decreased, the crusading spirit still remained.

Crusading was a traditional activity to which a large number of fifteenth-century knights had personal and familial ties. Many, for example, had predecessors who had participated during David II's active promotion of crusading in the mid fourteenth century. David wanted to 'set out for the Holy Land to tame the ferocity of the pagans with all his might' and 'had shown favour and affection to a great and exaggerated extent to his knights and men-at-arms (who were very numerous at this time), who had been assigned and enlisted for undertakings of this kind'.[6] David II's enthusiasm for crusading saw him rush from Norfolk to London in 1363, when he discovered that Peter I of Cyprus was recruiting for a crusade to recover Alexandria.[7] It would seem that at this meeting the Scottish king pledged to dispatch some of his key knights to join Peter I in the Holy Land. However, no preparations were made for their departure until 1365, by which time it was too late to join this crusade. Nevertheless, the Scottish party still departed and included Sir Archibald Douglas; Sir Alexander Lindsay; David of Mar, the treasurer of Moray and the Scottish Knights Hospitaller; Walter Wardlaw; Sir William Keith, the Marischal; Richard Comyn; Lawrence Gilliebrand; Nicholas Erskine, Sir Alexander Recklington, keeper of Dunbar castle; and various clerics. Sir Norman Leslie, Sir Walter Leslie, and Sir Thomas Bisset, lord of Fife, were already in Prussia by 1365, leaving shortly after the meeting in London.[8] Some remarkable knights were enlisted for David II's promotion of crusading in the fourteenth century. For example, Robert Erskine, David's closest counsellor, had taken a vow before 1359 to bear arms against the Saracens in the Holy Land and visit St Catherine's at Mount Sinai.[9] Erskine served variously as chamberlain, ambassador to England and France, sheriff and castle keeper of Stirling and Dumbarton and precentor of the lands of the Scottish Knights Hospitaller. He had a great deal of power and favour in the royal court and it is clear that crusading was still seen as a viable option for knights of all ranks. Erskine, however, later claimed that he was unable to fulfil his vow, due to the demands of the king's service and 'the wars everywhere going on'. In addition to this, he protested that the Scottish king had refused to grant him leave and he thus sought papal release from the obligation. The serious nature of these

---

[5] Macquarrie, *Scotland and the Crusades*, esp. pp. 92–116.

[6] *Chron. Bower*, book XIV, 34; Michael A. Penman, 'Christian Days and Knights: The religious devotions and court of David II of Scotland', *Historical Research* 75, 189 (2002), pp. 250–1.

[7] *Rot. Scot.*, I, pp. 876–7; *CDS*, IV, 93; Penman, *David II*, pp. 302–3. Present with David II in London were, amongst others, the earl of Douglas and Sir Robert Erskine.

[8] *Rot. Scot.*, I, pp. 875, 897; Penman, *David II*, p. 303.

[9] Penman 'Christian Days' pp. 262, 267.

pledges was demonstrated in the pope's rejection of his petition and Erskine was instead permitted to postpone his undertaking for one year.[10] Vows do not appear to have been made lightly and it was only in the most exceptional of circumstances that a knight sought to change the terms of his pledge. For example, in 1418 Sir Robert Keith, Marischal of Scotland, applied to the pope to commute his vow into 'another work of charity' and absolve him from his commitment:

> in the days of his youth [he] had vowed to visit the Holy Sepulchre, and planned many times to go, but because of his office and for other reasons he could never obtain licence of his superiors, and now, stricken in age, a septuagenarian, he is not able to go.

The papal response was to absolve him of his commitment, on the condition that he made a financial compensation to his preferred churches, to the value of what would have been spent in going to the Holy Sepulchre.[11] The Keith family appear frequently to have made crusading promises and in 1437 Sir William Keith, Robert's son, was granted papal permission to commute a pilgrimage to other pious acts on the grounds of his 'great infirmities and feebleness of his body'.[12]

By the late fourteenth century a number of Scottish knights were actively crusading. Sir Simon Preston of Craigmillar, Sir John Abernethy, Sir John Edmonstone of that Ilk, Sir John Towers of Dalry and Sir John of Monymusk were all known Prussian crusaders at this time and in 1389 the 'brave knight' Sir William Douglas of Nithsdale led a contingent of Scots to crusade in Prussia, including Sir James and Sir William Douglas of Strathbrock and Sir Robert Stewart of Durisdeer.[13] The force of the Teutonic Knights' cause was obviously strong, and the Order continued to encourage Scottish recruitment from their bases in Edinburgh and Linlithgow in the early fifteenth century.[14] Other participants in the 1389 crusade might perhaps be identified from the *Armorial de Gelre* and include Sir Walter Leslie; Sir Robert Erskine; his son, Sir Thomas Erskine; Sir David Lindsay; Sir Alexander Stewart of Darnley; Sir Patrick Hepburn; Sir James Lindsay; Sir Henry Preston of Craigmillar; Sir Alexander Ramsay of Dalhousie; and Sir John Stewart.[15] Sir Alexander Stewart also joined the Barbary crusade in 1390, whilst around 1395 Alexan-

---

[10] *CPP*, I, p. 326; Ditchburn, *Scotland and Europe*, p. 69; McRoberts, 'Scottish Pilgrims to the Holy Land', p. 89
[11] *Cal. Scot. Supp.*, I, p. 2.
[12] Ditchburn, *Scotland and Europe*, p. 59.
[13] *CDS*, IV, 593; Ditchburn, *Scotland and Europe*, pp. 69–70; Norman Housley (ed.), *Documents on the Later Crusades, 1274–1580* (Basingstoke & London, 1996), pp. 56, 103–4; *Chron. Bower*, book XIV, 54; Macquarrie, *Scotland and the Crusades*, pp. 85–7.
[14] Nicholson, *Scotland*, p. 266.
[15] Archibald Hamilton Dunbar 'Facsimiles of the Scottish Coats of Arms Emblazoned in the "Armorial de Gelre", with notes', *PSAS* 25 (1890–91), pp. 9–19; Ditchburn, *Scotland and Europe*, pp. 70–1. A number of these knights had been involved in a pilgrimage in 1382 to the Holy Land along with Alexander Lindsay and John Towers. McRoberts, 'Scottish Pilgrims to

der Lindsay and David Lindsay enrolled in Philip de Meziere's new chivalric order of the Knighthood of the Passion of Jesus Christ, which aimed to reconquer and garrison the Holy Land.[16]

A family heritage was often a key factor in the desire to go on crusade. Following in the footsteps of Sir Simon and Sir Henry Preston of Craigmillar, the family continued the tradition of defending the Christian faith.[17] Around 1455, Alexander Preston, canon of Glasgow, 'went lately with a notable company to the Holy Land to fight against the infidels, and whose father and many others of his kinsmen have fought against the infidels in the lands of the infidels and been made knights.'[18] Quite clearly the Preston family saw value in asserting that their kin had been made knights in the Holy Land. This was a long-standing tradition that took place in the Holy Sepulchre, although no records indicate that any Preston was actually knighted here. Knighting at the Holy Sepulchre represented perhaps the most powerful fusion of the chivalric and Christian ideals. Initially the practice was linked with the Knights of St John (Hospitallers), and later on men would regularly stop in Rhodes to request that a Hospitaller accompany him to Jerusalem, in order to carry out the dubbing. For example, Nompar de Caumont called at Rhodes on his way to the Holy Land and persuaded a Navarrese knight of the Order to join him on his visit to the Holy Sepulchre and dub him there as a Knight of St John. By 1480, newly dubbed knights were found stopping off at Rhodes on their return journeys and enrolling their names in a book kept by the king of Cyprus, for which they received a certificate in return. Gradually, knights who did not belong to the Order of the Hospital of St John, began to perform dubbings in the church, and by the fifteenth century it was an accepted practice over which the Hospitallers held no monopoly.[19] Although no record exists of Scots being knighted in Jerusalem, they were more than aware of the tradition, and Walter Bower, abbot of Inchcolm, related a story that Charles, the son of St Bridget of Sweden, was knighted at the Holy Sepulchre by Sir William Lindsay of the Byres.[20]

The enthusiasm and dedication to crusading appears to have waned during James I's absence from the throne (1406–24), and in the early fifteenth century there is a marked decline in Scottish knights taking up arms in defence of the Holy Land. The defeat of the Teutonic Knights at Tannenberg in 1410 must have contributed, but David Ditchburn has reasoned that the

---

the Holy Land', p. 90. Sir Alexander Lindsay died at Candia on Crete while on his pilgrimage to Jerusalem. *Chron. Bower*, book XIV, 42.
[16] Ditchburn, *Scotland and Europe*, p. 69.
[17] *CPL*, XI, pp. 158–9; Ditchburn, *Scotland and Europe*, p. 71.
[18] *CPL*, XI, pp. 158–9. Later in December 1458 it was said that Alexander Preston had been fighting for a year with twelve archers and more fighting men against the Infidel. *CPL*, XI, p. 519; Macquarrie, *Scotland and the Crusades*, p. 95.
[19] Jonathan Sumption, *Pilgrimage: An Image of Mediaeval Religion* (London, 1975), p. 266.
[20] *Chron. Bower*, book XIV, 39; McRoberts, 'Scottish Pilgrims to the Holy Land', p. 89; Boardman, *Early Stewart Kings*, p. 77.

decline in active crusading across the fourteenth and fifteenth centuries might be largely to do with Anglo-Scottish warfare. For lengthy periods Scottish knights were preoccupied with these wars and it was precisely those men who displayed crusading enthusiasm who became embroiled in the defence of the kingdom.[21] Of course, it was also part of a wider trend of decline across Europe. Only a small number of Scottish knights responded to the perpetual call to crusade and, even then, their efforts were largely focused on the Mediterranean areas where the links between the headquarters of the Knights of St John and the Scottish preceptory at Torphichen, West Lothian, may have been of significant assistance.

Both the military orders of the Knights of the Temple (Templars) and the Hospitallers had bases and property in Scotland during the late Middle Ages.[22] After the fall of the Templars in the early fourteenth century, the Hospitallers grew in strength and importance in Scotland, acquiring most of the lands previously held by the dissolved order.[23] The Hospitallers were an order dedicated to the treatment of the sick and the support of poor pilgrims, and by the early thirteenth century they had developed into a military order closely linked with the crusading movement.[24] P.H.R. Mackay and Jonathan Riley-Smith best explain how the military order could rationalise its dual function:

> For if the Hospitallers' service to the sick poor was an original expression of the concern for the *vita apostolica*, their military activities, like the crusades themselves, reflected another aspect of the same ideal [. . .] The best demonstration of love for one's neighbour is to die for him, and fighting on behalf of Christendom, in defence of Christians and the Church, was regarded as an expression of love and therefore as an act of charity and means of grace.[25]

The Hospitallers were a cosmopolitan and international group with preceptories and lands throughout Christendom. The Scottish preceptory at Torphichen was not part of a separate Scottish priory, but was in fact under English authority. Although there was regular contact between Torphichen and Rhodes during the fifteenth century, tensions were evident, and as late as 1513 James IV complained to the Master of Rhodes that appointments to Scottish preceptories were made by the English turcopolier and that Scottish

---

[21] Ditchburn, *Scotland and Europe*, p. 72.
[22] *Ibid.*, p. 44.
[23] John Edwards, 'The Templars in Scotland in the Thirteenth Century', *SHR* 5 (1908), pp. 13–25; Alfred Coutts, 'The Knights Templars in Scotland', *Records of the Scottish Church History Society* 7 (1938), pp. 126–40; John Edwards, 'The Hospitallers in Scotland in the Fifteenth Century', *SHR* 9 (1912), pp. 52–68; P.H.R. Mackay and Jonathan Riley-Smith, *The Knights of St John: The Story of the Order of St John of Jerusalem in Scotland* (Edinburgh, 1976), pp. 22–3.
[24] *Ibid.*, pp. 6–7.
[25] *Ibid.*, pp. 7–8.

brothers of the order must look to the prior of England as lord and protector. James was adamant that he would 'not allow either the English to establish their superiority over him and his kingdom, or Scotsmen elected by English votes to pry into his secrets and occupy positions of such great authority'.[26] James IV's concerns point to the close relationship between the Scottish crown and the knights at Torphichen: indeed, in December 1530 the Grand Master sent an official note to James V as 'a patron and protector' of the Order to indicate that the knights had moved their headquarters to Malta.[27]

Throughout the Order of the Hospitallers, brothers shared the same privileges, the same lifestyle and the same obedience to a common authority. They could be transferred between posts and places and lived the same life in each new home.[28] A preceptory was created as soon as it could perform a useful function and as soon as it had enough local property to justify its existence. The Hospitallers' principal purpose in placing a house in Scotland was for recruitment.[29] Entering an order was an attractive option for many, particularly younger sons of lesser nobles who sought the stability and experience that life in the order might bring. Indeed, the Hospitallers' popularity in Scotland caused Sir John Lauder to include in his sixteenth-century *Formulare* a specimen dispensation for a man who had imprudently vowed to go to the East and fight in the ranks of the Knights of St John.[30] The links with the Mediterranean that the Hospitallers facilitated no doubt assisted a number of Scottish knights to fulfil their crusading vows. Colin Campbell of Glenorchy, for example, was reported to have served with the Hospitallers in Rhodes, although he was never a member of the Order, and a number of other Scots are known to have taken up arms against Islam in the Mediterranean.[31] In some cases, financial contributions were made in place of actual physical service: Robert Arbuthnott of that Ilk and his wife, Mariota Scrymgeour, contributed financially to the war against the Turks. Robert and Mariota were also received into the privileges of the Observant Franciscans, as lay associates, and clearly saw patronage of religious orders as a serious expression of piety.[32]

In the late fifteenth century, James IV renewed the call to crusade with his characteristic zeal and vigour. Earlier attempts by Pope Sixtus IV in the 1470s

---

[26] *James IV Letters*, no. 535, pp. 296–7; Mackey and Riley-Smith, *The Knights of St John*, p. 18; Ian B. Cowan, P.H.R. Mackay and Alan Macquarrie (eds), *The Knights of St John of Jerusalem in Scotland*, SHS (Edinburgh, 1983), p. xvii.
[27] McRoberts, 'Scottish Pilgrims', p. 91.
[28] Mackay and Riley-Smith, *The Knights of St John*, p. 12.
[29] Cowan, Mackay and Macquarrie (eds), *The Knights of St John of Jerusalem*, pp. xxvii–xxviii.
[30] Gordon Donaldson and C. Macrae (eds), *St Andrews Formulare, 1514–1546* (Edinburgh, 1942), I, no. 234; McRoberts, 'Scottish Pilgrims to the Holy Land', p. 91.
[31] Ditchburn, *Scotland and Europe*, p. 69; Macquarrie, *Scotland and the Crusades*, pp. 93–5; Alan Macquarrie, 'Sir Colin Campbell of Glenorchy (1400–1480) and the Knights Hospitaller', *Notes and Queries of the Society of West Highland and Island Historical Research* 15 (1981), pp. 8–12; Alan Macquarrie, 'The Crusades and the Scottish *Gaidhealtachd* in Fact and Legend', in Loraine Maclean (ed.), *The Middle Ages in the Highlands* (Inverness, 1981), p.140.
[32] Ditchburn, *Scotland and Europe*, pp. 49, 69.

to preach the crusade in Scotland appear to have had little impact, but James's enthusiasm brought the crusading ideal to prominence.[33] James's interest in the crusade was, in part, to draw attention to Scotland and promote himself in Europe, but it also stemmed from his genuine desire to resuscitate the chivalric ideal and place it firmly at the forefront of Scottish knights' thoughts. Whilst countries lying on the peripheries of Europe have commonly been considered as showing only aspirational and cultural interest in the crusades in the latter part of the fifteenth century, scholars have viewed James IV's desire for crusade as 'sincere, though fanciful'.[34] Certainly, the crusading ideal had attracted James for a long time. As early as 1490, a Scottish contingent was pledged to join an army made up of men from France, Spain, Portugal, Navarre and England, to assist in Pope Innocent VIII's call to crusade against Bayezid II.[35] In December 1506 James made his desires apparent and a Scottish ambassador was received by the College of the Venetian Republic, announcing James's intentions of going to Jerusalem and requesting that the Signory provide him with galleys or with the artificers to build them.[36] At Easter 1507 James received as a gift from the pope a consecrated hat and sword along with the title of 'Protector of the Christian Faith'; after this experience his focus on crusade became even sharper.[37] In early 1508 Sir Bernard Stewart was invited back to Scotland to preside over the tournament of the Wild Knight and the Black Lady, a canny move given that Stewart was not only esteemed as a flower of chivalry throughout Europe, but also because he had been an active crusader who had been present at the final collapse of the Moorish kingdom of Granada in 1492.[38] By November 1508 the king had received papal permission to visit the Holy Land in person, with the additional stipulation that he was to pass via the papal court in Rome.[39] The journey was not to be funded solely out of the royal purse: the Bishopric of Dunkeld, presumably like many others, made payments in 1508, 1509 and 1510 to finance James 'to go on pilgrimage to Jerusalem and the sepulchre of Our Lord'.[40] Although James never made this trip, his enthusiasm for crusading remained. In response to a report from the king of France, that Pope Julius II intended to lead the expedition

---

[33] Norman Housley, *The Later Crusades, 1274–1580: From Lyons to Alcazar* (Oxford, 1992), pp. 405–6.
[34] *Ibid.*, pp. 124–5, 420.
[35] Housley (ed.), *Documents on the Later Crusades*, p. 165.
[36] *James IV Letters*, no. 65, pp. 45–6, no. 89, pp. 63–4, no. 103, pp. 69–70, no. 104, pp. 70–1, no. 122, pp. 79–80; McRoberts, 'Scottish Pilgrims to the Holy Land', p. 95; Macdougall, *James IV*, p. 199.
[37] McRoberts, 'Scottish Pilgrims to the Holy Land', p. 95; Peter Yeoman, *Pilgrimage in Medieval Scotland* (London, 1999), p. 105; Macdougall, *James IV*, p. 196.
[38] Ditchburn, *Scotland and Europe*, p. 68. For another Scot at the fall of Granada see Macquarrie, *Scotland and the Crusades*, p. 106.
[39] *James IV Letters*, no. 200, pp. 125–6; McRoberts, 'Scottish Pilgrims to the Holy Land', p. 95.
[40] Robert Kerr Hannay (ed.), *Rentale Dunkeldense: Being the Accounts of the Bishopric (A.D. 1505–1517) with Myln's 'Lives of the Bishops' (A.D. 1483–1517)*, SHS (Edinburgh, 1915), pp. 247, 250, 253; McRoberts, 'Scottish Pilgrims to the Holy Land', p. 95; Macdougall, *James IV*, p. 201.

against the Infidel in person, James urgently requested a timetable so that he might ready his fleet because he would 'gladly shed his last drop of blood in the cause of Christendom'.[41] Again, this never came to fruition. If James had survived Flodden, of course, the crusade planned on the accession of Pope Leo X in 1513 may perhaps have seen a contribution from Scotland.

Pilgrimage

With the decline of crusading, the most popular way of demonstrating Christian piety in the fifteenth century was through unarmed pilgrimage. Contact with the holy places associated with a saint and a saint's relics was an attractive offer for the devout and placed them in closer communion with the blessed.[42] Pilgrimage also afforded the penitent traveller with benefits in the afterlife. By far, the most visited pilgrimage sites in late medieval Christendom were Jerusalem, Rome and Santiago de Compostela, in Spain, but Scottish pilgrims also frequented Amiens in France and Canterbury in England.[43] The vast majority of pilgrims were from lower social backgrounds and due to the type of surviving sources, there is little indication of the number of Scottish pilgrims who ventured to England or the Continent. Of the knights who undertook pilgrimages only a small group are identifiable, but it is still clear that pilgrimage was an important activity for knights. Perhaps, for them, the desire to go on pilgrimage was undertaken in lieu of crusading and might have been motivated by genuine piety. Of course, very few knights engaged in pilgrimage in the true sense, by donning pilgrims outfits and travelling in a humble way; large companies, horses, servants and other costs ensured that the knight's pilgrimage was markedly different from the poor pilgrim's journey.[44]

Many knightly pilgrimages originated in a vow, such as in 1529 when George Preston of that Ilk vowed to Sir Simon Preston of that Ilk that he would visit the shrines of St Thomas of Canterbury and St John in Amiens.[45] Considerable arrangements were required prior to departure and pilgrims sought royal protection for their property and family until their safe return and made other provisions in the event of their death. A letter of licence from the crown was necessary before leave was granted, although it would seem unlikely that

---

[41] *James IV Papers*, no. 294, p. 166; Marguerite Wood (ed.), *Flodden Papers: Diplomatic Correspondence Between the Courts of France and Scotland, 1507–1517*, SHS (Edinburgh, 1933), pp. 6–10; McRoberts, 'Scottish Pilgrims to the Holy Land', p. 95; Macdougall, *James IV*, p. 203.
[42] Ditchburn, *Scotland and Europe*, p. 58.
[43] McRoberts, 'Scottish Pilgrims to the Holy Land', pp. 80–1, 84; Ian B. Cowan, 'Church and Society' in Jennifer M. Brown (ed.), *Scottish Society in the Fifteenth Century* (London, 1977), p. 113; a version of this essay appears in Ian B. Cowan, *The Medieval Church in Scotland*, James Kirk (ed.) (Edinburgh, 1995).
[44] Sumption, *Pilgrimage*, p. 264.
[45] *RSS*, I, 4064; Ditchburn, *Scotland and Europe*, pp. 58–9.

non-noble pilgrims went through the formality of obtaining these documents. Both clerics and laymen might obtain letters of recommendation to introduce themselves *en route* and safe-conducts through England were organised where required.[46] Immediately prior to their departure pilgrims were blessed in their church and received their pilgrim's staff and scrip from the altar. More wealthy pilgrims took the opportunity to simultaneously gift income or land to their church.[47] The level of preparation expended for these journeys clearly emphasised the piety of the undertaking and David McRoberts has argued that Chaucer's tales, which suggest that tourism and light-hearted companionship were elements of the pilgrimage, did not correspond to the reality of a normal pilgrimage. Whilst McRoberts concedes that individual motives varied,

> overseas pilgrimages were essentially a serious religious exercise from which the pilgrim could never be quite certain that he would return alive. For most pilgrims it was a dangerous expedition, undertaken with reluctance in a spirit of devotion and penitence to expiate some crime, to seek some indulgence, or, frequently, in fulfilment of a vow made in some emergency.[48]

In his *Scotichronicon* Walter Bower supported the idea that individual motivations did indeed inspire pilgrimages. For example, he reported that Alan Wyntoun, a man-at-arms, set out for the Holy Land 'because of the intrigues of the friends of his wife' following his contentious marriage to her around 1344.[49] Others, such as Thomas Clerk, left explicit statements of their motives for pilgrimage. In 1458 Clerk, in self-defence, had caused the death of his brother-in-law, William Strigale. He declared that he would make reparation to the kinsmen and friends of Striagle and that he would undertake a pilgrimage to Rome for his soul and do other works of charity.[50]

For many, however, there does seem to have been an element of 'tourism' involved in the pilgrimage. This was particularly the case for those of more wealthy backgrounds, who combined diplomatic, business and pleasure pursuits under the umbrella of pilgrimage. Pilgrims from all social backgrounds returned home with souvenir trinkets and badges, which were commonly sold at pilgrim centres. Pilgrims' badges have certainly been found throughout Scotland; for example, a fifteenth-century badge of jet in the form of a scallop shell shows that Scottish pilgrims did purchase these tokens of their travels.[51] A recent excavation of a skeleton on the Isle of May revealed it to

---

[46] Dunlop, *James Kennedy*, p. 411, n. 1; Yeoman, *Pilgrimage in Medieval Scotland*, pp. 110–12. See also copies of letters of recommendation printed in *St A Cop.*, pp. 30–2, 84–5.
[47] Yeoman, *Pilgrimage in Medieval Scotland*, pp. 110–12.
[48] McRoberts, 'Scottish Pilgrims to the Holy Land', p. 81.
[49] *Chron. Bower*, book XIII, 50; Ditchburn, *Scotland and Europe*, p. 58.
[50] Dunlop, *James Kennedy*, p. 411.
[51] National Museum of Antiquities of Scotland, *Angels, Nobles and Unicorns: Art and Patronage in Scotland, A Handbook Published in Conjunction with an Exhibition Held at the*

have a conch placed in its mouth – a clear indication that the person had undertaken a pilgrimage to St James's shrine at Compostela.[52] A wealthier pilgrim might secure a rare relic and donate it to their local church on their return, as William Preston did with the arm-bone of St Giles in 1455.[53] Jonathan Sumption has suggested that by the later Middle Ages, pilgrimage really combined spiritual motivations with a desire to travel. He warns, that 'it would be a gross exaggeration to suggest that simple curiosity had displaced the intensely spiritual feelings of an earlier age, but in the fifteenth century it was certainly the predominant motive of many pilgrims'.[54]

The most impressive and desirable achievement for a pilgrim was to reach the Holy Land, to be in Jerusalem and pray in the Holy Sepulchre. As David McRoberts remarked, 'no matter how the fashion in popular devotion might change, the perennial attraction of Christ's native country seems to have kept a constant stream of Scots pilgrims journeying to the Holy Land all through the medieval period.'[55] In the mid fourteenth century, Norman Leslie, esquire, who was the Scottish king's ambassador at Avignon, obtained permission for Sir Thomas Bissett, lord of Upsettlington, Sir Walter Leslie, and Simon de Balmelkine, esquire, along with another six esquires, 'to visit the Holy Sepulchre and other sacred places across the sea'.[56] The Leslies were also heavily involved in crusading at this time. Contingents of Scottish knights regularly visited the Holy Land and large entourages also went in 1366–67 and 1382.[57] During the fifteenth century, pilgrimages to the Holy Land continued, although they were in much smaller groups than travelled in the previous century. Often it was just an individual knight and his servants who travelled together. In the late 1420s, Sir John Stewart of Darnley, a Scottish knight in the service of the French king, journeyed to Jerusalem and prayed at the Holy Sepulchre; he returned to France where he was in the French king's service and died at the battle of Herrings in Orléans in 1429.[58] In March 1428 arrangements were made for John Liddale and two servants to go to Jerusalem and in

---

National Museum of Scotland August 12 – September 26, 1982 (Edinburgh, 1982), p. 92, E77 Badge of jet; 'Donations to the Museum and Library', *PSAS* 24 (1889–90), p. 411; Joseph Anderson, 'Notice of a Small Figure in Jet of St James the Greater, Recently Presented to the Museum by James Gibson Craig, Esq. FSA Scot, and Probably a Signaculum worn by a Leprous Pilgrim to St Jago di Compostella; with notes on "Pilgrim Signs" of the Middle Ages, and a Stone Mould for Casting Leaden Tokens, found at Dundrennan Abbey', *PSAS* 25 (1874–76), pp. 62–80.
[52] Ditchburn, *Scotland and Europe*, p. 58.
[53] *St Giles Reg.*, no. 77, pp. 106–7; McRoberts, 'Scottish Pilgrims to the Holy Land', p. 83.
[54] Sumption, *Pilgrimage*, p. 257.
[55] McRoberts, 'Scottish Pilgrims to the Holy Land', p. 84.
[56] W.H Bliss (ed.), *Calendar of Entries in the Papal Registers Relating to Great Britain and Ireland: Petitions to the Pope, Volume I, A.D. 1342–1419* (London, 1896), pp. 345–6; McRoberts, 'Scottish Pilgrims to the Holy Land', p. 89.
[57] *Rot. Scot.*, I, p. 901, II, pp. 31, 41; *Chron. Bower*, book XIV, 42; McRoberts, 'Scottish Pilgrims to the Holy Land', p. 90.
[58] *Ibid.*, p. 90.

March 1439 Sir Herbert Herries of Terregles made similar plans.[59] This development away from larger groups travelling together might either indicate that the cost of travel had escalated, making it more difficult to get a group assembled, or that knights were interested in making a more pious trip, with less ostentation and a smaller, more humble entourage. Of course there were notable exceptions to this, including the eighth earl of Douglas's trip to Rome in 1450 and Douglas, earl of Angus's trip to Amiens in 1489.

Mimicking the story described in *The Bruce*, in which James Douglas carried Robert I's heart on crusade, after James I's death the king's heart was taken to the Holy Land on pilgrimage by Sir Alexander Seton of Gordon. Seton travelled to Jerusalem via Bruges, Basle, Venice and Rhodes – stops that can be charted by the financial arrangements he made at these places for the return journey.[60] Seton of Gordon had been a close associate of James I (much like the good Sir James Douglas was of Robert Bruce) and it was a real honour to undertake the pilgrimage in this way. However, like Douglas, Seton did not survive the return trip, dying at Rhodes, where he bequeathed a legacy to the Hospitallers. James I's heart was returned to Scotland by an unnamed knight of this military order and was buried at the Charterhouse in Perth.[61]

James III, whilst not demonstrating much interest in crusading, was a keen, though aspirational, traveller (it is interesting that he had read and enjoyed the *Travels of Sir John Mandeville* in 1467).[62] Around this time the king had also developed a close relationship with the Brugeois ambassador Anselm Adornes and, at the Scottish king's bidding, Adornes undertook a pilgrimage to the Holy Land in 1470.[63] The journey not only appears to have been at James III's behest, but he also gave Anselm formal privilege to represent the Scottish court in these lands; James later spoke of Anselm having represented the kingdom at the Holy See and courts of Christian princes, as well as among the Saracens and Turks.[64] On his return in 1471, Anselm dictated an account of his pilgrimage to his son John, which he dedicated to James III.[65] Writing a

---

[59] *Rot. Scot.*, II, pp. 262, 313; McRoberts, 'Scottish Pilgrims to the Holy Land', p. 90.
[60] *Ibid.*, pp. 90–1; Dunlop, *James Kennedy*, p. 31, n. 6; Yeoman, *Pilgrimage in Medieval Scotland*, p. 119.
[61] Van Severen, *Inventaire de la Ville de Bruges*, I, no. 777; *ER*, V, pp. 156, 179; Dunlop, *Life and Time of James Kennedy*, pp. 31, n. 6, 390.
[62] *ER*, VII, p. 500.
[63] Macquarrie, 'The Impact of the Crusading Movement', p. 229; Macquarrie, *Scotland and the Crusades*, p. 97. Alasdair MacDonald suggests that James III's role in encouraging Adornes to take the journey was minimal and that Anselm sought the king's favour and approval to go, but for his own pious motivations. MacDonald claims that, while in Scotland, Anselm had fathered an illegitimate child, and his awareness of this carnal sin, combined with his conscience as a newly made knight, was enough to incite his pilgrimage. MacDonald, 'Chapel of Restalrig', p. 44.
[64] Bruges, Stadsarchief, Cartulaire Rodenboek, f. 270r–v, transcribed in Macquarrie, 'The Impact of the Crusading Movement', Appendix I, no. 6.
[65] Heers and de Groer (eds), *Itinéraire d'Anselme Adorno*, p. 30. The only surviving manuscript of Adornes' *Itinéraire* is in Lille, Bibliothèque Municipale, MS 330. David McRoberts has suggested that Anselm's diary was commissioned by Charles the Bold, but there are so

travel diary was a common occurrence amongst literate pilgrims and these itineraries were used by later pilgrims to navigate their routes or to obtain information about their destinations. After Anselm's return, and armed with his *Itinéraire*, James became increasingly preoccupied with the desire to travel or to go on pilgrimage, which was actively discouraged by the parliament of July 1473. Parliament advised James that he should give up his idea of visiting other countries, but if he absolutely insisted on going, then he should use the time to devote himself to making peace between the king of France and the duke of Burgundy. However, parliament warned that he should delay his departure until adequate provisions could be made for his absence and that he should in the meantime travel throughout Scotland to establish justice and policies to promote his governance, so that his fame as a great king might be known throughout other countries.[66] Three safe-conducts were issued to allow him to make the journey to the shrine of St John the Baptist at Amiens and in 1474 Louis XI wrote to James giving him permission to pass through France on his way to Rome.[67] In 1476, an elaborately worded safe-conduct issued by Edward IV for James indicated that the king was prone to seasickness and thus wished to visit Amiens via an overland route through England.[68] Unfortunately, James's ambitions were never realised and he was kept in Scotland to deal with domestic problems, having to content himself with the stories in Anselm's *Itinéraire*.

The Holy Land continued to attract Scottish pilgrims into the early sixteenth century. Sir Patrick Hume of Fastcastle is reported to have been there around 1509. This was about the time James IV was agitating for crusade and Hume's visit may have doubled as a reconnaissance trip.[69] The Humes were known as a highly chivalric family and were often found at the right hand of the king. Indeed Patrick Hume was an active participant in James's wars, including the sieges of Dumbarton and Duchal in 1489 and he had fought for him the previous year at the battle of Sauchieburn.[70]

Rome also proved to be a popular destination for Scottish knights. Sir Colin

---

few references to the Burgundian duke throughout the account that it seems highly unlikely that this was the case. In fact, not only was it dedicated to James III, but it was commissioned, approved by and directed principally towards him. McRoberts, 'Scottish Pilgrims to the Holy Land', p. 97; Macquarrie, 'The Impact of the Crusading Movement', p. 244; Macquarrie, *Scotland and the Crusades*, p. 99; Yeoman, *Pilgrimage in Medieval Scotland*, p. 120.

[66] *APS*, II, pp. 103–4; Macquarrie, 'The Impact of the Crusading Movement', p. 246; Tanner, *Late Medieval Scottish Parliament*, pp. 201–4.

[67] MacDonald, 'Chapel of Restalrig', p. 45; Macdougall, *James III*, pp. 114–15, 142–3.

[68] Diana Webb, *Pilgrims and Pilgrimage in the Medieval West* (London & New York, 1999), p. 214.

[69] Raphael Hollinshead, *The Scottish Chronicle: Or, a Complete History and Description of Scotland, being an Accurate Narration of the Beginning, Increase, Proceedings, Wars, Acts, and Government of the Scottish Nation, from the Original Thereof unto the Year 1585 &c* (Arbroath, 1805), II, pp. 131–2; McRoberts, 'Scottish Pilgrims to the Holy Land', p. 91.

[70] Stevenson, 'Knighthood, Chivalry and the Crown', Appendix C, Table One.

Campbell of Glenorchy was reportedly in Rome thrice during his life.[71] In 1456, Sir Alexander Sutherland of Dunbeath bequeathed £200 to his son, the archdeacon of Caithness, 'my said Son passand for me in pilgrimage to Sant Peter of Rome, and to do the thyngis for me and my saul that I have chargit hym under confessioun'.[72] As well as visiting the tombs of the apostles Peter and Paul, pilgrimages could be combined with visits to the papal court on personal or ambassadorial duties. Jubilee years were periodically called by later medieval popes in an attempt to stimulate the Roman pilgrim traffic. In these years pilgrim visitors were enticed by a general amnesty for sin: all who undertook such a pilgrimage were released from other penances yet to be undertaken for previously committed sins and from those penances that would have been undertaken in purgatory.[73] Scots certainly made an effort to attend and for the 1423 jubilee there were Scots in Rome, including Walter Stewart, earl of Atholl.[74] For the 1450 jubilee a significant number of Scots attended. In October 1449, safe-conducts were issued for Sir Henry Wardlaw and Sir John Maxwell, amongst others, to travel through England and cross at Calais on a pilgrimage to the Apostolic thresholds and it is most likely that they were planning to be in Rome for the jubilee. It has even been suggested that a Scottish church and hospice were founded at Sant' Andrea delle Frate in 1450 to cater for the large number of Scots who attended.[75]

William, eighth earl of Douglas, also visited Rome during the 1450 jubilee and took a large party with him. These men included Sir James Douglas (later ninth earl); Sir James, Lord Hamilton; Sir John Ogilvy of Lintrathen; Sir Alexander Hume; Sir William Cranston; Sir Colin Campbell of Glenorchy; Adam Auchinleck, cleric; Jonathan Clerk, cleric; Andrew Gray; William Lauder; Thomas Cranston; Andrew Kerr; Charles Murray; George Haliburton; Jonathan Haliburton; Jonathan Dodds; Jonathan Greenlaw; George Felawe; Alan Lauder; and James Bishop.[76] For the Douglas party this was no ordinary pilgrimage. They had visited the courts of Philip of Burgundy and Charles VII in Paris, and had participated in Jacques de Lalain's *pas d'armes* in Chalon sur Saône. In addition to this, a number of these knights took the opportunity to engage in some personal business whilst in Rome. Indeed, Lord Hamilton made no pretence of being just on pilgrimage and on 4 January 1451 he peti-

---

71 *Rot. Scot.*, p. 343; *CDS*, IV, 1229; McRoberts, 'Scottish Pilgrims to the Holy Land', p. 91.
72 'The Testament of Alexander Suthyrland of Dunbeath at Roslin Castle, 15 November 1456', *Bannatyne Misc. III*, p. 97; Dunlop, *James Kennedy*, p. 411.
73 Ditchburn, *Scotland and Europe*, p. 61.
74 *Cal. Scot. Supp.*, II, pp. 28–37; Ditchburn, *Scotland and Europe*, p. 62.
75 *CDS*, IV, 1217; Ditchburn, *Scotland and Europe*, p. 62.
76 *ER*, V, p. 439; Brown, *Black Douglases*, p. 287; Fraser, *Douglas*, I, p. 466; *Rot. Scot.*, II, p. 343; *CDS*, IV, 1229; NAS GD 16/46/3; Dunlop, *James Kennedy*, pp. 123–6; Yeoman, *Pilgrimage in Medieval Scotland*, p. 117. The eighth earl of Douglas returned to England just after 27 February 1451, when the Garter King of Arms was dispatched by Henry VI to the sea coast to await his arrival, to take him to the king's court and attend on him during his stay. *CDS*, IV, 1231.

tioned the pope to erect the parish church of Hamilton into a collegiate church. Two days earlier Sir Alexander Hume had received papal confirmation of the erection of the collegiate church of Dunglass, together with an indulgence to 'penitents who on the feast of the Assumption visit it and give alms for its conservation'.[77] The ninth earl of Douglas was clearly impressed by his trip to Rome for the jubilee. He obtained safe-conducts to return there in May 1453 with Archibald Douglas, earl of Moray; Hugh Douglas, earl of Ormond; John Douglas, lord of Balvenie; James, Lord Hamilton; James, Lord Livingston; and Archibald Dundas.[78] Douglas's actions were attributed to a number of causes, including the difficulties in the aftermath of the eighth earl's death and his attempts to negotiate the release of Malise Graham, earl of Menteith, still in captivity as a hostage for James I.[79]

Perhaps because France was more easily accessible than Rome and the Holy Land, a large number of knights set out on pilgrimage there. The shrine of St John the Baptist at Amiens proved to be an extremely popular destination for Scottish knightly pilgrims.[80] In November 1407, for example, a warrant for the granting of safe-conducts was issued to Alexander Lindsay, earl of Crawford, with twenty companions to pass through England *en route* to Amiens. In June 1412 safe-conducts were issued to pass through England on pilgrimage for the earl of Moray, twenty-four knights and esquires in his train and their servants.[81] In June 1464 Sir Alexander Forrester of Corstorphine applied for a safe-conduct to set out on pilgrimage in England to the shrine of St Thomas at Canterbury, and thence to the shrine of St John at Amiens, along with Sir John Lauder of Hawton, Henry Leverton of Sawny, John Wardlaw of Riccarton, Gilbert Forrester, and thirty servants.[82] In February 1489 Archibald, earl of Angus, requested a safe-conduct and protection for six months to set forth on pilgrimage to Amiens. His entourage was clearly considerable and included eighty attendants, horses and permission for one or more vessels.[83] In 1506 John, earl of Crawford, visited the shrine of St John at Amiens, as Alexander, earl of Crawford, had done in 1407. Indeed Earl John may have felt quite a connection with St John, and his family patronised an altar dedicated to this saint in the parish church of Dundee.[84]

It was not only Amiens, Rome and the Holy Land, however, that could draw Scottish knightly pilgrims. The shrine to St Thomas at Canterbury was also a major attraction. The dramatic story of Thomas Becket's murder had

---

[77] *CPL*, X, 75–6, 217–19; Dunlop, *James Kennedy*, pp. 405–6.
[78] *Rot. Scot.*, II, p. 362; Webb, *Pilgrims and Pilgrimage*, p. 223.
[79] McGladdery, *James II*, p. 83; Brown, *Black Douglases*, p. 302.
[80] Ditchburn, *Scotland and Europe*, p. 63.
[81] *CDS*, IV, 741, 826.
[82] *Ibid.*, IV, 1346; Webb, *Pilgrims and Pilgrimage*, p. 224.
[83] *CDS*, IV, 1547.
[84] *RSS*, I, 1251; Elizabeth P.D. Torrie, *Medieval Dundee: A Town and its People* (Dundee, 1990), p. 89; Ditchburn, *Scotland and Europe*, pp. 63–4.

spread throughout Western Christendom and the Church endeavoured to make a visit to Canterbury worthwhile for pilgrims. A beautiful shrine, where every relic of the tragedy was laid out, awaited those who entered the cathedral.[85] Scottish knights presumably visited Canterbury more regularly than the records show: ambassadorial trips to London and personal business in England may have been coupled with a trip to Canterbury cathedral. In addition, some journeys were made from Scotland specifically to visit St Thomas's shrine. In October 1390 the earl of March requested a safe-conduct for himself and thirty men, on horse or foot, to go on pilgrimage to Canterbury.[86] In 1404 Walter Stewart, earl of Atholl and Caithness, mounted an enormous pilgrimage to Canterbury, taking one hundred horsemen with him.[87] Much as was the case with pilgrimages to the Continent and the Holy Land, pilgrimages from Scotland to Canterbury were far less frequent whilst James I was held in English captivity and they did not increase in popularity until after his release.[88] In July 1426 Sir Patrick Dunbar and the squire Gilbert Hay, at the time hostages for James I in England, visited Canterbury with their wives.[89] It would seem that being a hostage did not restrict the freedom to undertake this journey and the codes of honour esteemed by the knightly class were clearly in effect here. Some years later, in 1444, Sir John Wallace, lord of Craigie, applied for a safe-conduct to Canterbury, which was granted with permission for him to take along twelve men.[90] In 1452, William, earl of Douglas; his brother James Douglas (later ninth earl); Sir William Crichton; Alexander Montgomery; James, Lord Hamilton; and Andrew, Lord Gray, were issued with safe-conducts to go to Canterbury (Douglas, James Douglas, Lord Hamilton, and Lord Gray had been on pilgrimage to Rome two years earlier) and in 1464 Sir Alexander Forrester and Sir John Lauder took the pilgrimage on their way to Amiens.[91]

Whilst international shrines were clearly a draw for Scottish knights, pilgrimage sites around Scotland attracted an ever-increasing local interest. St Andrews and shrines to St Andrew were always popular destinations and, as early as the fourteenth century, commercially minded Scots were selling cheap pilgrims' badges in the ferry port of North Berwick for pilgrims travelling to St Andrews and for those visiting the local church of St Andrew.[92] The trend towards encouraging pilgrimage to national shrines can be seen in sites favoured by royalty. From the second half of the fifteenth century, James III,

[85] S.C. Wilson, 'Scottish Canterbury Pilgrims', *SHR* 24 (1927), p. 258.
[86] *CDS*, IV, 417.
[87] *Ibid.*, IV, 655; Ditchburn, *Scotland and Europe*, p. 65.
[88] Wilson, 'Scottish Canterbury Pilgrims', p. 262.
[89] *CDS*, IV, 997, V, 999; *Rot.Scot.*, II, p. 257.
[90] *CDS*, IV, 1163.
[91] *Ibid.*, IV, 1346; Webb, *Pilgrims and Pilgrimage*, pp. 222–4; *Rot. Scot.*, II, pp. 354–5.
[92] *Angels, Nobles and Unicorns*, pp. 44–5, C49 Mould for Pilgrim's Badge. 'Notice of Portion of a Stone Mould for Casting Pilgrims' Signacula and Ring Brooches', *PSAS* 41 (1906–7), p. 431.

James IV and James V made frequent trips to the shrines of St Ninian at Whithorn (Dumfriesshire) and St Duthac at Tain (north of Inverness). Visits are also recorded to other, less significant shrines, such as St Serf's at Culross, St Fillan's at Scone, St Winin's at Kilwinning and St Adrian's on the Isle of May.[93] The popularity of 'local' pilgrimages was not a trend exclusive to Scotland and throughout Europe an emphasis on the worship of local saints had become common. These 'new' shrines were often dedicated to humble men who were acclaimed as saints by local people, with their cult rarely being recognised by the Church and their importance never extending beyond the immediate locality.[94] Some local shrines were also created by wealthy pilgrims who had returned from an overseas pilgrimage with a souvenir. For instance, as discussed above, Preston's gift of the arm-bone of St Giles to the parish church in Edinburgh in 1455 must have made this a considerably more worthwhile pilgrimage site.[95]

Of the Stewart kings it was James IV who particularly supported and engaged in local pilgrimage. His devout behaviour has often been attributed to his supposed feelings of remorse regarding his involvement in his father's death at the battle of Sauchieburn in 1488, but pilgrimage was also an appropriate activity in which a late-fifteenth-century king should engage.[96] From 1491 James's annual pilgrimage itinerary included visiting St Ninian's at Whithorn in spring or summer, and from 1493 he added an annual trip to St Duthac's at Tain in autumn. At times of particular personal stress, the king visited shrines more frequently; for example, in 1507 James was concerned over the health of his wife and twice visited Whithorn, as well as going to Tain and the Isle of May in the Firth of Forth.[97]

The king's personal patronage of these sites must have made them more popular amongst the Scots. Although it is far more difficult to ascertain whether knights also favoured pilgrimage to local sites, we can assume that they regularly visited them. Certainly the convenience of visiting local sites must have ensured a significant number of Scottish knights frequented local reliquaries. We know that James IV's visits to St Adrian's on the Isle of May were accompanied by Sir Andrew Wood of Largo. Wood was a naval captain for James III, but had sworn allegiance to James IV immediately after Sauchieburn in 1488. Both the king and parliament had been generous to Wood, and he had a privileged position in the king's favour. Obviously James's group travelled to the Isle of May on one of Wood's ships, but it can be assumed that Sir Andrew also took part in worship whilst he was there. Andrew Wood's services in this capacity were important to the king and, just

---

[93] David McRoberts, 'The Scottish Church and Nationalism in the Fifteenth Century', *IR* 19, 1 (1968), p. 11.
[94] Sumption, *Pilgrimage*, p. 269.
[95] McRoberts, 'Scottish Pilgrims to the Holy Land', p. 83.
[96] Yeoman, *Pilgrimage in Medieval Scotland*, chapter 'James IV: Scotland's Pilgrim King'.
[97] *Ibid.*, p. 101; Macdougall, *James IV*, p. 197.

two weeks before Flodden, James IV granted lands to him in return for which 'the grantee and his heirs should accompany the King and Queen on their pilgrimages to the May, whenever required'.[98]

Patronage of Churches

The interest in local churches was also reflected in knights' patronage of them. Wealth provided the nobility with the means to express their religious impulses freely and the regular incomes of landed estates allowed noblemen to make foundations and endowments.[99] As David Ditchburn has pointed out, churches and religious houses required and received secular support in Scotland, as they did throughout Europe. In giving this support, royalty and nobility demonstrated a full-hearted espousal of international fashions in religious patronage. Analysis of other devotional practices in Scotland, such as the collection of relics, the undertaking of pilgrimages and crusades, and even the popularity of certain cults, suggests a similar conformity with Christendom.[100]

The Church had always taught that its prayers could obtain forgiveness for the penitent. The growing late-medieval concern for the welfare of the soul after death encouraged wealthy individuals to make provision, by leaving money in their wills, for successions of priests to recite masses for their souls.[101] Sir Alexander Hume of that Ilk, for example, made provision in his last testimony for commemorative masses for his soul.[102] In 1456 Sir Alexander Sutherland of Dunbeath left an annual rent of £10 to pay for a priest to sing perpetually for his soul in Roslin collegiate church, near Edinburgh. He also left six merks to the canons of Fearn, four merks to the canons of the collegiate church of Tain, four merks to the canons at Dornoch cathedral, four merks to the abbey of Kinloss and six merks to Orkney cathedral. In addition to this he left the lands of Easter Kyndeiss to the canon of Ross for a priest to sing for his and his wife's souls. Six marks of his lands of Multayth and Drumnen were left to the canon of Fearn for a daily mass for his soul. The bishop of Caithness, who confirmed the testament, received £20 to sing for his soul.[103] Some arranged for masses to be said for others: in 1451 Sir John Forrester of Corstorphine founded masses for the soul of James Kennedy, bishop of St

---

[98] RMS, II, 3880; Yeoman, *Pilgrimage in Medieval Scotland*, p. 106.
[99] Jonathan Hughes, *Pastors and Visionaries: Religion and Secular Life in Late Medieval Yorkshire* (Woodbridge, 1988), p. 9.
[100] Ditchburn, *Scotland and Europe*, p. 49.
[101] Richard Fawcett, *Scottish Medieval Churches: An Introduction to the Ecclesiastical Architecture of the 12th to 16th Centuries in the Care of the Secretary of State for Scotland* (Edinburgh, 1985), pp. 25–6.
[102] Dunlop, *James Kennedy*, p. 404, n. 3.
[103] 'The Testament of Alexander Suthyrland of Dunbeath at Roslin Castle, 15 November 1456', *Bannatyne Misc. III*, pp. 96–7, 100; Dunlop, *James Kennedy*, p. 404.

Andrews, in the collegiate church of Corstorphine, near Edinburgh.[104] Sir Alexander Sutherland of Dunbeath also made a number of other provisions that would assist his soul and prove his piety. He left an additional £100 to the abbot of Fearn to repair Roslin collegiate church (at the time of the testament it had only recently been built) and for William Sinclair, earl of Orkney, to buy the stone to lie on his grave. Sir Alexander also left some personal possessions – a chalice to Roslin and a chalice to St Mungo's altar in Kirkwall, Orkney.[105] Other knights left personal possessions to churches on their death. For example, in 1506 Sir David Sinclair of Swinburgh left two parts of a black wolves' fur coat to St Magnus' church in Kirkwall and the third part to the church in Kinross. He also left his gold collar of the Danish Order of the Elephant to St George's altar at Roskilde Cathedral in Denmark.[106] Yet whilst these testaments show the types of provisions made after their deaths, knights also made sure to patronise churches during their lifetimes. Indeed, the Scrymgeour family, the hereditary constables of Dundee, patronised the altar of St James in Dundee's parish church, and George, first Lord Seton, added a new choir to the church at Seton in 1470.[107] Other ways of patronising a church might include establishing a chantry or providing an altar within their parish church. Gilbert Menzies of Pitfoddels, for example, emulated knightly fashions by founding a chantry in 1452 at St Sebastian's altar in St Nicholas's church in Aberdeen.[108]

However, by far the most popular and prominent way in which to demonstrate piety was through the founding of collegiate churches.[109] This was particularly the case from the mid fifteenth century when the earlier custom of founding altars and chantry chapels was replaced by an 'expensive spiritual premium' where the patron had control over the foundation and specifications of the residential college.[110] The collegiate church was a large chapel, most frequently erected in an existing parish church or chapel, organised into a college of secular canons or chaplains and presided over by a provost or dean. Once raised to collegiate status, the church was reconstructed or added to in order to accommodate its new purpose. There were over twenty collegiate churches founded in Scotland during the fifteenth century and the majority were created through the piety of the nobility.[111] Most of these were smaller churches founded specifically as a college of resident clergy, who were not cloistered, but resided in their own manses adjacent to the church they

[104] *CPL*, X, pp. 476–7; Dunlop, *James Kennedy*, p. 403.
[105] 'Testament of Alexander Suthyrland', pp. 96, 100.
[106] 'Testament of Sir David Synclar of Swynbrocht', pp. 108–9; Stevenson, 'Knighthood, Chivalry and the Crown', p. 267, n. 58.
[107] Richard Fawcett, *Seton Collegiate Church* (Edinburgh, 1985); Torrie, *Medieval Dundee*, p. 89.
[108] Scott, 'Dress in Scotland', p. 113.
[109] Fawcett, *Scottish Medieval Churches*, pp. 25–6.
[110] Stewart Cruden, *Scottish Medieval Churches* (Edinburgh, 1986), pp. 195–6.
[111] Cruden, *Scottish Medieval Churches*, p. 183; Cowan, 'Church and Society', pp. 116–17.

served. They officiated at the church's services, shared a common collegiate life and undertook parochial duties.[112] They were not founded for ministration to the laity in general, but were designed to have votive masses celebrated for the patron and his kin.[113]

As early as the late fourteenth century, the Douglas family had identified the benefits of founding colleges. In 1389 Archibald Douglas, lord of Galloway, petitioned for the erection of the collegiate church of Lincluden, near Dumfries. A decade later Archibald Douglas, earl of Douglas, petitioned for the parish church of Bothwell (near Hamilton in South Lanarkshire) to be raised to collegiate status, although this was not confirmed until May 1410.[114] Other noblemen soon followed suit and at the turn of the fifteenth century William Cunningham, lord of Kilmaurs, erected Kilmaurs collegiate church (near Kilmarnock in East Ayrshire). Shortly afterwards, in 1406, Sir James Douglas of Dalkeith founded the collegiate church of St Nicholas in Dalkeith, near Edinburgh. The church was rebuilt to accommodate the college before Sir James died in 1420.[115] 1420 also saw the petition for the erection of a college at St Cuthbert's parish church in Yester, (now known as Gifford, East Lothian), by co-lords of the lordship of Yester: Sir William Hay, sheriff of Peebles, Sir Thomas Boyd, Eustace Maxwell and Dougal McDowall.[116] A few years later, in 1424, Sir Thomas Somerville founded the collegiate church of Carnwath in South Lanarkshire.[117] At the same time he endowed the college with an annuity of ten merks for a provost and six prebendaries and commenced building the additional north transept, St Mary's aisle.[118]

The 1430s saw the foundation of two further colleges. In 1433 Walter Stewart, earl of Atholl, founded the collegiate church of Methven, near Perth, and by June 1436 the collegiate church of Corstorphine near Edinburgh had been erected by Sir John Forrester.[119] Around 1376 Sir Adam Forrester, Sir

---

[112] Cruden, *Scottish Medieval Churches*, p. 184; George Hay, 'The Architecture of Scottish Collegiate Churches', in G.W.S. Barrow (ed.), *The Scottish Tradition: Essays in Honour of Ronald Gordon Cant* (Edinburgh, 1974), p. 56.

[113] D.E. Easson, 'The Collegiate Churches of Scotland Part II – Their Significance', *Records of the Scottish Church History Society* 7 (1938), p. 31.

[114] Ian B. Cowan and David E. Easson, *Medieval Religious Houses Scotland with an Appendix on the Houses of the Isle of Man* (London & New York, 1976), pp. 216, 223; see also the Corpus MS appendix to Walter Bower's *Scotichronicon*, *Chron. Bower*, vol. IX, p. 27; J.S. Coltart, *Scottish Church Architecture* (London, 1936), pp. 150–2.

[115] Cowan and Easson, *Medieval Religious Houses*, p. 223; see also the Corpus MS appendix to Walter Bower's *Scotichronicon*, *Chron. Bower*, vol IX, p. 27; Donald Ferguson, *Six Centuries in and around the Church of Saint Nicholas, Dalkeith* (Bonnyrigg, 1951, reprinted 1992), p. 13.

[116] Cowan and Easson, *Medieval Religious Houses*, pp. 215–16; see also the Corpus MS appendix to Walter Bower's *Scotichronicon*, *Chron. Bower*, vol. IX, p. 27.

[117] Cowan and Easson, *Medieval Religious Houses*, p. 216; see also the Corpus MS appendix to Walter Bower's *Scotichronicon*, *Chron. Bower*, vol. IX, p. 28; Coltart, *Scottish Church Architecture*, p. 150.

[118] William Stark and George Paul, *A Short History of the Church in Carnwath* (n.p., 1967), 'The Auld Kirk 1167–1938'.

[119] Cowan and Easson, *Medieval Religious Houses*, pp. 217, 224; see also the Corpus MS

John's father, had erected a chapel connected to the parish church of Corstorphine and dedicated it to St John. Additional endowments by his widow and Sir John in 1424 and 1429 ensured the buildings were equipped to provide for a college.[120] When members of the nobility founded chapels and commissioned effigies of themselves, it was an assertion of their nobility and proof to the wider community that they had the wealth and the means to afford such public statements.[121] The founding of the college by the Forresters was part of the family's attempts to secure their relatively new-found noble status. By copying other noble families and emulating their patronage style, the Forresters ensured that their acceptance into noble society was complete.

However, it was the mid fifteenth century which saw the peak in popularity of founding collegiate churches. In 1444 Sir Walter Haliburton erected the collegiate church of Dirleton, near North Berwick in East Lothian and in 1446 Sir David Murray of Tullibardine allegedly founded the collegiate church of Tullibardine in Perthshire. Although there is no record of Tullibardine being granted collegiate status, around this time additional priests were added to the original complement and the church was eventually enlarged to a cruciform plan with a small western tower.[122] It is generally assumed that even if it had no papal sanction, Tullibardine was considered to be, and functioned as, a collegiate church. In 1449 Sir William Crichton of that Ilk, recently returned from diplomatic duties for James II in France and Burgundy, embarked upon extensive alterations to his castle at Crichton in Midlothian.[123] He simultaneously founded the collegiate church of Crichton 'out of thankfulness and gratitude to Almighty God' and 'to praise and honour of God Omnipotent and our Lord Jesus Christ, the ever Blessed and Glorious Virgin Mary, Kentigern and all the Saints and the Elect of God'. The foundation provided for a provost, eight prebendaries, two boys or clerks and a sacrist, clearly a large and well-endowed college.[124]

Around 1450 three more collegiate churches were erected: Dunglass, Hamilton and Roslin. Whilst visiting Rome for the papal jubilee, Sir Alexander Hume of that Ilk had sought papal ratification for the erection of a college at Dunglass, south-east of Dunbar in East Lothian.[125] Masses were also founded

---

appendix to Walter Bower's *Scotichronicon*, *Chron. Bower*, vol. IX, pp. 21, 28; Coltart, *Scottish Church Architecture*, pp. 138–9.
[120] Laing, 'Forrester Monuments at Corstorphine', p. 355.
[121] Scott, 'Dress in Scotland', p. 65.
[122] *Midl. Chrs.*, pp. 305–12; HMC, *12th Rep*, VIII, nos, 123–8. Cowan and Easson, *Medieval Religious Houses Scotland*, pp. 213–30, see also the Corpus MS appendix to Walter Bower's *Scotichronicon*, *Chron. Bower*, vol. IX, p. 28; Fawcett, *Scottish Medieval Churches*, p. 59; Coltart, *Scottish Church Architecture*, pp. 175–6.
[123] Dunlop, *James Kennedy*, p. 405.
[124] Colin F. Hogg, *Crichton Collegiate Church: A Short History from Foundation to Restoration* (n.p., 1974), pp. 4–5; *CPL*, X, pp. 64–5; *Midl. Chrs.*, pp. 305–12; Dunlop, *James Kennedy*, p. 405; Coltart, *Scottish Church Architecture*, pp. 118–21.
[125] *CPL*, X, p. 219; Fawcett, *Medieval Scottish Churches*, p. 55; see also the Corpus MS

in this new collegiate church by Hume and Sir Patrick Hepburn for the bishop of St Andrews, James Kennedy's soul.[126] Work had begun on structurally modifying the church in the 1440s, so this had clearly been a long-term plan. Initially Dunglass was laid out with a nave and a smaller choir, with a projection on the north of the choir for use either as a sacristy or a tomb chapel. Transepts and a central tower were then added.[127] James, Lord Hamilton, had also petitioned the pope to allow the parish church of Hamilton in South Lanarkshire to be erected to collegiate status when he was visiting Rome for the papal jubilee.[128] Hamilton made provision for a provost and six prebendaries in addition to the two chaplains who already served the parish church.[129] But it was the building of Roslin collegiate church, near Edinburgh, which was the most extravagant display of piety by a nobleman at this time.

Sir William Sinclair, earl of Orkney, founded St Matthew's at Roslin as a collegiate church around 1450.[130] This church was purpose-built and work had begun well before the mid 1440s. Indeed, in 1446 Sinclair requested that full-sized details and patterns be drawn on imported Baltic timber boards, after which he instructed his carpenters to carve the boards according to the drawings and gave them as patterns to the masons to cut into stone. As Cruden remarks: 'the architecture of the chapel indicates the work of an inspired amateur with pronounced heraldic tendencies.'[131] Roslin lacks a nave and consists only of the choir and sacristy. The east walls of the choir are raised, showing intended transepts, extending like wings to the north and south of the choir at its west end.[132] The most commented upon feature of Roslin, and what sets it apart from its contemporaries, is the richness of its ornamentation. There are no subtle contrasts of plain and decorated surfaces – there are simply no plain surfaces at all. Heraldic, religious and lay images abound on the interior and exterior of the church.[133]

The foundation of the church of Guthrie (east of Forfar in Angus) was started in 1456 by Sir David Guthrie of that Ilk, later James III's treasurer.[134] Sir David extended the church considerably, including adding the south transept, now known as the Guthrie aisle. Sir David died before the church was granted

---

appendix to Walter Bower's *Scotichronicon*, *Chron. Bower*, vol. IX, p. 28; Coltart, *Scottish Church Architecture*, pp. 109–10.
[126] Dunlop, *James Kennedy*, p. 403.
[127] Fawcett, *Scottish Medieval Churches*, p. 55.
[128] CPL, X, pp. 75–6; Cowan and Easson, *Medieval Religious Houses*, p. 222.
[129] Mairead Dougall, *The Old Parish Church of Hamilton* (n.p., 1987), p. 1.
[130] Cruden, *Scottish Medieval Churches*, pp. 186–94; Coltart, *Scottish Church Architecture*, pp. 121–7; Andrew Kerr, 'The Collegiate Church or Chapel of Rosslyn, Its Builders, Architect, and Construction', PSAS 12 (1876–78), pp. 218, 223; Easson, 'The Collegiate Churches of Scotland Part II', pp. 30–47; see also the Corpus MS appendix to Walter Bower's *Scotichronicon*, *Chron. Bower*, vol. IX, p. 28; Dunlop, *James Kennedy*, p. 405.
[131] Cruden, *Scottish Medieval Churches*, p. 196.
[132] *Ibid.*, p. 187.
[133] *Ibid.*, p. 188.
[134] Cowan and Easson, *Medieval Religious Houses*, p. 222.

collegiate status, and his son, Sir Alexander Guthrie regularly petitioned the pope until he consented in 1479.[135] James III's minority years saw little in the way of church patronage, but in 1470 George, first Lord Seton, commenced building the collegiate church at Seton parish church, just east of Prestonpans in East Lothian. Papal permission was sought from 1470 onwards to officially sanction its collegiate status, but this was not granted until 1492, to the second Lord Seton.[136] The majority of the building work was planned prior to Lord Seton's death in 1478, by which time most of the choir had been constructed. The first Lord Seton raised the walls of the choir and chancel and had it vaulted. The north wall of the choir was furnished with a tomb recess, but it is not known specifically for which Seton family member the recess was intended or if the effigies of a knight and lady which now repose there were designed for that position.[137] His son, the second Lord Seton, vaulted the choir and completed the sacristy between 1478 and 1507. The third Lord Seton roofed the vault with stone slabs, glazed the windows, paved the floors and provided furniture. His wife, Lady Janet Hepburn, added the transepts and tower.[138]

The flurry of building work for the new collegiate churches was not exclusive to the fifteenth century and did continue into the sixteenth. John, Lord Drummond, for example, rebuilt Innerpeffray in Perthshire to accommodate a college in the first decade of the sixteenth century.[139] Similarly John, Lord Semple, founded the collegiate church of Semple in Renfrewshire in 1504, and in 1527 Sir William Scott of Balweary made a similar foundation at Strathmiglo near Falkland in Fife.[140]

A number of other knights attempted to found colleges but for various reasons were unsuccessful. Some had trouble with the final financing of the project, whereas others failed to receive papal approval. This did not, however, preclude endowments for these churches to perform as colleges and doing so could be an adequate contribution for a knight. A number of foundations were never completed, including a petition from John Stewart, Lord Darnley, in 1422 for the parish church of Tarbolton (South Ayrshire) to be made into a collegiate church and Archibald, earl of Douglas's petition to the

---

[135] Brian Ramsay, *By Hill and Loch: A History of Guthrie and Rescobie Churches* (n.p., 1991), ch. 1, 'The Early Years'.
[136] Fawcett, *Seton Collegiate Church*; Fawcett, *Scottish Medieval Churches*, p. 26; Cowan and Easson, *Medieval Religious Houses*, p. 226; Cruden, *Scottish Medieval Churches*, pp. 184–6; Stewart Cruden, 'Seton Collegiate Church', *PSAS* 89 (1955–56), p. 424; Coltart, *Scottish Church Architecture*, pp. 116–7.
[137] Fawcett, *Seton Collegiate Church*; Brydell, 'Monumental Effigies of Scotland', pp. 407, 410.
[138] Fawcett, Scottish Medieval Churches, pp. 55–6; Cruden, 'Seton Collegiate Church', pp. 419–20, 424.
[139] Richard Fawcett, *Innerpeffray Chapel: Official Guide*, (Edinburgh, n.d.), pp. 1–2; Fawcett, *Scottish Medieval Churches*, p. 59.
[140] Cowan and Easson, *Medieval Religious Houses*, pp. 226–7; Fawcett, *Scottish Medieval Churches*, p. 26; Coltart, *Scottish Church Architecture*, p. 165.

pope in 1423 for permission to erect a collegiate church at Douglas (South Lanarkshire) and Sir John Lindsay petitioned the pope in May 1433 to found and endow a college of secular canons in Holy Trinity Church, St Andrews, in 1450 Alexander Livingston petitioned the pope to erect the collegiate church of Falkirk.[141] Andrew, second Lord Gray, intended to found a collegiate church at Fowlis, near Dundee but this never eventuated.[142]

Finance for the project was absolutely essential. Funds needed to be in place to expand the college and to pay for the required additional building work. An important part of the reconstruction of collegiate churches was to ensure that the patron was represented architecturally and an easy way to achieve this recognition was through the use of the coat of arms of the family throughout the church.[143] The early purpose of coats of arms was to identify knightly wearers otherwise anonymous in full armour, but heraldry was used increasingly for decorative effect, to mark property and ownership and to advertise the dignity of the dead in armorial shields sculpted on the walls of tombs.[144] Examples of heraldic arms in religious buildings are abundant. In the south transept of Seton church, for instance, is a baptismal font bearing the arms of Sir John Seton, who died in 1434. The Seton arms also appear on corbels throughout the church.[145] The engrailed cross, the armorial device of the Sinclairs, is prominent throughout the collegiate church of Roslin, appearing on shields along the wall heads and covering the altar frontals. The ribs of Roslin's vault are shaped like enlarged engrailed crosses and even the window tracery takes the form of the Sinclair's cross.[146] Amongst the Forrester arms at the collegiate church of Corstorphine are coats of arms on the exterior of the church: on the porch are arms showing Forrester and Forrester impaling Wigmer; and on the south transept gable are Forrester and Forrester impaling Wigmer reversed.[147] The use of heraldry was not exclusive to churches and was also found on other architectural structures. This was particularly the case at familial castles and surviving examples throughout the country are also abundant: for example, the Preston arms at Craigmillar, near Edinburgh.

One of the marked features of the collegiate churches is the effigial tombs of their founders and their families. It was customary for patrons and founders to make arrangements for their tombs and monuments, especially where new buildings or new choirs had been erected, but it was equally as common for effigies to be commissioned for pre-existing churches and niches. The tombs'

---

[141] Cowan and Easson, *Medieval Religious Houses*, p. 228; Dunlop, *James Kennedy*, p. 405; Coltart, *Scottish Church Architecture*, pp. 148–9.
[142] A. Jervise, 'Notice Regarding the Foundation of the Church of Fowlis in Gowrie', *PSAS* 7 (1867–68), pp. 241–8.
[143] Hughes, *Pastors and Visionaries*, pp. 13–16; Cruden, *Scottish Medieval Churches*, p. 195.
[144] *Ibid.*, pp. 194–5.
[145] Fawcett, *Seton Collegiate Church*; Cruden, 'Seton Collegiate Church', pp. 420–1.
[146] Cruden, *Scottish Medieval Churches*, pp. 194–5.

positions could vary, but in a church with a spacious choir, a common site for the founder's tomb was a central position between the high altar and the choir. This was a particularly popular position for effigies in English churches, where monuments were frequently free-standing.[148] Most frequently in Scotland, tombs were placed in recesses against the north wall of the sanctuary, as at Cullen, Lincluden, Semple, Seton and St Salvator's in St Andrews. At Corstorphine two of the Forrester monuments flank the sacristy door and with it fill the north wall of the mid-fifteenth-century sanctuary. In smaller collegiate churches, especially those founded within pre-existing buildings, a common addition was a transeptal aisle or chantry chapel to house the tomb, as at Carnwath, Guthrie and Methven.[149]

A large number of Scottish effigies have survived, many dating disproportionately to the mid fifteenth century. They tend to be made of ordinary stone, and occasionally marble, and stand in marked distinction to their English counterparts. Generally the English examples are made of brass and are etched images that sit flat over the tomb.[150] The Scottish effigies were originally fully coloured and gilt. Distinct vestiges of such can still be found, for example, on the upper part of James, seventh earl of Douglas's tomb at St Bride's. Often effigies were placed in couples of husband and wife, and in general the man wears full knightly regalia whilst his wife wears the height of fashion of the day. These are knights and nobles who achieved fame for themselves in battle, in the government of the realm, or had been liberal benefactors to the church.[151] An early fifteenth-century example is seen in the collegiate church at Seton. In 1434 Lady Catherine Sinclair, the widow of Sir John Seton, built a chapel on the south side of Seton parish church, to contain the tomb of her husband. She also built an altar at which masses could be said for the welfare of his soul. The two recumbent effigies which remain in the church today, however, date to later in the fifteenth century and can only be George, first Lord Seton, and his wife.[152] Sir George is clad in laminated full plate armour and an enriched sword-belt is girded about his hips. A misericord hangs from the dexter side, a long sword from the sinister, and the pommels of these two weapons are richly engraved. Like most Scottish knightly effigies, Sir George's feet repose upon a crouching lion, from whose mane an angel head emerges. His hands, clasping a reliquary, rest upon his breast, suggesting his devotion and piety.[153] Sir George is evidently a knight of station and presents himself as such by this effigy, but he ensures that his Christian beliefs are represented through the reliquary hung about his neck.

[147] *Corstorphine Parish Church Heraldry* (n.p., 1982), p. 2.
[148] Brydell, 'Monumental Effigies of Scotland', p. 337.
[149] Hay, 'Architecture of Scottish Collegiate Churches', p. 68.
[150] Brydell, 'Monumental Effigies of Scotland', p. 337.
[151] *Ibid.*, p. 334
[152] Cruden, 'Seton Collegiate Church', pp. 430–2; Scott, 'Dress in Scotland', p. 165.
[153] Cruden, 'Seton Collegiate Church', p. 431.

The effigies reveal much not only about the knight, but also about the values of the period. Sir John Ross of Hawkhead, who rose to chivalric fame in the 1449 tournament at Stirling, is buried at the parish church of Renfrew, where his effigy shows him in full plate armour and on his breast is a small shield bearing the Stewart fesse.[154] This tomb is a brilliant example of the use of heraldic images and there are nine coats of arms along the base of his monument: first the arms of Ross, followed by Erksine, Ramsay, Scotland quartering Stewart, Scotland, Stewart, Vans, Ross, and Ross.[155] Sir John's effigy is not unique and is almost identical to that of Sir Patrick Houston at Houston, Renfrewshire. The effigies there are thought to be Sir Patrick Houston who died in 1440 and his wife, Agnes Campbell, who died in 1456. The knight is depicted with plate defences on his arms and legs, and a bascinet with its visor removed. Protecting his body he has a mail habergeon with a breast plate, decorated with his coat-of-arms. His sword and dagger have been broken off, but his feet still rest on a miniature lion grasping a lamb in its claws.[156] The recurrence of similar effigies is not uncommon and suggests the repeated use of one mason and the emulation of desirable work. Similarities are seen between the effigies of Kenneth MacKenzie of Kintail and the bishop of Fortrose; and Sir Alexander Irvine of Drum at St Nicholas's in Aberdeen is similar to Provost Gilbert Menzies of Pitfoddels, also in Aberdeen, and Lord Seton at Seton.[157] Irvine of Drum is bareheaded, with, unusually, a small beard. According to Margaret Scott's study of dress in this period, his armour is out of vogue.[158] The mid-fifteenth-century effigy of Provost Gilbert Menzies of Pitfoddels shows him also bareheaded and dressed in full body armour, but he was never knighted and was simply a successful merchant. Menzies did, however, hold land in both the burgh and the countryside and built up a considerable estate.[159] Margaret Scott argues that Menzies' armour reflected the parliamentary act of 1430 stating the amount of armour required for different levels of society, but it is far more an indication that Menzies adhered to the codes of conduct of knightly society without being a formal member of it.[160]

In addition the raising of Corstorphine to collegiate status, the Forresters also commissioned effigies to prove their knightly and noble status. The Forrester family tombs at Corstorphine show Sir Adam Forrester, his son Sir John, and John's son, Sir John, in effigy, all dressed in full knightly armour with

---

[154] Brudell, 'Monumental Effigies of Scotland', pp. 369–70, 373–4.
[155] *Angels, Nobles and Unicorns*, p. 66, E6; Brydell, 'Monumental Effigies of Scotland', pp. 373–4; Scott, 'Dress in Scotland', pp. 162–4.
[156] *Angels, Nobles and Unicorns*, p. 66, E7; Brydell, 'Monumental Effigies of Scotland', pp. 397–8; Scott, 'Dress in Scotland', p. 151.
[157] Brydell, 'Monumental Effigies of Scotland', pp. 337, 384, 407; Scott, 'Dress in Scotland', p. 104.
[158] *Ibid.*, p. 108.
[159] *Ibid.*, p. 113.
[160] *Ibid.*, pp. 65, 111–13.

swords.[161] There are two recessed tombs in the chancel: to the west is Sir Adam's son Sir John and his wife; to the east, Sir John's son John and his wife. The first Sir John's tomb also uses heraldic imagery and is surmounted by the Forrester arms, on the front the five coats show first, third and fifth Forrester, second Forrester impaling Sinclair and fourth impaling a bend engrailed over the Stewart fesse. The Forrester bearings also appear on the breast of the knight.[162] His son's effigy is surmounted by the Forrester arms and a fragment of the crest; the same arms, borne by a cherub, appear at the terminations of the label over the moulded recess; on the front of the tomb the three shields show Forrester on the first and third and Forrester impaling a bend engrailed on the second. In the south transept the single figure of an old man in armour of a style not earlier than 1440 has been said to be Sir Alexander Forrester, the son of the second Sir John.[163]

From the latter end of the period with which we are concerned comes one of the most outstanding surviving tomb effigies belonging to a Scottish knight. The church of St Clement at Rodel on the island of Harris in the Outer Hebrides holds three knightly effigies. Two of these are recessed in the wall of the nave on each side of the south transept and one lies at the end of the transept. The most visually important of the three lies on the east wall of the transept and bears an inscription identifying the tomb as belonging to Sir Alexander Macleod of Dunvegan, who died in 1528. Sir Alexander wears the usual conical bascinet, surrounded by a jewelled wreath, short camail, close-fitting jupon, military belt, peaked knee-pieces, and short obtusely pointed sollerets. The armour on the thighs is dovetailed, but on the front instead of the usual position on the sides. The corresponding figure in the recess west of the transept is far more crude and simple, and the one within the transept seems to resemble that to the east of the transept. The guard of the sword, however, is reversed, while it is straight in the others, and a dagger sits at the left side. On each figure the sword, held by the hands, lies straight in front of the figures, with the pommel on the breast and the point between the feet.[164] The most notable element of the monuments is the back of the arched recess of Sir Alexander's tomb. This is elaborately decorated with carved panels of sacred and secular objects. On the left, over the feet of the effigy, there is a hunting scene, in which a huntsman on foot, armed with sword and spear, is followed by two attendants, each with two hounds in leash. In the panel immediately in front is a group of three stags. The panel adjoining the

---

[161] Brydell, 'Monumental Effigies of Scotland', pp. 334, 382; Laing, 'Forrester Monuments in the Church of Corstorphine', pp. 353–62; Scott, 'Dress in Scotland', pp. 104, 108–11, 143–50; *Corstorphine Parish Church Heraldry*, p. 1.
[162] Brydell, 'Monumental Effigies of Scotland', p. 383; *Corstorphine Parish Church Heraldry*, pp. 1–2; Laing, 'Forrester Monuments at Corstorphine', pp. 359–62.
[163] Brydell, 'Monumental Effigies of Scotland', pp. 383–4; Laing, 'Forrester Monuments at Corstorphine', pp. 360–2; *Corstorphine Parish Church Heraldry*, p. 1.
[164] Brydell, 'Monumental Effigies of Scotland', p. 334; Alexander Ross, 'Notice of St Clement's Church at Rowdill, Harris', *PSAS* 19 (1884–85), pp. 121, 123–5, 129.

inscription bears a representation of St Michael weighing souls, the devil sitting nearby and evidently taking a practical interest in the operation. In the second row of panels is first the representation of a castle, then three panels with canopied niches. The last panel in this row shows a galley in full sail. The three upper panels immediately underneath the crown of the arch contain figures of angels. The fronts of the voussoirs of the arch are also decorated with a series of religious sculptures.[165] This elaborate tomb shows the expense a knight was prepared to afford in order to promote himself in a particular fashion.

But not all knights chose to present themselves as such. The Douglas tombs at St Bride's church in Douglas are also well-known examples of fourteenth- and fifteenth-century effigies. Curiously, the yellow sandstone effigy of Archibald, fifth earl of Douglas, who died in 1438, does not show him in armour, even though he was a prominent knight and had won fame on the battlefield. Instead he wears robes of dignity, his left hand holds the baton of office and his right hand holds the cord which fastens his robe.[166] Margaret Scott has remarked that the non-military attire of the earl points to a greater pride in his non-knightly titles (Governor of Scotland, duke of Touraine etc.) than in his military campaigns in France and in a conventional depiction of knightly status.[167] Douglas's bare head is encircled by a flat, enriched band, the neck of the dress is embroidered, and a chain with oval links passes over the shoulders. The arms at the base of the tomb show firstly the Douglas arms, and secondly Douglas impaling the Scottish lion. These arms are repeated on the other side and ends of the tombs.[168] This is one of the few surviving Scottish effigies in civil costume, although Sir Alexander Seton, earl of Huntly, also chose to be represented in this way in the late fifteenth century.[169]

One effigial tomb in particular raises questions about the practice of chivalry in Scotland. This effigy is of Sir Anselm Adornes, who was close to James III. He was knighted by him in 1469 and held a privileged position at the king's court. Represented on Sir Anselm's effigial tomb in the Jerusalem Kirk in Bruges, Belgium, is a collar with clear associations with James III. The collar displays figure-of-eight links interspersed with the letter I and flanked by the numeral 3, from which hangs a pendant of a unicorn.[170] This collar is repeated on a sixteenth-century stained glass window on the inner east wall of the church, on a carved stone corbel frieze inserted into the brickwork on the

---

165 Ross, 'Notice of St Clement's Church', pp. 124–5; Fawcett, *Scottish Medieval Churches*, p. 60.
166 Brydell, 'Monumental Effigies of Scotland', p. 378; Scott, 'Dress in Scotland', p. 136.
167 *Ibid.*, pp. 137–8.
168 Brydell, 'Monumental Effigies of Scotland', p. 393.
169 *Ibid.*, pp. 393, 396.
170 Malden, 'Anselm Adornes and the Two Collars', pp. 6–7; John Malden, 'The Unicorn Collar and its English Contemporaries: The Saint Andrew Lecture, 1990', *The Double Tressure: Journal of the Heraldic Society of Scotland*, 13 (1991), pp. 8–9; Stevenson, 'Medieval Scottish Associations with Bruges', p. 102.

external west wall at the base of the church tower, and on the roof beam supports in the church and the adjoining hall, the Adorneshof. Much discussion has surrounded this unicorn collar and scholars have assumed, until recently, that it indicates that a Scottish chivalric order existed. However, this is by no means certain; the collar is most likely to have been a livery collar of James III's, especially given its direct reference to the ruling king. The receipt of a collar seems to have been a general way of signifying a special relationship with a king or monarch, and there is evidence to suggest that there were other numerous collars of this sort in Scotland.[171]

The evidence here suggests that the Christian component of the chivalric ideal did have meaning to the knights of Scotland. They recognised their place in the local Christian community, but also chose to represent themselves in this sphere as knights. That they were immortalised in full armour in effigy further supports this idea. Knights made efforts to behave in a Christian and pious way and if they could connect this with chivalry, then this was embraced even more so. For instance, in the fourteenth and fifteenth centuries the appeal of the crusade was attractive exclusively to knightly society. Although the evidence for knights' actions in the religious aspects of late-medieval life are less abundant, we can say with certainty that the practice of Christian ideals contributed towards Scottish chivalric culture.

---

[171] Stevenson, 'The Unicorn, St Andrew and the Thistle', pp. 3–22.

CHAPTER SIX

Chivalry in Scottish Literature

As we might expect, chivalric ideology heavily influenced literary representations of knights and literature helped to shape chivalric ideals. In some cases this was explicit, demonstrated particularly in the translations of romance literature. In other cases chivalry provided a more subtle framework for the description of events in which knights were involved, particularly apparent in chronicle sources. In general, the image of a truly chivalric knight that was widely promoted by European literature involved four main elements. Knights were bold and vigorous on the battlefield or in the lists; were ultimately loyal to their king; were inspired by their love for a lady to perform feats of arms; and upheld and defended the Christian faith.[1] Scottish writers portrayed knights largely along these lines and they subjected knights to tests of worth based upon them. The qualities that writers presented as ideal for knights, however, can only be partially revealing. We only learn from them what was considered to be knightly, not what was the reality. Richard Kaeuper warns that simply to draw up a list of knightly qualities that were esteemed is an inadequate approach. To do so does not consider the ideas presented by late medieval commentators as part of the wider movement for chivalric reform.[2] Critical expressions were made of the practice of chivalry in late medieval literature and ideals were continuously revised to make chivalry more relevant. This was evident in Scottish literature, and the changes throughout the fifteenth and early sixteenth centuries in the way knights were portrayed indicate a conscious development of the ideals of chivalric knighthood.

At first, consideration must be given to the issue of whether or not knights read or listened to the literature describing the world around them. Roger Mason has confirmed that in Scotland the noble household made up the audience for literature dealing with secular topics.[3] Evidence from the works

---

[1] Keen, *Chivalry*, pp. 112, 116–17; Kaeuper, *Chivalry and Violence*, pp. 33–5, 93–8, 103.
[2] *Ibid.*, p. 35.
[3] Mason, 'Chivalry and Citizenship', p. 58; Roger Mason, 'Laicisation and the Law: The Reception of Humanism in Early Renaissance Scotland', in L.A.J.R. Houwen, A.A. MacDonald and S.L. Mapstone (eds), *A Palace in the Wild: Essays on Vernacular Culture and Humanism in Late-Medieval and Renaissance Scotland* (Peeters, 2000), pp. 1–25. For more on book production and ownership in Scotland see R.J. Lyall, 'Books and Book Owners in Fifteenth-Century Scotland', in Jeremy Griffiths and Derek Pearsall (eds), *Book Production and Publishing in Britain 1375–1475* (Cambridge, 1989).

themselves proves that it was a knightly and noble audience to which they were principally presented. John Barbour, for example, addressed his audience directly as 'lordingis'.[4] After the death in 1497 of Robert, Lord Lyle, his son and heir sought to recover property which had belonged to the Lord. This included both a 'buke of storeis' and a 'buke of law'.[5] In 1390 James Douglas, lord of Dalkeith, agreed to leave his son and heir all his books, 'both of statutes of the kingdom and of romance', clearly indicating that the nobility held works of chivalry in their personal libraries. The lord of Dalkeith also requested that the books which he had borrowed from his friends be returned to their owners, so it is evident that books were freely circulated amongst peers and kin.[6] Kaeuper has argued that the ongoing debate surrounding audience is mainly with whether knights listened to (as opposed to read) the romances.[7] This they clearly did. According to John Barbour, whilst camped on the shores of Loch Lomond, Robert Bruce read his men the romance of Fierabras, part of the matter of Charlemagne compiled in the late twelfth century.[8] The anonymous *Pluscarden* chronicler wrote that after dinner a king should stand up and deliver a talk on a subject such as 'the relative merits of glorious deeds; and then let him hear the opinions of others'.[9] That ideals could be debated in this way suggests that knights took an active interest in the definition of chivalric behaviour and its relevance to their own lives.

Romance Literature

As Sonja Cameron has pointed out, romance is always closely associated with chivalry. The heroes of romance are frequently knights and the subject matter concerns their adventures, the challenge and confirmation of their knightly virtues and their interactions with other levels of society. Romances were addressed to a knightly audience and portrayed an ideal version of knight-

---

[4] Barbour, *Bruce*, Book I, line 445. In the second book of the *Bruce*, Barbour again addressed his audience saying 'Each of you is brave and worthy, full of great chivalry, and knows very well what honour is. Behave then, in such a way that your honour is always maintained.' II, lines 337–41.
[5] *ADC*, II, pp. 296–8; Mason, 'Laicisation and the Law', p. 9.
[6] *Mort. Reg.*, II, no. 193, pp. 171–2; Roger Mason, 'Laicisation and the Law', p. 9; Sellar, 'Courtesy, Battle and the Brieve of Right', p. 10.
[7] Kaeuper, *Chivalry and Violence*, pp. 30–1. Michael Clanchy has proved that lay literacy was much higher than originally calculated and most knights could read. Michael T. Clanchy, *From Memory to Written Record: England 1066–1307* (Oxford, 1993), esp. pp. 231–4, 246–51. See also Ruth Crosby, 'Oral Delivery in the Middle Ages', *Speculum* 11 (1936), pp. 88–110.
[8] Barbour, *Bruce*, Book III, line 437; Sonja Cameron, 'Chivalry and Warfare in Barbour's *Bruce*', in Matthew Strickland (ed.), *Armies, Chivalry and Warfare in Medieval Britain and France: Proceedings of the 1995 Harlaxton Symposium* (Stamford, 1998), p. 24.
[9] *Chron. Pluscarden*, II, p. 63.

hood that its audience could identify and to which they could aspire.[10] In light of this, it is no surprise that romance literature was widely available in Scotland. By the late thirteenth century, Continental tales of chivalrous knights had begun to be translated into vernacular Scots. The earliest surviving example is an anonymous version of the Tristan tale.[11] Whether or not this was still in circulation in the fifteenth century is difficult to establish, but it is highly probable that knights were familiar with the story and Tristan was used as a Christian name in some Scottish noble families well into the sixteenth century.[12] By the late fourteenth and fifteenth centuries romances were being regularly copied into Scots.[13] In 1438 a work on Alexander the Great was translated, although the identity of the translator has been long-contested amongst scholars.[14] In the mid 1460s, Gilbert Hay, under Thomas, second Lord Eskine's patronage, penned yet another version of the Alexander story.[15] A translation of *Lancelot of the Laik* was also made, probably in the later 1470s or early 1480s.[16] Towards the end of the fifteenth century chivalric poems were

[10] Cameron, 'Chivalry and Warfare in Barbour's *Bruce*', p. 24.
[11] George P. McNeill (ed.), *Sir Tristrem*, STS (Edinburgh & London, 1886). For more on the authorship of the poem see pp. xxxii–xlv.
[12] See for example Tristan Gorthy of that Ilk, *RMS*, II, 3141.
[13] Robert L. Kindrick, 'Politics and Poetry in the Court of James III', *Studies in Scottish Literature* 19 (1984), p. 44.
[14] Ritchie (ed.), *Buik of Alexander*. Ritchie attributed this version to John Barbour, but MacDiarmid comprehensively disproved this in his commentary on Barbour's *Bruce*, Ritchie (ed.), *Buik of Alexander*, esp. pp. lxxiii–xcviii, clvii–cclxvii; Matthew P. McDiarmid and James A.C. Stevenson (eds), *Barbour's Bruce: A fredome is a noble thing!*, STS (Edinburgh, 1985), I, pp. 27–32. See also Mapstone, 'Was there a Court Literature?', p. 416; John MacQueen (ed.), *Ballattis of Luve 1400–1570* (Edinburgh, 1970), pp. xxii, xxiv; and John MacQueen, 'The Literature of Fifteenth-Century Scotland', in Jennifer M. Brown (ed.), *Scottish Society in the Fifteenth Century* (London, 1977), p. 193. McDiarmid suggests that this may have been a juvenile work of Gilbert Hay, but Bitterling proves that Hay is not the author. See Klaus Bitterling, 'A Note on the Scottish *Buik of Alexander*', *Scottish Literary Journal* 23, 2 (1996), pp. 89–90.
[15] Gilbert Hay, *The Buik of King Alexander the Conqueror*, John Cartwright (ed.), STS (Edinburgh, 1986). This is preserved in two MSS., BL Add. MS 40732 and NAS GD112/71/90. For a discussion of the Alexander books and the Scottish attitude to a Greek heritage see Carol Edington, 'Paragons and Patriots', esp. pp. 70–3; and Fradenburg, *City, Marriage, Tournament*, p. 183.
[16] Gray (ed.), *Lancelot of the Laik*. Two other edited versions have been published: Joseph Stevenson (ed.), *The Scottish Metrical Romance of Lancelot du Lac. Now First Printed from a Manuscript of the Fifteenth Century Belonging to the University of Cambridge with Miscellaneous Poems from the Same Volume* (Maitland Club, 1839); and W.W. Skeat (ed.), *Lancelot of the Laik: A Scottish Metrical Romance, (About 1490–1500 AD), Re-edited from a Manuscript in the Cambridge University Library, with an Introduction, Notes and Glossarial Index* (London, 1865). It is not known who produced this translation, although Gray suggests that it was not a cleric, p. xx. For more on the dating and authorship of *Lancelot* see Walter W. Skeat, 'The Author of "Lancelot of the Laik"', *SHR* 8 (1911), pp. 1–4; M. Muriel Gray, 'Communications and Replies: Vidas Achinlek, Chevalier', *SHR* 8 (1911), pp. 321–6; Bertram Vogel, 'Secular Politics and the Date of *Lancelot of the Laik*', *Studies in Philology* 40 (1943), pp. 1–13. For more on the text see W. Schep, 'The Thematic Unity of Lancelot of the Laik', *Studies in Scottish Literature* 5 (1968) 167–75; Robin William Macpherson Fulton, 'Social Criticism in Scottish Literature 1480–1560' (Ph.D., University of Edinburgh, 1972), pp. 178–82; MacQueen, 'The Literature of Fifteenth-Century Scotland', p. 193; Sally Mapstone, 'The Scots, the French, and the English:

still proving popular, including 'The Knightly Tale of Golagros and Gawane' and 'The Tale of Syr Eglamaire of Artoys'. Both of these poems were amongst the first to be printed in Scotland.[17] There is also an indication that poems and stories were circulated which have not survived. Amongst them were 'The Tale of Syr Valtir the Bald Leslye', 'Ferrand erl of Flandris', 'The Tail of Syr Euan Arthours knycht', and 'The Tail of the Brig of Mantribil', which was part of the matter of Charlemagne.[18] Individually these works do not reveal a great deal about attitudes towards knighthood in Scotland. They are what Charles Moorman has called 'pedestrian romances' where the morality of chivalry and its contradictory code of ethics are not raised or questioned within the text.[19] However, they still reinforced chivalric ideals to knightly society and it is for this reason that they are crucial to any understanding of the new aspirations for knightly behaviour that may have appeared.

A salient feature of Scottish chivalric texts is the prominence of the cult of the Nine Worthies, popular in Scotland from at least the late fourteenth century. The Nine Worthies were upheld in knightly culture as the paragons of chivalric virtue. Traditionally they were Joshua, Judas, David, Hector, Alexander, Julius Caesar, Arthur, Charlemagne and Godfrey de Bouillon.[20] John Barbour was aware of the cult and included examples of the Worthies' acts of prowess in his 1370s work on Robert Bruce.[21] Around 1440 the author of the *Buik of Alexander* developed this further and wrote 'The Ballet of the Nine Nobles', introducing a tenth 'worthy' to his audience – Robert Bruce.[22] The

---

An Arthurian Episode', in Graham Caie, Roderick J. Lyall, Sally Mapstone and Kenneth Simpson (eds), *The European Sun: Proceedings of the Seventh International Conference on Medieval and Renaissance Scottish Literature and Language, University of Strathclyde, 1993* (East Linton, 2001); R.J. Lyall, 'Politics and Poetry in Fifteenth and Sixteenth Century Scotland', *Scottish Literary Journal* 3 (1976), esp. pp. 13–16.

[17] See George Stevenson (ed.), *Pieces from the Mackculloch and the Gray MSS together with the Chepman and Myllar Prints*, STS (Edinburgh, 1918). On 'Golagros and Gawane' see Fulton, 'Social Criticism in Scottish Literature', p. 176; Elizabeth Walsh, '*Golagros and Gawane*: A Word for Peace', in J. Derrick McClure and Michael R.J. Spiller (eds), *Bryght Lanternis: Essays on the Language and Literature of Medieval and Renaissance Scotland* (Aberdeen, 1989), p. 99.

[18] R.J. Lyall, 'The Lost Literature of Medieval Scotland', in J. Derrick McClure and Michael R.J. Spiller (eds), *Bryght Lanternis: Essays on the Language and Literature of Medieval and Renaissance Scotland* (Aberdeen, 1989), p. 41.

[19] Charles Moorman, *A Knyght There Was: The Evolution of the Knight in Literature* (Lexington, 1967), pp. 7–8.

[20] Keen, *Chivalry*, pp. 121–4.

[21] On Judas, see Barbour, *Bruce*, Book XIV, lines 313, on Hector, Book I, 395–404, on Alexander, Book I, lines 529–36, III, 83, X, 710–40, on Caesar, Book I, lines 537–48, III, 277, and on Arthur, Book I, lines 549–60. See also Sergi Mainer, 'A Comparison of Barbour's *Bruce* and John the Minstrel's *Histoire de Guillaume le Maréchal* as National Paradigms of Heroic-Chivalric Biographies' (M.Sc., University of Edinburgh, 2001), pp. 35–6, 74.

[22] 'The Ballet of the Nine Worthies', in Ritchie (ed.), *The Buik of Alexander*, I, pp. cxxxiv–cl. Ritchie attributes this poem to John Barbour, but Craigie convincingly claims it must have been written by the author of the *Buik of Alexander* in the later 1430s or early 1440s. W.A. Craigie, 'The "Ballet of the Nine Nobles"', *Anglia: Zeitschrift für Englische Philologie* 21 (1898–99), p. 365. McDiarmid agrees that it was not written by Barbour, but suggests that it may have been penned by Blind Harry. McDiarmid (ed.), *Barbour's Bruce*, I, p. 33.

elevation of Bruce to 'worthy' status meant, in effect, that the cult became even more relevant to the Scottish audience. Indeed, throughout all types of fifteenth-century literature, references to them are frequent.[23] Moreover, there was an emphasis placed upon the cult in James V's reign. Sir David Lindsay of the Mount compiled an *Armorial* where he represented the coats of arms of the noble families of Scotland, placing the arms of the Nine Worthies in a prominent location at the front of the roll.[24] By juxtaposing the Worthies with the Scottish nobility, Lindsay placed the Scottish knightly community firmly within the context of the heroes of chivalric legend.[25]

Chronicles

Most images of knights in the earlier part of the fifteenth century come from chronicle sources, in particular Andrew Wyntoun's *Original Chronicle*, dating to the 1420s, and Walter Bower's *Scotichronicon*, compiled in the 1440s. Both chroniclers had knightly patrons: Wyntoun's patron was Sir John Wemyss of Kincaldrum and Bower's was Sir David Stewart of Rosyth.[26] It has been suggested that in view of Bower's clear sympathies with James I, the king had some direct influence on the content of the chronicle, but this was not the case.[27] Although Sir David Stewart was knighted by James I at his coronation and he enjoyed a degree of royal favour, his relationship with the king was not especially strong and royal patronage was not filtered to Bower through this route.[28] Although Wyntoun and Bower's patrons belonged to a society which revered tales of prowess on the battlefield, this appears to have had little impact on the attitudes expressed in the chronicles. Wyntoun, as prior of St Serf's monastery in Loch Leven, and even more notably Bower as abbot of Inchcolm abbey, were both influenced by their clerical training and interests.

[23] For some examples see *Chron. Bower*, book I, 8, 34, book II, 10, 12, 16, 18, 19, 20, 23, 26, 45, book III, 16, 17, 20, 22, 24, 25, 26, 42, 54, 56, 57, 58, 61, book IV, 6, 8, 16, 25, book V, 22, 31, book VII, 34, 35, 55, *passim*; Blind Harry, *Wallace*, p. 295; William Dunbar, 'The Ballade of Barnard Stewart', pp. 222–7.
[24] Laing (ed.), *Facsimilie of an Ancient Heraldic Manuscript*, pp. 8–10; Charles J. Burnett, 'Outward Signs of Majesty, 1535–1540', in Janet Hadley Williams (ed.), *Stewart Style 1513–1542: Essays on the Court of James V* (East Linton, 1996), p. 297; Edington, *Court and Culture*, p. 37.
[25] Thomas, 'Renaissance Culture at the Court of James V', p. 273; H.A.B. Lawson, 'The Armorial Register of Sir David Lindsay of the Mount', *The Scottish Genealogist* 4 (1957), pp. 12–19; Edington, *Court and Culture*, pp. 37–9.
[26] *Chron. Wyntoun.*, I, pp. xli–xlii, II, pp. 6–7; *Chron. Bower*, book VII, 1, book XVI, 39; Alan Borthwick, 'Bower's Patron, Sir David Stewart of Rosyth', in *Chron. Bower*, Vol 9, pp. 354–62; MacQueen, 'The literature of fifteenth-century Scotland', p. 196; Mapstone, 'Was there a Court Literature?', p. 413. For more on Wyntoun see R. James Goldstein, ' "For he wald vsurpe na fame": Andrew of Wyntoun's Use of the Modesty *Topos* and Literary Culture in Early Fifteenth-Century Scotland', *Scottish Literary Journal* 14 (1987), pp. 5–18; Grace G. Wilson, 'Andrew of Wyntoun: More than Just "That Dreich Clerk"', *Scotia: American-Canadian Journal of Scottish Studies* 10 (1986), pp. 189–201.
[27] Mapstone, 'Was there a Court Literature?', p. 417.
[28] See Borthwick, 'Bower's Patron', pp. 357–8.

Yet both chroniclers demonstrate, in distinct ways, how they felt about knighthood and chivalry.

Wyntoun had a keen interest in chivalric lifestyles, as was apparent in his recounting of the deeds of Scottish knights.[29] Most writers in the later medieval period concentrated on the behaviour and exploits of knights during warfare and Wyntoun was no exception. As his intended audience was the nobility, his focus on aspects of knightly life is understandable. Indeed, Wyntoun made it explicit that he was writing for a knightly audience and that he intended for them to hear his work. This extended to interrupting his narration to include stories which he felt were of interest to his audience, like an account of the tournament of Brittany where

> That for the nobilitie of the deid
> Is worthy baith to wryit and reid.
> All cum it nocht to this mateir,
> Methink it speidfull to wryt heir,
> That men of armys may reiosing
> Haue, quhen it cummis till hering.[30]

The chronicler wrote in vernacular rhyming couplets that, to an extent, constrained his ability to record accurately and affected the vocabulary with which he depicted knights and discussed their attributes. As a consequence of this, many of the supplementary descriptions of knights must be viewed as a by-product of the need to rhyme. Nevertheless, these attributes were not chosen for purely poetic reasons because Wyntoun considered that they were appropriate and they were displayed by the knights of whom he approved. We are thus afforded an insight into what was considered, by this chronicler at least, as chivalrous. The chronicler's praise of worthy knights could provide a model to which other knights might aspire. Indeed, the importance of chronicles to knightly reputations must not be underestimated. Being named in a chronicle was considered highly desirable, as illustrated in a poem by Thomas Barry, canon of Glasgow and first provost of Bothwell. Prior to the battle of Otterburn in 1388, Archibald 'the Grim', third earl of Douglas, said to his men:

> So, having considered all these reasons for fighting,
> fight boldly on behalf of your fellow-countrymen.
> You will be the victors, have no doubt of that.
> And the evening will turn out a successful one for you,
> and martial glory will crown you,
> Your names will be written in the chronicles.[31]

---

[29] Wilson, 'Andrew of Wyntoun', p. 11.

[30] *Chron. Wyntoun*, VI, pp. 209–11. For another example of this type of interruption see VI, p. 348. See also Stephen Boardman, 'Chronicle Propaganda in Fourteenth-Century Scotland: Robert the Steward, John of Fordun and the "Anonymous Chronicle" ', *SHR* 76 (1997), p. 27.

[31] *Chron. Bower*, book XIV, 52. For more on this poem and its relationship to the 'Anonymous Chronicle' in Wyntoun, see Boardman, 'Chronicle Propaganda in Fourteenth-Century Scotland', p. 25.

Barry did not, however, expand on what he considered to be 'martial glory' and his descriptions of knights on the battlefield were essentially in simplistic terms. In Barry's mind, knights were brave, loyal, bold, noble and courageous and Wyntoun's descriptions do not differ significantly from these.[32]

The pages of Wyntoun's chronicle are strewn with references to knightly acts, especially during warfare. In these accounts Wyntoun highlighted the qualities he valued and those which were prized in knights. Of these, worthiness occupied the most prominent place.[33] Other admired qualities included stoutness, vigour, manliness, boldness, hardiness, wisdom, honesty, generosity, honour, loyalty and virtuousness.[34] Sir Andrew Murray, warden of Scotland, was considered worthy of extensive description and we find in him a combination of ideal qualities – making him, in Wyntoun's opinion, a 'worthy' knight:

> He was a man of gret bownte,
> Off sobyr lif and of chastite,
> Wysee and wertuousse of consaille,
> And of his gudie liberalle.
> He was of gret dewocione
> In prayer and in orysone;
> He was of mekyl almus deide,
> Stout and hardy of manheide.[35]

Murray's great devotion to prayer demonstrated that this knight paid attention to the Christian element of knighthood, making him, for the prior of St Serf's, an example of an ideal, well-rounded knight and thus more worthy. The qualities that Wyntoun valued can be divided into qualities of personal character and those which were displayed on the battlefield. Nevertheless, many of these qualities are never made manifest in the actions undertaken by the knights Wyntoun described. They are simply stated to belong to a particular knight, and although not rendered void of meaning, no examples are given of how he demonstrated these qualities in practice.

The most important possession a knight could have was a good reputation and Wyntoun makes this abundantly clear in his chronicle. Sir Alexander Ramsay of Dalhousie, for example, was deemed to be worthy and of good renown, suggesting that a military reputation was covetable. His reputation is well recorded, and later chroniclers maintained the tradition of referring to his high esteem.[36] Of Sir Andrew Murray, Wyntoun claimed that he was such a 'gud' knight that there was 'nane bettyr [. . .] in his day'.[37] William Douglas of Nithsdale through 'wit and worschep' did 'mony douchty' deeds and had

---

[32] *Chron. Bower*, book XIV, 52.
[33] *Chron. Wyntoun*, VI, pp. 19, 51, 79, 225, 372, 373.
[34] *Ibid.*, V, pp. 331, 429, VI, 69, 85, 123, 199, 225, 251, 265, 371, 372, 373, 403, 411, 412.
[35] *Ibid.*, VI, p. 99.
[36] *Ibid.*, VI, p. 51; *Chron. Pluscarden*, II, p. 221.
[37] *Chron. Wyntoun*, V, p. 429.

such a good reputation that the earl of Derby challenged him to a jousting match.[38] Squires were referred to using the same terminology: John Haliburton was called 'a nobil sqwyar of gret ranowne' and Ingram Wyntoun was recorded to be 'a manly sqwyar of ranowne'.[39] Obviously not all knights could have been 'the best knight' and the chroniclers clearly took considerable liberties in their descriptions. John Barbour avoided this problem by numbering his favourites in order, for instance, saying that Sir Giles d'Argentan, 'was the third best knight who lived in his time known to men; he achieved many a fine feat of arms'.[40] By mentioning their reputations, the chroniclers implicitly approved of the actions and deeds of these particular men and thus they became exemplars for other knights.

Simply claiming that a knight was of great renown without expanding upon his achievements was a tool used by Wyntoun and other writers. This solved the problem of how to present a seemingly informed view when a knight was not personally known to the author, nor the details of how his individual deeds led to him being considered worthy. For example, Wyntoun records nothing of the deeds of Sir Thomas Roslin, nor how he came to be held in high regard. Instead, he simply wrote:

> That throw al Inglande callit wes
> Ane of the best knychtis of hande,
> That men mycht fynde in ony lande.[41]

In other cases, suggesting that a knight had a good reputation added legitimacy to the acts that he was reported to have performed. Sir William Keith was one such knight: allegedly a knight 'of gret ranowne', he took an active part in besieging Stirling castle.[42] According to Wyntoun, before the main attack could be made, the knight got the urge to climb the walls fully armed. In the course of his attack he was hit with a stone that was thrown down from the castle and, in his consequent fall, he stabbed himself with his spear. He died of this wound, and

> of his dede was gret pete;
> For he was bathe wicht and hardy,
> And full of al gud chewalry.[43]

This action embraced chivalry insofar as it demonstrated the pursuit of individual glory on the battlefield with the aim of securing success. Keith's actions, however, contravened the laws of war, which stipulated that knights

---

[38] *Ibid.*, VI, p. 103.
[39] *Ibid.*, VI, pp. 209, 251.
[40] Barbour, *Bruce*, Book XIII, lines 320–7. We can assume that, in Barbour's opinion, the first best knight was Robert Bruce, and the second best, Sir James Douglas.
[41] *Chron. Wyntoun*, VI, p. 61.
[42] *Ibid.*, VI, p. 125.
[43] *Ibid.*, VI, p. 135. His son, Robert Keith, was later described as a mighty man of lineage, a direct reference to William, VI, p. 375.

should not pursue spontaneous acts of prowess without the leave of their commander or considering the overall goals of the campaign.[44]

Walter Bower's descriptions of knights do not differ significantly from Wyntoun's in vocabulary, although he writes in Latin prose and not in vernacular Scots. However, the manner in which he records their deeds is in contrast to Wyntoun's praise of chivalric ideals. In part this was due to Bower's intended audience, which was predominantly clerical. Bower's main distinction from other chroniclers lay in his lesser emphasis on chivalric matters. His opinions on politics and his clerical preoccupations are far more apparent. Bower spends considerably fewer words in describing the qualities of the knights he discusses and the variations between his depictions of different knights are negligible. Bower's lack of extensive description is especially significant when he can be shown to have been working from the same source as Wyntoun.[45] For example, in describing the May 1390 tournament in London between Sir David Lindsay, earl of Crawford, and Lord Wells, Bower recorded only that it took place in the presence of Richard II. He also noted that Lindsay was 'a worthy knight' but spent less than ten lines on the section. Wyntoun, on the other hand, recorded the jousting in detail, tilt-by-tilt, taking upwards of one hundred lines of description.[46] Despite having fewer constraints upon expression through his choice of prose, Bower quite significantly did not elaborate freely. To an extent, this supports the idea that Bower was not especially concerned with the characterisation of Scottish knights. He consciously omitted detail he thought was unnecessary and which might 'arouse boredom' in his audience.[47] Although Bower did spend a reasonable portion of his chronicle detailing knights' activities, this is possibly more of an indication of the type of sources he was working from than personal interest in the event. Wyntoun, on the other hand, often made digressions in his narrative to include tales of chivalric deeds that he thought might have engaged and interested his audience.[48]

Bower did, however, record knights who were deemed to be 'worthy' in a similar manner to Wyntoun. These descriptions were of knights such as Sir David Lindsay, who was 'extremely distinguished in every military skill'.[49] In Bower's opinion desirable qualities included respectability, nobility, good sense, liveliness, spirit and wisdom.[50] Reputation was again considered crucial and something knights were encouraged to pursue. Patrick Hepburn

---

[44] Stevenson (ed.), *Buke of the Law of Armys*, pp. 82–4.
[45] For more on this see Boardman, 'Chronicle Propaganda in Fourteenth-Century Scotland', esp. pp. 25–8.
[46] *Chron. Bower*, book XV, 4; *Chron. Wyntoun*, VI, pp. 359–62.
[47] *Chron. Bower*, book XIV, 38.
[48] *Chron. Wyntoun*, VI, pp. 209–11; Boardman, 'Chronicle Propaganda in Fourteenth-Century Scotland', p. 27.
[49] *Chron. Bower*, book XV, 4. Bower does not expand on this, so we are not told what these military skills were.
[50] *Ibid.*, book XV, 6, 13, 14, book XVI, 12.

of Hailes, for example, 'desired an extension of the fame of his name'.[51] Of Sir John Gordon, who was renowned for his 'vigorous prowess', Bower wrote that 'to entrust even just a selection of [his] remarkable deeds individually would arouse boredom – if not in military men, certainly in other refined readers among churchmen'.[52] Bower's comments here further indicate that he, and his intended audience, might not have found the deeds of worthy knights particularly relevant and that he did not wish to waste words describing them. In this instance, simply stating that Gordon had a fine knightly reputation was considered to be adequate.

Walter Bower did, however, expand upon what he perceived to be ideal knighthood. This was exemplified for the chronicler by Sir William Douglas of Nithsdale, who had earned his renown by 1385, although at this date he was still 'young in years'.[53] Bower described Sir William as 'a dark-skinned man, not very heavy but spare, gigantic in appearance, erect and tall, energetic and approachable, charming and amiable, generous and cheerful, reliable and clever.'[54] William Douglas's stature gave the impression of physical dominance and his energetic nature would have been suitably directed towards the battlefield where he surpassed all 'others in prowess, and [. . .] was indefatigable in harrying the English by land and sea'.[55] Douglas's function as a warrior was considered by Bower to be his most important accomplishment and he described William's prowess on the battlefield as exemplary.

> He was said to be so strong that whomsoever he had struck with a blow of his mace or sword or a thrust of his lance fell dead to the ground, or if protected by some kind of armour, fell on his back scarcely half alive.[56]

Given the level of description of William Douglas, an unusual digression for Bower, the chronicler was clearly using a source that had an interest in chivalric exploits. The source was one that he shared with Wyntoun, but Wyntoun's presentation of Douglas was not as elaborate as Bower's, suggesting that Bower may also have been influenced by additional sources.[57] Douglas's rep-

---

[51] *Ibid.*, book XV, 13.
[52] *Ibid.*, book XIV, 37, 38. The Pluscarden chronicler avoided describing acts of military prowess by simply writing of William Douglas, 'it would be impossible to recount and tedious to tell all the valiant and warlike deeds he achieved against the men of England'. *Chron. Pluscarden*, II, p. 209.
[53] *Chron. Bower*, book XIV, 48.
[54] *Ibid.*, book XIV, 48.
[55] *Ibid.*, book XIV, 48.
[56] *Ibid.*, book XIV, 48.
[57] Compare *Chron. Wyntoun*, VI, pp. 316–32 and *Chron. Bower*, book XIV, 48, 49. Wyntoun described Douglas as 'a man of great bounte,/Honorabil, wise, and richt worthi'. He also called him 'sturdy' and 'stowt'. *Chron. Wyntoun*, VI, pp. 225, 323. Fordun, Bower's main source, does not describe Douglas at all. Bower did use sources which it does not appear Wyntoun had access to. At XV, 5 and 6, Bower told a story of how a Scottish knight outwitted English knights in an after-dinner conversation, and described a joust between this Scottish knight and Sir Peter Courtney in February 1390. These episodes do not appear in Wyntoun's chronicle.

utation certainly seems to have been justified. He received pensions and cash grants for his service in the wars of the 1370s and 1380s and 'on account of his skill' in war he was given the earl of Carrick's 'beautiful' sister Egidia as his bride.[58] He was an active military leader during his father's attack on Lochmaben in 1384 and in 1388 Douglas attacked Carlingford, on the coast of Ireland, as part of a Scottish offensive.[59] He was also given the responsibility of overseeing the 1390 truce in the Borders.[60]

Throughout his chronicle, Bower avoided extended descriptions of knights and we are rarely privy to what he deemed to be good evidence of chivalric knighthood. He did, however, hold some strong opinions about knights who acted against the chivalric code and spoke out against Sir James Lindsay who committed a 'wrongful act' by changing 'from a knight to a tyrant' when he murdered Roger Kirkpatrick in his own home.[61] Other chroniclers, roughly contemporary with Bower, spent even less time discussing knightly qualities. The Pluscarden chronicler, who abridged Bower's work, remarked on knights in general that 'it is a good thing in warfare to act not always with valour and might, but sometimes with shrewdness and ingenuity'.[62] The Pluscarden chronicler did not expand upon much of Bower's commentary and he generally avoided describing any qualities of knighthood. In the early 1460s, the fragmentary *Auchinleck Chronicle* asserted that knights should be gentle and virtuous but dealt little with other desirable qualities.[63] Nevertheless, the role of the chronicler in the reportage of chivalrous deeds was regarded as essential, even as late as 1531. At this time, John Bellenden added a postscript to his translation of Boece's *Chronicles of Scotland* into vernacular Scots, writing

> Schew now quhat kingis bene maist viciouss,
> And quhay has bene of cheuelry the roiss,
> Quhay has thair realme in honoure maist reioss,
> And with thair blude oure liberties has coft.[64]

One of the purposes of the chronicle, according to Bellenden, was to educate knights on the desired codes of conduct.

> Schaw how young knychttis suld be men of were,
> With hardy spreit at euery ieoparde,
> Like as thair eldaris bene sa mony yere,

---

[58] *RMS*, I, 752, 753, 770; *Mort. Reg.* II, pp. 158–9; *Chron. Bower*, book XIV, 49; *Chron. Pluscarden*, II, p. 248; Brown, *Black Douglases*, p. 70.
[59] *Ibid.*, pp. 150, 173. The Pluscarden chronicler, abridging Bower's work, simply recorded that Douglas 'was a very celebrated and gallant warrior'. *Chron. Pluscarden*, II, p. 248.
[60] *Rot. Scot.*, II, p. 112; *CDS*, IV, 416; Brown, *Black Douglases*, p. 87.
[61] *Chron. Bower*, book XIV, 20.
[62] *Chron. Pluscarden*, II, p. 237.
[63] *Chron. Auchinleck*, p. 52.
[64] Edith C. Batho and H. Winifred Husbands (eds), *The Chronicles of Scotland Compiled by Hector Boece, Translated into Scots by John Bellenden, 1531*, STS (Edinburgh & London, 1941), II, p. 403.

Ay to defend thair realme and liberte,
That thai nocht be thair sleuth and cowardrye
The fame and honour of thair eldaris tyne.
Apprise ilk state into thair awyne degree,
Ay as thair in morall desciplyne.[65]

Bellenden's remarks demonstrate beyond doubt that these ideas were still considered relevant for inclusion in chronicles.

Chivalric Manuals

By the 1450s, chivalric manuals were being produced in Scotland. These were designed to set down very specific ideals and outline how a truly chivalric lifestyle could be achieved. Moreover, they presented objectives for the improvement of knightly conduct. In 1456 William Sinclair, earl of Orkney, commissioned Sir Gilbert Hay to translate Continental chivalric manuals at Roslin Castle, near Edinburgh. These were *The Buke of the Law of Armys, The Buke of the Ordre of Knychthede* and a further treatise, *The Buke of the Gouernaunce of Princis*, which appeared in Hay's manuscript in this order.[66] The juxtapostion of the *Law of Armys* and the *Ordre of Knychthede* was not Hay's innovation and the two works appeared side by side for the first time in a late-fourteenth-century manuscript, which may have been the source Hay used.[67] Of particular interest is that Hay did not translate these works literally and he added a significant amount of his own thoughts and opinions to the text.[68] Moreover, these manuals had strikingly different messages. The *Law of Armys* suggested ideas for making knights more efficient on the battlefield

---

[65] *Ibid.*, II, p. 408.
[66] Stevenson (ed.), *Gilbert of Haye's Prose Manuscript (A.D. 1456) Volume I.*, Glenn (ed.), *The Prose Works of Sir Gilbert Hay Volume III*, NLS Acc 9253. This was sometime before William Caxton translated these texts into English in 1483. NLS MS TD 209. For more on Continental martial manuals see Sydney Anglo, 'How to Kill a Man at Your Ease: Fencing Books and the Duelling Ethic', in Sydney Anglo, *Chivalry and the Renaissance* (Woodbridge, 1990).
[67] St John's College, Cambridge, MS 102; Mapstone, 'The Advice to Princes Tradition', p. 56.
[68] As yet no comprehensive study of the differences between the versions has been undertaken, which would be a useful tool in ascertaining precisely what Hay added to the works. Sally Mapstone spent part of her doctoral thesis exploring some of the differences between the translation of the *Buke of the Ordre of Knychthede* and the original, see Mapstone, 'The Advice to Princes Tradition', esp. pp. 88–99. Stevenson argues that at times Hay simplified and confused French syntax, Stevenson (ed.), *Gilbert of Haye's Prose Manuscript*, II, pp. viii–x, but Jonathan Glenn has pointed out that this is a difficult conclusion to draw unless we know which manuscript he translated from. He claims that Stevenson is misguided in his comments and editorial conclusions, as his own understanding of French text was poor. See Jonathan A. Glenn, 'Gilbert Hay and the Problem of Sources: The Case of the "Buke of the Ordre of Knychthede" ', in Graham Caie, Roderick J. Lyall, Sally Mapstone and Kenneth Simpson (eds), *The European Sun: Proceedings of the Seventh International Conference on Medieval and Renaissance Language and Literature, University of Strathclyde, 1993* (East Linton, 2001), pp. 106, 108.

and the *Buke of the Ordre of Knychthede* promoted knighthood, especially in times of peace, firmly within its social and civic setting.

Considering that these manuals were introduced to Scotland as part of an increased interest in the practices of chivalry, some value may also be obtained from looking at the role of Hay's patron. Richard Kaeuper has argued that literature was 'no simple mirror reflecting society, it is itself an active force', and it seems that the earl of Orkney's intentions in commissioning the translations were to bring revised and relevant ideas to knightly society.[69] In 1456, William Sinclair was Chancellor of Scotland. He had spent much of 1455 and 1456 engaged in James II's military campaigns against the Black Douglases and in his war with England.[70] James II's motivations and desire to wage war cannot be dissociated from the production of these chivalric manuals and Sinclair's relationship with the king further supports this. At the peak of his personal power and royal favour, Sinclair was clearly influenced by James's attitudes. The interest in the texts may also have been brought about by the period of civil and international conflict in which some of the cohesive values of noble society had been severely tested and possibly needed to be reasserted. Indeed, Sinclair may have been attempting to encourage renewed social order, perhaps in his capacity as Chancellor, after a period of great political instability.

Hay's translations were widely read in Scotland. Sally Mapstone suggests that they reached a more extensive audience in the fifteenth and sixteenth centuries than just those with access to Sinclair's library at Roslin. Between 1485 and 1490 additional copies were made for Sir Oliver Sinclair, son of William, earl of Caithness, a 'familiar knight' of James III.[71] Further copies may also have been made and Mapstone claims that Hay's later reputation and appearance by name in the works of William Dunbar and Sir David Lindsay of the Mount is ample evidence to prove that Hay's translations were well known and widely distributed throughout the country.[72]

The Buke of the Law of Armys, Honoré Bonet's French work of 1382, was a practical guide to warfare, concerned primarily with the laws of war and the position of the soldier in society.[73] Unlike many treatises which glorified knighthood, the work disapproved of some of the ideals of chivalric virtue. Sir Gilbert Hay's translation of the work also carried this tone, unsurprisingly given Hay's own knightly career. He had led a particularly military-based

---

[69] Kaeuper, *Chivalry and Violence*, p. 22.
[70] Crawford, 'William Sinclair', p. 232; Mapstone, 'The Advice to Princes Tradition', p. 66; *HBC*, p. 182; *Chron. Auchinleck*, p. 53.
[71] *RMS*, II, 1665; NLS MS TD 209; Mapstone, 'The Advice to Princes Tradition', p. 47.
[72] William Dunbar, 'The Lament for the Makaris', in Bawcutt (ed.), *William Dunbar*, p. 109; David Lindsay, 'The Testament and Complaynt of the Papyngo', in Hamer (ed.), *Works of Sir David Lindsay of the Mount*, I, p. 56; Stevenson (ed.), *Gilbert of Haye's Prose Manuscript*, p. xxiii; Mapstone, 'The Advice to Princes Tradition', p. 47.
[73] N.A.R. Wright, 'The "Tree of Battles" of Honoré Bouvet and the Laws of War', in C.T. Allmand (ed.), *War, Literature and Politics in the Late Middle Ages* (Liverpool, 1976), p. 14.

career, spending a considerable amount of time in France as a member of Charles VII's household, and his experience of war may have been extensive. Walter Bower recorded that Hay had been knighted by Sir Patrick Ogilvy of Auchterhouse in 1429, but Hay himself annotated a later copy of the *Scotichronicon* and made it clear that he was knighted by the French king.[74] Other knights who had served at the French court returned to Scotland with ideas promoting the latest chivalric fashions and ideas and the influence of these knights' experiences in France must be taken into account.[75]

The major points of which the *Law of Armys* disapproved were designed to promote ideas enhancing the knight's effectiveness on the battlefield, whilst rationalising chivalric qualities. The *Law of Armys* thus spoke out against the search for individual glory in combat. Praise for an act which was motivated by personal ambition was regarded as inappropriate. The *Law of Armys* warned:

> For suppose a knycht wald be sa hardy and sa presumptuous that he wald assailye ane hundreth knychtis him allane, that wald nocht be repute till him to the vertew of nobless, bot erar to fuliche hardiness and presumptuousnes.[76]

It was upheld that true boldness in a knight was derived from a proper understanding of the reason and justice of his cause (although these points are not expanded upon in the text), not from the base motives of vainglory, anger or fear of dishonour.[77] These ideas tied into wider notions of just warfare. Knightly violence was deemed acceptable by commentators when in the context of a war directed by the crown's interests. Commentators, on the basis of the greater purpose of the conflict, thus decided what was considered to be a praiseworthy act of violence.

The *Law of Armys* highlighted the tensions between the practice of warfare and chivalric knighthood. It stated that knights should not engage in spontaneous acts of individual prowess to show their 'great courage' although these were deemed central to proving oneself as a knight. The *Law of Armys* suggested that soldiers should instead stay with the host unless they had permission from their military commander.[78] This clearly ran counter to the ideals promoted in romance literature and epic poetry, where knights often leapt into combat without permission from their superiors. Whether or not knights

---

[74] *Chron. Bower*, book XVI, 16; Mapstone, 'The *Scotichronicon*'s First Readers', pp. 32–3; Forbes-Leith, *Scots Men-at-Arms*, I, pp. 43, 158; Stevenson (ed.), *Gilbert of Haye's Prose Manuscript*, pp. xxvii–xxviii.
[75] De Comminges (ed.), *Traité dur L'Art de la Guerre de Bérault Stuart*, see also MacDonald, 'Chivalry as a Catalyst', pp. 153–5, for a recent discussion of the French influence on Scottish literature.
[76] Stevenson (ed.), *Buke of the Law of Armys*, p. 84.
[77] *Ibid.*, pp. 82–4, 168; Wright, 'The "Tree of Battles" ', p. 18.
[78] Stevenson (ed.), *Buke of the Law of Armys*, pp. 114–16; Wright, 'The "Tree of Battles" ', p. 18.

upheld these prescriptions is debatable. However, commentators frequently addressed this problem. John Barbour, for instance, wrote of Bruce's anger when Colin Campbell was guilty of spontaneous prowess in Ireland. Bruce responded by hitting Campbell with a truncheon and saying, 'the breaking of orders can lead to defeat'.[79] By acting in a 'chivalric' way through seeking opportunities to display individual expertise on the battlefield, knights could earn renown and be 'written in the chronicles'.[80] Where the contradictions in the chivalric code lay, was that in some instances when they might pursue this course of action, they contravened the effective conduct of their commander's war.

Above all, the single most important quality a knight could display was loyalty. This was a theme that emerged in romance literature, the epic poetry of James III's reign, and Hay's manuals. The *Law of Armys* demanded that knights should be loyal to their lords.

> Sen it is sa that he has maid him athe, and gevin him his faith, than suld he stand with him to the utterest, and tak lyf and dede, and presoune and othir fortune, as it may cum till hand to sauf his honour and his lawtee, and for defens of justice and rychtwis querele.[81]

The *Law* also makes it clear that a knight's loyalty to the crown should override all obligations to any other lord.[82] This message had a special resonance for the Scottish political community in 1456. When James II, supported by Hay's patron Sinclair, attacked the Black Douglases, loyalty to the crown above all other loyalties was a key issue. Sinclair himself turned his back on the Douglas earls with whom he had so many links through kinship and marriage.[83] Emphasising this quality in the *Law of Armys* suggests that Hay's manual was providing not only a guide to the correct knightly behaviour during war, but also ideas for the reintegration of the traumatised knightly society.

The second treatise in Hay's manuscript is the *Buke of the Ordre of Knychthede*, a translation of Ramon Llull's late-thirteenth-century work. This was not a literal translation and Hay made substantial additions to the text.[84] The *Ordre of Knychthede* was predominantly concerned with the knight's relationship to the king and it opened with the story of a young squire who wanted to be made a knight. On his way to the dubbing ceremony, the squire

---

[79] Barbour, *Bruce*, Book XVI, lines 135–6.
[80] *Chron. Bower*, book XIV, 52.
[81] Stevenson (ed.), *Buke of the Law of Armys*, p. 87.
[82] *Ibid.*, pp. 113, 122–6; Wright, 'The "Tree of Battles" ', p. 18.
[83] See Brown, *Black Douglases*, p. 98, Genealogical Table 4.
[84] The Catalan original was 13,500 words, the French version, 17,000 words and Hay's version is 34,000 words. Mapstone, 'The Advice to Princes Tradition', p. 57; Kaeuper, *Chivalry and Violence*, pp. 275–80; Elspeth Kennedy, 'The Knight as Reader of Arthurian Romance', in Martin B. Shichtman and James P. Carley (eds), *Culture and the King: The Social Implications of the Arthurian Legend, Essays in Honour of Valerie M. Lagorio* (New York, 1994), esp. pp. 83–7.

met an ancient hermit knight who gave him a book of the codes and conducts of knighthood. He asked the young squire to distribute the book to those who wished to know more about the order that they would be joining. The old knight was introduced as an expert on chivalry and knighthood as

> be the nobless and the force of his noble and hie curage throu grete wisdome and hye gouernaunce – had auenturit his persone to pursue and manetene justis tournaymentis and weirs – and throu his gude fortune and prowess had opteynit grete honour and glore and victorious loving.[85]

The *Ordre of Knychthede* expressed concern that 'cheritee leautee justice and veritee was failit jn the warld' and set out to rectify this by outlining what was expected of a knight.[86] Knights were told that they should feel the privilege of their status and honour their postion by behaving in a noble way. The book warned that 'na suld nane be maid knychtis yat had contrarious condiciouns to that worthy and noble ordre'.[87]

Unlike the *Law of Armys*, the *Ordre of Knychthede* concentrated mainly on the privileged status of knights and their chivalric duties. Its stated purpose was to correct wayward knights through educating them and ensuring that new knights remained true to the order: 'thou yat art a knycht and will correk otheris defaultis correk thine awin faultis fyrst'.[88] The main advice for knights was that they were defined not only by their military function, but also by their place in society as paragons of chivalric virtue and qualities. The Christian component of knighthood was overtly emphasised and the *Ordre* makes it clear that 'first and formast knychthede was ordanyt to manetene and defend halykirk and the faith'.[89] The idea that the knight was bound to the Christian faith was also present in other fifteenth-century literature. In the 1440s, Walter Bower remarked that the sword was given to a knight 'when he was invested for the defence of the Church and its members'.[90]

Hay's *Ordre of Knychthede* also covered the qualities a knight should possess. It specified that a knight must hold all of the desired physical traits and all of the necessary personal qualities in order to be a true knight and not an enemy of knighthood.[91] Knights should be well ridden and should hunt and hawk, 'and sa mayntenand the office of the ordre of knychthede worthily'. Force was considered to be 'a grete vertu jn all noble actis'. Of qualities of the soul, wisdom, renown and discretion 'ar the ledaris and gouernouris of cheualrye' and prudence was considered especially important. Hay also esteemed charity, verity, loyalty, humility, faith and subtlety.[92]

[85] Glenn (ed.), *Buke of the Ordre of Knychthede*, p. 3.
[86] *Ibid.*, p. 8.
[87] *Ibid.*, p. 9.
[88] *Ibid.*, p. 23.
[89] *Ibid.*, p. 13.
[90] *Chron. Bower*, book XVI, 13.
[91] Glenn (ed.), *Buke of the Ordre of Knychthede*, p. 17.
[92] *Ibid.*, pp. 17, 20, 42, 41.

Quhen a knycht has all strenthis and habiliteis yat appertenis to the corps – and had nocht thame yat appertenis to the saule he is nocht verray knycht – bot is contrarious to the ordre and jnymy of knychthede.[93]

Within this text, the notion that the knight should not only be fit and able on the battlefield, but also a well-rounded man, seems to steer the definition of knighthood towards the humanistic ideals which were increasingly influential in later fifteenth- and early-sixteenth-century Scotland.[94]

Moral Literature

The qualities of knightly nobleness that were esteemed by writers such as Hay were tested to the full in James III's reign. Traditionally it has been argued that James III's political ineptitude was reflected in the moral and court poetry of the period.[95] However, what is more relevant to this study is the debate in this literature regarding the attributes that were admired and desired in the nobility. Questions were raised as to whether the quality of nobleness could be achieved without being of noble birth. This had a direct impact on knightly culture, as many of the qualities used to define nobility were inextricably bound up with the codes of chivalry. The traditional standards of chivalric prowess remained as knightly ideals, but the automatic association between them and the hereditary ethics of knightly society were challenged.[96] Under this pressure the nobility patronised literature which emphasised the associations between chivalry and nobility.[97] Amongst these texts were chivalric stories such as *Lancelot of the Laik*.

Some debate surrounds the dating of the anonymous translation of *Lancelot of the Laik*. The orginal editors argued that it dated to the late fifteenth or early sixteenth century. More recently Kindrick supported this view and argued that the *Lancelot* dated to the mid 1490s. Other scholars have convincingly argued that it dated to James III's reign and Sally Mapstone and John

---

[93] *Ibid.*, p. 17.
[94] For more on the humanist movement in Scotland see John Durkan, 'The Beginnings of Humanism in Scotland', *IR* 4 (1953), pp. 5–24; Mason, 'Laicisation and the Law', pp. 1–25; A.A. MacDonald, Michael Lynch and Ian B. Cowan (eds), *The Renaissance in Scotland: Studies in Literature, Religion, History and Culture Offered to John Durkan* (Leiden, NY and Köln, 1994); John MacQueen (ed.), *Humanism in Renaissance Scotland* (Edinburgh, 1990).
[95] Kindrick, 'Politics and Poetry', p. 40; Marshall W. Stearns, *Robert Henryson* (New York, 1949), esp. pp. 14–25, 106–29; Robert L. Kindrick, *Robert Henryson* (Boston, 1979), esp. pp. 19–22; Robert L. Kindrick, 'Lion or Cat? Henryson's Characterisation of James III', *Studies in Scottish Literature* 14 (1979), pp. 123–36; Steven R. McKenna, 'Legends of James III and the Problem of Henryson's Topicality', *Scottish Literary Journal* 17 (1990), pp. 5–20.
[96] Robert L. Kindrick, 'Kings and Rustics: Henryson's Definition of Nobility in *The Moral Fabillis*', in Roderick J. Lyall and Felicity Riddy (eds), *Proceedings of the Third International Conference on Scottish Language and Literature (Medieval and Renaissance), University of Stirling, 2–7 July 1981* (Stirling & Glasgow, 1981), p. 272.
[97] Moorman, *A Knyght There Was*, p. 97.

MacQueen have suggested that it may even have been earlier than this. The political content of the poem, especially when Arthur is given advice on good government, would seem to place the poem firmly in the 1470s or 1480s. Indeed, Bertram Vogel argues that as the content of the poem is so specific and apparently directed entirely at James III, it cannot have been written before 1482.[98] *Lancelot* is an adaptation of the French *Prose Lancelot*, detailing the relationships between Arthur and Lancelot, and Lancelot and Guinevere. In the Scottish version, the love component is notably absent, particularly the initial stages of Lancelot's love for Guinevere. One of the most prominent themes in the text is the criticism of Arthur's kingship and the Scottish poet amplified the advice on good governance from its French original. In *Lancelot of the Laik*, Arthur is explicitly criticised for not choosing his ministers carefully. Rich and poor subjects, he was told, were to be treated with equal consideration. The king must visit the various estates and towns of his realm and must interest himself in his people's welfare. He was told not to be proud or arrogant and that he must lavish gifts upon his tenants, vassals and the worthy poor.[99] These were all criticisms that were also directed specifically at James III, suggesting that there was a connection between the king and the translation of the poem. The poet may have chosen a traditionally chivalric romance as his vehicle for these ideas because it might also have highlighted James III's refusal to engage with chivalric ideology. Additionally, exposing these ideas in this text rehearsed the debate in a form with which the nobility might engage.

With the possibilities for increased social and financial mobility during James III's reign, the nobility was forced to find ways to preserve its social standing.[100] This concern may have been exacerbated by the behaviour of James III, who was extensively criticised for favouring 'low-born' men. This criticism had a wide variety of outlets, with satirical literature providing a powerful means of expression. The theme running through some of this literature was that those of noble and knightly status could not pursue activities appropriate to their social rank and function because they had to rectify the king's oversights and supervise the aspects of governance that he neglected. In the *Thre Prestis of Peblis* the king asks the barons why they were not abroad

---

[98] Gray (ed.), *Lancelot of the Laik*, pp. xxxv–xxxvi; Skeat, 'The Author of "Lancelot of the Laik" ', p. 1; Kindrick, 'Politics and Poetry', p. 52; Mapstone, 'Was there a Court Literature?', pp. 412, 420; MacQueen, 'The Literature of Fifteenth-Century Scotland', p. 193; MacQueen, *Ballattis of Luve*, p. xxv; Vogel, 'Secular Politics', pp. 8–10.

[99] *Ibid.*, p. 3. Similar criticisms were made in other 'chivalric' literature at the time: in 'Golagros and Gawane', Arthur is criticised, amongst other things, for his pride and arrogance. Walsh, '*Golagros and Gawane*', p. 93.

[100] Often members of the mercantile class could gain entry into lower-level nobility through being dubbed. See Scaglione, *Knights at Court*, p. 21; Robert Fulton, '*The Thre Prestis of Peblis*', *Studies in Scottish Literature* 11 (1973–74), p. 24. See J.H. Hexter, 'The Myth of the Middle Class in Tudor England', in J.H. Hexter, *Reappraisals in History* (London, 1961), who disagrees that there was a rise of the middle classes in the late-medieval period.

proving their might and performing noble deeds (the implication being that as men of knightly status they should be doing so). They responded that

> Your Justice ar sa ful of sucquedry,
> Sa covetous and ful of avarice
> That they your Lords impaires of thair pryce.[101]

The complaint was bitter and reflected a genuine social grievance caused by James III's ineffectual leadership. The nobles went on to argue that no matter how loyal a man might be to his king, he would be driven to extremes by capricious administration.

As much as the nobility may have been trying to reinforce the traditional conflation of noble status with virtues of chivalric knighthood, some commentators presented the argument that nobleness did not necessarily come from heredity. This was not a debate exclusive to the fifteenth century, nor to Scotland. During the thirteenth century, moves were made to establish that noble descent was a requirement of eligibility for knighthood; yet at the same time ideas were still being put forward that any man 'has a right to the title of knighthood who has proved himself in arms and thereby won the praise of men'.[102] The resurrection of these ideas towards the end of the fifteenth century indicates that these concerns were still relevant, but in a new social context. 'The Porteous of Noblenes' printed by Chepman and Myllar in 1508, but probably dating earlier than this, contributed significantly to this debate. The 'Porteous' listed twelve virtues of nobleness: faith, truth, honour, reason, worthiness, love, courtesy, diligence, cleanliness, largesse, soberness and perseverance.[103] The author clearly felt that these 'noble' virtues belonged naturally to those of noble birth. His message to the nobility was that they must realise the importance of these virtues and display them in their conduct, as these qualities were being readily attained by members of other social groups.[104] These ideas were still being questioned in the mid sixteenth century, when Dame Scotia said in the *Complaynt of Scotland*:

> ane person may succeid to heretage and to movabill guids of his predecessours, bot no man can succeid to gentreis nor to vertue; for vertu and gentreis most proceid fra the spreit of hym self, and nocht fra his predecessours.[105]

---

[101] T.D. Robb (ed.), *The Thre Prestis of Peblis, how thair tald thar talis: Edited From the Asloan and Charteris Texts* (Edinburgh & London, 1920), pp. 18, 19; Kindrick, 'Politics and Poetry', pp. 48–9; Fulton, 'The Thre Prestis of Peblis', pp. 23–46.
[102] E. Stengel (ed.), *Li Romans de Durmart le Galois* (Stuttgart, 1873), quoted in Keen, *Chivalry*, p. 80.
[103] 'The Porteous of Noblenes', in W.A. Craigie (ed.), *The Asloan Manuscript: A Miscellany in Prose and Verse written by John Asloan in the Reign of James the Fifth*, Vol. I (Edinburgh & London, 1923).
[104] *Ibid.*, p. 272.
[105] James A.H. Murray (ed.), *The Complaynt of Scotland with Ane Exortatione to the Thre Estaits to be Vigilante in the Deffens of Their Public Veil, 1549* (London, 1872), p. 150; Fulton, 'The Thre Prestis of Peblis', p. 27.

Dame Scotia does, however, insist on the righteousness of the social order in which other classes are subjected to the authority of the nobility and distinction between classes was still viewed as essential. Robert Henryson, on the other hand, was of the opinion that the quality of nobleness (the personal characteristic) was achievable by anyone from any social class. He expressed in many of his poems the idea that there was no inherent relationship between nobleness and high social position.[106]

Epic Poetry

Epic poems, with a markedly different agenda, were also produced during James III's reign. Blind Harry wrote the *Actis and Deidis of the Illustere and Vailyeand Campioun, Schir William Wallace, Knicht of Ellerslie* between 1474 and 1479, although by whom it was commissioned is not known.[107] Although Wallace is a knight this was not a chivalric tale of glorious knighthood but a story of warfare and violence between the Scots and the English. Harry's poem is also clearly a political commentary on his own time and it has been seen as a denunciation of James III's policy of peace with England.[108] The narrative is emotive rather than instructive and Harry's work is so intensely nationalistic that he is not concerned with the ideals and morals of the stories he relates, but instead with the feelings that the episodes evoke.[109]

This, in effect, renders the poem devoid of extensive commentary on chivalry or knightly behaviour. Blind Harry did not judge knights by their adherence to the codes of chivalric practice nor by their violations of it; instead he portrayed good knights as those who were loyal to Wallace because they were fighting for the right cause, thus implying that all of Wallace's enemies were not knights who should be considered worthy. Harry's use of adjectives to describe knights is constrained by his vernacular rhyming couplets. Given that the poet cannot have been describing the 'real' characters (as Wallace was executed in 1305), the qualities he listed must be viewed as those that were considered appropriate for knights to hold in the 1470s and 1480s.[110] Wallace

---

[106] Kindrick, 'Kings and Rustics', p. 281.
[107] Harry himself proclaims that no one paid him to write the poem. Blind Harry, *Wallace*, pp. 376–7; MacQueen, 'The Literature of Fifteenth-Century Scotland', p. 195; Matthew P. McDiarmid, 'The Date of the *Wallace*', *SHR* 34 (1955), p. 31. For more on Blind Harry's *Wallace* see Goldstein, 'Blind Harry's Myth of Blood', pp. 70–82; Grace G. Wilson, 'Barbour's "Bruce" and Hary's "Wallace": Complements, Compensations and Conventions', *Studies in Scottish Literature* 25 (1990), pp. 189–201.
[108] Kelham, 'Bases of Magnatial Power', p. 240; Macdougall, *James III*, pp. 269–70.
[109] Kindrick, 'Politics and Poetry', p. 44; Lois A. Ebin, 'John Barbour's *Bruce*: Poetry, History and Propaganda', *Studies in Scottish Literature*, 9 (1972), pp. 235–6.
[110] Harry clearly used earlier sources – see Blind Harry, *Wallace*, p. 168, where he writes of Sir Alexander Ramsay 'quhen it wes wer, till armes he him kest;/Wndir the croun he wes ane off the best:/In tyme of pees till courtlynes he yeid;/Bot to gentrice he tuk nayne othir heid./Quhat gentill man had nocht with Ramsay beyne;/Off courtlynes thai cownt him

was worthy, wise and 'wicht', he was kind, well taught, debonair and good looking.[111] Other knights were described as worthy, vigorous, hardy, wise, true and gentle.[112] Although many of his adjectives are alliterative, repetitive and formulaic, Harry's use of these phrases to describe his knights indicates that they did have meaning. These qualities were traditionally esteemed in the chivalric code and their appearance in the text represents the reinforcement of ideas of appropriate knighthood.

Wallace is often contrasted with 'false' knights, in this case the knights and squires who did not support the hero's cause. More often than not these episodes are designed to show his good, though rather elemental, characteristics and dedication to his goals. Early in the text when Wallace was fishing, he was approached by some Englishmen who attempted to steal the fish he had caught. Wallace appealed to their knightly charity, claiming that the fish were for an 'agyt knycht';[113] the Englishmen ignored his pleas and Wallace promptly drew out his sword and killed three of them. Wallace's actions were justified in two ways. Firstly, the men were not acting in a chivalric manner and thus Wallace's violence was a legitimate response. Secondly, they were English, and as such were Wallace's 'natural' enemies, and thus their deaths were acceptable. However, Wallace's violence was not always 'knightly'. In one episode he met the squire, Selbie, the son of the sheriff of Dundee, who habitually loitered around Dundee with 'thre men or four thar went with him to play'.[114] Selbie challenged Wallace because he was wearing green clothing, which Selbie considered to be too 'gay' for a Scot to wear.[115] Wallace immediately responded to these insults by stabbing and killing Selbie and his friends.[116] His impulsiveness and aggressiveness, which would have been appropriate in a battlefield context, contravened chivalric codes of conduct. Off the battlefield, chivalric knights were expected to display civil behaviour and as Wallace's actions here appear to be motivated by personal insult, his violence was not controlled by the chivalric ideal. However, Wallace's actions were presented to Harry's audience as honourable because they were motivated by his higher purpose and Harry himself may have viewed this type of violence as ideal. Unlike similar acts of irrational and extreme violence carried out by the young James Douglas in Barbour's *Bruce*, the Dundee episode was not part of Wallace's character development.[117] During the poem we do not

---

nocht a preyne./Fredome and treuth he had as men would ass;/Sen he begane na bettyr squier was.' This is clearly drawn from Wyntoun and Bower, who both wrote similarly of Ramsay. *Chron. Wyntoun*, VI, p. 147; *Chron. Bower*, book XIII, 47.
[111] Blind Harry, *Wallace*, pp. 7, 11, 102, 114, 116.
[112] See for example *Ibid.*, pp. 88, 159, 165, 263.
[113] *Ibid.*, p. 14.
[114] *Ibid.*, p. 8.
[115] *Ibid.*, p. 8.
[116] *Ibid.*, pp. 8–9.
[117] In an early episode of the *Bruce*, James Douglas killed the bishop of St Andrews' stableman because he insulted him. Barbour, *Bruce*, Book II, lines 134–9. By the end of the

find Wallace becoming a more refined knight and therefore Blind Harry's characterisation of him is not as a model of chivalric and courtly knighthood.

The story of Robert Bruce, another hero from the Wars of Independence, was also revived towards the end of James III's reign. Alongside the struggle for freedom from English oppression, loyalty was one of the key themes of John Barbour's epic poem the *Bruce*.[118] It is no coincidence that the only two surviving manuscripts of Barbour's poem date to 1487 and 1489, a time when loyalty to the crown was an issue at the heart of Scottish politics.[119] The *Bruce* was written around 1375 and the poem comprises a collection of episodic adventures.[120] These are brought together with the chivalric code and the pursuit of independence as a series of examples intended to instruct and inspire Barbour's audience.[121] The *Bruce* is largely an account of the lives and activities of Robert Bruce and one of his nobles, Sir James Douglas. Barbour intended that his audience view Robert Bruce as the ideal warrior king and James Douglas as the ideal knight and, consequently, the ideal loyal vassal.[122]

Barbour was not especially creative in describing the model attributes of his knightly characters: his extensive use of adjectives associated with them is often formulaic, repetitive and alliterative, a product of his use of vernacular rhyming couplets. Barbour constructed the linear and simplistic identities of his characters through the use of particular descriptions to emphasise to the audience which traits they embodied. He seldom uses individual terms excessively and he uses a variety of particularising adjectives.[123] His characters are uncomplicated by other features such as wives or romantic interests, civic duties or political aspirations; instead, they are designed specifically and definitively to be warriors, partial to large-scale warfare as much as one-to-one skirmishes, and they are always on the threshold of violent out-

---

poem, Douglas had learnt to control and channel his violence to chivalric and worthy pursuits.

[118] Barbour placed more emphasis on loyalty in the poem than any other single quality. Barbour, *Bruce*, Book I, lines 365–74; Ebin, 'John Barbour's *Bruce*', p. 224; McKim, 'James Douglas and Barbour's Ideal of Knighthood', p. 173; Kliman, 'The Idea of Chivalry', pp. 489–90. For more on Barbour's *Bruce* see Anne M. McKim, ' "Gret Price Off Chewalry": Barbour's Debt to Fordun', *Studies in Scottish Literature* 24 (1989), pp. 7–29; Wilson, 'Barbour's "Bruce" and Hary's "Wallace" ', pp. 189–201; Kurt Wittig, *The Scottish Tradition in Literature* (Edinburgh & London, 1958), esp. pp. 13, 26; Purdon and Wasserman, 'Chivalry and Feudal Obligation', p. 77; Bernice W. Kliman, 'John Barbour and the Rhetorical Tradition', *Annuale Mediaevale* 18 (1977), pp. 106–35.

[119] NLS Adv. MS 19.2.2, St John's College, Cambridge, MS G23.

[120] A.M. Kinghorn has argued that the *Bruce* is a romance, as Barbour calls it such, and it is a characteristically classical epic not historical. Lois A. Ebin says that it is a carefully planned narrative, neither chronicle written as a romance nor an epic. A.M. Kinghorn, 'Scottish Historiography in the 14th Century: A New Introduction to Barbour's *Bruce*', *Studies in Scottish Literature* 6 (1969), pp. 134–5; Ebin, 'John Barbour's *Bruce*', pp. 219–20. However, the *Bruce* is not a romance, as it contains no love component, but instead is an epic poem.

[121] Mason, 'Chivalry and Citizenship', pp. 57–8.

[122] Väthjunker, 'A Study in the Career of Sir James Douglas', p. 242; McKim, 'James Douglas and Barbour's Ideal of Knighthood', p. 169; Ebin, 'John Barbour's *Bruce*', p. 222.

[123] Kliman, 'John Barbour and the Rhetorical Tradition', pp. 31–3.

bursts. In this way the characters are only described in terms of the violent culture to which they belonged, the same culture from which Barbour's audience was drawn.

In general, Barbour gave his knights three types of qualities: physical, personal (of the soul), and those that were used on the battlefield (the traditional knightly attributes). Knights were esteemed if they were of fine bearing. The personal qualities they required were varied, but worthiness was the most commonly desired attribute for a knight to hold; other attributes that were esteemed were wisdom and generosity. Knights were also courteous, debonair, affectionate and loving, prudent, chivalrous, curious, noble, cunning, caring, cheerful, amicable, gentle, honest, stern and of good judgement. Qualities which were prized in knights on the battlefield included valour, boldness, courage, bravery, strength, powerfulness, sturdiness, manliness, distinction and prowess. A good knightly reputation was also considered to be important and Barbour often mentions that knights were of high renown, of great esteem and of good repute.[124] Barbour wrote 'when Bruce was pitted against three of his enemies that whosoever wins the prize in chivalry, be he friend or foe, men should speak faithfully of it. And assuredly, in all my life, I never heard tell, in song or verse, of a man who achieved great chivalry so vigorously.'[125] James Douglas reportedly believed that if he achieved 'great things, hard struggles and combats' his reputation would be doubled.[126]

> Even now I have heard it often said that he was so greatly feared then that when women wanted to scold their children, they would consign them with a very angry face to the Black Douglas, for in their reckoning, he was more dreadful than was any devil in hell. Because of his great valour and courage he was so feared by his foes that they were terrified by the mention of his name.[127]

Barbour wrote that 'those men should be highly esteemed who in their own day were bold and wise, who led their lives in great travail, and often in the hard press of battle won a great reputation for chivalry, who were free from cowardice'.[128] Sir Ingram Umfraville 'was famed for such great prowess, that he passed the rest in reputation; for that reason he always had carried about a red bonnet upon a spear, as a sign that he was set at the apex of chivalry'.[129] Umfraville was not a supporter of Bruce and Barbour's treatment of him must reflect a level of genuine admiration for Umfraville's knightly skills. A.A.M. Duncan also suggests that Barbour may have had access to a pro-English source that spoke of Umfraville in this way.[130]

[124] Barbour, *Bruce*, passim.
[125] Ibid., Book, III, lines 174–180.
[126] Ibid., Book I, lines 305–7.
[127] Ibid., Book XV, lines 558–65.
[128] Ibid., Book I, lines 21–6.
[129] Ibid., Book IX, lines 507–13.
[130] Ibid., pp. 28–30.

A good reputation, nevertheless, was not simply held by a knight for great military achievements, but for the display of a range of qualities. For Barbour the best knights distinguished themselves by their martial prowess, noble birth and the qualities of leadership they displayed.[131] Anne McKim has pointed out that Barbour's ideal knights are loyal and responsible towards each other and martial prowess was their most valued collective quality. This differs markedly from the knight of courtly romance who sought personal glory in the name of his lady through individual feats of arms. According to McKim, Barbour's ideal of knighthood was based more upon the rules governing the real practice of war than upon chivalric violence.[132] This may, in part, be due to Barbour's desire to record what he perceived to be historical accuracy, rather than to provide a set of exemplars. However, Archie Duncan, the most recent editor of the *Bruce*, argues that it

> is a poem about chivalry, about valour and fidelity, about personal qualities which secure the repute of a man without validation by his fighting for a corporate political destiny. As with other fourteenth century historical writings, the real enemy is not the other country or people, but cowardice and treachery.[133]

Barbour himself modified the practice of chivalry to fit with his stories. His greatest difficulty stemmed from having to present ideal knighthood with the realities of his subject matter.[134] So Barbour 'limited' the chivalric ideal to comply with his overall purpose. Bernice Kliman has pointed out that by doing so, Barbour's modified chivalry is

> truly significant, because while the courtly ideal bears the seed of its own decay in its all too elevated idealism, the ideal that Barbour describes is close enough a possibility to be capable of setting a standard for real behaviour. The heroes of Barbour's *Bruce*, the embodiment of practical chivalry, are models that the Scots could follow. By his skill he is able to transform chivalry, the ideal so loved by medieval men at least in theory, without blurring its essential outlines.[135]

---

[131] Matthew Strickland, 'Arms and the Men: War, Loyalty and Lordship in Jordan Fantosme's Chronicle', in Christopher Harper-Bill and Ruth Harvey (eds), *Medieval Knighthood IV: Papers from the Fifth Strawberry Hill Conference, 1990* (Woodbridge, 1992), p. 203; Sally North, 'The Ideal Knight as Presented in Some French Narrative Poems, c.1090–c.1240: An Outline Sketch', in Christopher Harper-Bill and Ruth Harvey (eds), *The Ideals and Practice of Medieval Knighthood: Papers from the First and Second Strawberry Hill Conferences* (Woodbridge, 1986), pp. 122–8.
[132] McKim, 'James Douglas and Barbour's Ideal of Knighthood', pp. 170–1. This view is supported by Bernice Kliman and Sonja Cameron. See Kliman, 'The Idea of Chivalry', p. 484; Sonja Cameron, 'Chivalry and Warfare in Barbour's *Bruce*', p. 14.
[133] A.A.M. Duncan, 'Introduction', to John Barbour's *Bruce* (Edinburgh, 1997), p. 13.
[134] Kliman, 'The Idea of Chivalry', pp. 478–9; Sonja Cameron, 'Chivalry and Warfare in Barbour's *Bruce*', pp. 13–14.
[135] Kliman, 'The Idea of Chivalry', p. 507.

Kliman argues that because Barbour modified but did not discard chivalry, he reconciled the contradictions between the reality of warfare and the idealism of the chivalric code.[136]

How, then, did Barbour present his modified version of chivalric knighthood? Sir James Douglas's importance in the poem as the 'ideal' knight has been explored by many scholars and much emphasis has been placed upon his role within the text. Douglas was developed as the ideal knight by the attention Barbour gave to the education and qualities of a good knight, the ideal knightly conduct and his criticism of vices opposed to this ideal.[137] Douglas was passionate, glad and jolly, and in his youth 'was up to such dissolute behaviour as nature expects of youth and [was] sometimes in low company', a stage which Barbour considers important to his education.[138] This idea was picked up by Sir David Lindsay of the Mount, who portrayed Squyer Meldrum's youth as a selfish, almost hedonistic, phase where he acted like a passionate, headstrong, heroic knight and, most essentially, broke some ladies' hearts.[139] Barbour described Douglas as worthy, generous, hardy, valorous, bold, good and strong. He was said to be of merit, courteous and debonair, cheerful, stout, honest, sweet, noble, and above all loyal.[140] Most of Douglas's actions in the poem take place on the battlefield and demonstrate his courage, his strength and his physical endurance.[141] For example, when he besieged Roxburgh and Jedburgh castles, Douglas made 'many attacks and showed feats of chivalry', and even Barbour says that his deeds were so many that he could not recount them all for there was so much to tell.[142]

There is, however, some question as to why James Douglas was so prominent in this narrative, especially as he never held as close a position to the king as Barbour suggested. A.A.M. Duncan attributes this to Barbour working from a voluminous source that described Douglas in such honourable and noble terms that the poet could not possibly exclude him from the story.[143] In his work on the Douglas family, Michael Brown says little about Barbour's routine treatment of James Douglas, pointing out that although Douglas had acquired and maintained a great deal of power in the south of Scotland, the

---

[136] *Ibid.*, p. 508; Mainer, 'A Comparison of Barbour's *Bruce*', p. 34.
[137] McKim, 'James Douglas and Barbour's Ideal of Knighthood', p. 167.
[138] Barbour, *Bruce*, Book I, lines 332, 333–5; McKim, 'James Douglas and Barbour's Ideal of Knighthood', p. 167; Mainer, 'A Comparison of Barbour's *Bruce*', p. 37.
[139] 'Historie of Squyer Meldrum', pp. 149–64.
[140] Barbour, *Bruce, passim*.
[141] For more on other literary heroes' battlefield actions see North, 'The Ideal Knight', pp. 121–2.
[142] Barbour, *Bruce*, Book X, lines 345–6.
[143] Duncan, 'Introduction', p. 14; Edington, 'Paragons and Patriots', p. 19. In her doctoral thesis, Patricia McRaven argues that the *Bruce* is not historically accurate but is 'conscious artistry'. 'It appears to represent deliberate manipulation of characters, events, and movement in time and space'. Patricia A. McRaven, 'John Barbour's Narrative Technique in *The Bruce*' (Ph.D., University of Iowa, 1979), pp. 6–7.

king favoured others as close counsellors.[144] Indeed, Douglas was not always a loyal vassal to Robert I – for example, on 15 May 1307 he considered submission to Edward I.[145] However, Brown does point out that between 1307 and 1315 Douglas became one of the most significant supporters of Robert I and he was usually the first knight to witness documents for him.[146] Whilst the poem may not have been an accurate reflection of Bruce and Douglas's relationship, Barbour's elevation of Douglas is significant.

Barbour clearly puts James Douglas forward as the ideal knight, but scholars are still arguing whether this characterisation is in accordance with fourteenth-century, or indeed fifteenth-century, notions of chivalry and knighthood.[147] Sonja Väthjunker concluded that Douglas was not the ideal knight because he did not behave in a chivalric way. This was because he often did not serve the king's interests, particularly in earlier episodes, but instead pursued his own cause. The Douglas Larder, for instance, is the most striking and appalling example of Douglas's capacity for vindictive violence, motivated entirely by his own agenda of regaining his rights to the lands of Douglas. Whilst Väthjunker argued that during the planning stages Douglas co-operated harmoniously with his vassals, and during the battle he demonstrated outstanding bravery:

> an episode such as the Douglas Larder [. . .] raises the question how 'knightly virtues' and the 'ideal of knighthood' are to be defined. The obvious recourse to the courtly code with its emphasis on serving a lady and on chivalrous combat is evidently of little use. Douglas serves not a lady but his king, and his methods cannot be called chivalrous by the longest stretch of the imagination.[148]

Väthjunker argues that even when Douglas responded to knightly challenges he did so with unchivalric military tactics. He did not fight for knightly honour – he fought to win. Väthjunker says:

> for these reasons, it is impossible to call Douglas an 'ideal knight' without redefining the concept of chivalry beyond recognition; the 'ideal subject', however, seems more appropriate in view of Douglas's services and his loyalty.[149]

However, Väthjunker does not identify the ideas for the recasting of chivalry contained within the text. Barbour did present a chivalric hero in Douglas but aspects of the codes of conduct were clearly ignored, as Barbour considered that they did not apply in encounters such as the Douglas Larder where per-

---

[144] Brown, *Black Douglases*, p. 26.
[145] *CDS*, II, 1979; Väthjunker, 'A Study in the Career of Sir James Douglas', pp. 37–40.
[146] Brown, *Black Douglases*, p. 17; Väthjunker, 'A Study in the Career of Sir James Douglas', p. 156.
[147] *Ibid.*, p. 21.
[148] *Ibid.*, pp. 177–8.
[149] *Ibid.*, p. 258.

sonal motivations outweighed others.[150] Moreover, Barbour was presenting what was, in his mind, an 'historically' accurate portrayal of Douglas, where contradictions in ethical codes were likely to occur. Indeed Douglas, like Harry's Wallace, demonstrated two types of violent behaviour. On the battlefield, especially against the English, his violence could be accepted as keeping broadly in line with appropriate knightly behaviour, but off the battlefield his 'uncontrollable' violence, especially when used in defence of personal honour or property, was not criticised by Barbour, and therefore must have been viewed as legitimate by him and his audience.

It has been argued by some scholars that the most traditionally chivalric knight in the poem is Sir Edward Bruce, King Robert's brother.[151] Lois Ebin has pointed out that Edward Bruce's character is designed to highlight the qualities in his brother and although Edward possessed the courage and strength of a knight, he does not have the corresponding prudence and wisdom essential to a king.[152] Edward Bruce is referred to by Barbour as hardy, valorous, generous, good, worthy, wise, strong, noble, chivalrous and bold.[153] However, Barbour strongly criticised Edward, particularly when he discussed his death. Ignoring better advice, Edward refused to wait for reinforcements when faced with a stronger enemy. Barbour presents this as an abandonment of a key part of chivalric knighthood, that is, that he should not pursue individual glory if it might be detrimental to the overall goal of winning.[154] Whilst Barbour claimed that Edward 'had a great desire to do deeds of chivalry always', the poet still presented him as more concerned with attaining individual glory, especially evident on the Irish campaign.[155] Kliman has viewed Barbour's characterisation of Edward less harshly and claims that Barbour simply presents him as 'human', arguing that Edward's major downfall was that he lacked wisdom and therefore at times acted foolishly.[156]

Court Poetry

The evident concern with the values of chivalry in literary works produced and reworked in James III's reign continued in the reign of James IV. James IV certainly seems to have patronised the production of literature reflecting ideal

---

[150] Kliman, 'The Idea of Chivalry', p. 484.
[151] Väthjunker, 'A Study in the Career of Sir James Douglas', p. 178. See also Kliman, 'The Idea of Chivalry', pp. 479, 507; Cameron, 'Chivalry and Warfare in Barbour's *Bruce*', p. 16.
[152] Ebin, 'John Barbour's *Bruce*', p. 223; Mainer, 'A Comparison of Barbour's *Bruce*', p. 45.
[153] Barbour, *Bruce, passim*.
[154] *Ibid.*, XVIII, lines 28–210; Väthjunker, 'A Study in the Career of Sir James Douglas', p. 179; Cameron, 'Chivalry and Warfare in Barbour's *Bruce*', p. 19. This is a point which the *Buke of the Law of Armys* also made. Stevenson (ed.), *Buke of the Law of Armys*, pp. 82–4.
[155] Barbour, *Bruce*, IX, lines 588–9; Purdon and Wasserman, 'Chivalry and Feudal Obligation', p. 81.
[156] Kliman, 'The Idea of Chivalry', p. 493.

knightliness and adherence to conventional chivalric codes. One interesting forum for the discussion of these themes was court poetry, the emergence of which was, in itself, a reflection of the increased importance of the royal court as a centre for cultural and social discourse. The knights at James IV's court would have almost certainly heard the poems of William Dunbar and Dunbar's attitude towards knighthood reflected what he saw around him. Dunbar's portrayal of knighthood in 'Fasternis Evin in Hell' has already been explored and it is clear from that poem that he thought that chivalric activities should be left to knights and that knights should be men who were noble and worthy. This outlook may have been a direct response to the criticisms that had flourished in the literature of James III's reign. Dunbar also indicated that knighthood was a responsibility that should only be undertaken by those fitted to that station.[157] Part of his justification for such opinions lay within his poems directed at the king. He explicitly lay down that 'men of armes and vailyeand knychtis' had a prominent place at court as the king's 'profitable' servants.[158] In other commentaries he remarked that life in Edinburgh was superior to that in Stirling because at the court in Edinburgh one could be in the company of lords and knights.[159] Dunbar also lamented the consequences of warfare in fairly conventional terms, observing that death was the only real victor in battles as knights were often killed.[160] However, these views were not usually upheld within knightly culture as death on the battlefield was regarded as preferable to any other.

Dunbar's opinions are most clearly seen in his poems on knightly men. 'Schir Thomas Norny', a mock eulogy of a member of James IV's household, was written some time between 1503 and June 1506. The poem itself described Norny in traditional knightly terms. Dunbar used the same alliterative and repetitive descriptions of knights as other writers, saying of Norny:

> Now lythis of ane gentill knycht,
> Schir Thomas Norny, wys and wycht,
>   And full of gret chevelry,
>   Quhais father was ane giand keyne;

---

[157] For Dunbar's background see Jean-Jacques Blanchot, 'William Dunbar in the Scottish Guard in France? An Examination of the Historical Facts', in Roderick J. Lyall and Felicity Riddy (eds), *Proceedings of the Third International Conference on Scottish Literature and Language (Medieval and Renaissance), University of Stirling, 2–7 July 1981* (Stirling & Glasgow, 1981).
[158] 'To the King', Bawcutt (ed.), *William Dunbar*, p. 283, lines 7, 10, 20.
[159] William Dunbar, 'The Dregy of Dunbar', in Bawcutt (ed.), *William Dunbar*, line 15. For more on this poem see Judith Ting, 'A Reappraisal of William Dunbar's *Dregy*', *Scottish Literary Journal* 14 (1987), pp. 19–36; Elizabeth Archibald, 'William Dunbar and the Medieval Tradition of Parody', in Roderick J. Lyall and Felicity Riddy (eds), *Proceedings of the Third International Conference on Scottish Language and Literature (Medieval and Renaissance), University of Stirling, 2–7 July 1981* (Stirling & Glasgow, 1981); Joanne S. Norman, 'Thematic Implications of Parody in William Dunbar's "Dregy" ', in Roderick J. Lyall and Felicity Riddy (eds), *Proceedings of the Third International Conference on Scottish Language and Literature (Medieval and Renaissance), University of Stirling, 2–7 July 1981* (Stirling & Glasgow, 1981).
[160] William Dunbar, 'The Lament for the Makaris', in Bawcutt (ed.), *William Dunbar*, p. 107.

>His mother was ane farie queyne,
>   Gottin be sossery.[161]

Dunbar paid tribute to chivalric verse but his ironic tone is apparent. He describes Norny as an excellent knight, in fact, 'ane fairar knycht nor he was ane' and says that he did many valiant deeds throughout Ross and Moray.[162] At feasts and weddings throughout the country, Norny won the prizes and the garlands, indicating that he participated in tournaments and was a champion jouster. Norny was a braver man than Robin Hood or Roger of Cleknishkleuch (of whom no records survive), and he was a better archer than Guy of Gisbourne and Adam Bell.[163] However, it is extremely unlikely that Norny was involved in any of the mentioned deeds, which gives Dunbar's mocking tone a greater emphasis.

Problems in identifying Norny are apparent as he appeared in official records styled both as a knight and as a fool. Although Priscilla Bawcutt argues that it was not impossible that he was both a knight and a fool, her view is extremely implausible. The treasurer's accounts record that Norny was generally called a 'fool' and was associated with the entertainers, but in four entries, on 9 August 1505, 12 October 1505, 18 March 1507 and 5 August 1512, he is referred to as Sir Thomas Norny.[164] James Kinsley has suggested an explanation for this discrepancy, positing that Norny's title was probably a short-lived joke initiated by Dunbar's poem. However, Kinsley only considers the entries of 'Sir' in the accounts of 1505 and 1507. He failed to include the 1512 example in his hypothesis, whereby it becomes apparent that the joke was not 'short-lived' at all.[165] Bawcutt has argued that some real-life incident may have provoked Dunbar's poem. Alternatively, Bawcutt further suggested, if two men shared the same name, the joke might lie in deliberately confusing one with the other. This again seems rather unlikely. The most attractive possibility she offered was that Norny the fool acted the part of a knight in some entertainment or was knighted in a mock ceremony at a court event.[166] Elizabeth Eddy also argued convincingly that Norny was a fool and the poem stemmed from James IV's taste for elaborate practical jokes. One such joke was the provision of incongruously dignified attire for entertainers.

---

161 'Schir Thomas Norny', in Bawcutt (ed.), *William Dunbar*, no. 31, stanza 1, p. 162.
162 *Ibid.*, line 7, p. 162. Dunbar's use of irony might also be seen in this reference to Ross and Moray, as Norny's chasing of the Catterans and Highland ghosts among those 'dully glennis' might not be considered to be knightly.
163 *Ibid.*, lines 19–21, 25–7, 31–3, 38–40, p. 163. Although Adam Bell is called Allan in the poem, see Bawcutt's notes, p. 385. Adam Bell appears in the exchequer accounts in 1506. *ER*, XII, pp. 432, 695, 696, though not styled as a knight. See also *RMS*, II, 1600, 2800.
164 *TA*, III, pp. 155, 166, 375, IV, pp. 184, 358.
165 James Kinsley (ed.), *The Poems of William Dunbar* (Oxford, 1979), p. 300; Bawcutt, *Dunbar the Makar*, p. 60.
166 *Ibid.*, p. 60; Bawcutt (ed.), *William Dunbar*, p. 161.

For instance, a doctor's gown and hood was created as a costume for the fool John Bute, presumably to wear in some court spectacle.[167]

Throughout the poem Dunbar played on the fool/knight theme. He reported that a man called Quentin had called Norny a foul chamber pot and had said that he was a lecherous bull, but Dunbar argued that Quentin's claims were unfounded because Norny was a wise and worthy knight.[168] Dunbar, also reporting that Quentin would have made Norny a court jester, himself says

> I pray to God better his honour saiff
> Na to be lychtleit swa.[169]

Dunbar compared Norny with the court jester, Curry, and wrote that Norny had never dirtied his saddle in his life, whereas Curry had befouled two.[170] This motif is similar to that which Dunbar used in the soutar and the tailor's tournament poem where the tailor 'left his sadill all beschittin' after jousting.[171] Dunbar did favour scatological terms, playing on the primal joke of the undignified nature of the human body, and images like this are common in his comic poetry.[172] He clearly used this example to show that those who were not brave, noble and worthy knights became afraid when acting as a knight: if Curry had twice shown his lack of suitability for such pursuits, then Norny must have been a true knight as he had never done such a thing. The comparison between Norny and Curry may also have been a reference to their treatment at court. Although Curry was the senior court jester, Norny was treated with considerable favour by James IV and he was obviously more popular with him. Curry and Norny seem to have been clothed to the same standard, for example both receiving red and yellow coats. Norny's cost more, however, at twenty-seven shillings, while Curry's cost just over twenty shillings.[173] Dunbar further emphasised the fool/knight joke in this poem, writing that at every Easter and Christmas

> I cry him [Norny] lord of evere full
> That in this regeone dwellis.[174]

This was a clear reference to the Feast of Fools which was traditionally held at Christmas.[175] Dunbar finished his poem by saying that this renowned knight

---

[167] *TA*, III, pp. 301, 308; Bawcutt, *Dunbar the Makar*, p. 59; Elizabeth Eddy, 'Sir Thopas and Sir Thomas Norny: Romance Parody in Chaucer and Dunbar', *Review of English Studies* NS 22 (1971), pp. 401–9.
[168] 'Schir Thomas Norny', stanza 7, pp. 163–4.
[169] *Ibid.*, lines 44–5, p. 164.
[170] *Ibid.*, lines 46–8.
[171] 'Fasternis Evin in Hell', line 191, p. 188.
[172] Eddy, 'Sir Thopas and Sir Thomas Norny', p. 408.
[173] *TA*, II, p. 321, III, 143, 186.
[174] 'Schir Thomas Norny', lines 50–1.
[175] Anna Jean Mill, *Medieval Plays in Scotland: Thesis Submitted for the Degree of Ph.D. of the University of St Andrews, July 1924* (Edinburgh & London, 1927), p. 17.

'wanttis no thing bot bellis', inverting the situation and allowing Norny to revert to his true position of fool.[176]

In 1508 the arrival of Sir Bernard Stewart allowed Dunbar to discuss chivalric ideals in more straightforward and conventional terms. In 'The Ballade of Barnard Stewart', the famous knight was praised for his 'chevalry' and compared to the heroes of classical antiquity, Achilles, Hector, Arthur, Agamemnon, Hannibal and Caesar.[177] Dunbar's association of Stewart with these figures is an interesting variation on the cult of the Nine Worthies. Joshua, Judas and David, the biblical captains of the Israelites, were left out by Dunbar, along with Alexander, Charlemagne and Godfrey de Bouillon. Achilles, however, was a new addition. Hector, Achilles, David and Alexander appeared along with Absolon, Hercules and Samson in another of Dunbar's poems, 'Quod tu in cinerem reverteris', so the author was familiar with both the Worthies and the heroes of classical mythology.[178] His modification of the traditional Worthies may have been a result of the increasing emphasis on and familiarity with classical history during the Renaissance, but in that case Alexander's exclusion may be problematic.[179]

Through his treatment of Stewart, Dunbar indicated what he held as precious commodities in a knight. Bellicosity, ability in the field, renown, nobleness, adventurousness, doughtiness, lineage, valiant actions and energy were all qualities which Dunbar emphasised and he claimed that Stewart was

> most cristin knight and kene,
> Most wise, most valyand, moste laureat hie victour.[180]

As Dunbar welcomed Stewart home he wrote:

> Welcum, in stour most strong, incomparable knight,
> The fame of armys and floure of vassalage,
> Welcum, in were moste worthi, wyse and wight.[181]

> Welcum, thow knight moste fortunable in field,
> Welcum, in armis moste aunterus and able
> Undir the soun that beris helme or scheild.[182]

Dunbar called Stewart, 'the prince of knightheyd and flour of chevalry', a common term for writers to use for knights who had displayed martial

---

[176] 'Schir Thomas Norny', line 54.
[177] 'The Ballade of Barnard Stewart', stanza 8, p. 223; see also MacDonald, 'Chivalry as a Catalyst', p. 163.
[178] 'Quod tu in cinerem reverteris', in Bawcutt (ed.), William Dunbar, p. 144.
[179] See MacDonald, Lynch and Cowan (eds), The Renaissance in Scotland, for essays covering a broad range of literature influenced by the Humanist movement, and Mason, 'Laicisation and the Law', pp. 1–25. There is a noticeable absence of references to the Worthies in sixteenth-century histories. See for example, Buchanan who mentions only Arthur, History, I, p. 243–8.
[180] 'The Ballade of Barnard Stewart', pp. 223, 226, lines 3–4, 89–93.
[181] Ibid., p. 223, lines 9–11.
[182] Ibid., p. 224, lines 41–3.

prowess and won themselves great renown.[183] He also paid tribute to Stewart's military achievements:

> Prynce of fredom and flour of gentilnes,
> Sweyrd of knightheid and choise of chevalry,
> This tyme I lefe, for grete prolixitnes,
> To tell quhat feildis thow wan in Pikkardy,
> In France, in Bretan, in Naplis and Lumbardy.[184]

To an extent Dunbar was giving an accurate portrayal of Stewart who had won some renown as captain of the Scots guards in France and who had excelled himself in the Italian wars. He also commemorated Stewart's death and he claimed that Stewart was:

> In deid of armes most anterous and abill,
> Most mychti, wyse, worthie and confortable.[185]

Dunbar requested that:

> Complaine sould everie noble valiant knycht
> The death of him that douchtie was in deid,
> That many ane fo in feild hes put to flight,
> In weris wicht be wisdome and manheid.[186]

He finally suggested that Stewart was the epitome of the ideal knight:

> The prince of knychtheid, nobill and chevilrous,
> The witt of weiris, of armes and honour,
> The crop of curage, the strenth of armes in stoir,
> The fame of France, the fame of Lumbardy,
> The schois of chiftanes, most awfull in airmour,
> The charbuckell cheif of every chevelrie?[187]

Dunbar's opinions here reinforced views of chivalric knighthood, where the emphasis on good knighthood lay predominantly in his abilities in war. Bernard Stewart's promotion as a 'military' knight may have been part of James IV's focus on more conventional chivalric duties, especially as Dunbar's poems were written around the time of the 1508 tournament of the Wild Knight and the Black Lady.

Dunbar's status at court and central role in the promotion of early-sixteenth-century Scottish chivalry was built on by his successor Sir David Lindsay of the Mount. Lindsay was not only a court poet for James V, but also central in the practical expressions of chivalry as Snowdon Herald and later Lyon King of Arms. Lindsay held a great deal of authority over chivalric

---

[183] *Ibid.*, p. 223, line 18.
[184] *Ibid.*, p. 225, lines 81–5.
[185] 'Elegy on Barnard Stewart', lines 4–5.
[186] *Ibid.*, lines 9–12.
[187] *Ibid.*, lines 19–24.

matters and wrote extensively about the society in which he lived. From his works it is apparent that knighthood was still important and that chivalry was ever present. Carol Edington has remarked that

> much ink has been spilled debating the extent to which chivalry animated lay culture in this period, but it seems clear that, in Scotland at least, the ethos exerted a powerful hold. Within this context, the royal court was the prime focus for the most elaborate and impressive expressions of chivalric mores.[188]

Indeed, Lindsay's chivalric expertise was made manifest not only in his *Armorial* but also in his poems, such as the 'Historie of Squyer Meldrum', which describes at considerable length a tournament and a variety of heroic, chivalric deeds.[189]

Like Dunbar, Lindsay felt that chivalric activities should be left to those of knightly rank. Lindsay's 1538 'Iusting of Watsoun and Barbour' made it clear that jousting and tournaments were only a suitable pursuit for those who were members of knightly society.[190] In the same way as Dunbar approached the topic, Lindsay pitted two stereotypical members of the lower classes against each other in a duel. Failing in a spectacular way to prove their worth in the lists, Lindsay's basic point remained that they could not overturn the natural social order.[191] As a member of the knightly ranks, Lindsay's stance differed from Dunbar's in one essential way – whereas Dunbar was observing this behaviour at court, Lindsay had a vested interest in preserving the exclusivity of knighthood. But from this position Lindsay could also be the most critical of knighthood. He recognised that military might was limited and suggested a number of situations where physical prowess was futile.[192]

However, like Dunbar, Lindsay still framed his writings on knights in the military arena. 'The Historie of Squyer Meldrum', for instance, was written around 1550 and its hero, William Meldrum of Cleish and Bynnis, was a close, personal friend of the poet. This poem was written in memory of Meldrum after his death and is a tribute to his adventures as a soldier in 1513, in Ireland and France, and his much-troubled love affair with Lady Gleneagles.[193] The poem is based on allegedly real episodes of Meldrum's life, but it is heavily weighted towards his 'knightly' exploits. We enter Meldrum's life when he is twenty years of age and watch him kick up a storm in tales of knight-errantry, only to find him quickly back in Scotland, in love with Lady Gleneagles and in

---

[188] Edington, *Court and Culture*, p. 102.
[189] *Ibid.*, p. 103.
[190] 'The Iusting of Watsoun and Barbour', in Hamer (ed.), *Works of Sir David Lindsay*, I, pp. 114–16.
[191] Edington, *Court and Culture*, p. 116.
[192] 'The Deploration of the Deith of Quene Magdalene' in Hamer (ed.), *Works of Sir David Lindsay of the Mount*, I, p. 108, lines 64–70.
[193] Hamer (ed.), *Works of Sir David Lindsay*, IV, pp. xxxiii, 186.

the fast lane to social responsibility and 'gentlemanly' behaviour.[194] Lindsay was clearly familiar with the construction of chivalric romances and he plunders these to incorporate practically every motif imaginable: the rescue of a maiden, victory against all odds, the prophetic dream, the sleepless lover, the dawn walk and the feminine lament over the fallen hero.[195] We are left wondering why Lindsay was resurrecting these seemingly outdated chivalric themes. If it was part of a nostalgic desire to reinstate the traditional values of chivalry, then Lindsay did himself no justice. His works betray the developments in Scottish chivalry and make it apparent that in the sixteenth century physical skill was no longer enough. Indeed Meldrum's personal development might reflect Lindsay's wider observations on the maturation of Scottish chivalry.

Lindsay's description of Squyer Meldrum at the outset of the poem does not even take into consideration the qualities which had become 'essential' for knights from the later fifteenth century. Meldrum is described as being of noble descent and

> Proportionat weill, of mid stature,
> Feirie, and wicht, and micht indure,
> Ouirset with trauell, both nicht and day,
> Richt hardie baith in ernist and play,
> Blyith in countenance, richt fair of face,
> And stude weill ay in his Ladies grace;
> For he was wounder amiabill,
> And, in all deidis, honorabill.[196]

Absent from this description are any notions of his personal qualities – those which would have been approved by humanists. Indeed, this description, mildly reminiscent of the description of William Wallace by Blind Harry, focused only on the qualities that would have made Meldrum a great fighter. Whilst effectively promoting conventional knightly skills, Lindsay was, in fact, heavily criticising this way of life.

Later in his career Lindsay became increasingly uneasy with the traditional chivalric tenets. He became anxious to play down the chivalric and martial elements of training for social leadership. Carol Edington remarked that:

> The cult of chivalry had always represented a somewhat uneasy alliance between an aggressive individualism on the one hand and a sense of social responsibility on the other: the lone knight-errant in search of adventure was hardly the best guardian of public order. It is perhaps significant that in Scotland individual achievement and bravery were often downplayed in favour of Christian obligation toward the community. For Lindsay, though, this

---

[194] Edington, *Court and Culture*, pp. 122, 124.
[195] Ibid., p. 122; Riddy, *'Squyer Meldrum'*, p. 26.
[196] 'Historie of Squyer Meldrum', p. 148, lines 67–86.

sense of social responsibility was expressed in the language of the commonweal rather than that of chivalric morality.[197]

This was apparent in 'Squyer Meldrum' where he did not reject chivalric ideology outright but incorporated some of its fundamental concepts into a new understanding of social responsibility. Fyndlaw the Fute Band, the comic knight of Lindsay's 'Satyre of the Thrie Estaitis', boasts of his bravery on the battlefield but is the first to flee at Pinkie Cleugh. At the very end of the play, however, his real purpose becomes clear during Folie's diatribe against war, which places Fyndlaw and everything that he implies in the context of humanist disillusion with militarism.[198] This development offered Scots an alternative manner of viewing and expressing traditional notions of service. No longer was the stress upon duty to a military overlord (or even to the lady of chivalric romance); in Lindsay's work heroes were to be found in the local community, administering justice, dispensing charity, and generally ensuring public well-being. This was very much an observation of contemporary knighthood.

Edington has concluded in her work on Lindsay that he 'dechivalrised' the knightly ideal by emphasising ideas that had been expressed earlier by the likes of Sir Gilbert Hay and William Dunbar, namely that military skill was not enough. Lindsay, however, made these ideas far more apparent in his works, assisted perhaps by the acceptance and belief in humanist ideals. Lindsay was uncomfortable about many of the aspects of Scottish chivalric ideology, but appreciated the stress it laid upon the common profit.

> He therefore sought to isolate and to elevate this particular tenet of the knightly code, thereby providing a revised pattern for secular achievement and one more appropriate for men of his own social background [. . .] Lindsay [. . .] attempted 'dechivalization' of the knightly ideal, the elements of martial prowess, courtly love, and elaborate ceremonial being stripped away to leave the core concepts of justice and public service relocated in the commonweal.[199]

Edington has suggested that the answer to the problem of how the knight developed into the Renaissance courtier might lie in this change: humanism was not solely responsible for these developments and it is clear that 'the impulse for change also lay within traditional chivalric thinking'.[200] The way in which Lindsay's 'Squyer Meldrum' uses and discards chivalric romance is an acknowledgement of the growth in the sixteenth century of new evaluations of the place of the knight in society.[201]

---

[197] Edington, *Court and Culture*, p. 122.
[198] Riddy, *'Squyer Meldrum'*, p. 26.
[199] Edington, *Court and Culture*, p. 122.
[200] *Ibid.*, p. 122.
[201] Riddy, *'Squyer Meldrum'*, p. 36.

Chivalry in Scottish Literature

In European literary traditions, knights were bold and vigorous on the battlefield, loyal to the king, inspired by their love for a lady and defended the Christian faith. These ideas were also apparent in the literature produced in late medieval Scotland, but to varying extents. The degree to which they were present differs between authors and the genre in which they were writing. From what we have seen of the literature produced outside the romance genre, knights were usually portrayed in their warrior role. The adjectives describing their qualities were largely associated with this function. In some texts, however, there was an increasing emphasis on qualities of the soul and the ability of the individual to function in peacetime society. It was no longer adequate for a knight to be good with a sword alone – he also had to perform other tasks and duties that required more than brute force. This was apparent in literary descriptions of knights such as Sir Patrick Ogilvy of Aucherhouse, whom Bower described as 'a man of acute mind, distinguished speech, manly spirit, small in stature, but notable and trustworthy in every kind of upright behaviour'.[202] This change, moreover, was also seen in 'real' descriptions of knights. The squire John Paston wrote in a letter of 1472 that Thomas Boyd, earl of Arran, was, amongst other things, courteous, gentle, wise, well spoken and the most perfect knight. He was only attributed with one military characteristic, which was that he was a good archer.[203] The implication in this description is that during the fifteenth century the emphasis on purely martial qualities changed markedly. To an extent, Dunbar's poetry reflected a re-emphasis on and celebration of the martial skills of a particular knight, but the humanist ideals were well entrenched in knightly society by this time and they are never far removed from his writings.

Loyalty was a major theme of most of the works and Christian consciousness is also evident. Courtly love, at first glance, seems distinctly absent.[204] Although Dunbar wrote that 'lufe makis knychtis hardy at assey', in most of the texts reviewed knights did not fight for the love of a lady but for their king.[205] Nevertheless, there is evidence from the literature of the fifteenth century to indicate that courtly love as an inspiration for martial prowess was a recognised theme in Scottish chivalry. James I, himself, presented his love for Joan Beaufort in largely courtly terms. He described how he suffered for his love before he had proved himself and won her.[206] According to Wyntoun, at

---

[202] *Chron. Bower*, XVI, 26.
[203] Gairdner (ed.), *Paston Letters*, V, p. 144.
[204] Mainer, 'A Comparison of Barbour's *Bruce*', pp. 39–40, 74.
[205] William Dunbar, 'A Lusty Lyfe in Luves Service Bene', in Bawcutt (ed.), *William Dunbar*, line 83.
[206] Walter W. Skeat (ed.), *The Kingis Quair Together with A Ballad of Good Council by King James I of Scotland* (Edinburgh & London, 1884), pp. xiii, 46, 47.

the siege of Dunbar, William Montague fought for the love of a lady and was reported to have said:

> This is ane of my ladyis pynnis;
> His amouris to my hert [th]us rynnis.[207]

A similar theme was illustrated by John Comyn and Simon Fraser at the battle of Roslin in 1302. They spoke directly to their men, saying:

> And als for our lemmannys luf
> Off pres yhit apayit we pruff.[208]

John Barbour wrote that 'love is such a great strength that it makes light of all suffering, and often gives strength and such power to easy-going men that they can endure great tribulations and not give up, come what may'.[209] He also described the siege of Douglas castle where Sir John Webiton was killed.

> When he was dead [...] they found in his purse a letter sent to him by a lady whom he loved and would serve. The letter was in the following terms, saying that when he had guarded for a year in war, as a good bachelor, the hazardous castle of Douglas, which was so dangerous to keep, and had managed it well, in every way, then he could ask a lady for her love and her service.[210]

So the idea was present in some texts, but it was not used to move the story forward and it was not the goal of a knight's actions. The theme was indeed explicitly identified and rejected in the *Wallace*. Although Wallace fell deeply in love, he viewed the feeling as potentially distracting to his mission. Eventually he surrendered to his feelings but his wife was subsequently killed. This served to fuel Wallace's hatred for the English and his goals became refocused.[211] Perhaps due to the increase of interest in traditional or 'Arthurian' chivalry promoted by James IV and James V, the love theme re-emerged in works of the early sixteenth century. In the 1537 'Deploration of the Deith of Quene Magdalene', courtly love elements are apparent. James V is alleged to have been distraught at his inability to save Madeleine's life:

> The potent Prince, hir lustie lufe and knicht,
> With his most hardie Noblis of Scotland,
> Contrair that bailfull bribour had no micht.
> Thocht all the men had bene at his command,
> Of France, Flanderis, Italie, and Ingland,

---

[207] *Chron. Wyntoun*, VI, p. 82.
[208] *Ibid.*, V, p. 339.
[209] Barbour, *Bruce*, Book II, lines 523–30.
[210] *Ibid.*, Book VIII, 488–98.
[211] Blind Harry, *Wallace*, pp. 92–3, 96, 116–17; Elizabeth Walsh, 'Hary's Wallace: The Evolution of a Hero', *Scottish Literary Journal* 11 (1984), pp. 13–14.

> With fiftie thousand Millioun of tresour,
> Mycht nocht prolong that Ladyis lyfe ane hour.[212]

The themes were similarly apparent in the 'Historie of Squyer Meldrum', where Lindsay evidently pays significant tribute to courtly love.[213] But he also showed discomfort with the use of courtly love and rejects outright an important component of Arthurian romance by suggesting that the relationship between Lancelot and Guinevere, held up as the epitome of the courtly love ideal, was in fact little more than a sordid, adulterous liaison.[214] Thus whilst writers and their audience were clearly familiar with the ideals of courtly love, Scottish writers outside the romance genre did not consider that it fitted with their presentation of knighthood. Knights were first and foremost warriors and the preoccupation of love was something of a distraction.

The main genres of literature reviewed here all reflect differing views on what 'ideal' knighthood constituted and how chivalry might be expressed in practice. There are, however, some trends that are apparent throughout the texts. Over the course of the century, the emphasis on military qualities as being the most prominent requirement of good knighthood was augmented by a desire to see knights embody certain peaceable and civic qualities as well. However, the two main 'bloodthirsty' and martial works, the *Bruce* and the *Wallace* were written nearly a century apart, and their emphasis on qualities in warriors must be viewed as distinct from any developments in chivalric ideals. Instead, the vernacular verses were written primarily as entertainment for men of violence in their own terms. Nevertheless, the other literature dealing with chivalric ideology forced a modification of the ideals of knighthood, taking into account social changes and the relative decline of their primacy on the battlefield. Literature proved itself to be the forum where new ideas about knighthood could be asserted. The texts generally show that chivalric ideals were still relevant in the fifteenth and early sixteenth centuries and that they could be manipulated to suit changing social and political needs. In many ways, the texts were also modified, particularly during translations and adaptations, to suit the new social and political objectives. The Scottish texts were not entirely typical of their various genres as they were adapted very carefully to make criticisms of the practice of chivalry and at times of the crown being unwilling to support chivalric society. James IV's increasing engagement with chivalry brought the expression of these ideas into the royal court and influenced the type of images being presented. By the end of the fifteenth century it was firmly established that the ideal knight needed to incorporate a wide range of qualities and that skills on the battlefield alone were no longer adequate. The redrawing of the image of the knight

---

[212] 'The Deploration of the Deith of Quene Magdalene' in Hamer (ed.), *Works of Sir David Lindsay of the Mount*, I, p. 108, lines 64–70.
[213] 'Historie of Squyer Meldrum', pp. 149–51.
[214] Edington, *Court and Culture*, p. 123; 'Historie of Squyer Meldrum', pp. 147–8, lines 48–64.

as an ideal warrior, an administrator and a courtier, indicates that general social changes did have an impact on knightly society. More importantly, this literature reveals the qualities that should be held by the type of knight who was thought to be appropriate and useful in the service of the crown. These were not changes just imposed by the king, of course, but part of a wider reassessment of the way in which society functioned.

CHAPTER SEVEN

The Crown's Use of Chivalry

James I, 1424–1437

During the fifteenth century the Scottish chivalric ethos developed and was revised to fit the varying social and political climates. Each king used chivalry in their own way for their own goals.

In 1424 James I returned to Scotland after eighteen years as a hostage in England. In the years prior to his release James had been exposed to the lavish displays and use of chivalry and knighthood at the English court of Henry V. For many, Henry was the epitome of the ideal medieval king. He embodied a number of desirable knightly qualities, having a reputation for prowess in arms and success in warfare.[1] Moreover, he was the leader of his knights and ruled his kingdom with this in mind. When James reached the age of twenty-five, Henry's attitude to his royal prisoner changed and he began to treat him more as if he were a foreign visitor to his court: in 1420 James even accompanied Henry to the siege of Melun in France.[2] After they returned to England, Henry's queen, Catherine, was crowned on 23 February 1421. At the coronation banquet, held at Westminster Hall, James was seated on her immediate left, demonstrating his high status at court and allowing him to be a close observer of proceedings.[3] In March 1421, Henry began a tour of the major towns of England, a demonstration of his royal authority, and James accompanied him as a guest of honour. It was whilst on this tour that Henry dubbed James at Windsor Castle on St George's Day, carefully articulating that James was more than just a prisoner and that his royal status was a consideration in his treatment by the English king.[4] By July 1421 James and Henry were back in France where James spent another year assisting Henry in his

---

[1] G.L. Harriss, 'Introduction: the Exemplar of Kingship', in G.L. Harriss (ed.), *Henry V: The Practice of Kingship* (Oxford, 1985), pp. 19–20.
[2] Wylie and Waugh, *Reign of Henry the Fifth*, p. 212.
[3] *Ibid.*, p. 269. There is no indication that there were any knightings at this ceremony.
[4] John Shirley, 'The Dethe of the Kynge of Scotis', in Lister M. Matheson (ed.), *Death and Dissent: Two Fifteenth-Century Chronicles* (Woodbridge, 1999), p. 25; Wylie and Waugh, *Reign of Henry the Fifth*, pp. 270–1. For James's knighting see NA E.101.407.4, 17. James was not made a Knight of the Order of the Garter, although the Order's annual meeting took place on this day at Windsor. See Shaw (ed.), *Knights of England*, I, p. 10, where James would have been listed if he had joined the Order.

military campaigns.[5] After prolonged negotiations James finally returned to Scotland in early 1424, undoubtedly with an increased awareness of how he too could use knighthood to create a strong kingship and further his political goals.[6]

James's coronation was a display of restored royal prestige and power following years under the Albany regency, with its primary intention being to emphasise the king's leadership of a politically united kingdom.[7] Alasdair MacDonald supports this idea and claims that James I attempted to assert his authority on his return by engaging in chivalric ritual similar to that which he had witnessed in Henry V's court. One such demonstration was the dubbing of new knights.[8] MacDonald describes the return of James I to Scotland in 1424 as the start of innovations and developments effected by the 'dynamic new ruler with personal experience of life'. He claims that James's cultivation of chivalric attitudes and his subsequent attempt to implement a royal monopoly on knighthood was part of these new departures.[9]

As previously discussed, James I made a number of new knights at his coronation at Scone on 21 May 1424.[10] Bower recorded the names of twenty-five men whom James knighted although only eighteen of them actually received the honour at this time. These men were prominent nobles of the kingdom and included Alexander Stewart, son of the duke of Albany; Archibald Douglas, earl of Wigtown and son of the fourth earl of Douglas; William Douglas, earl of Angus; George Dunbar, earl of March; Adam Hepburn of Hailes; Thomas Hay of Yester; David Stewart of Rosyth; Patrick Ogilvy of Auchterhouse, sheriff of Angus; John Red Stewart of Dundonald; David Murray of Gask; John Stewart of Cardney; William Erskine of Kinnoul; William Hay of Errol; John Scrymgeour, constable of Dundee; Walter Ogilvy of Lintrathen; Herbert Herries of Terregles; Alexander Ramsay of Dalhousie, and

---

[5] Wylie and Waugh, *Reign of Henry the Fifth*, pp. 326–7, 358.
[6] In February 1424, approximately sixty hostages for the king and other nobles met James on his release at Brancepeth, near Durham. *CDS*, IV, 941, 942; *Rot. Scot.*, II, p. 245. For more on the hostages see Michael Brown, *James I*, p. 40; *Rot. Scot.*, II, pp. 242, 244; *CDS*, IV, 942, 947, 948, 950, 952, 954; and for a discussion on the monetary worth of nobles see A.A.M. Duncan, *James I King of Scots, 1424–1437* (Department of Scottish History, University of Glasgow, 1984), esp. p. 7.
[7] Brown, *James I*, p. 48.
[8] MacDonald, 'Chivalry as a Catalyst for Cultural Change', pp. 151–2; Jennifer M. Brown, 'Introduction', in Jennifer M. Brown (ed.), *Scottish Society in the Fifteenth Century* (London, 1977), p. 5. David II did knight some 'nobles of the kingdom of Scotland' at his coronation in 1331, so the practice was not unheard of in Scottish coronation ceremonies. See *Chron. Fordun*, II, p. 346. However, Robert II and Robert III do not appear to have done so at their coronations, although the evidence for what went on in these assemblies is hardly full. See *Chron. Bower*, book XIV, 36, book XV, 1.
[9] MacDonald provides little evidence to support this assertion, and his study concentrates mainly on the reigns of James III and James IV. MacDonald, 'Chivalry as a Catalyst of Cultural Change', pp. 152–3. Indeed, James's father, Robert III was heavily criticised for being a politically insecure and weak monarch, particularly in his relations with his magnates. See Boardman, *Early Stewart Kings*, esp. 'Conclusion: The Kindly King', pp. 302–13.

William Crichton of that Ilk. These men were all drawn from the upper nobility and most of them were hereafter employed in the crown's service in diplomatic, administrative or military roles. A significant point of this communal ceremony was to bind these men together in a formal and honorific sense. An underlying component of this unification through the bonds of knighthood was the control of factional dissent. Indeed, James's choice of men to dub was dictated by his desire to ensure political stability now that he had returned and to assert his royal authority, and he clearly knighted these men to ensure that they would be loyal to him. According to Fionn Pilbrow, in England the king rewarded service rather than solicited it. The mutual chivalric culture of king and nobility centred on loyal service to the king and the monarch was required to recognise prowess and virtue exercised in his service.[11] However, the political circumstances in Scotland meant that the king really had to use all the devices available to him to retain and encourage loyalty, particularly in James I's case when he had been absent from the country for such a long period of time.

James used similar tactics at the baptism of his twin sons in 1430 and he dubbed the sons of men over whom he wished to reassert his control, including sons of Archibald, fifth earl of Douglas; Sir James Douglas of Balvenie; Simon Logan of Restalrig; James Edmonstone of that Ilk; Sir William Crichton; and Sir William Borthwick.[12] The fifth earl of Douglas and Sir William Crichton had both been knighted by the king at his coronation. By binding their sons together James made the clear political message that he sought to tie these men to the crown and reassert his bonds with them. As a result this reinforced his power base in the Lothians. When James I dubbed his nobles he gave the honour to ensure political allegiance and bind the recipients to his lordship. The situations in which he bestowed these knighthoods suggest a highly politicised agenda, understandably so, given his prolonged absence from his kingdom. His actions were expressed in the only way that the social norms could allow, through the conventions of courtly culture. Hence the bestowal of knighthood placed James's nobles clearly and unquestionably in a context which they understood and to which they could respond appropriately. James did not knight these men for show and he did use them in high status positions at court as well as in their traditional military capacity.

[10] *Chron. Bower*, book XVI, 2; *Chron. Pluscarden*, II, p. 279.
[11] Pilbrow, 'Knights of the Bath', pp. 209–10.
[12] *Chron. Bower*, book XVI, 16, and notes p. 365; Brown, *James I*, p. 117. Simon Logan's father, Robert Logan of Restalrig, is thought to have died on 6 March 1440 and since the John who was knighted in 1430 is not found as the lord of Restalrig until 25 October 1444, Bower may have known Simon as holder of the estate between 1440 and 1444 before he wrote this passage, although Simon has commonly been thought to have predeceased Robert. Stephen Porcari came from a noble family of Rome, employed in the services of Popes Martin V and Eugene IV. He was captain of Florence in 1428. His visit to Scotland was followed by visits to France and Germany before returning to Rome in 1431. *Chron. Bower*, book XVI, 16, notes p. 364.

James I deployed his knights on military campaigns, as he had witnessed at the English court. By 1428 he had succeeded in intimidating a great number of the Scottish nobility and, to an extent, the political climate had stabilised. Alexander, Lord of the Isles, however, remained outside royal control and James set about trying to force Alexander to pay homage to him.[13] James called on the military service due from the nobles, especially those who stood to benefit territorially or politically from the campaign. Along with their own retinues, Alexander Stewart, earl of Mar; Sir James Douglas of Balvenie; Sir Alexander Keith; Sir John Forrester of Corstorphine; Sir Walter Ogilvy of Lintrathen; Patrick Ogilvy of Auchterhouse; John, earl of Buchan; Sir William Douglas, earl of Angus; Alexander Ogilvy; Sir David Stewart; and John Brown of Midmar were all members of the expedition to the Highlands. Some of these men had been personally knighted by James I and were clearly being called upon through this bond.[14] Michael Brown argues that this group was James's personal entourage rather than a full host, since the king had only called on east-coast burghs to provide contingents and provisions. Brown also suggests that James was not planning an open conflict as he had taken the queen with him.[15] Indeed, when James met Alexander at Inverness at the end of August 1428 no battle took place, although they had both brought large armies with them.[16] Instead James seized the Lord of the Isles, imprisoned him, and arrested 'nearly all of the notable men of the north'.[17] The knights accompanying James were given little opportunity to display their martial ability and had essentially served as an impressive and intimidating force behind the king. However, some managed to achieve strong chivalric reputations throughout their careers, such as Sir Patrick Ogilvy of Auchterhouse who 'was very highly regarded by the king and his subjects', and 'was a man of acute mind, distinguished speech, manly spirit, small in stature, but notable and trustworthy in every kind of upright behaviour.'[18]

After negotiations with James I, Alexander was released from royal custody in 1429, but he did not fulfil his promises and in spring 1429 he rebelled against the king by attacking Inverness.[19] In response to this James again raised a host, significantly larger than the one he had led in 1428.[20] The

---

[13] *St A Cop.*, no. 26, pp. 48–53; Tanner, 'The Political Role of the Three Estates', pp. 50–1. James's plans were not greeted enthusiastically and he held a general council to discuss them. According to Michael Brown only Alexander Stewart, earl of Mar, and Walter Stewart, earl of Atholl, supported him. Brown, *James I*, p. 96, see also Brown, 'Regional Leadership in North-East Scotland', pp. 40–1 for Mar's motivations.
[14] *RMS*, II, 109–15.
[15] *APS*, II, p. 17; *ER*, IV, p. 473; Brown, *James I*, pp. 96–7.
[16] *Chron. Bower*, book XVI, 15.
[17] *Ibid.*, book XVI, 15; Brown, *James I*, p. 97.
[18] *Chron. Bower*, book XVI, 26. In the early years of the fifteenth century many knights had achieved chivalric reputations through bold and valiant deeds on the battlefield, including Archibald Douglas, fourth earl of Douglas, Alexander Stewart, earl of Mar, and Sir John Swinton.
[19] *Chron. Bower*, book XVI, 16; *ER*, IV, pp. 516, 634; Brown, *James I*, pp. 100–1.

crown's tenants-in-chief were required to attend by their annual forty-day obligation and included in his host were Archibald, fifth earl of Douglas; William, earl of Angus; Alexander Lindsay, earl of Crawford; Sir Walter Haliburton of Dirleton; Sir Alexander Seton of Gordon; Sir William Crichton of that Ilk; Sir Adam Hepburn of Hailes; William Borthwick; and Sir Walter Ogilvy of Lintrathen; along with Walter Davidson; Sir William Forbes; and his brother Alexander, lord of Forbes, who was one of the earl of Mar's closest supporters and a close councillor of James I.[21] Again, many knights in this party had been personally knighted by the king and it is clear that James was calling upon the services of men whom he could trust, but who were also bound to him through the lord-knight ties. Like the 1428 campaign, there is no evidence that there was a general call-out of infantry forces. Instead this appears to be a force of noble retinues who would have been more mobile because they were horsed and who would thus have been more likely to find and engage the Lord of the Isles' forces.

James did not, however, take his knights' service without any recognition of their contribution. Indeed, after the encounter at Badenoch he granted Sir William Forbes the lands of Kynnaldy, Gordy, Davach, Manach, Petnamone and Knochsoul *pro servitio ejus* in the highlands.[22] James also punished those who had not undertaken their promised service and in parliament of March 1430 legislation was passed against deserters from the royal host. This was especially directed at the king's lieges who had taken payments, which James I had been forced to grant, but who had not served on the campaign.

> It is ordanyt anent the matar of the kyngis legis that warnyt war and schargyt to pas with hyme in the northt cuntre aganys hys rebellouris and bade at hame withowtyne the kyngis leife or turnyt agayne be the way withowtyne lefe or tuk payment and held it [at] thar awne oyse and made na serwys tharfor that the Justice sal mak a dyt within thar Justrie and punyst thaim that ar fawtise as the caus requeris the baronys makkande requestis to the kynge for thar lywyss that beis conuikkyt.[23]

---

[20] *Ibid.*, p. 102.

[21] *RMS*, II, 127. Sir Alexander Seton of Gordon did not just serve on this campaign for James, but also because he was a close adherent of the earl of Mar. Being a member of Mar's retinue, he owed him military service. Brown, 'Regional Lordship in North-East Scotland', pp. 36–7, 40–1; *ER*, IV, p. 510; *RMS*, II, 55–9, 127. Walter Bower provides a contemporary account of the 1429 campaign. However, he does not report on who was involved in the expedition, recounting only that James I was faced with Alexander's force of ten thousand men from Ross and the Isles, *Chron. Bower*, book XVI, 16.

[22] *RMS*, II, 127.

[23] This act does not appear in the printed *APS* under the March 1430 parliament, although it does appear identically at c. 3 of the parliament held at Perth on 15 October 1431. *APS*, II, p. 20. However, Croft Dickinson thinks the legislation was probably enacted at the 1430 parliament, as it was the first parliament held after James's successful campaign, although a general council had been held in October 1429 directly after the success in the Highlands. W. Croft Dickinson, 'The Acts of Parliament at Perth, 6 March 1429/30', *SHR* 29 (1950), p. 9; Tanner, 'The Political Role of the Three Estates', p. 56.

The problems with desertion by paid lieges made the knight's service even more attractive, as the crown could rely on the codes of honour-based mutual exchange which knighthood esteemed.[24] The 1456 *Law of Armys* made it clear that 'na man of armis [should] leve the ost under payne of dede'.[25] Desertion from the host, however, remained a problem that all kings faced. The serious defeat at the battle of Flodden (Northumberland) in September 1513 has been attributed to a loss of significant numbers of the host after the siege of Norham (Northumberland) in the August prior to the battle.[26] By all assessments the host expected that they could go home after Norham as they had done their work and only plunder was left to be retrieved.[27] Although the crown's reliance upon a body of knights who owed military service was crucial, as warfare changed and arsenal developed, the skills that the chivalric code esteemed were no longer enough. Instead Scottish knights adapted to these changes by acquiring new skills.

Before the arrival of guns in Scotland, James I had been concerned with keeping the level of skill of the able-bodied men of his realm relatively high, especially in essential arts like archery. James had been witness to the English use of archers in Henry V's war-making, where archers could make up towards two-thirds of the English army.[28] In his first parliament in May 1424, James decreed that all boys over twelve should practise archery and would be fined if they did not. Practice targets were ordered to be setup near parish churches and in every ten pounds' worth of land. In March 1426 parliament declared that all yeomen were to be sufficiently 'bowit' at wapinschawings.[29] In the 1440s Bower wrote that:

> There was certainly one statute among the others which the king [James I] issued that was most useful for the kingdom and the public interest, namely

[24] James made his favouritism of knights and their prestige apparent at the same parliament, setting sumptuary statutes against 'ordinary' men dressing in silk or fur without his permission. Parliament specified that the only men entitled to do so were knights and lords of two hundred merks of yearly rent and their eldest sons and heirs, legislation designed to reinforce social prestige. *APS*, II, p. 18. Whilst it is difficult to ascertain which knights and lords were worth this amount, in 1424, David Ogilvy and David Menzies were valued at two hundred English marks, (worth significantly more than Scots merks) Alexander Seton, lord of Gordon, was valued at four hundred marks, whereas the earl of Atholl was valued at one thousand, two hundred marks, Thomas earl of Moray at one thousand marks, and William Douglas, the son and heir of the lord of Dalkeith, at one thousand, five hundred marks. *CDS*, IV, 952; *Foedera*, X, p. 327.
[25] See Stevenson (ed.), *Gilbert of Haye's Prose Manuscript*, pp. 114–16.
[26] W. Mackay Mackenzie, *The Secret of Flodden, with 'The Rout of the Scots', a Translation of the Contemporary Italian Poem La Rotta De Scocesi* (Edinburgh, 1931), p. 48; *Edin. Recs.*, I, p. 143.
[27] Macdougall, *James IV*, p. 273.
[28] According to Matthew Bennett, at Agincourt in 1415 archers made up to four-fifths of the army. Matthew Bennett, *Agincourt 1415: Triumph Against the Odds* (London, 1991), p. 18. See also Stewart, *Henry V*, pp. 70, 99.
[29] *APS*, II, pp. 6, 11. Similar legislation was passed by James II in 1456, by James III in 1481 and by James IV in April 1491, when parliament declared that football and golf should be forbidden, and butts erected in the parishes for archery and shooting practice. *APS*, II, p. 226.

that the archer's art should be practised by nearly everybody, at least on feast days, under threat of fixed money fines, with targets for shooting prepared and erected in every village, especially at the parish churches,[30]

confirming that the parliamentary legislation was practised throughout the kingdom. Bower, however, criticised the developments in warfare and decline of archery in the 1440s claiming that:

after and as a consequence of his [James I's] sad death, nearly everyone gave up bows and archery equipment without a thought, and devoted themselves to riding with lances, with the result that now at a meeting for magnates you [usually] find out of one hundred men some eighty lances and scarcely six archers. For this reason the English can now truly say about the Scots: 'The bow of the brave has been overcome'; and we in turn say of them: 'and the weak have been equipped with strength.' You should therefore read the old chronicles if you will, and you will find that the English have often beaten the Scots by means of their bows.[31]

Whilst archery is not traditionally considered to be a knightly skill, there is ample evidence to suggest that in Scotland it was practised by knights. Robert Bruce reportedly used the bow of one of his squires to defend himself against three of his enemies while he was in Carrick.[32] Sir Thomas Boyd, earl of Arran, was considered the 'fayrest archer' by English knights and indeed James I himself was reputed as the 'best of archers'.[33] More convincingly, James, second Lord Hamilton, a prominent participant in tournaments throughout James IV's reign, won the prize for the best archer on horseback or on foot at the tournament of the Wild Knight and the Black Lady in 1508, proving that amongst jousting with swords, spears and axes, archery also had a place in Scottish chivalric sports.[34] Of course, knights were not involved in the initial onslaught of arrows at the start of a battle or siege, nor were they part of archers' formations, but it remains that Scottish knights saw fit to prepare themselves in all the arts of warfare.

Walter Bower's view that archery should not be abandoned was part of his contribution to the ongoing international debate on the legitimacy of war. Like other commentators, Bower generally warned against military careers, particularly in favour of a life devoted to religion. He tells the story of Waltheof, later abbot of Melrose, and his older brother Simon.

When the brothers were children, they understood, behaved and played as children do. Simon the elder boy was in the habit of collecting little twigs

---

[30] *Chron. Bower*, book XVI, 15.
[31] *Ibid.*, XVI, 15. This is the only explicit comparison made by Bower between James I's reign and the 1440s. For more on this see Michael Brown, ' "Vile Times": Walter Bower's Last Book and the Minority of James II', *SHR* 79 (2000), pp. 165–88.
[32] Barbour, *Bruce*, Book V, 582–657.
[33] Gairdner (ed.), *Paston Letters*, V, p. 144; *Chron. Bower*, book XVI, 28.
[34] Pitscottie, *Historie*, I, p. 243.

and branches to build a castle to his own little design, and mounting his horse or steed, and grasping and brandishing a little stick like a lance, he painstakingly engaged in pretend warfare with boys of his own age based on the guarding and defending of a make-believe and imaginary castle. But Waltheof as a small boy made buildings like churches out of small sticks and stones, and stretching out his hands played the part of a priest celebrating mass; and because he did not know how to pronounce the words, he used to utter sounds in imitation of the chant. The boys would often indulge in this game, and they would cause many people to watch and laugh. On one occasion a certain wise monk who was standing and watching with the others said to the onlookers: 'What do you make of this children's game?' They declared that he was merely a simpleton, in that he was one of those who cannot tell their right hand from their left. He said: 'Not so, not so! For this game acts as a kind of prelude that foretells the life and end of each boy. For the first will entangle his life with warfare until his death, while the second will live as a monk and crown his days with good.' None of these words went unfulfilled.[35]

Bower's stories and commentaries contributed to the wider theological and social discussions that had been brought about by the introduction of guns in warfare.[36] The decline of the use of bows and the dwindling of the need for cavalry necessitated the need for knights to adapt to the changing technologies on the battlefield and Scottish knights embraced this new technology. The question remained that if war was the playing field for chivalrous knights, was it possible for knights to display their worth once guns had become the main siege weapons?

The first time guns were used in Scotland to any significant extent was in 1436 during the siege of Roxburgh.[37] James was confident in the ability of his guns to take the castle. He had hired specialised gunners and artillery workers

---

[35] *Chron. Bower*, book VI, 5. For a discussion on Jocelin of Furness's *Life of Waltheof* see Derek Baker, 'Legend and Reality: The Case of Waldef of Melrose', in Derek Baker (ed.), *Church, Society and Politics: Papers Read at the Thirteenth Summer Meeting and the Fourteenth Winter Meeting of the Ecclesiastical History Society* (Oxford, 1975). One English commentator warned his son against a military career saying that 'he that sets up his rest to live by that profession can hardly be an honest man or a good Christian'. Quoted by J.R. Hale, 'War and Public Opinion in the Fifteenth and Sixteenth Centuries', *Past and Present* 22 (1962), p. 23.
[36] *Ibid.*, p. 21. Hale argues that the influence of commentators heralding the defence of the bow was limited to England. p. 30. However, Bower clearly subscribed to similar views.
[37] *Chron. Bower*, book XVI, 15; *Chron. Pluscarden*, II, p. 287; David H. Caldwell, *Scotland's Wars and Warriors: Winning Against the Odds* (Edinburgh, 1998), p. 49. Guns were normally made of wrought iron, and many were loaded by wedging a separate chamber with the powder and shot at the breech end. This meant that guns could achieve a good rate of fire by having more than one chamber for each, but it meant there was a weakness in their design by having a join in the barrel where the powder exploded. In the second half of the fifteenth century guns began to be made with cast bronze which was much stronger and they fired metal shot which created a bigger force than the wrought iron guns. By 1474 James III was casting bronze guns in Edinburgh. Caldwell, *Scotland's Wars and Warriors*, pp. 49–50, 53; Geoffrey Stell, 'Late Medieval Defences in Scotland', in David H. Caldwell, *Scottish Weapons and Fortifications, 1100–1800* (Edinburgh, 1981), p. 39.

from Germany, whom he placed under the command of Johannes Paule, Master of the King's Engines.[38] The host which James gathered was large and Walter Bower recorded that all men between the ages of sixteen and sixty were summoned to the army to assist in the attack, a typical call-to-arms.[39] Bower's account of the siege informs us that over two hundred thousand horsemen and as many foot soldiers were counted.[40] Although this was a gross exaggeration, the knightly presence was obviously strong. One commentator reported that Robert Stewart of Atholl, a squire and the king's cousin, was made the constable of the host.

> for [th]is same Robart Stuard aboode euyre in [th]e kingez presens, fulle famulyer abowte hym at all owrez & most prive aboue al o[th]er, & was a ful ientiel squier, ffresche & lusti & right amyable, whome [th]e king entierly louyd as his owne sune, & for [th]e tendre love [th]at he had to him he made hym conestable for al his oost at [th]e seege of Edinburgh [Roxburgh].[41]

In Michael Brown's opinion, this promotion of a young and inexperienced squire to such a senior role in the borders may have caused significant hostilities between the king and his magnates, and especially with the earl of Douglas and the earl of Angus, who as wardens of the Marches would have had grounds to feel demoted. Both Douglas and Angus had military experience and extensive local interests and may have resented Robert Stewart's authority.[42]

James I's use of his knights in a military capacity might also have extended to their participation in tournaments and jousting. Although the treasurer's accounts for this period no longer exist, and if extant might have suggested a number of tourneys, the king is only recorded to have held one tournament in October 1433 at Perth.[43] However, James was reputed as a 'knowledgeable jouster' and it is likely that he paid some attention to this aspect of chivalric

---

[38] *ER*, IV, pp. 677, 678, 679, 680. James had received military engines and armour from Flanders specifically for Roxburgh. Bower reports that in 1430 James had a huge brass bombard gun brought from Flanders, with an inscription around its girth in gold lettering saying: 'For the illustrious James, worthy prince of the Scots./Magnificent king, when I sound off, I reduce castles./I was made at his order; therefore I am called "Lion" '. *Chron. Bower*, book XVI, 16.

[39] Sir Harris Nicolas (ed.), *Proceedings and Ordinances of the Privy Council of England* (London, 1835), IV, pp. 310–13; Brown, *James I*, p. 162; *Chron. Bower*, book XVI, 26. The only legitimate absentees from the host at Roxburgh were 'shepherds and keepers who out of necessity of for legal reasons had to be excused'.

[40] Bower obviously exaggerated these numbers, as they seem impossibly large.

[41] Both surviving manuscript versions make the error of recording the siege as at Edinburgh, but they should read Roxburgh. Shirley, 'The Dethe of the Kynge of Scotis', p. 32.

[42] Brown suggests that the disaffection with James, leading to his murder in 1437, may have begun here, as his reliance upon foreigners and close familiars who had limited military experience, especially in what was essentially a border campaign, may have caused political tensions between the March magnates and royal authority. Brown, *James I*, p. 164.

[43] *ER*, IV, p. 561; *Chron. Bower*, book XVI, 23; *Chron. Pluscarden*, II, pp. 285–6; Tanner, 'The Political Role of the Three Estates', pp. 75–6; Tanner, *Late Medieval Scottish Parliament*, pp. 58–9.

life.[44] Nevertheless, if, as we suppose, he was influenced by Henry V, then James may have felt that chivalrous sports should not be pursued if there was a chance of real warfare.[45]

James I returned to Scotland in 1424 having witnessed the English approach to kingship. In many aspects of governance, he attempted to employ modified English models in order to bring the kingdom under his control. Alasdair A. MacDonald described James's return as a turning point in crown power and he has argued that 1424 saw the redefining of chivalry.[46] However, James had not been exposed to an active promotion of the chivalric ideal at the English court and he does not appear to have attempted to 'revive' chivalric culture at this time. In contradistinction to this, James redefined knighthood. With this came the assertion that loyalty to the crown was ultimately more important than obligations to lords, enabling James to consolidate his nobility on the strength of a common bond with the crown and thus with each other. James I used knighthood as a way of unifying his political community by ensuring that his knights were bound to him through an honorific relationship, thus enabling him to further his own political goals. He especially used the men he knighted at his coronation in this way, giving them important administrative, diplomatic and judicial duties. He formed close friendships and alliances with them, Sir William Crichton of that Ilk being just one example. Although he recognised the usefulness of knights, James I appears to have had very little interest in promoting chivalric ideals. The ultimate expression of chivalry off the battlefield was the tournament and yet there is only evidence that James held one such event during his reign.

James II, 1437–1460

With significant changes in the waging of warfare around 1436 and the murder of James I in 1437 by Albany-Stewart partisans, James II was forced to reassess knighthood and his father's approach to it. Like James I, he did promote and emphasise knights' engagement in administrative duties, with men such as the Livingstons becoming his close counsellors. However, James II encouraged a more traditional policy for his knights, patronising a range of expressions of chivalric knighthood. In conjunction with the Douglases, he held a large-scale tournament with visiting participants of high chivalric renown and he engaged in full-scale wars from the time of his majority. Alasdair A. MacDonald has recently argued that in the mid fifteenth century hubs of chivalric culture existed away from the royal court and, that after the collapse of the Douglas earls, the Sinclair castle of Roslin was the most promi-

---

[44] *Chron. Bower*, book XVI, 28.
[45] Barber and Barker, *Tournaments*, p. 37.
[46] MacDonald, 'Chivalry as a Catalyst', p. 153.

nent example of such a centre.[47] Sir Gilbert Hay's translations produced at Roslin demonstrate that the endorsing of chivalric culture in the 1450s was not exclusive to the crown.

Unlike the coronation of James I which contemporary and near contemporary chroniclers record with a fair amount of detail and at least partial accuracy, the coronation of James II goes almost unnoticed.[48] James II had been knighted by his father at his own baptism in 1430 and he was only seven at the time of his coronation.[49] He was crowned on 25 March 1437 at Holyrood Abbey but the chroniclers make no mention of him bestowing any knighthoods. This is understandable given that their main concern was with recording the details of the aftermath of the murder of James I and the subsequent prosecution of the assassins.[50] Knightings at coronations were the usual practice but it may be possible that James's guardians and the queen had more pressing concerns than who was a suitable candidate for the receipt of a royal bestowal of knighthood.[51] However, James II did need to assert his authority in the face of the confusion and chaos of the aftermath of James I's murder, and the easiest way to achieve this was through knightings and sworn oaths of fealty.

Assuming that James II did confer knighthoods at his coronation ceremony, then there is certainly some indication of who these men may have been. They might have included a number of men such as: William Cranston; Walter Scott of Kirkurd; John Lindsay de Byres; Alexander Hume of that Ilk; Norman Leslie of Fithkill, lord of Rothes; James Hamilton of Fingaltoun; David Lindsay of Meikle; Walter Ogilvy of Deskfurd; Andrew Ogilvy of Inchmartin; George Seton, lord Seton; George Crichton of Blackness; David Hay of Yester; Patrick Hepburn of Wauchtoun.[52] More detailed information about others suggests that James certainly did bestow knighthoods at his coronation. Colin Campbell of Glenorchy, for instance, is widely believed to have been knighted in Rhodes where he fought against the Turks in the 1460s, but strong evidence

---

[47] *Ibid.*, p. 159.
[48] If Roderick Lyall is correct, then the source he uses detailing the coronation of Robert II was actually a description to legitimise James II's coronation at Holyrood. See Roderick J. Lyall, 'The Medieval Scottish Coronation Service: Some Seventeeth-Century Evidence', *IR* 28 (1977), pp. 6–11.
[49] *Chron. Bower*, book XVI, 16; Fraser, *Douglas*, I, pp. 478–9; Michel, *Les Écossais en France*, pp. 206–8.
[50] *Chron. Bower*, Harleian MS Additions, ch. 9, p. 139; *Chron. Extracta*, p. 237. This addition to Bower's text is only found in Harleian MS in the British Library, MS Harleian 712, composed c. March 1473.
[51] Roderick Lyall makes no reference to knightings as a significant part of the coronation ceremony. However, Lyall uses predominantly seventeenth-century evidence for the fifteenth-century ceremonial and disregards the contemporary chronicle evidence which proves that knightings were a common feature of the ceremony. Lyall, 'The Medieval Scottish Coronation Service', pp. 3–21.
[52] *RMS*, II, 12, 102, 119, 182, 201, 203, 204, 206, 210, 211, 212, 215, 218, 239, 246, 399, 438, 497, 558, 588, 768; HMC, *4th Report*, p. 495, no. 17; NAS GD20/1/13 2 May 1454.

indicates that he was actually dubbed at James II's coronation in 1437.[53] Robert Livingston of Drumry was also knighted by James II at this time.[54] Indeed, the Livingstons were well represented at James's coronation and Alexander Livingston of Callander was also probably knighted at the ceremony.[55] James II also utilised highly public celebrations to bestow knighthood and assert himself as the leader of the chivalric community. In February 1449, at the Stirling tournament with the Burgundian knights, James dubbed James Douglas, the brother of the eighth earl of Douglas, and later ninth earl; John Ross of Hawkhead; and another James Douglas, the brother of Sir Henry de Douglas of Loch Leven.[56] Later in that year at his wedding to Mary of Gueldres, James II probably included a knighting ceremony and dubbed David Bruce of Clackmannan and Alexander Boyd of Drumcoll.[57]

The evidence surviving from James II's reign indicates that he knighted his nobles predominantly at royal events such as his marriage and the 1449 tournament. James II's focus, however, appears to have been on the chivalric aspects of knighthood, using elaborate court displays as a way of impressing royal power on his subjects. Indeed, the knights who were dubbed by him also tended to have careers focused on more 'traditional' knightly duties like military service. Sir Alexander Boyd of Drumcoll, for example, took part in the siege of Hatton (Aberdeenshire) in 1452 and the siege of Threave (Dumfriesshire) in 1455, becoming Warden of Threave Castle in 1456.[58] He had earned enough of a chivalric reputation that by the sixteenth century it was claimed that he was responsible for teaching the young James III the arts of chivalry.[59] Similarly, John Ross of Hawkhead later became the Keeper of Blackness Castle (West Lothian), although he had very little role in royal

---

[53] NAS GD112/3/2; *Black Book of Taymouth*, p. 13; see McRoberts, 'Scottish Pilgrims to the Holy Land', p. 91, for the assertion that Campbell was a Knight of St John; and Macquarrie, *Scotland and the Crusades*, pp. 93–5. Macquarrie comes to the conclusion that Campbell did not receive membership of the Order. 'The assertion that he was a Knight of Rhodes may spring from a misunderstanding of the nature of Hospitaller knighthood in later family tradition, or from some honour that was conferred on him during his service, other than reception into the knightly fraternity', p. 94. For more on Campbell see Macquarrie, 'Sir Colin Campbell of Glenorchy (1400–1480) and the Knights Hospitaller', pp. 8–12.
[54] *Registrum de Dumfermline*, no. 406; Alan Borthwick, 'The King, Council and Councillors in Scotland c. 1430–1460' (Ph.D., University of Edinburgh, 1989), p. 66. On 11 September 1448 Robert Livingston of Drumry again witnessed a charter for James II as knight. HMC, *Mar and Kellie*, II, p. 18.
[55] *RMS*, II, 203, 205, 206 208, 209, 210, 211, 212, 215–22, 224, 226–8, 230–42, 245, 247–51, 253, 254, 256–73, 275, 276, 278–82, 284, 285, 287–9, 325, 326.
[56] *Chron. Bower*, Harleian MS Additions, ch. 9, p. 141; *Chron. Auchinleck*, p. 40; *Chron. Extracta*, p. 238; Michel, *Les Écossais en France*, p. 207. A long-standing tradition of Shrovetide tournaments throughout Europe existed, and Tuesday was the traditional day to commence a tournament. In the earlier Middle Ages, the traditional day to commence was Monday. See Bumke, *Courtly Culture*, p. 253.
[57] *RMS*, II, 352; *ER*, V, 329, 356.
[58] *Ibid.*, IV, pp. 199, 202, 203, 204, 208–9, V, pp. 607; *Chron. Auchinleck*, p. 47.
[59] Buchanan, *History*, II, pp. 125–6.

administration.[60] As James II was heavily involved in military activity in the 1450s, this trend may simply reflect their increased attendance on the battlefield, but it remains that the king's knights were focused on their martial duties.

James also relied on his knights to support him against factional dissent. In his attack against the Douglases a number of men he had dubbed, including some who had previously supported the Douglases, assisted the king in quashing their power. These men included Sir Walter Scott of Kirkurd; Sir Alexander Boyd of Drumcoll; John Stewart, Lord Darnley; Sir Andrew Stewart; Sir Alexander Hume of that Ilk and Sir William Cranston, both previously Douglas supporters; Sir Simon Glendenning; and Andrew, first Lord Gray, Master of the Household.[61] Whilst there were more pressing political reasons for James's desire to crush the Douglases' power, their promotion of chivalric culture must also have contributed to James's cause. This becomes more believable when we consider that William Sinclair, earl of Orkney, was quickly ousted from royal favour when he took an interest in chivalry in the mid 1450s. It would seem then that James II wanted to keep, or tried to bring, chivalry and its manifestations under royal control and used political manipulation as a way of ensuring this could happen. No other noble families sought to attempt decentralisation after this time, even though James III's lack of enthusiasm about chivalry could have facilitated an active chivalric culture away from the royal court.

James III, 1460–1488

Although there had been some attempt by James II and his nobles to sponsor and support the chivalric ideals of knighthood, James III did not concern himself with them. He did not bestow knighthoods at celebratory events, a precedent established earlier in the fifteenth century, and as such the opportunity for knights to gain social prestige in this way was limited. He only seems to have knighted men for very specific purposes – for example, when he needed immediate military power at his coronation in 1460 (although as he was still in his minority, this would have been directed by his advisors) or when he needed to secure loyalty, such as at parliament in 1488. During his majority, at a time when the social exclusivity of knighthood was under threat, the Scottish nobility pursued crown patronage. When James did not provide

---

[60] *ER*, VII, pp. 365, 404, 500, 506, 589.
[61] *Ibid.*, V, p. 607; *Chron. Auchinleck*, p. 47. Alexander Hume of that Ilk, Walter Scott of Kirkurd and William Cranston had all received their knighthoods from James II at his coronation in 1437 and appear to have been very close to the king. However, Hume and Cranston had both accompanied Douglas to Rome for the Papal Jubilee in 1450. According to the Auchinleck chronicler these men had participated in the earl's murder and would have been keen to demonstrate their loyalty to the king at this time.

this, he was heavily criticised. There is no surviving record of tournaments being held in James III's reign and given his attitude to chivalric pastimes it is probable that none were held. Despite this, James III was not unaware of traditional chivalric attitudes. Both he and his brother, Alexander Stewart, duke of Albany, a 'fadir in chevalry', were members of chivalric orders of knighthood, although, as has recently been proven, James III did not found an order in Scotland.[62]

We have already established that James III's war-making played a more significant role in his decisions to make knights than the political value of the men that he dubbed. James III was crowned at Kelso on 10 August 1460, immediately after his father's death, and the queen mother and the bishops and nobles of the kingdom attended the ceremony. During the proceedings James created one hundred knights.[63] Only a handful of these knights can be identified: Patrick Maitland; James Crichton of Carnis; John Colquhoun of that Ilk; William Wallace of Craigie; Alexander Napier of Merchiston; John Herries, lord of Terregles; Alexander Forrester of Corstorphine; William Hay of Nactane; Alexander Lauder of Hatton; and William, Thane of Cawdor.[64] Although clearly men were still being knighted, we hear barely anything of the other dubbings throughout James III's reign, apart from Anselm Adornes' investiture, of which much has been written. On 15 January 1469 the king knighted the Brugeois ambassador who was attached to the court of the duke of Burgundy, Philip the Good.[65] Some historians, however, have concluded that Anselm was not just knighted, but that he actually became a member of a Scottish order of knighthood at the same time. This conclusion is based on comments John Adornes made in 1471, where he made reference to the knightly insignia which his father, Anselm, received from James III. As membership of an order of chivalry was usually displayed by the receipt and wearing of a collar and pendant which symbolised the order, the knightly insignia to which Adornes refers has been assumed by scholars to be the collar of James III's chivalric order. However, there is no official record that he received such a collar from James III at this time. Instead, John Adornes was referring to his father's dubbing, a quite common expression of receipt of the general order of knighthood and it in no way implies that Anselm was a member of the Order of the Unicorn. Indeed, recent scholarship has proven without question that no such Order existed in Scotland at this time.

[62] Lesley, *History*, p. 51.
[63] *Chron. Auchinleck*, p. 21; Macdougall, *James III*, p. 51. See also 'The Short Chronicle of 1482' in MacDougall, *James III*, Appendix A, pp. 311–13.
[64] *RMS*, II, 679, 758, 797, 692, 1108, 700, 734, 765, 771, 786, 815, 921, 1088, 1656; NAS GD430/14, GD430/13, GD305/1/79/8; *ER*, VII, p. 34; Jean Munro and R.W. Munro (eds), *Acts of the Lords of the Isles 1336–1493*, SHS (Edinburgh, 1986), no. 79. The *Scots Peerage* suggests that John Wemyss of that Ilk was also created a knight at this ceremony, but provides no supporting evidence, *SP*, VIII, p. 484.
[65] Bruges, Stadsarchief, Fonds de Limburg Stirum, 15 January 1469, transcribed in Macquarrie, 'The Impact of the Crusading Movement', Appendix I, no. 3.

Anselm Adornes' knighting appears to be the exception rather than the rule, although it does demonstrate that knights could be dubbed away from large public ceremonials. In almost all recorded instances where he knighted men in state, it was under the immediate pressure of war or rebellion. For example, the hundred men James knighted at his coronation were used immediately at the siege of Wark castle in Northumberland. Most telling, during the beginnings of the disruptions in 1488, James III raised the status of many of his nobles and knighted three of them at his last parliament.[66] In this instance his choice of new knights was primarily motivated by his desire to retain the support of these men and their families. The lack of records from this period makes it impossible to draw firm conclusions about the policy that James III had towards making knights and the use of knights' service. In fact, all that can really be said is that as the duke of Albany was also bestowing knighthoods during this time, there was almost certainly no exclusive monarchical control over dubbing.

James's preference for knighting for military purposes broadly influenced these knights' future careers as well. We find a limited number of knights involved in diplomatic or administrative positions for James III, but instead a large number of knights being employed in their military capacity. This was never 'chivalric' warfare, however, and whilst James III paid tribute to knightly society by upholding the value of knighthood as a commodity, he did little to promote the chivalric ethos. Indeed, Andrew Wood of Largo, whose naval achievements were considerable during his reign, did not receive recognition for this by being dubbed. In fact, he was only raised to knightly status by James IV, in an attempt to ensure his loyalty. Nevertheless, James III's employment of knights in warfare certainly placed them in the front line.

For example, James III was embroiled in war with England in 1482 and his main concern was with the defence of the borders. He proposed to finance personally a garrison of five hundred soldiers and the estates agreed to pay the wages of an additional six hundred.[67] James Borthwick of Glengelt was placed in command of garrisons at Blackadder, Wedderburn and Hume. Borthwick was asked to choose two deputies to oversee the twenty-strong garrisons of Blackadder and Wedderburn and he held Hume himself with sixty men. James Stewart, earl of Buchan, was entrusted with the guardianship of the middle marches with commanders under him: James Edmonstone of that Ilk, who was appointed captain of Cessford (with a garrison of sixty), Ormiston (with twenty) and Edgarston (with twenty); John Cranston of that Ilk was given Jedburgh (with sixty), Cocklaw (with twenty) and Dolphinstoun (with twenty); and William Bailey of Lamington was given the command of Hermitage castle with a garrison of one hundred men, because parliament

---

[66] *APS*, II, 181; Macdougall, *James III*, p. 237.
[67] *Ibid.*, pp. 148–50. Two hundred and fifty were to be paid for by the clergy, two hundred and fifty by the barons and one hundred by the burghs.

considered it to be 'in maste dangere'.[68] In the west borders John Stewart, first Lord Darnley, was entrusted with the Wardenship.[69] Thomas Kilpatrick, laird of Closeburn, was given the captaincy of Lochmaben castle, the main strongpoint of the west borders, and a garrison of one hundred men. Robert Charteris, laird of Amisfield, a squire, was also given one hundred soldiers to split between Castlemilk, Annan, and Bell's Tower.[70] Apart from the earl of Buchan and Lord Darnley, little more is known about the military careers of these men and why they were selected for these positions, although they were presumably regarded as militarily competent.

James III's martial interests, however, did not extend to the lists or tournament field. In contrast to his predecessors, the king appears to have entirely avoided all chivalric sports and made no provision for their staging in Scotland. Of course, James's neglect of chivalric pastimes may have been simply because he was not personally interested in them and he does not appear to have discouraged others from pursuing knightly glory in a joust. His brother, for example, was a renowned jouster and met his end at a tournament in Paris in 1485, a fitting demise for a 'chivalric' knight.[71] Remarkably however, James III did recognise the value of membership in the European orders of chivalry. Like his brother, he was a knight of the Order of St Michael, and the Danish Order of the Elephant.[72] James's membership in these orders does not indicate that he had a significant interest in chivalry, nor that he actively promoted himself as a chivalric king, but instead it suggests that he sought the political value that came with membership of a European elite.

James IV, 1488–1513

Felicity Riddy has considered the assertion that there was a general trend in the second half of the fifteenth century towards a revival of chivalry and she argued that this was also evident in Scotland. Indeed many scholars have asserted that from the mid fifteenth century there was a revival of traditional chivalric sentiments throughout Europe.[73] These ideas were based upon the mythical court of King Arthur and took their inspiration from the Arthurian romances of the twelfth century. Riddy claimed that the Scottish revival was not a nostalgic renewal of outdated beliefs in order to declare class-conscious ideals, but that it was a response to the humanistic ethos that promoted men

---

[68] *APS*, II, pp. 132–5; *RMS*, II, 1418.
[69] *APS*, II, p. 140; Macdougall, *James III*, pp. 152–3.
[70] *ADC*, I, p. 60, Appendix B, Table Three, no. 478.
[71] Lesley, *History*, p. 51; *SP*, I, p. 152; Nicholson, *Scotland*, p. 517; Macdougall, *James III*, p. 212; *ER*, IX, p. lvi; Michel, *Les Écossais en France*, p. 264.
[72] *TA*, I, pp. 81, 8; Boulton, *Knights of the Crown*, pp. 427, 436, 443–4.
[73] See for example Ferguson, *Indian Summer of English Chivalry*, esp. ch. 1, 'A Chivalric "Revival"?', pp. 3–32, where he argues that this was a reaction of the nobility to social developments which threatened their exclusivity.

as learned warriors.[74] Indeed there was a resuscitation of chivalry in the late fifteenth century and it was firmly crown-sponsored.

Possibly as a response to the complaints laid against his father, or perhaps due to a genuine interest in chivalric pastimes, James IV undertook a programme of chivalric patronage in more extravagant forms than had previously been seen. This was due to a desire to do justice to the ideals which the knightly classes valued, a redressing of his father's failings.[75] James IV bestowed knighthood for especially knightly reasons, such as a reward for excellence on the battlefield or for participating in tournaments. For example, during the border wars of the late 1490s, James IV bestowed a number of knighthoods. Men who benefited from this patronage included John Ogilvy of Finglask; Patrick Blackadder; Peter Houston of that Ilk; Sir John Somerville of Cambusnethan; Sir Robert Erskine of Ellem; Thomas Hume of Langshaw; William Colville of Ochiltree; John Ross of Malevyn; David Sinclair; Alexander Seton of Touchfraser; William Douglas of Drumlanrig; Baldred Blackadder; and Walter Forrester of Torwood.[76] Notably, many of these men came from the lesser nobility and we can draw a clear distinction between the status of men knighted at court and of those dubbed on the battlefield. What this tells us about James IV's attitude to knighthood is revealing, as whilst there is little indication that he bestowed knighthoods at state ceremonies, his dubbing of men during wars and campaigns highlights his emphasis on the martial aspect of knighthood.

James IV certainly retained these men in military-type service. John Ogilvy of Finglask, for example, held positions of considerable military responsibility. Ogilvy seems to have retained royal favour after the border wars and in 1501 he was appointed constable of Inverness Castle.[77] In February 1506 he became sheriff of Inverness, at which point he was also acting as a royal messenger for James IV.[78] He also dubbed men for service to the crown in less martial spheres. James's appreciation for the cult of chivalry was strong and, amongst other things, he sponsored court poetry emphasising chivalric virtues in knights. James IV also promoted the tournament as a key domain for the demonstration of chivalric abilities. As developments in warfare left knights without a space to prove their 'knightly' worth, and knighthood had taken on increasingly political qualities, the tournament was the remaining space where knights could demonstrate chivalrous attributes. In part this was to compensate for the changes in 'knightly' warfare and to encourage knights to

---

[74] Felicity Riddy, 'The Revival of Chivalry in Late Medieval Scotland', in Jeans-Jacques Blanchot and Claude Grad (eds), *Actes du 2e Colloque de Lanque et de Litterature Écossaises (Moyen Age et Renaissance)* (Strasbourg, 1978), esp. pp. 54, 61.
[75] Keen, *Chivalry*, pp. 216–17.
[76] *TA*, I, pp. 207, 211, 332, 354; NAS GD6/12, GD124/1/167, GD32/8/3, GD39/39/5/6; *RSS*, I, 40, 97, 130, 182, 473; *RMS*, II, 618, 2252, 2408, 2384, 2499, 2680, 3312; *Prot. Bk. Young*, no. 986, 1580; *ER*, X, p. 766, XI, p. 4; *SP*, V, p. 608.
[77] *ER*, XI, p. 356.
[78] *RSS*, I, 1214, *APS*, II, pp. 263–4, Macdougall, *James IV*, p. 188.

participate fully in war, as it was their 'chivalric duty'. In part it was also a direct response to the nobility, who were attempting to assert their elitism in the face of increasing upward social mobility. Primarily, however, it was part of a campaign headed by James IV to promote himself on the international stage as a chivalric king and patron.

James began on a small scale, with simple jousts in the early 1490s, but by 1496 his appetite had been whetted for the power of opulent display when he staged a lavish tournament for the marriage of Perkin Warbeck to Lady Catherine Gordon. Upon his marriage to Margaret Tudor in 1503, James launched a programme of tournaments to demonstrate his chivalric personal policy. The first of these, held on Margaret's bridal journey to Edinburgh, was an overtly courtly display, reintroducing to his knights the courtly love element of tournaments. However, much of this must be attributed to James IV's desire to revive Arthurian concepts of chivalry. Whether or not further expressions of courtly love were made by knights around James IV's court is not known. The royal wedding celebrations also incorporated three days of jousting in Holyrood Palace courtyard, a prime opportunity to parade James's tribute to revived forms of chivalric expression.

James IV's favouring of the tournament as the ultimate chivalric playground is apparent and he even had a team of royal knights who participated in his tournaments. He held a series of annual tournaments, the first of which was held on Shrove Tuesday in 1503. This marked the commencement of celebrations, which were held again in 1505 and 1506. These tournaments, however, seem not to have had the desired effect and in 1507 James completely changed his approach to staging chivalric games. Instead of having Shrovetide celebrations, in early summer 1507 James IV orchestrated his most extravagant tournament to date. This was the tournament of the Wild Knight and the Black Lady in which James himself appeared in the allegorical role of the Wild Knight. He also paid specific tribute to the Arthurian legend 'with counterfutting of the round tabill of King Arthour of Jngland'.[79] Johan Huizinga has pointed out that these expressions were significant as they indicated a tendency to recreate in reality an ideal image of the past.[80] James repeated the tournament in 1508 with increased expense and pageantry. This tournament may not have provided ultimate success in achieving his desired goals and it is more likely that it fell short of James's expectations. Whatever the case, he held no further tournaments.

There is no doubt that there was a revival of traditional chivalry in James IV's reign. This effort at revival could not resuscitate an exclusively Arthurian model, as the ethos of chivalry had developed in line with social and political

---

[79] Lesley, *History*, p. 154; Fradenburg, *City, Marriage, Tournament*, p. 232.
[80] Johan Huizinga, 'The Political and Military Significance of Chivalric Ideas in the Late Middle Ages', James S. Holmes and Hans van Marle (trans), *Men and Ideas: History, the Middle Ages, the Renaissance* (London, 1960).

pressures throughout the fifteenth century. Scottish knighthood changed over the century from a career and a way of life which esteemed heroics on the battlefield to one which demanded equally martial skills and administrative, political and diplomatic abilities. These changes were exploited and at times apparently directed and encouraged by the Scottish crown, which used knighthood and the promotion of chivalry, in varying degrees, for political gain.

Under James IV a strong emphasis seems to have been placed upon chivalry in day-to-day court life. In both his personal qualities as a king and in his administrative rule, James IV seems to have sought a revival of the glory days of chivalry based loosely around the ideals of the Arthurian legend, reworked and refashioned since the twelfth century. James IV encouraged a chivalric dynasty and this was almost seamlessly incorporated into his interest in the military, the navy and the knightly. Gavin Douglas dedicated his *Palice of Honour* to James IV and wrote that he

> mot haue Eternallie
> Supreme Honour, Renoun of Cheualrie.[81]

With so much emphasis placed on chivalric and courtly ideals, it would be expected that there would be evidence of James bestowing knighthoods at large-scale, public, royal and chivalric events, but this is not the case. The most obvious aspect of James IV's bestowal of knighthood was that he did so for particularly 'knightly' reasons: for participation in tournaments and especially as a reward for fighting well in battle. Like James II, James IV knighted his nobles at public and royal events, but with the primary intention of supporting his own chivalric image, combining dubbing ceremonies with tournaments and battles, the ultimate knightly activities.

In addition there were other events where knighthoods were granted. In August 1503, on the third day of his extravagant and costly wedding celebrations, James IV knighted forty-one men after which a three-day joust in the courtyard of Holyrood Palace began.

> After the Othe sworne and taken, the Erle Bothwell [gave] them the gylt spourneys, and the Kynge gaffe them the Stroke of his Swerde, wich was born before hym. This doon, he sayed to the Qwene, the Lady – these are your knyghts.[82]

Although no indication of the identity of the men knighted is given in any descriptions of the celebrations, there are, nevertheless, some men who were knighted around this time and can be linked closely enough to the crown to conclude that they probably received the honour at the wedding: Alexander Lauder, provost of Edinburgh; Robert Lauder of the Bass; Sir Robert Bruce of

---

[81] Douglas, *Palice of Honour*, p. 71; MacDonald, 'Chivalry as a Catalyst', p. 167.
[82] Younge, 'The Fyancells of Margaret', p. 298. Bothwell was given prominence at this tournament because he had been crucial in securing the marriage treaty.

Airth; Alexander Ramsay of Cockpen; John Hay of Belltown; David Bruce of Clackmannan; John Forman of Rutherford; William Lindsay; John Melville of Raith; and Thomas Borthwick of Collielaw.[83] The courtly love overtones of this declaration, that the knights were bound in service to the queen, are unusual in a Scottish context. However, what cannot be overlooked is that the report comes from an English herald. Whilst courtly romance was popular in Scotland, there is no indication from Scottish sources that these themes were ever ritually expressed at the Scottish court. There is certainly no indication that the men knighted at this time were ever bound in service to the queen, but this may be a problem with the sources that have survived.[84]

The nobility's passion for chivalry, which James IV had so actively encouraged, did not fade after Flodden. James V continued the traditions embraced by his father and fostered the cult of chivalry at the royal court. Prominence was given to mounted joust and tournaments, the art of heraldry and the European orders of knighthood. James V presented himself as the ideal Christian knight and was eager for crusading duties, and he led his army on military campaigns.[85] Yet the values of the Renaissance court were also felt and James V's nobles, through education and emphasis on less 'military' skills, developed less as knights and more as courtiers.

Chivalry and Knighthood in Scotland

At the outset of this study, Maurice Keen's definition of chivalry could be adequately applied to Scotland. Keen's emphasis directed historians to consider the martial function of knights, the elitism of chivalric ideals promoted through emphasis on nobility and the importance of model Christianity. Alastair J. MacDonald suggested that in the fourteenth century in Scotland, the major emphasis of the chivalric code was on 'glory and renown through military feats and the enjoyment of martial endeavour for its own sake'.[86] However, during the fifteenth century Scottish chivalry developed other traits.

The martial function of knights was always central to chivalric culture, but Scottish chivalry was not just a military ideal. Throughout the century, knights were expected to provide military service through the agreements they had with their lords. This was maintained even though the crown had begun to

---

[83] Ibid., p. 298; *TA*, II, pp. 182, 270, 364, 385–9; R.L. Mackie, *King James IV of Scotland: A Brief Survey of His Life and Times* (Edinburgh, 1958), p. 112; *Prot. Bk. Foular*, nos. 206, 258; Fradenburg, *City, Marriage, Tournament*, p. 106; *RMS*, II, 2608, 2781, 3046, 2745, 2759; *Prot. Bk. Young*, nos. 193, 1357; *RSS*, I, 922, 993; Fraser, *Melville*, I, p. 38; *SP*, VI, p. 86; *CDS*, IV, Appendix no. 38.
[84] *RMS*, II, 3007, sees John Hay of Belltown (de Snaid) and *RMS*, II, 3339, sees John Melville of Raith, witnessing charters for James IV.
[85] Thomas, 'Renaissance Culture at the Court of James V', p. 13.
[86] MacDonald, *Border Bloodshed*, p. 178.

pay skilled workmen to attend its campaigns and perform tasks that knights and men-at-arms could not. The greatest problem in assessing the martial aspect of knighthood stems from the changes that came with the development of new technologies for warfare and the decrease in formal pitched battles. The decline in Anglo-Scottish hostilities meant that a large body of military men had little to do except in the context of local feuds and highland campaigning. Even though contemporary commentators indicated that there was an ongoing debate surrounding the knights' place in these developments, knights were still very much present on the battlefield. Apart from positions of command, however, it is not possible to determine what their roles were specifically. There is, nevertheless, evidence that knights did adapt to retain their place on the battlefield and by the end of the fifteenth century new positions, such as Master of the King's Artillery, were held by Scottish knights. As warfare developed, the role of the knight on the battlefield changed and knights looked to other ways in which they could demonstrate and prove their military skills and prowess. Participating in jousting and tournaments became the focus for these demonstrations. The advantages of this were attractive, as a knight not only had an audience, but the dangers of warfare were not present. Jousting had strict rules and the emphasis was on winning prizes and esteem for the display of skill. In the 1440s sharp weapons were still being used at jousts in Scotland and serious injuries could be sustained. As the emphasis shifted from winning the joust to proving martial worth through display, blunted weapons began to be used and by the 1490s their use was standard practice. As this reduced the need to concentrate on avoiding serious injury, knights were able to focus on increasingly elaborate displays and pageantry. Consequently the knight's performance at tournaments became increasingly ritualised.

The changes knights faced in their military capacity also enhanced the necessity to look to diplomatic and administrative careers. This significant development, which has hitherto been underemphasised by historians, was incorporated into the Scottish chivalric ethos. Men who were knighted by a king often held offices and positions of responsibility in his administration. By the 1450s, the idea that knights were public figures with public duties to perform was so entrenched in knightly society that Sir Gilbert Hay heavily emphasised it in his chivalric manuals.[87] In the second half of the fifteenth century, humanist educationalists persuaded the nobility that they needed new skills to strengthen their involvement in public life and service, thereby encouraging knights to combine their skills in warfare with the more learned skills previously seen as the preserve of the clergy.[88] Although there was a distinct anti-martial thrust to humanist scholarship, in practice the traditionally

[87] Glenn (ed.), *Buke of the Ordre of Knychthede*, p. 18; Mason, 'Chivalry and Citizenship', p. 58.
[88] Brown, *Noble Society in Scotland*, p. 181.

lauded skills were still accepted as long as they co-existed with the virtues of humanism.[89] Nobles were encouraged to embrace the new learning of the universities to help them become refined gentlemen and to be of use in governmental offices where martial skills alone were not adequate.[90] Knights like Sir John Ross of Montgrenan were quick to heed the humanist advice.[91] Even Sir Bernard Stewart was affected by the trend to increase and demonstrate 'educated' skills, penning a treatise on war in the early sixteenth century.[92] During the fifteenth century, civic responsibility emerged as another component added to the ever-changing concept of the chivalric ideal. However, civic responsibility never outweighed the importance of martial duty. Instead, this development of skills from and beyond the battlefield simply served to make knights a more useful body of men for the crown.

The later fifteenth century also saw a conscious addressing of whether or not hereditary nobility should be part of the chivalric ideal and if the elitism of knighthood could be justified. Under the influence of humanist philosophy, the non-noble classes forced the questioning of whether the traditional virtues of chivalry were an expression of true nobility. If a non-nobleman could display the virtues and qualities esteemed in the chivalric code, it was asked, ought he to be excluded from eligibility for knighthood on the basis of his social status. Alasdair A. MacDonald has argued that these questions came largely from the Burgundian influence and claims that chivalry came to be regarded as an inspiration and expression of true nobility: 'central to this notion is that the essence of true nobility was seen as stemming from virtue rather than any accident of birth, rank or fortune'.[93] MacDonald's views, however, are limited by his agenda of proving that the Burgundian influence in Scotland in the later fifteenth century was more prominent than the French influence. His position that non-nobles could legitimately achieve the chivalric ideal is only part of the picture, as noble descent was considered an essential element of Scottish knighthood that should be preserved.

At the time these questions were being raised, James III was certainly dubbing non-nobles. He was heavily criticised by his nobility for favouring 'low-born' men and their concerns that knighthood was losing its exclusivity were particularly relevant. The nobility attempted to assert its elitism, but

---

[89] Edington, *Court and Culture*, p. 81.
[90] Brown, *Noble Society in Scotland*, pp. 196–7.
[91] Ross made a notable career as a lawyer and administrator in royal service. He acted as king's advocate for the last decade of James III's reign. Brown, 'The Scottish "Establishment" ', p. 99; Mason, *Kingship and Commonweal*, p. 115. The post of king's advocate was, in general, held by a layman, although during the years immediately following Sir John Ross's tenure of the office, its holders noticeably became both more professional and more obviously exponents of humanistic skills. John Finlay has recently argued that the office of King's Advocate did not exist until 1493, but he recognises Sir John Ross's role in the law. Finlay, *Men of Law in Pre-Reformation Scotland*, ch. 7, 'The Office of the King's Advocate', esp. pp. 170, 208.
[92] De Comminges (ed.), *Traité dur L'Art de la Guerre*.
[93] MacDonald, 'Chivalry as a Catalyst', p. 158.

entry to the lower nobility could be assured via knighthood (as knighthood and nobility were still inherently linked). Dubbing of the upper nobility occurred at official crown events, and lesser nobles, in general, appear to have been knighted on the battlefield and for military service. In this context, dubbings were often made for displays of skill and non-nobles could enter knighthood via this route. Burgesses certainly took part in the crown's military campaigns and some even designated themselves as squires.[94] Knighthoods were also granted to non-nobles for service to the crown in administrative and diplomatic duties. The crown thereby endorsed the view that the display of chivalric virtue was an adequate expression of nobility that conferred eligibility for knighthood. This was particularly apparent in James III's and James IV's reigns.

The Christian component of chivalry was also still relevant to late-medieval Scottish knightly society. Christian consciousness was never far removed from the practice of chivalry and knights did endeavour to defend the faith, or at least visit the Holy Land on pilgrimage.[95] Scottish knights also patronised the Church to demonstrate their Christian commitment, favouring, in particular, the founding of collegiate churches.[96] The knight's ultimate service to God was also emphasised in chivalric and vernacular literature produced throughout the century. The courtly love component was notably absent from the Scottish chivalric model. In his recent exploration of chivalry, Richard Kaeuper argued that courtly love was an essential element. It was implicitly linked to the emphasis on martial prowess, as knights sought to secure the love of their lady.[97] This was not part of Scottish chivalry to the same extent. There were a number of translations made of Continental chivalric tales which contained love themes, but these were often diluted from their original and were no longer central to the text. Some Scottish literary sources do suggest that knights could be inspired by their love for a lady, but these ideas appear to be far removed from practice. Fifteenth-century Scottish chivalry thus comprised four main components. As the principal ingredients necessary in defining Scottish chivalry, these components were linked and knights were expected to embody all of them. Scottish chivalry comprised, first and foremost, military skill and prowess, followed by public duty and service in crown administration, noble status and Christian consciousness.

---

[94] *RMS*, II, 737, 1477; Scaglione, *Knights at Court*; p. 21; Scott, 'Dress in Scotland', pp. 65, 111–13.
[95] For example see *CDS*, IV, 1346.
[96] See for example *Midl. Chrs.*, pp. 305–12.
[97] Kaeuper, *Chivalry and Violence*, p. 302.

BIBLIOGRAPHY

Mannuscript Sources

British Library, London
Add. MS 40732
Ashmolean MS 763
Cotton Caligula, B. III, 19

City Archives, Edinburgh
Protocol Book of John Foular, Volume III, June 1519–April 1528

National Archives, London
E.101.407.4, 17

National Archives of Scotland, Edinburgh
AD1   Crown Office Writs
E21   Exchequer Records
GD1   Miscellaneous Accessions
GD3   Eglinton Muniments
GD4   Benholm and Hedderwick Writs
GD6   Biel Muniments
GD16   Airlie Muniments
GD20   Crawford Priory Collection
GD26   Leven and Melville Muniments
GD28   Yester Writs
GD32   Viscounts and Barons of Elibank
GD33   Haddo Muniments
GD39   Glencairn Muniments
GD45   Dalhousie Muniments
GD47   Ross Estate Muniments
GD52   Lord Forbes Collection
GD78   Hunter of Barjarg Muniments
GD98   Douglas Collection
GD101   Wigtown Charters
GD112   Breadalbane Muniments
GD124   Earls of Mar and Kellie
GD135   Earls of Stair
GD137   Earls of Dundee
GD160   Drummond Castle Muniments
GD172   Fordell Muniments
GD176   Mackintosh Muniments

GD198   Haldane of Gleneagles
GD305   Earls of Cromartie
GD430   Napier Muniments

National Library of Scotland, Edinburgh
Acc. 9253
Adv. MS 19.2.2
Adv. MS 31.3.20
Adv. MS 31.5.2
Adv. MS 31.7.22
Adv. MS 80.4.15
MS TD 209
MS 20771

Primary Printed Sources

Alighieri, Dante, *The Divine Comedy: Volume I, Inferno*, Mark Musa (ed.) (New York, 1984).
Anderson, Joseph, 'Notice of a Small Figure in Jet of St James the Greater, Recently Presented to the Museum by James Gibson Craig, Esq. FSA Scot, and Probably a Signaculum worn by a Leprous Pilgrim to St Jago di Compostella; with notes on "Pilgrim Signs" of the Middle Ages, and a Stone Mould for Casting Leaden Tokens, found at Dundrennan Abbey', *PSAS* 25 (1874–76), pp. 62–80.
Armstrong, C.A.J. (ed.), 'A Letter of James III to the Duke of Burgundy', *Miscellany of the Scottish History Society VIII* (Edinburgh, 1951).
Bain, J. (ed.), *Calendar of Documents relating to Scotland A.D. 1108–1516* (Edinburgh, 1881–88).
'The Ballet of the Nine Worthies', in Graeme Ritchie (ed.), *The Buik of Alexander the Most Noble and Valiant Conquerour Alexander the Grit by John Barbour, Archdeacon of Aberdeen*, I, STS (Edinburgh, 1925).
Barbour, John, *The Bruce*, A.A.M. Duncan (ed.) (Edinburgh, 1997).
Barclay, William and David Donald Turnbull (eds), *Extracta e Variis Cronicis Scocie: From the Ancient Manuscript in the Advocates Library at Edinburgh*, Abbotsford Club (Edinburgh, 1842).
Batho, Edith C., and H. Winifred Husbands (eds), *The Chronicles of Scotland Compiled by Hector Boece, Translated into Scots by John Bellenden, 1531*, STS (Edinburgh & London, 1941).
Bawcutt, Priscilla (ed.), *William Dunbar: Selected Poems* (London & New York, 1996).
Baxter, James Houston (ed.), *Copiale Prioratus Sanctiandree: The Letter-Book of James Haldenstone, Prior of St Andrews (1418–1443)* (Oxford, 1930).
Beattie, William (ed.), *The Chepman and Myllar Prints: Nine Tracts from the First Scottish Press, Edinburgh 1508 Followed By the Two Other Tracts in the Same Volume in the National Library of Scotland* (Edinburgh, 1950).
Bellaguet, M.L. (ed.), *Chronique du Religieux de Saint-Denys, Contenant Le Règne de Charles VI, De 1380 A 1422* (Paris, 1844).

BIBLIOGRAPHY

Bergenroth, G.A. (ed.), *Calendar of Letters, Despatches, and State Papers, Relating to the Negotiations between England and Spain, Preserved in the Archives of Simancas and Elsewhere* (London, 1862–1954).

The Black Book of Taymouth with Other Papers from the Breadalbane Charter Room (Edinburgh, 1855).

Blind Harry, *The Actis and Deidis of the Illustere and Vailyeand Campioun Schir William Wallace, Knicht of Ellerslie*, STS (Edinburgh & London, 1889).

Bliss, W.H. et al. (eds), *Calendar of Entries in the Papal Registers relating to Great Britain and Ireland: Papal Letters* (London, 1893–1960).

——, *Calendar of Entries in the Papal Registers Relating to Great Britain and Ireland: Petitions to the Pope, Volume I, A.D. 1342–1419* (London, 1896).

Bower, Walter, *Scotichronicon*, D.E.R. Watt (ed.), (Aberdeen, 1993–98).

Brodie, R.H. (ed.), *Letters and Papers, Foreign and Domestic of the Reign of Henry VIII, Preserved in the Public Record Office, the British Museum and Elsewhere* (London, 1920).

Brown, P. Hume (ed.), *Early Travellers in Scotland* (Edinburgh, 1978).

Buchanan, George, *The History of Scotland*, J. Aikman (trans), (Glasgow & Edinburgh, 1827–29).

Campbell, Colin (ed.), *The Scots Roll: A Study of a Fifteenth Century Roll of Arms* (Heraldic Society of Scotland, 1995).

Certaine Matters Composed Together (Edinburgh, 1594).

Charters of the Hospital of Soltre, of Trinity College, Edinburgh, and Other Collegiate Churches in Mid-Lothian, Bannatyne Club (Edinburgh, 1861).

Chastellain, George, 'Historie du bon chevalier Messire Jacques de Lalain frère et compagnon de l'ordre de la Toison d'Or', in P. Hume Brown (ed.), *Early Travellers in Scotland* (Edinburgh, 1978).

Clouston, Joesph Storer (ed.), *Records of the Earldom of Orkney*, SHS (Edinburgh, 1914).

Comminges, Élie de (ed.), *Traité dur L'Art de la Guerre de Bérault Stuart Seigneur D'Aubigny* (The Hague, 1976).

Constable, Archibald (ed.), *A History of Greater Britain as Well England as Scotland, Compiled from Ancient Authorities by John Major, by Names Indeed a Scot, but by Profession a Theologian, 1521*, SHS (Edinburgh, 1892).

Corstorphine Parish Church Heraldry (n.p., 1982).

Craigie, W.A., 'The "Ballet of the Nine Nobles"', *Anglia: Zeitschrift für Englische Philologie* 21 (1898–99), pp. 359–65.

Dickson, T. and Sir J. Balfour Paul (eds), *Accounts of the Lord High Treasurer of Scotland* (Edinburgh, 1877–1916).

Don Pedro de Ayala, 'Letter to Ferdinand and Isabella of Spain, 25 June 1498', in P. Hume Brown (ed.), *Early Travellers in Scotland* (Edinburgh, 1978).

Donaldson, Gordon (ed.), *Protocol Book of James Young 1485–1515*, SRS (Edinburgh, 1952).

—— and C. Macrae (eds), *St Andrews Formulare, 1514–1546* (Edinburgh, 1942).

'Donations to the Museum and Library', *PSAS* 24 (1889–90), p. 411.

Douglas, Gavin, *Palice of Honour*, Bannatyne Club, (Edinburgh 1827, reprinted New York, 1971).

Easson, D.E. and Angus MacDonald (eds), *Charters of the Abbey of Inchcolm*, SHS (Edinbugh, 1938).

'The Errol Papers', *Miscellany of the Spalding Club*, II, (Aberdeen, 1842).
Extracts from the Council Register of the Burgh of Aberdeen, 1398–1570, Spalding Club (Aberdeen, 1844).
Extracts from the Records of the Burgh of Edinburgh AD1403–1528, SBRS (Edinburgh, 1869–92).
Faques, Richard, 'The Trewe Encountre of Batalyle Lately Don Betwene Englande and Scotlande' in David Laing, 'A Contemporary Account of the Battle of Flodden, 9th September 1513', *PSAS* 7 (1866–67), pp. 141–52.
Favine, Andrew, *The Theater of Honour and Knighthood or a Compendious Chronicle and Historie of the Whole Christian World* (London, 1620).
Fraser, William (ed.), *Memoirs of the Maxwells of Pollock* (Edinburgh, 1863).
———, *The Book of Caerlaverock* (Edinburgh, 1873).
———, *The Red Book of Menteith* (Edinburgh, 1880).
———, *The Melvilles Earls of Melville and the Leslies Earls of Leven* (Edinburgh, 1880).
———, *The Douglas Book* (Edinburgh, 1885).
Froissart, Jean, *Chronicles*, Geoffrey Brereton (ed.) (London, 1978).
Fryde, E.B., D.E. Greenway, S. Porter and I. Roy (eds), *Handbook of British Chronology*, third edition (London, 1986).
Gairdner, James (ed.), *The Paston Letters A.D. 1422–1509* (London, 1904).
Geoffrey of Monmouth, *The History of the Kings of Britain*, Lewis Thorpe (trans.) (London, 1966).
Glenn, Jonathan A. (ed.), *The Prose Works of Sir Gilbert Hay Volume III: 'The Buke of the Ordre of Knychthede' and 'The Buke of the Governaunce of Princis'*, STS (Edinburgh, 1993).
Gray, Margaret Muriel (ed.), *Lancelot of the Laik from Cambridge University Library MS*, STS (Edinburgh, 1912).
Hamer, Douglas (ed.), *The Works of Sir David Lindsay of the Mount 1490–1555*, STS (Edinburgh & London, 1931).
Hannay, Robert Kerr (ed.), *Rentale Dunkeldemse: Being the Accounts of the Bishopric (A.D. 1505–1517) with Myln's 'Lives of the Bishops' (A.D. 1483–1517)*, SHS (Edinburgh, 1915).
Hay, Denys (ed.), *The Anglica Historia of Polydore Vergil, A.D. 1485–1537* (London, 1950).
———, *The Letters of James V: Collected and Calendared by the late Robert Kerr Hannay* (Edinburgh, 1954).
Hay, Gilbert, *The Buik of King Alexander the Conquerour*, John Cartwright (ed.), STS (Edinburgh, 1986).
Heers, Jacques and Georgette de Groer (eds), *Itinéraire d'Anselme Adorno en Terre Sainte (1470–1471)* (Paris, 1978).
Hinds, Allen B. (ed.), *Calendar of Papers and Manuscripts, existing in the Archives and Collections of Milan* (London, 1912).
Housley, Norman (ed.), *Documents on the Later Crusades, 1274–1580* (Basingstoke & London, 1996).
Houwen, L.A.J.R. (ed.), *The Deidis of Armorie: A Heraldic Treatise and Beastiary* (Edinburgh, 1994).
Illustrations of the Topography and Antiquities of the Shires of Aberdeen and Banff, Spalding Club (Aberdeen, 1847–69).

Innes, C. (ed.), *The Book of the Thanes of Cawdor: A Series of Papers Selected from the Charter Room at Cawdor, 1236–1742* (Edinburgh, 1869).
Jervise, A., 'Notice Regarding the Foundation of the Church of Fowlis in Gowrie', *PSAS* 7 (1867–68), pp. 241–8.
Johnston, Alfred W. and Amy Johnston (ed.), *Orkney and Shetland Records* (London, 1907–13).
Kindersley, Edward Cockburn (ed.), *The Very Joyous, Pleasant and Refreshing History of the Feats, Exploits, Triumphs and Achievements of the Good Knight without Fear and without Reproach the Gentle Lord de Bayard* (London, 1848).
Kinsley, James (ed.), *The Poems of William Dunbar* (Oxford, 1979).
Laing, David (ed.), *Facsimilie of an Ancient Heraldic Manuscript Emblazoned by Sir David Lyndsay of the Mount, Lyon King of Armes, 1542* (Edinburgh, 1878).
Lesley, John, *De Origine, Moribus, et Rebus Gestis Scotorum Libri Decem* (Rome, 1578).
———, *The History of Scotland from the Death of King James I in the Year 1424 to the Year 1561*, Bannatyne Club (Edinburgh, 1830).
Letts, Malcolm (ed.), *The Diary of Jörg von Ehingen* (London, 1929).
Lindsay, E.R. and A.I. Cameron (eds), *Calendar of Scottish Supplications to Rome 1418–1422*, SHS (Edinburgh, 1934).
Livingstone, M. et al. (eds), *Registrum Secreti Sigilli Regum Scotorum* (Edinburgh, 1908).
McDiarmid, Matthew P., and James A.C. Stevenson (eds), *Barbour's Bruce: A fredome is a noble thing!*, STS (Edinburgh, 1985).
McNeill, George P. (ed.), *Sir Tristrem*, STS (Edinburgh & London, 1886).
Mackie, R.L., *The Letters of James the Fourth, 1500–1513*, SHS (Edinburgh, 1953).
Macleod, W. and M. Wood (eds), *Protocol Book of John Foular 1501–28*, SRS (Edinburgh, 1927).
MacPhail, J.R.N. (ed.), *Highland Papers*, SHS (Edinburgh, 1914–34).
Macpherson, D. et al. (eds), *Rotuli Scotiae in Turri Londinensi et in Domo Capitulari Westmonasteriensi Asservati* (London, 1814–19).
MacQueen, John (ed.), *Ballattis of Luve 1400–1570* (Edinburgh, 1970).
Marwick, James D., *Charters and Other Documents Relating to the City of Edinburgh, A.D. 1143–1540*, SBRS (Edinburgh, 1871).
Miscellany of the Spalding Club, Spalding Club (Aberdeen, 1841–52).
Munro, Jean and R.W. Munro (eds), *Acts of the Lords of the Isles 1336–1493*, SHS (Edinburgh, 1986).
Murray, James A.H. (ed.), *The Complaynt of Scotland with Ane Exortatione to the Thre Estaits to be Vigilante in the Deffens of Their Public Veil, 1549* (London, 1872).
National Museum of Antiquities of Scotland, *Angels, Nobles and Unicorns: Art and Patronage in Scotland, A Handbook Published in Conjunction with an Exhibition Held at the National Museum of Scotland August 12–September 26, 1982* (Edinburgh, 1982).
Nicolas, N. Harris, *The Siege of Caerlaverock in the XXVIII Edward I. A.D. MCCC: with the arms of the Earls, Barons and Knights, who were present on the occasion* (London, 1828).
———, *The Controversy between Sir Richard Scrope and Sir Robert Grosvenor in the Court of Chivalry A.D. MCCCLXXXV–MCCCXC* (London, 1832).
———, *Proceedings and Ordinances of the Privy Council of England* (London, 1835).

'Notice of Portion of a Stone Mould for Casting Pilgrims' Signacula and Ring Brooches', *PSAS* 41 (1906–07), p. 431.

'The Order of Combats for Life in Scotland as they are anciently recorded in ane old Manuscript of the Law Arms and Offices of Scotland pertaining to James I King of Scots', *The Miscellany of the Spalding Club*, II (Aberdeen, 1842).

Paton, Henry M. (ed.), *Accounts of the Masters of Works for Building and Repairing Royal Palaces and Castles, Volume I, 1529–1615* (Edinburgh, 1957).

Paul, J. Balfour (ed.), *The Scots Peerage* (Edinburgh, 1904–14).

Pinkerton, John, *The History of Scotland from the Accession of the House of Stewart to that of Mary with Appendixes of Original Papers* (London, 1797).

Pitcairn, Robert, *Ancient Criminal Trials in Scotland from 1488 to 1624* (Edinburgh, 1833).

Pitscottie, Robert Lindsay of, *The Historie and Cronicles of Scotland from the Slauchter of King James the First to the Ane Thousande Fyve Hundreith Thrie Scoir Fyftein Zeir*, STS (Edinburgh & London, 1899–1911).

Pollard, A.F. (ed.), *The Reign of Henry VII from Contemporary Sources* (London, 1913).

'The Porteous of Noblenes', in W.A. Craigie (ed.), *The Asloan Manuscript: A Miscellany in Prose and Verse written by John Asloan in the Reign of James the Fifth*, Vol. I (Edinburgh & London, 1923).

Registrum Cartarum Ecclesie Sancti Egidii de Edinburgh, Bannatyne Club (Edinburgh, 1859).

Registrum de Dunfermline (Bannatyne Club, 1842).

Registrum Episcopatus Aberdonensis, Maitland Club (Edinburgh, 1845).

Registrum Honoris de Morton, Bannatyne Club (Edinburgh, 1853).

Reports of the Royal Commission on Historical Manuscripts (London, 1870–).

Ritchie, Graeme (ed.), *The Buik of Alexander the Most Noble and Valiant Conquerour Alexander the Grit by John Barbour, Archdeacon of Aberdeen*, 4 vols, STS (Edinburgh, 1925).

Robb, T.D. (ed.), *The Thre Prestis of Peblis, how thair tald thar talis: Edited From the Asloan and Charteris Texts* (Edinburgh & London, 1920).

Rogers, C. (ed.), *The Earl of Stirling's Register of Royal Letters Relative to the Affairs of Scotland and Nova Scotia from 1615 to 1635* (Edinburgh, 1885).

'The Rout of the Scots', in W. Mackay Mackenzie, *The Secret of Flodden, with 'The Rout of the Scots', a Translation of the Contemporary Italian Poem La Rotta De Scocesi* (Edinburgh, 1931).

Rymer, T. (ed.), *Foedera, Conventiones, Litterae et Cuiuscunque Generis Acta Publica* (London, 1816–69).

Shaw, William A. (ed.), *The Knights of England: A Complete Record from the Earliest Times to the Present Day of the Knights of All the Orders of Chivalry in England, Scotland and Ireland, and of Knights Bachelors* (London, 1906).

Severen, Gilliodts van (ed.), *Inventaire des Archives de la Ville de Bruges* (Bruges, 1876).

Shirley, Janet (trans.), *A Parisian Journal 1405–1449, translated from the Anonymous 'Journal d'un Bourgeois de Paris'*, (Oxford, 1968).

Shirley, John, 'The Dethe of the Kynge of Scotis', in Lister M. Matheson (ed.), *Death and Dissent: Two Fifteenth-Century Chronicles* (Woodbridge, 1999).

'The Short Chronicle of 1482', in Norman Macdougall, *James III: A Political Study* (Edinburgh, 1982), Appendix A.

BIBLIOGRAPHY

Skeat, W.W. (ed.), *Lancelot of the Laik: A Scottish Metrical Romance (About 1490–1500 AD), Re-edited from a Manuscript in the Cambridge University Library, with an Introduction, Notes and Glossarial Index* (London, 1865).

———, *The Kingis Quair Together with A Ballad of Good Council by King James I of Scotland* (Edinburgh & London, 1884).

Skene, F.J.H. (ed.), *Liber Pluscardenis, The Book of Pluscarden* (Edinburgh, 1877–80).

Skene, W.F. (ed.), *Johannis de Fordun, Chronica Gentis Scotorum, John of Fordun's Chronicle of the Scottish Nation* (Edinburgh, 1871–72).

Stevenson, George (ed.), *Pieces from the Mackculloch and the Gray MSS together with the Chepman and Myllar Prints*, STS (Edinburgh, 1918).

Stevenson, J.H. (ed.), *Gilbert of Haye's Prose Manuscript (A.D. 1456), Volume I, The Buke of the Law of Armys or Buke of Bataillis* (Edinburgh, 1901).

Stevenson, Joseph (ed.), *The Scottish Metrical Romance of Lancelot du Lac. Now First Printed from a Manuscript of the Fifteenth Century Belonging to the University of Cambridge with Miscellaneous Poems from the Same Volume* (Maitland Club, 1839).

———, *Letters and Papers Illustrative of the Wars of the English in France During the Reign of Henry the Sixth, King of England* (London, 1861–64).

Stow, John, *A Survey of London: Written in the Year 1598*, Henry Morley (ed.) (Stroud, 1994).

Stuart, J. et al. (eds), *The Exchequer Rolls of Scotland* (Edinburgh, 1878–1908).

'The Testament of Sir David Synclar of Swynbrocht Knycht at Tyngwell, 10 July 1506', *Bannatyne Miscellany III* (Aberdeen, 1960).

Teulet, Alexandre, *Relations Politiques de la France et de l'Espagne avec L'Écosse au XVIe siècle: papiers d'état, pièces et documents inédits ou peu connus tirés de bibliothèque et des archives de France* (Paris, 1862).

Thomson, J.M. et al. (ed.), *Registrum Magni Sigilii Regum Scotorum* (Edinburgh, 1882–1914).

Thomson, Thomas (ed.), *The Auchinleck Chronicle, ane Schort Memoriale of the Scottis Corniklis for Addicioun* (Edinburgh, 1819/1877).

——— and C. Innes (eds), *The Acts of the Parliaments of Scotland* (Edinburgh, 1814–75).

———, *The Acts of the Lords of Council in Civil Causes* (Edinburgh, 1839).

Wood, Marguerite (ed.), *Flodden Papers: Diplomatic Correspondence Between the Courts of France and Scotland, 1507–1517*, SHS (Edinburgh, 1933).

Wyntoun, Andrew, *The Original Chronicle of Andrew of Wyntoun, Printed on Parallel Pages from the Cottonian and Wemyss MS*, F.J. Amours (ed.), STS (Edinburgh & London, 1903–14).

Younge, John, Somerset Herald, 'The Fyancells of Margaret, Eldest Daughter of King Henry VIIth to James King of Scotland: Together with her Departure from England, Journey into Scotland, her Reception and Marriage There, and the Great Feasts Held on that Account', in Thomas Hearne (ed.), *Joannis Leland Antiquarii de Rebus Britannicis Collectanea* (London, 1770).

Secondary Sources

Adams, J. du Quesnay, 'Modern Views of Chivalry, 1884–1984', in H. Chickering and T.H. Seiler (eds), *The Study of Chivalry* (Kalamazoo, 1988).
Anglo, Sydney, 'How to Kill a Man at Your Ease: Fencing Books and the Duelling Ethic', in Sydney Anglo, *Chivalry and the Renaissance* (Woodbridge, 1990).
Archibald, Elizabeth, 'William Dunbar and the Medieval Tradition of Parody', in Roderick J. Lyall and Felicity Riddy (eds), *Proceedings of the Third International Conference on Scottish Language and Literature (Medieval and Renaissance), University of Stirling, 2–7 July 1981* (Stirling & Glasgow, 1981).
Aurell, Martin, 'The Western Nobility in the Late Middle Ages: A Survey of the Historiography and Some Prospects for New Research', in Anne J. Duggan (ed.), *Nobles and Nobility in Medieval Europe: Concepts, Origins, Transformations* (Woodbridge, 2000).
Ayton, Andrew, *Knights and Warhorses: Military Service and the English Aristocracy Under Edward III* (Woodbridge, 1994).
Baker, Derek, 'Legend and Reality: The Case of Waldef of Melrose', in Derek Baker (ed.), *Church, Society and Politics: Papers Read at the Thirteenth Summer Meeting and the Fourteenth Winter Meeting of the Ecclesiastical History Society* (Oxford, 1975).
Baldick, Robert, *The Duel: A History of Duelling* (London, 1965).
Balfour-Melville, E.W.M., *James I, King of Scots, 1406–1437* (London, 1936).
Barber, Richard, *The Knight and Chivalry* (Woodbridge, 1995).
—— (ed.), *The Pastons: A Family in the Wars of the Roses* (Harmondsworth, 1981).
Barber, Richard, *The Reign of Chivalry* (Newton Abbot & London, 1980).
—— and Juliet Barker, *Tournaments: Jousts, Chivalry and Pageants in the Middle Ages* (Woodbridge, 1989).
Barker, Juliet R.V., *The Tournament in England 1100–1400* (Woodbridge, 1986).
Barnie, John, *War in Medieval Society: Social Values and the Hundred Years War 1337–99* (London, 1974).
Barron, Caroline, 'Chivalry, Pageantry and Merchant Culture in Medieval London', in Peter Coss and Maurice Keen (eds), *Heraldry, Pageantry and Social Display in Medieval England* (Woodbridge, 2002).
Barrow, G.W.S., *Robert Bruce and the Community of the Realm of Scotland* (3rd edn, Edinburgh, 1988).
Bartlett, Robert, *Trial by Fire and Water: The Medieval Judicial Ordeal* (Oxford, 1986).
Bawcutt, Priscilla, *Dunbar the Makar* (Oxford, 1992).
Bennett, Matthew, 'The Status of the Squire: the Northern Evidence', in ChristopherHarper-Bill and Ruth Harvey (eds), *The Ideals and Practice of Medieval Knighthood: Papers from the First and Second Strawberry Hill Conferences* (Woodbridge, 1986).
——, *Agincourt 1415: Triumph Against the Odds* (London, 1991).
——, 'Military Masculinity in England and Northern France c.1050–c.1225', in D.M. Hadley (ed.), *Masculinity in Medieval Europe* (London, 1999).
Bennett, Michael, *The Battle of Bosworth* (Gloucester, 1985).
Bentley-Cranch, Dana, and Rosalind K. Marshall, 'Iconography and Literature in the Service of Diplomacy: The Franco-Scottish Alliance, James V and Scotland's

Two French Queens, Madeleine of France and Mary of Guise', in Janet Hadley Williams (ed.), *Stewart Style 1513–1542: Essays on the Court of James V* (East Linton, 1996).

Bernheimer, Richard, *Wild Men in the Middle Ages: A Study in Art, Sentiment, and Demonology* (Harvard, 1952).

Bingham, Caroline, *James V King of Scots 1512–1542* (London, 1971).

Bitterling, Klaus, 'A Note on the Scottish *Buik of Alexander*', *Scottish Literary Journal* 23, 2 (1996), pp. 89–90.

Blanchot, Jean-Jacques, 'William Dunbar in the Scottish Guard in France? An Examination of the Historical Facts', in Roderick J. Lyall and Felicity Riddy (eds), *Proceedings of the Third International Conference on Scottish Literature and Language (Medieval and Renaissance), University of Stirling, 2–7 July 1981* (Stirling & Glasgow, 1981).

Bloch, Marc, *Feudal Society II: Social Classes and Political Organisation* (London, 1962).

Blyth, Charles R., *"The Knychtlyke Stile": A Study of Gavin Douglas's Aeneid* (New York & London, 1987).

Boardman, Stephen, *The Early Stewart Kings: Robert II and Robert III, 1371–1406* (East Linton, 1996).

———, 'Chronicle Propaganda in Fourteenth-Century Scotland: Robert the Steward, John of Fordun and the "Anonymous Chronicle" ', *SHR* 76 (1997), pp. 23–43.

Borst, Arno, 'Knighthood in the Middle Ages: Ideal and Reality', in Fredric L. Cheyette (ed.), *Lordship and Community in Medieval Europe* (New York, 1968).

Borthwick, Alan, 'Bower's Patron, Sir David Stewart of Rosyth', in D.E.R. Watt (ed.), *Walter Bower's Scotichronicon* (Aberdeen, 1993–98), vol. 9, pp. 354–62.

Boulton, D'Arcy Jonathan Dacre, *The Knights of the Crown: The Monarchical Orders of Knighthood in Later Medieval Europe, 1325–1520* (Woodbridge, 1987).

Brown, A.L., 'The Scottish "Establishment" in the Later 15th Century', *JR* 23 (1978), pp. 89–105.

Brown, Jennifer M. (ed.), *Scottish Society in the Fifteenth Century* (London, 1977).

Brown, Keith M., 'The Vanishing Emperor: British Kingship and Its Decline 1603–1707', in Roger A. Mason (ed.), *Scots and Britons: Scottish Political Thought and the Union of 1603* (Cambridge, 1994).

———, *Noble Society in Scotland: Wealth, Family and Culture from Reformation to Revolution* (Edinburgh, 2000).

Brown, Michael, *James I* (Edinburgh, 1994).

———, 'Scotland Tamed? Kings and Magnates in Late Medieval Scotland: A Review of Recent Work', *IR* 45 (1994), pp. 120–46.

———, 'Regional Lordship in North-East Scotland: The Badenoch Stewarts. II. Alexander Stewart Earl of Mar', *Northern Scotland* 16 (1996), pp. 31–53.

———, *The Black Douglases: War and Lordship in Late Medieval Scotland,1300–1455* (East Linton, 1998).

———, ' "Vile Times": Walter Bower's Last Book and the Minority of James II', *SHR* 79 (2000), pp. 165–88.

Brydell, Robert, 'The Monumental Effigies of Scotland from the Thirteenth to the Fifteenth Century' *PSAS* 29 (1894–95), pp. 329–410.

Bumke, Joachim, *Courtly Culture: Literature and Society in the High Middle Ages* (Berkeley, 1991).
Burnett, Charles J., 'Outward Signs of Majesty, 1535–1540', in Janet Hadley Williams (ed.), *Stewart Style 1513–1542: Essays on the Court of James V* (East Linton, 1996).
Caldwell, David H., *Scotland's Wars and Warriors: Winning Against the Odds* (Edinburgh, 1998).
Cameron, Jamie, *James V: The Personal Rule 1528–1542* (Edinburgh, 1994).
Cameron, Sonja, 'Chivalry and Warfare in Barbour's *Bruce*', in Matthew Strickland (ed.), *Armies, Chivalry and Warfare in Medieval Britain and France: Proceedings of the 1995 Harlaxton Symposium* (Stamford, 1998).
Cartellieri, Otto, *The Court of Burgundy: Studies in the History of Civilisation* (London & New York, 1929).
Church, S.D., *The Household Knights of King John* (Cambridge, 1999).
Clanchy, Michael T., *From Memory to Written Record: England 1066–1307* (Oxford, 1993).
Clephan, R. Coltman, *The Tournament: Its Periods and Phases* (London, 1919).
Cline, Ruth Huff, 'The Influence of Romances on Tournaments in the Middle Ages', *Speculum: A Journal of Medieval Studies* 20 (1945), pp. 204–11.
Coltart, J.S., *Scottish Church Architecture* (London, 1936).
Contamine, P., 'The War Literature of the Late Middle Ages: The Treatises of Robert de Balsac and Béraud Stuart, Lord of Aubigny', in C.T. Allmand (ed.), *War, Literature and Politics in the Late Middle Ages* (Liverpool, 1976).
Cooke, T. Etherington, 'Notice of the Heraldic Painted Ceilings in a House at Linlithgow, Now Destroyed', *PSAS* 7 (1867–68), pp. 409–12.
Coss, Peter and Maurice Keen (eds), *Heraldry, Pageantry and Social Display in Medieval England* (Woodbridge, 2002).
Coss, Peter, 'Knighthood, Heraldry and Social Exclusion in Edwardian England', in Peter Coss and Maurice Keen (eds), *Heraldry, Pageantry and Social Display in Medieval England* (Woodbridge, 2002).
Coutts, Alfred, 'The Knights Templars in Scotland', *Records of the Scottish Church History Society* 7 (1938), pp. 126–40.
Cowan, Ian B., 'Church and Society' in Jennifer M. Brown (ed.), *Scottish Society in the Fifteenth Century* (London, 1977).
———, *The Medieval Church in Scotland*, James Kirk (ed.) (Edinburgh, 1995).
——— and David E. Easson, *Medieval Religious Houses Scotland with an Appendix on the Houses of the Isle of Man* (London & New York, 1976).
———, P.H.R. Mackay and Alan Macquarrie (eds), *The Knights of St John of Jerusalem in Scotland*, SHS (Edinburgh, 1983).
Crawford, Barbara E., 'William Sinclair, earl of Orkney, and His Family: A Study in the Politics of Survival', in K.J. Stringer (ed.), *Essays in the Nobility of Medieval Scotland* (Edinburgh, 1985).
Crosby, Ruth, 'Oral Delivery in the Middle Ages', *Speculum: A Journal of Medieval Studies* 11 (1936), pp. 88–110.
Cruden, Stewart, 'Seton Collegiate Church', *PSAS* 89 (1955–56), pp. 417–37.
———, *Scottish Medieval Churches* (Edinburgh, 1986).
Dickinson, W. Croft, 'The Acts of Parliament at Perth, 6 March 1429/30', *SHR* 29 (1950), pp. 1–12.

BIBLIOGRAPHY

Ditchburn, David, *Scotland and Europe: The Medieval Kingdom and its Contacts with Christendom, c.1215–1545* (East Linton, 2000).

Dougall, Mairead, *The Old Parish Church of Hamilton* (n.p., 1987).

Duby, Georges, *The Three Orders: Feudal Society Imagined* (Chicago & London, 1980).

Dunbar, Archibald Hamilton, 'Facsimiles of the Scottish Coats of Arms Emblazoned in the "Armorial de Gelre", with notes', *PSAS* 25 (1890–91), pp. 9–19.

Duncan, A.A.M., *James I King of Scots, 1424–1437* (Department of Scottish History, University of Glasgow, 1984).

Dunlop, Annie I., *The Life and Times of James Kennedy, Bishop of St Andrews* (Edinburgh & London, 1950).

Dunlop, David, 'The "Masked Comedian": Perkin Warbeck's Adventures in Scotland and England from 1495 to 1497', *SHR* 70 (1991), pp. 97–128.

Durkan, John, 'The Beginnings of Humanism in Scotland', *IR* 4 (1953), pp. 5–24.

———, 'Education: The Laying of Fresh Foundations', in John MacQueen (ed.), *Humanism in Renaissance Scotland* (Edinburgh, 1990).

Easson, D.E., 'The Collegiate Churches of Scotland Part II – Their Significance', *Records of the Scottish Church History Society* 7 (1938), pp. 30–47.

Ebin, Lois A., 'John Barbour's "Bruce": Poetry, History and Propaganda', *Studies in Scottish Literature* 9 (1972), pp. 218–42.

Eddy, Elizabeth Roth, 'Sir Thopas and Sir Thomas Norny: Romance Parody in Chaucer and Dunbar', *Review of English Studies* NS 22 (1971), pp. 401–9.

Edington, Carol, *Court and Culture in Renaissance Scotland: Sir David Lindsay of the Mount (1486–1555)* (East Linton, 1994).

———, 'Paragons and Patriots: National Identity and the Chivalric Ideal in Late-Medieval Scotland', in Dauvit Broun, R.J. Finlay and Michael Lynch (eds), *Image and Identity: The Making and Re-making of Scotland Through the Ages* (Edinburgh, 1998).

———, 'The Tournament in Medieval Scotland', in Matthew Strickland (ed.), *Armies, Chivalry and Warfare in Medieval Britain and France: Proceedings of the 1995 Harlaxton Symposium* (Stamford, 1998).

Edwards, John, 'The Templars in Scotland in the Thirteenth Century', *SHR* 5 (1908), pp. 13–25.

———, 'The Hospitallers in Scotland in the Fifteenth Century', *SHR* 9 (1912), pp. 52–68.

Ewan, Elizabeth, *Townlife in Fourteenth-Century Scotland* (Edinburgh, 1990).

Fawcett, Richard, *Innerpeffray Chapel: Official Guide*, (Edinburgh, n.d.).

———, *Scottish Medieval Churches: An Introduction to the Ecclesiastical Architecture of the 12th to 16th Centuries in the Care of the Secretary of State for Scotland* (Edinburgh, 1985).

———, *Seton Collegiate Church* (Edinburgh, 1985).

Ferguson, Arthur B., *The Indian Summer of English Chivalry: Studies in the Decline and Transformation of Chivalric Idealism* (London, 1960).

Ferguson, Donald, *Six Centuries in and around the Church of Saint Nicholas, Dalkeith* (Bonnyrigg, 1951, reprinted 1992).

Ffoulkes, Charles, *The Amourer and his Craft from the XIth to the XVth Century* (New York, 1912 reprinted 1988).

———, 'Some Aspects of the Craft of Armourer', *Archaeologia or Miscellaneous Tracts Relating to Antiquity* 79 (1929), pp. 13–28.

Finlay, John, *Men of Law in Pre-Reformation Scotland* (East Linton, 2000).
Finlayson, W.H., 'The Boyds in Bruges', *SHR* 28 (1949), pp. 195–6.
Forbes-Leith, William (ed.), *The Scots Men-at-Arms and Life-Guards in France From Their Formation until their Final Dissolution* (Edinburgh, 1882).
Fradenburg, Louise Olga, *City, Marriage, Tournament: Arts of Rule in Late Medieval Scotland* (Wisconsin, 1991).
Fraser, James E. ' "A Swan from a Raven": William Wallace, Brucean Propaganda, and *Gesta Annalia* II', *SHR* 81 (2002), pp. 1–22.
Fulton, Robert, 'The Thre Prestis of Peblis', *Studies in Scottish Literature* 11 (1973–74), pp. 23–46.
Gies, Francis, *The Knight in History* (New York, 1984).
Glenn, Jonathan A., 'Gilbert Hay and the Problem of Sources: The Case of the "Buke of the Ordre of Knychthede" ', in Graham Caie, Roderick J. Lyall, Sally Mapstone and Kenneth Simpson (eds), *The European Sun: Proceedings of the Seventh International Conference on Medieval and Renaissance Language and Literature, University of Strathclyde, 1993* (East Linton, 2001).
Goldstein, R. James, 'Blind Harry's Myth of Blood: The Ideological Closure of "The Wallace" ', *Studies in Scottish Literature* 25 (1990), pp. 70–82.
———, ' "For he wald vsurpe na fame": Andrew of Wyntoun's Use of the Modesty *Topos* and Literary Culture in Early Fifteenth-Century Scotland', *Scottish Literary Journal* 14 (1987), pp. 5–18.
Goodare, Julian, *State and Society in Early Modern Scotland* (Oxford, 1999).
Grant, Alexander, 'The Development of the Scottish Peerage', *SHR* 57 (1978), pp. 1–27.
———, *Independence and Nationhood: Scotland 1306–1469* (London, 1984).
———, 'To the Medieval Foundations', *SHR* 73 (1994), pp. 4–24.
———, 'Service and Tenure in Late Medieval Scotland, 1413–1475', in Anne Curry and Elizabeth Matthew (eds), *Concepts and Patterns of Service in the Later Middle Ages* (Woodbridge, 2000).
Gray, Douglas, 'The Royal Entry in Sixteenth-Century Scotland' in Sally Mapstone and Juliette Wood (eds), *The Rose and the Thistle: Essays on the Culture of Late Medieval and Renaissance Scotland* (East Linton, 1998).
———, 'A Scottish "Flower of Chivalry" and his Book', *Words: Wai-Te-AtaStudies in Literature* 4 (1974), pp. 22–34.
Gray, M. Muriel, 'Communications and Replies: Vidas Achinlek, Chevalier', *SHR* 8 (1911), pp. 321–6.
Hale, J.R., 'War and Public Opinion in the Fifteenth and Sixteenth Centuries', *Past and Present* 22 (1962), pp. 18–33.
Hamilton, George, *A History of the House of Hamilton* (Edinburgh, 1933).
Harriss, G.L., 'Introduction: the Exemplar of Kingship', in G.L. Harriss (ed.), *Henry V: The Practice of Kingship* (Oxford, 1985).
Hay, George, 'The Architecture of Scottish Collegiate Churches', in G.W.S. Barrow (ed.), *The Scottish Tradition: Essays in Honour of Ronald Gordon Cant* (Edinburgh, 1974).
Hexter, J.H., 'The Education of the Aristocracy in the Renaissance', in J.H. Hexter, *Reappraisals in History* (London, 1961).
———, 'The Myth of the Middle Class in Tudor England', in J.H. Hexter, *Reappraisals in History* (London, 1961).

Hicks, Michael A., *Bastard Feudalism* (London, 1995).

Higgit, John, 'From Bede to Rabelais – or How St Ninian got his Chain', in Paul Binski and William Noel (eds), *New Offerings, Ancient Treasures: Studies in Medieval Art for George Henderson* (Stroud, 2001).

Hogg, Colin F., *Crichton Collegiate Church: A Short History from Foundation to Restoration* (n.p., 1974).

Hollinshead, Raphael, *The Scottish Chronicle: Or, a Complete History and Description of Scotland, being an Accurate Narration of the Beginning, Increase, Proceedings, Wars, Acts, and Government of the Scottish Nation, from the Original Thereof unto the Year 1585 &c* (Arbroath, 1805).

Housley, Norman, *The Later Crusades, 1274–1580: From Lyons to Alcazar* (Oxford, 1992).

Hughes, Jonathan, *Pastors and Visionaries: Religion and Secular Life in Late Medieval Yorkshire* (Woodbridge, 1988).

Huizinga, Johan, 'The Political and Military Significance of Chivalric Ideas in the Late Middle Ages', in James S. Holmes and Hans van Marle (trans.), *Men and Ideas: History, the Middle Ages, the Renaissance* (London, 1960).

———, *The Waning of the Middle Ages: A Study of the Forms of Life, Thought, and Art in France and the Netherlands in the Fourteenth and Fifteenth Centuries*, Fritz Hopman (trans.) (Harmondsworth, 1972).

———, *The Autumn of the Middle Ages*, Rodney J. Payton and Ulrich Mannitzsch (trans.) (Chicago, 1996).

Jackson, William H., 'Tournaments and the German Chivalric *renovation*: Tournament Discipline and the Myth of Origins' in Sydney Anglo (ed.), *Chivalry in the Renaissance* (Woodbridge, 1990).

Kaeuper, Richard W., *War, Justice and Public Order: England and France in the Later Middle Ages* (Oxford, 1988).

———, *Chivalry and Violence in Medieval Europe* (Oxford, 1999).

Keen, Maurice, 'Chivalry, Nobility, and the Man-at-Arms', in C.T. Allmand (ed.), *War, Literature and Politics in the Late Middle Ages* (Liverpool, 1976).

———, *Chivalry* (New Haven & London, 1984).

———, 'War, Peace and Chivalry', in Maurice Keen, *Nobles, Knights and Men-at-Arms in the Middle Ages* (London & Rio Grande, 1996).

Kennedy, Elspeth, 'The Quest for Identity and the Importance of Lineage in Thirteenth-Century French Prose Romance', in Christopher Harper-Bill and Ruth Harvey (eds), *The Ideals and Practice of Medieval Knighthood II: Papers from the Third Strawberry Hill Conference* (Woodbridge, 1988).

———, 'The Knight as Reader of Arthurian Romance', in Martin B.Shichtman and James P. Carley (eds), *Culture and the King: The Social Implications of the Arthurian Legend, Essays in Honour of Valerie M. Lagorio* (New York, 1994).

Kerr, Andrew, 'The Collegiate Church or Chapel of Rosslyn, Its Builders, Architect, and Construction', *PSAS* 12 (1876–78), pp. 218–44.

Kiernan, V.G., *The Duel in European History: Honour and the Reign of Aristocracy* (Oxford, 1988).

Kilgour, Raymond Lincoln, *The Decline of Chivalry as Shown in the French Literature of the Late Middle Ages* (Harvard, 1937).

Kim, Hyonjin, *The Knight Without the Sword: A Social Landscape of Malorian Chivalry* (Cambridge, 2000).

Kindrick, Robert L., 'Lion or Cat? Henryson's Characterisation of James III', *Studies in Scottish Literature* 14 (1979), pp. 123–36.

——, *Robert Henryson* (Boston, 1979).

——, 'Kings and Rustics: Henryson's Definition of Nobility in *The Moral Fabillis*', in Roderick J. Lyall and Felicity Riddy (eds), *Proceedings of the Third International Conference on Scottish Language and Literature (Medieval and Renaissance), University of Stirling, 2–7 July 1981* (Stirling & Glasgow, 1981).

——, 'Politics and Poetry in the Court of James III', *Studies in Scottish Literature* 19 (1984), pp. 40–55.

Kinghorn, A.M., 'Scottish Historiography in the 14th Century: A New Introduction to Barbour's "Bruce" ', *Studies in Scottish Literature* 6 (1969), pp. 131–45.

Kliman, Bernice W., 'The Idea of Chivalry in John Barbour's *Bruce*', *Mediaeval Studies* 35 (1973), pp. 477–508.

——, 'John Barbour and the Rhetorical Tradition', *Annuale Mediaevale* 18 (1977), pp. 106–35.

Lachaud, Frédérique, 'Armour and Military Dress in Thirteenth- and Early Fourteenth-Century England', in Matthew Strickland (ed.), *Armies, Chivalry and Warfare in Medieval Britain and France: Proceedings of the 1995 Harlaxton Symposium* (Stamford, 1998).

Laing, David, 'The Forrester Monuments in the Church of Corstorphine', *PSAS* 11 (1876), pp. 353–62.

Lawson, H.A.B., 'The Armorial Register of Sir David Lindsay of the Mount', *The Scottish Genealogist* 4 (1957), pp. 12–19.

Legge, M.D., 'The Inauguration of Alexander III', *PSAS* 80 (1948), pp. 73–82.

Leonard, H.H., 'Distraint of Knighthood: The Last Phase, 1625–41', *History* 63 (1978), pp. 23–37.

Lindsay, Lord, *Lives of the Lindsays, or A Memoir of the Houses of Crawford and Balcarres* (London, 1849).

Lyall, Roderick J., 'Books and Book Owners in Fifteenth-Century Scotland', in Jeremy Griffiths and Derek Pearsall (eds), *Book Production and Publishing in Britain 1375–1475* (Cambridge, 1989).

——, 'The Lost Literature of Medieval Scotland', in J. Derrick McClure and Michael R.J. Spiller (eds), *Bryght Lanternis: Essays on the Language and Literature of Medieval and Renaissance Scotland* (Aberdeen, 1989).

——, 'The Medieval Scottish Coronation Service: Some Seventeenth-Century Evidence', *IR* 28 (1977), pp. 3–21.

——, 'Politics and Poetry in Fifteenth and Sixteenth Century Scotland', *Scottish Literary Journal* 3 (1976).

Lynch, Michael, *Scotland: A New History* (London, 1992).

MacDonald, A.A., Michael Lynch and Ian B. Cowan (eds), *The Renaissance in Scotland: Studies in Literature, Religion, History and Culture Offered to John Durkan* (Leiden, New York & Köln, 1994).

——, 'The Chapel of Restalrig: Royal Folly or Venerable Shrine?', in L.A.J.R. Houwen, A.A. MacDonald and S.L. Mapstone (eds), *A Palace in the Wild: Essays on Vernacular Culture and Humanism in Late-Medieval and Renaissance Scotland* (Peeters, 2000).

——, 'Chivalry as a Catalyst of Cultural Change in Late-Medieval Scotland', in

Rudolf Suntrup and Jan R. Veenstra (eds), *Tradition and Innovation in an Era of Change* (Frankfurt am Main & Oxford, 2001).

MacDonald, Alastair J., *Border Bloodshed: Scotland and England at War, 1369–1403* (East Linton, 2000).

———, 'Profit, Politics and Personality: War and the Later Medieval Scottish Nobility', in Terry Brotherstone and David Ditchburn (eds), *Freedom and Authority, Scotland c. 1050–c.1650: Historical and Historiographical Essays Presented to Grant G. Simpson* (East Linton, 2000).

Macdougall, Norman, 'The Sources: A Reappraisal of the Legend', in Jennifer M. Brown (ed.), *Scottish Society in the Fifteenth Century* (London, 1977).

———, *James III: A Political Study* (Edinburgh, 1982).

———, 'Response: At the Medieval Bedrock', *SHR* 73 (1994), pp. 25–6.

———, *James IV* (East Linton, 1997).

Macfarlane, Leslie J., *William Elphinstone and the Kingdom of Scotland, 1431–1514: The Struggle for Order* (Aberdeen, 1985).

Mackay, P.H.R., and Jonathan Riley-Smith, *The Knights of St John: The Story of the Order of St John of Jerusalem in Scotland* (Edinburgh, 1976).

Mackenzie, W. Mackay, *The Secret of Flodden, with 'The Rout of the Scots', a Translation of the Contemporary Italian Poem La Rotta De Scocesi* (Edinburgh, 1931).

Mackie, R.L., *King James IV of Scotland: A Brief Survey of His Life and Times* (Edinburgh, 1958).

Macquarrie, Alan, 'Sir Colin Campbell of Glenorchy (1400–1480) and the Knights Hospitaller', *Notes and Queries of the Society of West Highland and Island Historical Research* 15 (1981), pp. 8–12.

———, 'The Crusades and the Scottish *Gaidhealtachd* in Fact and Legend', in Loraine Maclean (ed.), *The Middle Ages in the Highlands* (Inverness, 1981).

———, *Scotland and the Crusades, 1095–1560* (Edinburgh, 1985).

———, 'Anselm Adornes of Bruges: Traveller in the East and Friend of James II', *IR* 33 (1982), pp. 15–22.

MacQueen, John (ed.), 'The Literature of Fifteenth-Century Scotland', in Jennifer M. Brown (ed.), *Scottish Society in the Fifteenth Century* (London, 1977).

———, *Humanism in Renaissance Scotland* (Edinburgh, 1990).

Malden, John, 'Anselm Adornes and the Two Collars', *The Double Tressure: Journal of the Heraldic Society of Scotland* 10 (1988), pp. 6–10.

———, 'The Unicorn Collar and its English Contemporaries: The Saint Andrew Lecture, 1990', *The Double Tressure: Journal of the Heraldic Society of Scotland* 13 (1991), pp. 5–16.

Mapstone, Sally, 'Was There a Court Literature in Fifteenth-Century Scotland', *Studies in Scottish Literature* 26 (1991), pp. 410–22.

———, 'The *Scotichronicon*'s First Readers', in Barbara E. Crawford (ed.), *Church, Chronicle and Learning in Medieval and Early Renaissance Scotland: Essays Presented to Donald Watt on the Occasion of the Completion of the Publication of Bower's Scotichronicon* (Edinburgh, 1999).

———, 'The Scots, the French, and the English: An Arthurian Episode', in Graham Caie, Roderick J. Lyall, Sally Mapstone and Kenneth Simpson (eds), *The European Sun: Proceedings of the Seventh International Conference on Medieval and Renaissance Scottish Literature and Language, University of Strathclyde, 1993* (East Linton, 2001).

Mason, Roger, 'Kingship, Tyranny and the Right to Resist in Fifteenth Century Scotland', *SHR* 66 (1987), pp. 125–51.

———, 'Chivalry and Citizenship: Aspects of National Identity in Renaissance Scotland', in Roger Mason and Norman Macdougall (eds), *People and Power in Scotland: Essays in Honour of T.C. Smout* (Edinburgh, 1992).

———, *Kingship and the Commonweal: Political Thought in Renaissance and Reformation Scotland* (East Linton, 1998).

———, 'This Realm of Scotland is an Empire? Imperial Ideas and Iconography in Early Renaissance Scotland', in Barbara E. Crawford (ed.),*Chronicle and Learning in Medieval and Early Renaissance Scotland: Essays Presented to Donald Watt on the Occasion of the Completion of the Publication of Bower's* Scotichronicon (Edinburgh, 1999).

———, 'Laicisation and the Law: The Reception of Humanism in Early Renaissance Scotland', in L.A.J.R. Houwen, A.A. MacDonald and S.L. Mapstone (eds), *A Palace in the Wild: Essays on Vernacular Culture and Humanism in Late-Medieval and Renaissance Scotland* (Peeters, 2000).

McCoy, Richard C., *The Rites of Knighthood: The Literature and Politics of Elizabethan Chivalry* (Berkeley, Los Angeles & London, 1989).

McDiarmid, Matthew P., 'The Date of the *Wallace*', *SHR* 34 (1955), pp. 26–31.

McGladdery, Christine, *James II* (Edinburgh, 1990).

McKenna, Steven R., 'Drama and Invective: Traditions in Dunbar's "Fasternis Evin in Hell" ', *Studies in Scottish Literature* 24 (1989), pp. 129–41.

———, 'Legends of James III and the Problem of Henryson's Topicality', *Scottish Literary Journal* 17 (1990), pp. 5–20.

McKim, Anne M., 'James Douglas and Barbour's Ideal of Knighthood', *Forum for Modern Language Studies* 17 (1981), pp. 167–80.

———, 'James Douglas and Barbour's Ideal of Knighthood', in W. H. Jackson (ed.), *Knighthood in Medieval Literature* (Woodbridge, 1981).

———, ' "Gret Price Off Chewalry": Barbour's Debt to Fordun', *Studies in Scottish Literature* 24 (1989), pp. 7–29.

McRoberts, David, 'The Scottish Church and Nationalism in the Fifteenth Century', *IR* 19, 1 (1968), pp. 3–14.

———, 'Scottish Pilgrims to the Holy Land', *IR* 20 (1969), pp. 80–106.

Michel, Francisque, *Les Écossais en France, les Français en Écosse* (London, 1862).

Mill, Anna Jean, *Medieval Plays in Scotland: Thesis Submitted for the Degree of Ph.D. of the University of St Andrews, July 1924* (Edinburgh & London, 1927).

Moorman, Charles, *A Knyght There Was: The Evolution of the Knight in Literature* (Lexington, 1967)

Mortimer, Richard, 'Knights and Knighthood in Germany in the Central Middle Ages', in Christopher Harper-Bill and Ruth Harvey (eds), *The Ideals and Practice of Medieval Knighthood: Papers from the First and Second Strawberry Hill Conferences* (Woodbridge, 1986).

Murray, Athol L., 'The Procedure of the Scottish Exchequer in the early Sixteenth Century', *SHR* 40 (1961), pp. 89–117.

———, 'The Comptroller, 1425–1488', *SHR* 52 (1973), pp. 1–29.

Murray, Peter J., 'The Lay Administrators of Church Lands in the 15th and 16th Centuries', *SHR* 74 (1995), pp. 26–44.

Neilson, George, *Trial by Combat* (Glasgow, 1890).

Neville, Cynthia J., *Violence, Custom and Law: The Anglo-Scottish Border Lands in the Later Middle Ages* (Edinburgh, 1998).

Nichols, Francis Morgan, 'On Feudal and Obligatory Knighthood', *Archaeologia: Or, Miscellaneous Tracts Relating to Antiquity* 39 (1863), pp. 189–244.

Nicholson, Ranald, *Scotland: The Later Middle Ages* (Edinburgh, 1974).

Norman, Joanne S., 'Thematic Implications of Parody in William Dunbar's "Dregy" ', in Roderick J. Lyall and Felicity Riddy (eds), *Proceedings of the Third International Conference on Scottish Language and Literature (Medieval and Renaissance), University of Stirling, 2–7 July 1981* (Stirling & Glasgow, 1981).

———, 'William Dunbar's Rhetoric of Power', in Graham Caie, Roderick J. Lyall, Sally Mapstone and Kenneth Simpson (eds), *The European Sun: Proceedings of the Seventh International Conference on Medieval and Renaissance Scottish Language and Literature, University of Strathclyde, 1993* (East Linton, 2001).

North, Sally, 'The Ideal Knight as Presented in Some French Narrative Poems, c.1090–c.1240: An Outline Sketch', in Christopher Harper-Bill and Ruth Harvey (eds), *The Ideals and Practice of Medieval Knighthood: Papers from the First and Second Strawberry Hill Conferences* (Woodbridge, 1986).

Oakley, Stewart, *The Story of Denmark* (London, 1972).

Orme, Nicholas, *From Childhood to Chivalry: The Education of the English Kings and Aristocracy 1066–1530* (London & New York, 1984).

Penman, Michael A., 'Christian Days and Knights: The religious devotions and court of David II of Scotland', *Historical Research* 75, 189 (2002), pp. 249–72.

———, *David II, 1329–71* (East Linton, 2004).

Pierce, Ian, 'The Knight, his Arms and Armour in the Eleventh and Twelfth Centuries', in Christopher Harvey-Bill and Ruth Harvey (eds), *The Ideals and Practice of Medieval Knighthood: Papers from the First and Second Strawberry Hill Conferences* (Woodbridge, 1986).

Pilbrow, Fionn, 'The Knights of the Bath: Dubbing to Knighthood in Lancastrian and Yorkist England', in Peter Coss and Maurice Keen (eds), *Heraldry, Pageantry and Social Display in Medieval England* (Woodbridge, 2002).

Purdon, Liam O. and Julian N. Wasserman, 'Chivalry and Feudal Obligation in Barbour's "Bruce"', in Liam O. Purdon and Cindy L. Vitto (eds), *The Rusted Hauberk: Feudal Ideals of Order and their Decline* (Gainsville, 1994).

Ramsay, Brian, *By Hill and Loch: A History of Guthrie and Rescobie Churches* (n.p., 1991).

Riddy, Felicity, 'The Revival of Chivalry in Late Medieval Scotland', in Jeans-Jacques Blanchot and Claude Grad (eds), *Actes du 2e Colloque de Langue et de Littérature Écossaises (Moyen Age et Renaissance)* (Strasbourg, 1978).

Ross, Alexander, 'Notice of St Clement's Church at Rowdill, Harris', *PSAS* 19 (1884–85), pp. 118–32.

Ross, Ian Simpson, *William Dunbar* (Leiden, 1981).

Saul, Nigel, *Knights and Esquires: The Gloucestershire Gentry in the Fourteenth Century* (Oxford, 1981).

Scaglione, Aldo, *Knights at Court: Courtliness, Chivalry and Courtesy from Ottonian Germany to the Italian Renaissance* (Berkeley, Los Angeles & Oxford, 1991).

Schep, W., 'The Thematic Unity of Lancelot of the Laik', *Studies in Scottish Literature* 5 (1968), pp. 167–75.

Scott, Tom, *Dunbar: A Critical Exposition of the Poems* (Edinburgh & London, 1966).

Sellar, David, 'Courtesy, Battle and the Brieve of Right, 1368 – A Story Continued', in David Sellar (ed.), *The Stair Society Miscellany II* (Edinburgh, 1984).
Seton, George, *The Law and Practice of Heraldry in Scotland* (Edinburgh, 1863).
———, *A History of the Family of Seton* (Edinburgh, 1896).
Shenton, Caroline, 'Edward III and the Symbol of Leopard', in Peter Coss and Maurice Keen (eds), *Heraldry, Pageantry and Social Display in Medieval England* (Woodbridge, 2002).
Skeat, Walter W., 'The Author of "Lancelot of the Laik" ', *SHR* 8 (1911), pp. 1–4.
Stark, William, and George Paul, *A Short History of the Church in Carnwath* (n.p., 1967).
Stearns, Marshall W., *Robert Henryson* (New York, 1949).
Stell, Geoffrey, 'Late Medieval Defences in Scotland', in David H. Caldwell, *Scottish Weapons and Fortifications, 1100–1800* (Edinburgh, 1981).
Stevenson, Alexander, 'Medieval Scottish Associations with Bruges', in Terry Brotherstone and David Ditchburn (eds), *Freedom and Authority, Scotland c.1050–c.1650: Historical and Historiographical Essays Presented to Grant G. Simpson* (East Linton, 2000).
Stevenson, Katie, 'The Unicorn, St Andrew and the Thistle: Was there an Order of Chivalry in Late Medieval Scotland?', *SHR* 83 (2004), pp. 3–22.
Strickland, Matthew, 'Arms and the Men: War, Loyalty and Lordship in Jordan Fantosme's Chronicle', in Christopher Harper-Bill and Ruth Harvey (eds), *Medieval Knighthood IV: Papers from the Fifth Strawberry Hill Conference, 1990* (Woodbridge, 1992).
———, 'Provoking or Avoiding Battle? Challenge, Duel and Single Combat in Warfare in the High Middle Ages', in Matthew Strickland (ed.), *Armies, Chivalry and Warfare in Medieval Britain and France: Proceedings of the 1995 Harlaxton Symposium* (Stamford, 1998).
Strong, Roy, *Art and Power: Renaissance Festivals 1450–1650* (Woodbridge, 1984).
Sumption, Jonathan, *Pilgrimage: An Image of Mediaeval Religion* (London, 1975).
Swinton, George S.C., 'John of Swinton: A Border Fighter in the Middle Ages', *SHR* 16 (1919), pp. 261–79.
Tanner, Roland, *The Late Medieval Scottish Parliament: Politics and the Three Estates, 1424–1488* (East Linton, 2001).
Ting, Judith, 'A Reappraisal of William Dunbar's *Dregy*', *Scottish Literary Journal* 14 (1987), pp. 19–36.
Torrie, Elizabeth P.D., *Medieval Dundee: A Town and its People* (Dundee, 1990).
Vale, Malcolm, *War and Chivalry: Warfare and Aristocratic Culture in England, France and Burgundy at the End of the Middle Ages* (London, 1981).
Vaughan, Richard, *John the Fearless: The Growth of Burgundian Power* (London & New York, 1979).
Vogel, Bertram, 'Secular Politics and the Date of *Lancelot of the Laik*', *Studies in Philology* 40 (1943), pp. 1–13.
Walsh, Elizabeth, 'Hary's Wallace: The Evolution of a Hero', *Scottish Literary Journal* 11 (1984), pp. 5–19.
———, '*Golagros and Gawane*: A Word for Peace', in J. Derrick McClure and Michael R.J. Spiller (eds), *Bryght Lanternis: Essays on the Language and Literature of Medieval and Renaissance Scotland* (Aberdeen, 1989).

Warner, M., 'Chivalry in Action: Thomas Montagu and the War in France, 1417–1428', *Nottingham Medieval Studies* 42 (1998), pp. 146–73.
Webb, Diana, *Pilgrims and Pilgrimage in the Medieval West* (London & New York, 1999).
Wilson, Grace G., 'Andrew of Wyntoun: More than Just "That Dreich Clerk"', *Scotia: American-Canadian Journal of Scottish Studies* 10 (1986), pp. 189–201.
———, 'Barbour's "Bruce" and Hary's "Wallace": Complements, Compensations and Conventions', *Studies in Scottish Literature* 25 (1990), pp. 189–201.
Wilson, S.C., 'Scottish Canterbury Pilgrims', *SHR* 24 (1927).
Wittig, Kurt, *The Scottish Tradition in Literature* (Edinburgh & London, 1958).
Wormald, Jenny, *Lords and Men in Scotland: Bonds of Manrent, 1442–1603* (Edinburgh, 1985).
———, 'Taming the Magnates?', in K.J. Stringer (ed.), *Essays on the Nobility of Medieval Scotland* (Edinburgh, 1985)
———, 'Lords and Lairds in Fifteenth-Century Scotland: Nobles and Gentry?' in Michael Jones (ed.), *Gentry and Lesser Nobility in Late Medieval Europe* (Gloucester & New York, 1986).
Wright, N.A.R., 'The "Tree of Battles" of Honoré Bouvet and the Laws of War', in C.T. Allmand (ed.), *War, Literature and Politics in the Late Middle Ages* (Liverpool, 1976).
Wylie, James Hamilton and William Templeton Waugh, *The Reign of Henry the Fifth* (Cambridge, 1929).
Yeoman, Peter, *Pilgrimage in Medieval Scotland* (London, 1999).

Unpublished Theses

Boardman, Stephen I., 'Politics and the Feud in Late Medieval Scotland' (Ph.D., University of St Andrews, 1989).
Borthwick, Alan, 'The King, Council and Councillors in Scotland c.1430–1460' (Ph.D. University of Edinburgh, 1989).
Chalmers, Trevor M., 'The King's Council, Patronage, and the Governance of Scotland, 1460–1513' (Ph.D., University of Aberdeen, 1982).
Fulton, Robin William Macpherson, 'Social Criticism in Scottish Literature 1480–1560' (Ph.D., University of Edinburgh, 1972)
Kelham, Charles Adrian, 'Bases of Magnatial Power in Later Fifteenth-Century Scotland' (Ph.D., University of Edinburgh, 1986).
Macquarrie, Alan Denis, 'The Impact of the Crusading Movement in Scotland, 1095–c.1560' (Ph.D., University of Edinburgh, 1982).
Mainer, Sergi, 'A Comparison of Barbour's *Bruce* and John the Minstrel's *Histoire de Guillaume le Maréchal* as National Paradigms of Heroic-Chivalric Biographies' (M.Sc., University of Edinburgh, 2001).
Mainer, Sergi, 'The Scottish Romance Tradition within the European Context, c.1375–c.1536' (Ph.D., University of Edinburgh, 2004).
McRaven, Patricia A., 'John Barbour's Narrative Technique in *The Bruce*' (Ph.D., University of Iowa, 1979).
Mapstone, Sally, 'The Advice to Princes Tradition in Scottish Literature, 1450–1500' (D.Phil., University of Oxford, 1987).

Rosie, Alison, 'Ritual, Chivalry and Pageantry: The Courts of Anjou, Orléans and Savoy in the Later Middle Ages' (Ph.D., University of Edinburgh, 1989).

Scott, Margaret Cochrane, 'Dress in Scotland 1406–1460' (Ph.D., University of London, 1987).

Stevenson, Katherine C., 'Knighthood, Chivalry and the Crown in Fifteenth-Century Scotland, 1424–1513' (Ph.D., University of Edinburgh, 2003).

Tanner, Roland J., 'The Political Role of the Three Estates in Parliament and General Council in Scotland, 1424–1488' (Ph.D., University of St Andrews, 1999).

Thomas, Andrea, 'Renaissance Culture at the Court of James V, 1528–1542' (Ph.D., University of Edinburgh, 1997).

Väthjunker, Sonja, 'A Study in the Career of Sir James Douglas' (Ph.D., University of Aberdeen, 1992).

INDEX

Abercorn Castle 32 n.103
Aberdeen 15, 120
Abernethy, John 105
Absolon 161
Achilles 161
administrative service 16, 17, 25–6, 29, 32, 34–9, 184, 190–1
Adornes, Anselm, of Bruges 49–50, 113–14, 129, 183–4
Adornes, John, of Bruges 49–50, 113–14, 183
Adorneshof 130
Agamemnon 160
Aire 79 n.74
Airth, Robert 17
Albany-Stewart family 61, 70, 170, 179
Alexander III, king of Scotland (1249–86) 43–4
Alexander the Great 134, 161
Alexandria 104
Angus 24
Annan 185
Arbroath, abbot of 25
Arbuthnott, Robert, of that Ilk 108
archery 175–6
Armorial de Gelre 105
armour 17, 19, 20, 23, 63, 68, 74, 78, 96, 128
Argyll 24
arsenal 32–3, 175, 179, 186, 190
Arthur and Arthurian legend 2, 69, 72, 134, 148, 161, 167, 168, 185, 187, 188
Atholl 24
Auchinleck, Adam 79 n.72, 115
Auchinleck Chronicle 141
Avignon 112
Ayala, Don Pedro de, Spanish ambassador 23, 26

Bailey, William, of Lamington 184
The Ballet of the Nine Nobles 134
Balmelkine, Simon de 112
Bannockburn 45, 50
banquets and feasts 76, 90, 92, 94, 96, 160, 170
baptisms 18, 47–8, 54, 172
Barbour, John, archdeacon of Aberdeen (c.1330–95), *The Bruce* 5, 26, 45–6, 61, 113, 132, 134, 138, 145, 151–7, 167, 168
Barclay, Alexander 35 n.115, 59
Barry, Thomas, canon of Glasgow 136–7
Battlehaugh 64
battles 7, 41, 50, 131
  Roslin 1302 167
  Bannockburn 1314 45, 50
  Otterburn 1388 51, 136
  Humbleton Hill 1402 50, 57–8
  Tannenberg 1410 106
  Verneuil 1424 50 n.40
  Herrings 1429 112
  Bosworth 1485 25
  Sauchieburn 1488 30, 31, 50, 114
  Flodden 1513 97, 110, 175, 189
  Pinkie 1547 165
Bayard, Chevalier 79 n.74
Bayezid II 109
Beaufort, Edmund, count of Mortain 71 n.38
Beaufort, Joan, wife of James I 71 n.38, 166
Bellenden, John 141–2
bellmen 24
Bell's Tower 185
Benedict XIII 14
Bishop, James 79 n.72, 115
Bisset, Thomas 104, 112
Black Douglases *see* Douglas family

213

INDEX

Black Lady 95
Blackadder 184
Blackadder, Baldred 186
Blackadder, Patrick 186
Blackness Castle 62, 181
Blind Harry (c.1440–c.1493) 7, 21
   The Wallace 14–15, 81, 150–2, 157, 167, 168
Boece, Hector 141–2
Bolomer, John 70
Bonet, Honoré 143
Book of Pluscarden 14, 21, 41–2, 44, 132, 141
Book of the Order of Chivalry 82
Borthwick, James, of Glengelt 184
Borthwick, Thomas, of Collielaw 189
Borthwick, Willam, of that Ilk 47, 172, 174
Borthwick, William 47
Boswell, Thomas 95
Bosworth 25
Bothwell 121
Bouillon, Godfrey de 134, 161
Boutard, Jean 15
Bower, Walter, abbot of Inchcolm Abbey (d.1493) 7, 14, 21, 54, 103, 106
   Scotichronicon 14, 43, 47–8, 53, 57, 59, 64, 70, 89, 111, 135, 139–42, 144, 166, 175–6, 177, 178
bowyers 21, 66, 83
Boyd, Alexander, of Drumcoll (d.1469) 36 n.126, 37–9, 181, 182
Boyd, Robert, Lord Boyd 38 n.137
Boyd, Thomas, earl of Arran 22, 121, 166, 176
Bretel 67
Brochton, Thomas 50
Bromwich, John 18
Brown, John, of Midmar 173
The Bruce see Barbour, John
Bruce, Alexander, of Earlshall 25
Bruce, Edward, brother of Robert I 26, 157
Bruce, David, of Clackmannan 181, 189
Bruce, Henry 93
Bruce, Robert *see* Robert I

Bruce, Robert, of Airth 188–9
Bruges 76–7, 113, 129
Buchan, John, earl of 173
Buchanan, George, *History* 59
The Buik of Alexander 5, 133, 134
The Buik of King Alexander the Conqueror 133
The Buke of the Gouernaunce of Princis see under Hay, Gilbert
The Buke of the Law of Armys see under Hay, Gilbert
The Buke of the Ordre of Knychthede see under Hay, Gilbert
Bull, Stephen 31 n.95
Buonconsiglio Castle 89
burgesses 9, 16–17, 30 n.84, 192
Bute, John 160

Caesar, Julius 134, 161
Calais 77, 115
campaigns, military 7, 54, 84, 141, 189
   Liège 1407 58
   Highlands 1428 & 1429 25, 27, 35, 173–4
Campbell, Agnes 127
Campbell, Colin 145
Campbell, Colin, earl of Argyll, chancellor 24
Campbell, Colin, of Glenorchy 79, 108, 114–15, 180–1
Canterbury 36, 110, 116–7
cards 90
Carlyle, John, first Lord of Carlyle 48
Carlyle, William 48
Carnwath 121, 126
Catherine, wife of Henry V 170
Caumont, Nompar de 106
Caupance, John, French squire 85, 97
Castlemilk 185
Cawdor, William, Thane of 183
Caxton, William 82
Certaine Matters Composed Together 42–3
Cessford 184
Chalmers, Christian 35 n.115
Chalmers, William 15
Chalon sur Saône 36 n.55, 78–9, 115
Charlemagne 100, 132, 134, 161

INDEX

Charles of Sweden 106
Charles VI, king of France (1380–1422) 58
Charles VII, king of France (1422–61) 35, 35 n.115, 79
Charles VIII, king of France (1483–98) 28, 82
Charny, Geoffrey de 10, 28, 34
Charteris, John, of Amisfield 65
Charteris, Robert, laird of Amisfield 185
Chastellain 53, 73
Chaucer 111
Chepman & Myllar 28 n.76, 134, 149
chivalric culture 5, 6, 69, 73, 77, 78, 82, 172, 179, 182, 186, 188
chivalric heroes 5, 57, 131, 132, 134, 135, 137, 138 139, 141, 150–1, 156–7
chivalric ideal 3, 4, 5, 6, 12, 21, 22, 34, 38, 89, 94, 106, 109, 131, 132, 134, 136, 137, 138, 141, 144, 147, 151–5, 156, 157, 158, 164, 165, 168, 179, 186, 188, 190–1
chivalric literature 1, 5, 9, 50, 54, 131–5, 143, 147–8, 192
chivalric manuals 20, 142–7
chivalry
 and kingship 4, 7, 11, 42, 70, 170–92
 centres of 6–7, 143, 158, 179–80, 182
 Christian component 3, 7, 11–12, 130, 131, 137, 166, 189, 192
 codes of conduct 1, 3, 11, 13, 17, 20, 64, 70, 141, 145, 146–7, 152, 156
 definition 3–12, 41, 170, 189
 martial component 3, 6, 7, 26, 34, 189, 192
 noble component 3, 7, 8, 189, 192
 school of chivalry 21-2
 social exclusivity 2, 6, 7, 8, 82, 88, 187
Christian I, king of Denmark, Norway and Sweden 82
Chronica Gentis Scotorum see Fordun, John of
chronicles 135–42

Chronicles of Scotland 141–2
Church 12, 192
churches 103, 111, 119–30, 177
 Bothwell 121; Bruges 129; Carnwath 121, 126; Corstorphine 15, 120, 121–2, 125, 126, 127; Crichton 36, 122; Cullen 126; Dalkeith 121; Dirleton 122; Dornoch 119; Douglas 125; Dundee 116, 120; Dunglass 116, 122–3; Falkirk 125; Fowlis 125; Guthrie 123, 126; Hamilton 116, 122, 123; Holy Trinity, St Andrews 125; Houston 127; Innerpeffray 124; Kilmaurs 120; Kinross 120; Lincluden 121, 126; Methven 121, 126; Ratho 14; Renfrew 127; Rodel 128; Roslin 68, 119, 120, 122, 123; Roskilde 120; St Giles, Edinburgh 118; St Magnus, Kirkwall 119, 120; St Nicholas, Aberdeen 120, 127; St Salvator, St Andrews 126; Sant Andrea delle Frate 115; Semple 124, 126; Seton 120, 124, 125, 126, 127; Strathmiglo 124; Tarbolton 124; Tullibardine 122; Yester 121
Clackmannan 24
Cleansing of the Causeway 39
Clerk, Jonathan 79 n.72, 115
Clerk, Thomas 111
coats of arms 27, 45, 51, 73 n.47, 125, 127–8, 129, 135, *see also* heraldry
Cockburn, Adam 96
Cockburn, William, of Langton 93
Cocklaw 184
Colleime, David 51–2
Colquhoun, John, of that Ilk 183
Colville, William, of Ochiltree 186
Complaint of the Black Knight 28 n.76
Complaynt of Scotland 149–50
Comyn, John 167
Comyn, Richard 104
Comyn, Walter, earl of Menteith 43–4
constable of England 20, 75
constable of Scotland 66, 93

215

INDEX

coronations 41–6, 54, 59, 70, 102, 170, 180, *see also* Alexander III; James I; James III; Charles VII
Corry, Gilbert 73
Corry, James 73
Corstorphine 15, 120, 121–2, 125, 126, 127
court
  Burgundian 7, 69, 79, 100, 183
  English 6, 79 n.72, 100, 170, 173, 179
  French 6, 27–8, 71, 79, 81, 100, 144
  Scottish 1, 2, 6–7, 9, 19, 26, 29, 39, 40, 49, 50, 80, 81, 89, 100, 113, 129, 158, 163, 168, 179, 181, 189
court of chivalry 18
court jesters 159–61, *see also* Norny, Thomas; Curry; Bute, John
court poetry 157–65
court poets *see* Dunbar, William; Lindsay, David
courtly love 4, 7, 53–4, 91–2, 131, 166–8, 187, 188–9, 192
Cranston, John, of that Ilk 184
Cranston, Thomas, of that Ilk 36, 79 n.72, 115
Cranston, William, of that Ilk 36, 62, 78, 79, 115, 180, 182
Crichton 36, 122
Crichton Castle 122
Crichton, George, of Blackness 180
Crichton, James, of Carnis 30, 183
Crichton, James, of that Ilk 47
Crichton, Patrick, of Cranstonriddel 39
Crichton, William, of that Ilk 27, 35–6, 47, 117, 122, 172, 174, 179
crown 41, 43
crusades & crusading 1, 4, 12, 48, 103–10, 130, 189
Cumming, William, of Inverallochy 68
Cunningham, Alexander 65
Cunningham, John 60
Cunningham, Robert, of Kilmaurs 45, 46
Cunningham, Robert, of Polmaise 48

Cunningham, William, lord of Kilmaurs 121
Curry 160
Cutlar, Robert 90, 92

D'arcy, Anthony, de la Bastie 85–6
D'argentan, Giles 138
Dalkeith 121
Dalrymple 65
Dalrymple, John 17
Dalzel, William de 89
Dame Scotia 149–50
dances 90
David 134, 161
David II, king of Scotland (1329–71) 1, 72, 104
Davidson, Walter 174
Derby, earl of *see* Henry IV, king of England
Dingwall Castle 25
diplomacy 22, 32, 34, 35–6, 37, 49–50, 54, 69, 71, 73, 104, 109, 122, 184, 186, 190–1
Dirleton 122
Dodds, Jonathan 79 n.72, 115
Dolphinstoun 184
Douglas 15, 125
Douglas, Archibald 104
Douglas, Archibald, earl of Moray 116
Douglas, Archibald, fifth earl of Angus 32, 116, 124–5
Douglas, Archibald, fifth earl of Douglas (d.1439) 27, 35 n.114, 47, 60, 129, 171, 172, 174
Douglas, Archibald, fourth earl of Douglas (d.1424) 35 n.113, 50 n.40, 56, 64, 121, 173 n.18
Douglas, Archibald, lord of Galloway 121
Douglas, Archibald, third earl of Douglas (d.1400) 136
Douglas, Gavin, *Palice of Honour* 92, 188
Douglas, Hugh, earl of Ormond 116
Douglas, James, of Ralstoun (also of Loch Leven and Lugton) 52–3, 72–6, 181

216

INDEX

Douglas, James, ninth earl of Douglas (c.1427–88)   18, 52–3, 72–6, 79, 115, 116, 117, 181
Douglas, James, of Balvenie   27, 47, 172, 173
Douglas, James, of Dalkeith   121, 132
Douglas, James, of Drumlanrig   65
Douglas, James, of Strathbrock   105
Douglas, James, second earl of Douglas (d.1388)   51
Douglas, James, seventh earl of Douglas (d.1443)   126
Douglas, James 'the Gud' (d.1330)   9, 45, 50, 56 n.66, 113, 151, 153, 155–6
Douglas, John, lord of Balvenie   116
Douglas, William, earl of Angus (d.1437)   35 n.114, 56, 60, 171, 173, 174
Douglas, William, eighth earl of Douglas (d.1452)   36, 37, 47, 52, 65 n.9, 72, 73, 79, 113, 115–16, 117
Douglas, William, of Cavers   48
Douglas, William, of Drumlanrig   186
Douglas, William, of Nithsdale   105, 137–8, 140
Douglas, William, of Strathbrock   105
Douglas, William, sixth earl of Douglas (1425–40)   47, 59, 172
Douglas family (Black Douglases)   15, 21, 27, 37, 39, 61, 65, 70, 72–3, 73 n.47, 75, 78, 80, 113, 121, 129, 143
Doune Castle   30
Drummond, John Lord   124
dubbing   9, 13, 16, 17–19, 28, 29, 30, 32, 35, 41–62, 74, 84, 106, 145, 146, 171–2, 179, 181, 183–4, 186, 188, 191–2
dubbing ceremony   17, 28, 30, 41–62, 145, 159, 181
Duchal   97, 114
duels, judidcial   64–5, 70, *see also* tournaments
Dumbarton Castle   24, 37, 57 n.70, 97, 114
Dunbar, James, of Cumnock   62
Dunbar, Gavin   61
Dunbar, George, earl of March (d. c.1455)   35 n.114, 60, 117, 171

Dunbar, Patrick   117
Dunbar, William (c.1460–c.1513)   28, 86–9, 158, 165, 166
  Ballade of Barnard Stewart   28, 86, 96, 161–2
  Fasternis Evin in Hell   86–9, 158
  The Lament for the Makaris   143
  Quod tu in cinerem reverteris   161
  Schir Thomas Norny   86, 158–61
  Thrissill and the Rois   92
Dunbar Castle   32, 104, 167
Dundas, Archibald   116
Dundas Castle   36
Dunkeld   109
Dunlop, John   95
Duns   51
Dunstable   95
Durham   54
Durham, bishop of   93
Durward, Sir Alan   43

Edinburgh   17, 20, 53, 105, 158
Edinburgh Castle   35, 37, 38, 39, 64, 85
Edgarston   184
Edmonstone, James, of that Ilk   47, 172, 184
Edmonstone, John, of that Ilk   105
education   19–22, 37–8, 39, 131–2, 146, 191, *see also* military training
Edward I, king of England (1272–1307)   29
Edward III, king of England (1327–77)   1, 95
Edward IV, king of England (1461–83)   75, 114
effigies   15, 17, 125–30
Egidia, sister of the earl of Carrick   141
Ellem   24
Elphinstoun, Alexander   95
epic poetry   145, 150–7
Eric, king of Denmark and Norway (1396–1442)   35
Erskine, Nicholas   104
Erskine, Robert   58 n.75, 104–5
Erskine, Robert, of Ellem   186
Erskine, Thomas   50, 56–7, 58, 62, 105
Erskine, Thomas, second Lord   133

217

Erskine, William, of Kinnoul   34, 171
Eskdale, raid of   97
espionage   34

Falkirk   125
Falkland   102
Feast of Fools   160
Felawe, George   79 n.72, 115
Ferrand erl of Flandris   134
Ferrers, Ralph   20
feudalism   23
Fife   24
Fitzgilbert, John   56 n.66
Fleming, Robert, Lord Fleming   38 n.137
fletchers   21
Flodden   97, 110, 175, 189
The Flower   31
Foggo, David   79 n.74
football   21
Forbes, Alexander, Lord Forbes   24, 174
Forbes, Alexander   23, 58
Forbes, James, Lord Forbes   58
Forbes, William   25, 174
Fordun, John of   14, 44
Forman, Andrew   32 n.99
Forman, John   96
Forman, John, of Rutherford   189
Forrester, Adam   121–2, 127–8
Forrester, Alexander, of Corstorphine   116, 117, 128, 183
Forrester, Gilbert   116
Forrester, John   127–8
Forrester, John, of Corstorphine   15, 27, 119, 121, 127–8, 173
Forrester, Walter, of Torwood   186
Forrester family of Corstorphine   9, 15, 122, 125, 126, 127–8
forty-day service   23–4, 27, 174
Fowlis   125
France, Scots in   27–8, 35, 58–9, 60, 81, 112, 122, 144, 161–2, 163, 170
Fraser, Simon   167
Frederick II   8
Frendraught, James Lord   73
Froissart, Jean   51–2, 72
Fulk Fitzwarin   67

Fyndlaw the Fute Band   165

Galbraith, Patrick   56–7
Galford, David   65
games *see* tournaments; football; golf; cards
Gaunt, John of   57
Gawain   28 n.76, 134
Gentleman of the Bedchamber *see* Crichton, William, of that Ilk
Gesta Annalia   14
Gilliebrand, Lawrence   104
Glasgow, archbishop of   32 n.99
Glendenning, Simon   36 n.126, 182
Gleneagles, Lady   163–4
Gloucester, duke of   45, 60
Golagros   28 n.76, 134
golf   21
Gordon, Adam, of that Ilk   50, 57–8
Gordon, Alexander, earl of Huntly   58
Gordon, Lady Catherine   187
Gordon, George, second earl of Huntly   24, 25
Gordon, John   140
government *see* kingship, practice of
Graham, Malise, earl of Menteith   54, 116
Granada   109
Gray, Andrew   79 n.72, 115
Gray, Andrew, of Foulis, Lord Gray   36, 182
Gray, Andrew, second Lord Gray   97, 98, 117, 125
Gray, Patrick, master of Gray   36 n.126
Greenlaw   79 n.72, 115
Greenside   20, 80, 91
Greensward   91, 93, 97
Grymslaw, John de   65
Gueldres, Mary of   36, 76–8, 181
Guinevere   148, 168
Guise, Mary of   101
gunners   24, 32–3, 32 n.103, 177–8
Guthrie   123, 126
Guthrie, Alexander, of that Ilk   124
Guthrie, David, of that Ilk   30 n.81, 123
Guyane, French gunner   32

INDEX

Hacket, William 65
Haddington 17, 91
Haliburton, George 79 n.72, 115
Haliburton, John, squire 138
Haliburton, Jonathan 79 n.72, 115
Haliburton, Patrick 84
Haliburton, Walter, of Dirleton 19, 27, 36, 122, 174
Hamilton, James 79
Hamilton, James, of Fingaltoun 180
Hamilton, James, of Finnart 39–40
Hamilton, James, Lord Hamilton, earl of Arran 32, 85–6, 91–2, 93, 97, 98, 115, 116, 117, 123, 176
Hamilton, Patrick, of Kincavil 85, 91–2, 93, 97, 98
Hamilton family 39
Hannibal 160
Hans, gunner from the Low Countries 32
Hans, king of Norway, Denmark and Sweden 82
Hardy, John 64
Hartilton, Roger 50
Hatton 181
Hay, David, of Yester 180
Hay, Gilbert 10, 12, 23, 34, 35 n.115, 39, 59, 80, 142–3, 145, 165, 190
 Buik of King Alexander the Conqueror 133
 Buke of the Gouernaunce of Princis 142
 Buke of the Law of Armys 142–5, 146, 175
 The Buke of the Ordre of Knychthede 9, 12, 20, 22, 29, 42, 47, 50, 61, 64, 77, 92, 103, 142, 143, 145–7
Hay, Gilbert 58, 117
Hay, John, of Belltown 54 n.57, 189
Hay, Thomas, of Yester 171
Hay, William, lord of Nauchton 58, 183
Hay, William, of Errol 171
Hay, William, sheriff of Peebles 120
Hay, William, third earl of Errol 24, 35 n.114, 74, 93
Hays of Erroll, hereditary constables 66

Heartshead, John 90
Hector 134, 161
Henric, gunner from the Low Countries 32
Henry III, king of England (1216–72) 44
Henry IV, king of England (1399–1413) 2, 70
Henry V, king of England (1413–22) 2, 70–1, 170, 171, 175, 179
Henry VI, king of England (1422–71) 65 n.9, 71, 79 n.72
Henry VII, king of England (1485–1509) 25, 34, 61
Henry VIII, king of England (1509–47) 99
Henryson, Robert 150
Hepburn, Adam, of Hailes 27, 171, 174
Hepburn, Alexander 17
Hepburn, Archibald 17
Hepburn, Janet 124
Hepburn, Patrick 105
Hepburn, Patrick, Lord Hailes, first earl of Bothwell 32 n.99, 53, 91–2, 93, 97, 123, 188
Hepburn, Patrick, of Hailes 140
Hepburn, Patrick, of Wauchton 180
Hepburn, Thomas 17
heraldry 67–9, 123, 125, 127–8, 129, 189
heralds 78
 Garter King of Arms 79 n.72; Lyon King of Arms 23, 65, 73, 162; Marchmont 68; Snowdon 162; Somerset 53–4, 67–9, 92–3, 189, *see also* Lindsay, David; Nairn, Alexander, of Sandford; Cumming, William, of Inverallochy; Holmes, Thomas
Hercules 161
Heriot, William 65
Hermitage Castle 184
Herries, Herbert, of Terregles 35 n.114, 113, 171
Herrie, John, lord of Terregles 183
Herrings 112

Historie du bon chevalier Messire Jacques de Lalain 53, 73
Historie de Guillaume le Maréchal 17 n.23, 67
Hogg, James 90
Holmes, Thomas, English herald 68
Holy Sepulchre 41, 48–50, 105, 106, 112
Holyrood Abbey 65, 77, 180
Holyrood Palace 53, 96, 99, 187, 188
Homildon *see* Humbleton Hill
horses 19, 75, 88, 100, 101, 146, 176
Hospitallers 104, 107, 108, 113, 181 n.53
household, noble 11, 19, 21, 60, 131–2, 179
household, royal 9, 10, 25, 34, 36, 158
Houston 127
Houston, Patrick 127
Houston, Peter, of that Ilk 186
humanism & humanists 2, 22–3, 42, 147, 161, 164, 165, 185, 190–1
Humbleton Hill 50, 57–8
Hume 33, 83, 184
Hume, Alexander, of that Ilk 19, 79, 115, 116, 119, 122, 180, 182
Hume, David 56
Hume, David, of Wedderburn 25
Hume, David, of Weddernburn 93, 98
Hume, Patrick, of Fastcastle 114
Hume, Patrick, of Polwarth 30, 50–1, 61, 84, 93, 97, 98
Hume, Thomas, of Langshaw 186
Hume family 50–1, 114
hunting 146

Inchcolm, abbey of 135
Innerpeffray 124
Innocent VIII 109
Inverness 54, 173, 186
Inverness Castle 32, 186
Irvine, Alexander 58
Irvine, Alexander, of Drum 15, 45, 46, 127
Isle of May 31 n.95, 118

James I, king of Scotland (1406–37)
  in English captivity 2, 44, 59, 70, 106, 117, 170, 172; *Kingis Quhair* 166; return to Scotland 6, 59, 70, 170, 171, 179; coronation 18, 27, 34, 35, 44–6, 54, 171, 179, 180; hostages 19, 54, 116, 117; charter witnesses 29; overseeing duel 64; and Bower 135; reputation 70, 176, 178–9; promotion of chivalry 6, 170–9; death 113, 180
James II, king of Scotland (1437–1460)
  baptism 18, 47–8, 172; coronation 180–1; wedding 37, 77–8, 181; charter witnesses 29; warmaking 17, 20, 80, 143, 179, 181–2; the Black Douglases 79, 80, 143, 145, 179, 182; murder of earl of Douglas 36, 79; nobles 37; overseeing duel 65; overseeing tournaments 73–6; public celebrations 52; reputation 72; use of chivalry 182
James III, king of Scotland (1460–88)
  coronation 28, 29, 30, 182, 183; education 37–8, 181; dubbing 183–4; order of chivalry 6, 81–2, 183, 185; warmaking 183–4; peace policy 81; exile of Arran 22; Bosworth 25; agreement with Darnley 27; charter witnesses 29; celebration of Shrove Tuesday 89–90; crusading 113; pilgrimages 118; criticism 147–50, 183; neglect of chivalry 182–3, 185; death at Sauchieburn 30
James IV, king of Scotland (1488–1513)
  comparison with James III 82; marriage 53–4, 91–3, 187, 188; birth of first son 91, 95; warmaking 24; dubbing on battlefield 50; coins great chain 24; silver spear tax 24; criticisms of 26; Sir Thomas Todd 16; Patrick Hume 30; Sir John Ramsay 34; public celebrations 53–4, 56; celebration of Shrove Tuesday 90–2, 187; as Wild Knight 94–5, 187; crusades 108–10, 114; and

INDEX

Hospitallers 107–8; pilgrimages 118–19; court poetry 157–8; revival of chivalry 168, 185–6, 187–8
James V, king of Scotland (1513–1542) 40, 55, 99–102, 118, 167, 189
Jedburgh Castle 155, 184
Jerusalem 41, 48–50, 106, 109, 110, 111, 112, 113, 114, 192
jesters *see* court jesters
John the Fearless, duke of Burgundy (d.1419) 58
Joshua 134, 161
jousts *see* tournaments
Judas 134, 161
Julius II 109–10

Keith, Alexander 58, 173
Keith, Robert 104
Keith, William 138
Keith, William, third earl of Marischal 24, 104, 105
Keith family 105
Kelso Abbey 28, 183
Kennedy, David 48
Kennedy, Gilbert, Lord Kennedy 38 n. 137
Kennedy, James 119–20, 123
Kennedy, John 38, 48
Kerr, Andrew 79 n.72, 115
Kerr, Cuthbert, lord of St Quentin 79 n.74
Kerr, James 73
Kerr, Robert, of Cessford, also of Ferniehirst 24, 33, 84, 97
Kilmaurs 120
Kilmaurs, Cuthbert, third Lord, earl of Glencairn 93, 97, 98
Kilpatrick, Thomas, laird of Closeburn 185
Kilwinning 118
King, Nicholas 35 n.115, 59
The Kingis Quhair 166
kingship, practice of 2, 6, 10, 11, 23, 70, 132, 148, 170–92
Kinloss Abbey 119
Kinross 24, 120
Kintyre pursuivant 68
Kirkpatrick, Roger 141

knight banneret 45–6, 60
knighthood
 age dubbed 17–19, 47; and the Church 12, 146; and kingship 4, 10, 42, 156; benefits of 25, 146–7; crown monopoly 56, 59, 60–2; eligibility for 8, 9, 10, 13–17, 47, 147, 149, 158, 191; development of 13, 16, 29–30, 167–8, 179, 188; lifestyle 2, 8, 9, 11–12, 13, 15, 17, 63, 136; oath 42–3; obligations of 13, 15, 16, 23, 25–39, 42–3, 146–7; public duties 8, 10, 29, 34-9, 146, 152, 169, 192; recruitment 12; social status 8, 9, 13 47, 87, 146, 158, 182
The Knightly Tale of Golagros and Gawain 28 n.76, 134
knights
 of England 13, 151; of France 13, 71, 86; of Germany 13; of Portugal 71
 as warriors 7, 13, 15, 23, 25, 26–34, 39, 107, 136, 152–3, 168, 176, 189–90; and ordinary soldiers 8, 21
Knox, Henry 64

Lalain, Jacques de 52–3, 72–7, 78–9, 115
Lalain, Simon de 52–3, 72–6
Lancelot 148, 168
Lancelot of the Laik 5, 133, 147–8
land grants 25, 30, 31, 51, 56, 61–2, 174
landownership 14 n.5, 15, 23
Lauder 51
Lauder, Alan 79 n.72, 115
Lauder, Alexander 13–14
Lauder, Alexander, of Hatton 183
Lauder, Alexander, provost of Edinburgh 188
Lauder, John 108
Lauder, John, of Hawton 116, 117
Lauder, Robert, of the Bass 188
Lauder, William 79 n.72, 115
law & lawyers 19, 39, 55, 69, 132, 191
Leckie, Walter 35 n.115, 59

INDEX

Leith 20, 94
Lennox 24, 27
Leo X 110
Leslie, Norman 104, 112
Leslie, Norman, of Fithkill 180
Leslie, Walter 104, 105, 112
Leslie family 112
Leverton, Henry, of Sawny 116
Liddale, James, of Halkerston 59–60, 81 n.81
Liddale, John 112
Liddale, John, squire 78
Liddale, Robert 73
Liège 58
Lincluden 121, 126
Linlithgow 68, 105
Linsday, Alexander 56, 61
Lindsay, Alexander 104, 105–6
Lindsay, Alexander, earl of Crawford (d.1439) 27, 54–5, 60, 116, 174
Lindsay, David 105, 106
Lindsay, David, lord of Crawford 56, 139
Lindsay, David, of Meikle 180
Lindsay, David, of the Mount (1486–1555) 23, 162
   Ane Satyre of the Thrie Estaitis 165
   Armorial 68, 135, 163
   Deploratioun 69, 100, 101, 167
   Historie of Squyer Meldrum 69, 155, 163–5, 168
   Iusting betuix Iames Watsoun and Ihone Barbour 88–9, 101–2, 163
   Testament of Papyngo 99, 143
Lindsay, James 105
Lindsay, James 141
Lindsay, John 125
Lindsay, John, de Byres 19, 180
Lindsay, John, earl of Crawford 116
Lindsay, Thomas 60
Lindsay, Walter, of Kinneff 58
Lindsay, William 189
Lindsay, William, of the Byres 106
Lioun the tailor 92
literacy 131–2, 143
literature *see* chivalric literature; romance literature; moral literature
Livingston, Alexander 125

Livingston, Alexander, of Callander 25, 181
Livingston, James, Lord Livingston 116
Livingston, Robert, of Drumry 181
Livingston family 73 n.47
Livre de chevalerie 10, 28, 34
Llull, Ramon 145
Loch Leven 135
Loch Lomond 132
Lochmaben Castle 185
Logan, James 65
Logan, John, of Restalrig 47
Logan, Simon, of Restalrig 47, 172
London 22, 104
Louis XI, king of France (1461–83) 28, 81, 114
Louis XII, king of France (1498–1514) 28, 109
Loutfut, Adam 68
Louvre 100
Lovell, Dominic 50
Lovell, Thomas 35 n.115, 59
Lundy, Robert, of Balgony 32, 51
Luxembourg, Jean de, bastard of St Pol 77
Lydgate, John 28 n.76
Lyle, Robert Lord 132

Madeleine of France 68–9, 100, 101, 167
Mair, John, *History of Greater Britain* 19
MacCulloch, Alexander 95, 97
MacDonald, Alexander, earl of Ross and Lord of the Isles 27, 173–4
MacDonald, John, earl of Ross and Lord of the Isles 25, 46 n.24
MacKenzie, Kenneth, of Kintail 127
Macleod, Alexander, of Dunvegan 128
Maitland, Patrick 183
Malta 108
Mar, David of 104
Marche, Olivier de la 77
The Margaret 94
marischal 66, 104, 105

INDEX

Marshal, William the (1147–1219)   17, 56 n.66
martial careers   26–34, 46
masons   24
Master of the King's Artillery *see* Kerr, Robert, of Cessford; Sandilands, John, of Hillhouse
Master of the King's Engines *see* Paule, Johannes
Master of the King's Household *see* Crichton, William, of that Ilk; Ogilvy, Walter, of Lintrathen; Gray, Andrew, of Foulis
Master of the Queen's Avery *see* Liddale, James, of Halcerston
Master Waxmaker to the King *see* Todd, William
Maxwell, Eustace   121
Maxwell, Herbert, of Caerlaverock   45, 46
Maxwell, John   115
McDowall, Dougal   121
Meldrum, William, of Cleish and Bynnis   163–4
Melrose   51
Melrose Abbey   176
Melun   170
Melville, John, of Raith   54 n.57, 189
Menteith   24, 30
Menteith, John of   58
Menzies, Gilbert, of Pitfoddels   17, 120, 127
Mercer, Andrew   15
merchants (mercantile class)   2, 16–17, 31 n.95, 49–50, *see also* burgesses
Meriadet, Hervey de   52–3, 72–6
Methven   121, 126
Methven Castle   25, 48 n.29
Meziere, Philip de   105
military orders
    Knights of the Hospital of St John   104, 107, 108, 113, 181 n.53
    Knighthood of the Passion of the Christ   106
    Knights of the Temple   107
    Teutonic Knights   105, 106
military service   16, 17–25, 26–37, 47–8, 50–2, 97, 98, 162, 172–3, 176–7, 181, 184–5, 186, 189–90, 192
military training   17–25, 37–8, 80, *see also* education
minstrels   68
Montague, William   167
Montgomery, Alexander   117
Montgomery, John, of Corscrag   55
Monymusk, John of   105
Monypenny, William   50 n.40
Moor, Peter the   90
moral literature   147–50
Morley, Lord   93
Mount Sinai   104
Mowbray, John, lord of Drummany   50, 58, 62
Murray, Adam   60
Murray, Andrew, warden of Scotland   137
Murray, Charles   79 n.72, 115
Murray, David, of Gask   171
Murray, David, of Tullibardine   122

Nairn, Sir Alexander, of Sandford   65, 73
Napier, Alexander, of Merchiston   183
national identity   4–5
Newcastle   37
Nine Worthies   134, 135, 161
nobility   8, 9, 69, 187
    Scottish   1, 2, 4, 10–11, 13, 21, 37, 40–1, 72, 80, 148, 172, 173, 182, 186, 189, 191–2
nobility, virtue of   7, 8, 147–50, 191
Norfolk   104
Norham   51, 175
Norny, Thomas   158–61
North Berwick   117
Northumberland, earl of   60
Nottingham   70

Observant Franciscans   108
Ogilvy, Alexander   173
Ogilvy, Andrew, of Inchmartin   180
Ogilvy, John, of Airlie   46 n.24
Ogilvy, John, of Finglask   32, 51, 186
Ogilvy, John, of Lintrathen   79, 115

223

INDEX

Ogilvy, Patrick, of Auchterhouse 27, 34–5, 35 n.114, 59, 144, 166, 171, 173
Ogilvy, Walter, of Deskfurd 180
Ogilvy, Walter, of Lintrathen 9, 27, 37, 171, 173, 174
Ogilvy, William 95
Ogistoun, Alexander of 23
Order of Combats for Life in Scotland 66–7, 70
orders of chivalry 189
   in Scotland 6, 49, 81, 129–30, 183
   Order of the Elephant 81, 120, 185
   Order of the Garter 55 n.62, 77 n.62, 170 n.4
   Order of St Michael 81, 185
ordinary soldiers 8, 21
Ormiston 184
Ormond, marquis 48
Otterburn 51, 136
Otterburn, Adam, of Redhall 55

pageantry 63, 69, 91–2, 94, 99, 100–1, 188
Palice of Honour 92, 188
Paris 79, 100, 185
parliament
   legislation and statutes 17, 18, 19, 20–1, 24, 132; sumptuary laws 68; general council 1433 71
   of James I 46; of 1424 175; of 1426 46, 175; of 1428 46; of 1430 54, 174; of 1463 37; of 1464 37; of 1482 184–5; of 1488 48, 182, 184; of 1491 31
Passion of the Christ *see under* military orders
Paston family 15
Paston, John, squire 22, 166
Paston, Sir John 22
patronage, noble 80, 119–30
patronage, royal 4, 9, 12, 157–65, 182
Paule, Johannes 178
Percy, Sir Henry 65
Perth 71–2, 113, 178
Perthshire 24, 25
Peter I of Cyprus 104, 106
Philip the Good, duke of Burgundy (d.1466) 77, 78, 79, 115, 183

piety 11, 12, 36, 103–30
pilgrim badges 111–12
pilgrim sites
   Amiens 110, 113, 114, 116, 117
   Canterbury 36, 110, 116–17
   Isle of May 118
   Jerusalem 41, 48–50, 106, 109, 110, 111, 112, 113, 114, 192
   Rome 36, 78–9, 109, 110, 113, 114–16
   Santiago de Compostela 110, 112
   Tain 118, 119
   Whithorn 95, 118
pilgrimage 36, 41, 48–50, 78, 95, 103, 105, 110–19, 192
Pinkie 165
Pitscottie, *Historie* 31, 53, 85, 96
plague 30
Pluscarden chronicle *see Book of Pluscarden*
poetry *see* epic poetry; court poetry
poets *see* court poets
Porcari, Stephen 47
The Porteous of Noblenes 149
Preston, Alexander, canon of Glasgow 48, 106
Preston, Archibald 49 n.35
Preston, George, of that Ilk 110
Preston, Henry, of Craigmillar 105, 106
Preston, John 49 n.35
Preston, Simon, of Craigmillar 105, 106
Preston, Simon, of that Ilk 110
Preston, William 49, 111, 118
Preston family 106
Prose Lancelot 148
Prussia 104
pursuivants 68, *see also* heralds

quarriers 24
Quentin 160

Ramsay, Alexander, of Cockpen 189
Ramsay, Alexander, of Dalhousie (d.1342) 21–2, 105, 137
Ramsay, Alexander, of Dalhousie 171
Ramsay, John 33

INDEX

Ramsay, John, Lord Bothwell (d.1513) 33–4
Randolph, Thomas, earl of Moray 61
Rannoch 24
Ratho 14
Recklington, Alexander 104
Rednach 51, 61
Rhodes 106, 107, 113
Richard II, king of England (1377–99) 139
Richard III, king of England (1483–85) 82
Robert I (Robert the Bruce), king of Scotland (1306–29) 1, 26, 50, 61, 113, 132, 134, 152, 156, 176
Robert II, king of Scotland (1371–90) 1
Robert III, king of Scotland (1390–1406) 1, 18
Rodel 128
romance literature 132–5, 147–8, 164, 167–8, 192
Rome 36, 78–9, 109, 110, 113, 114–16
Roslin, battle of 167
Roslin, Sir Thomas 138
Roslin Castle 80, 143, 179–80
Roslin Chapel 68, 119, 120, 122, 123
Ross, John, Lord of Hawkhead 93, 97, 127
Ross, John, of Hawkhead 18, 52–3, 62, 93, 97, 181
Ross, John, of Malevyn 186
Ross, John, of Montgrennan 39, 191
Rossy, William 35 n.115, 59
Rothesay Castle 28
Rouen 50 n.40
Round Table, knights of the 72, 187
royal court *see* court
royal entries 68–9, 92, 100, 101
royal household *see* household, royal
royal service 15, 16, 25–6, 29–30, 31, 32, 34–9, 55, 59–60, 172
Roxburgh 36, 155, 177–8
Renaissance, ideals and influence in Scotland 2, 7, 39–40, 42, 86, 100, 161, 165, 189
Rutherford, John 60

St Adrian, shrine of 118
St Andrew, shrines of 117
St Andrews 101, 117
St Andrews, archbishop of 93
St Andrews, bishop of 44, 119–20, 123
St Bernard of Clairvaux 89
St Bridget of Sweden 106
St Duthac, shrine of 118
St Fillan, shrine of 118
St George, altar of 120
St Giles 112, 118
St James, altar of 120
St John 122
St John, shrine of 110, 114, 116
St Michael 129
St Mungo, altar of 120
St Ninian, shrine of 95, 118
St Paul 115
St Peter 115
St Sebastian, altar of 120
St Serf, priory of 135, 137
St Serf, shrine of 118
St Thomas, shrine of 110, 116
St Winin, shrine of 118
Samson 161
Sandilands, John, of Hillhouse 32–3
Sauchieburn 30, 31, 50, 114
Scone 44, 118, 171
Scotichronicon see Bower, Walter
Scotland, influences from
   Low Countries 6, 32, 49–50, 52–3, 69, 72 191
   Denmark and Norway 80
   England 6, 22, 45–6, 179
   France 6, 32, 32 n.103 191
   Germany 69
Scott, Walter, of Kirkurd 180, 182
Scott, William, of Balweary 124
Scrope *v.* Grosvenor, 1386 18
Scrope, John 18
Scrope, John, of Masham 71 n.38
Scrymgeour, John 171
Scrymgeour, Mariota 108
Scrymgeour family 120
Selbie 151
Semple 124, 126
Semple, John Lord 124

INDEX

Senlis 59
Sens 71
service *see* military service; royal service; administrative service
Seton 120, 124
Seton, Alexander, earl of Huntly 129
Seton, Alexander, master of Montgomery 93
Seton, Alexander, of Gordon 27, 113, 174
Seton, Alexander, of Touchfraser 186
Seton, George, first Lord Seton 18, 120, 124, 126, 127, 180
Seton, John 125, 126
Seton, Jonathan 65
ships 31, 94, 109
shooting 21
Shrove Tuesday 52 n.51, 76, 86–92, 98, 187
sieges 7, 24, 25, 34, 36, 50, 65, 138, 167, 170, 177–8, 181
silver spear tax 24
Simon, brother of Waltheof 176–7
Sinclair, Catherine 126
Sinclair, David 186
Sinclair, David, of Swinburgh 120
Sinclair, Oliver 100–1, 143
Sinclair, Patrick 91–2, 93, 95, 97
Sinclair, William 84
Sinclair, William, earl of Orkney 68, 80, 120, 123, 142, 143, 145, 182
Sinclair family 179
Sir Tristrem 133
Sixtus IV 108–9
Smith, Thomas 64
smiths 24
Snowdon *see* Stirling; heralds
soldiers *see* ordinary soldiers
Somerville, John, of Camusnethan 186
Somerville, Thomas 121
squires 8, 17, 19–20, 21, 22, 23, 29, 39, 51–2, 56, 61, 76–7, 78, 112, 116, 138, 145, 151, 192
Stanley, Lord, English steward 60
Stewart, Alan, of Darnley (d.1439) 27
Stewart, Alexander 105

Stewart, Alexander, earl of Mar (d.1435) 23, 27, 35 n.113, 58, 173, 173 n.18
Stewart, Alexander, duke of Albany 25, 45, 59–60, 81, 183, 185
Stewart, Alexander, of Darnley 105
Stewart, Alexander, son of Murdac, duke of Albany 171
Stewart, Andrew 36 n.126, 58, 182
Stewart, Bernard, third Seigneur d'Aubigny (1447–1508) 28, 39, 96, 109, 161–2
  Traité dur L'Art de la Guerre 28, 39, 191
Stewart, David 173
Stewart, David, duke of Rothesay, earl of Carrick and Atholl 18, 52
Stewart, David, of Rosyth 135, 171
Stewart, James 95
Stewart, James, earl of Buchan 184
Stewart, James, of Auchterhouse 30 n.81
Stewart, John 105
Stewart, John, earl of Atholl 30 n.84
Stewart, John, first Lord Darnley (d.1495) 27–8, 182, 185
Stewart, John, of Cardney 18, 171
Stewart, John, of Darnley (d.1429) 27, 112, 124
Stewart, John, Red, of Dundonald (d.1425) 18, 171
Stewart, Margaret, daughter of James I, wife of Louis XI 36
Stewart, Murdac, duke of Albany (d.1425) 35, 44
Stewart, Robert, of Atholl 178
Stewart, Robert, of Durisdeer 105
Stewart, Thomas, earl of Angus (d. c.1362) 56, 61
Stewart, Walter 50, 56 n.66
Stewart, Walter, earl of Atholl 115, 117, 121
Stewart, Walter, of Strathavon 55
Stewarts of Darnley 27–8
Stirling 65, 85, 86, 99, 158
Stirling Castle 30, 52, 72, 73, 78
Stormonth 24
Strathearn 24
Strathmiglo 124

226

INDEX

Strigale, William   111
Surrey, lord of   93
Sutherland, Alexander, of
    Dunbeath   115, 119, 120
Sutherland, John of   58
Swinton, Sir John   35 n.113, 50, 57–8,
    173 n.18

The Tail of the Brig of Mantribil   134
tailor   64
The Tale of Syr Eglamaire of Artoys   134
The Tale of Syr Valtir the Bald Leslye
    134
Tannenberg   106
Tarbolton   124
Taylor, Christopher   87
Templars   107
Teutonic Knights   105, 106
Thre Prestis of Peblis   148–9
Threave Castle   37, 181
Todd, Sir Thomas   15, 16
Todd, Thomas   16
Todd, William   16
tomb effigies *see* effigies
Torphichen   107, 108
tournaments   7, 16, 20, 34, 39, 45,
    52–4, 56, 63–102, 131, 163, 176, 178,
    179, 183, 185, 186, 187, 189, 190;
    organisation of   65–7; royal
    team   84, 97–8, 187
    Brittany   136; Chauvency   67;
        Spanish   67
    Dunstable 1334   95
    1390s   72, 138, 139
    Edinburgh 1398   18
    Perth 1433   71–2, 178
    Stirling 1449   37 n.128, 52–3, 72–6,
        78, 89, 127, 179, 181
    Bruges 1449   76–7
    Calais 1449   77
    Holyrood 1449   77–8
    Chalon sur Saône 1450   36 n.55,
        78–9, 115
    Paris 1485   185
    1491   83
    Aire 1494   79 n.74
    for Perkin Warbeck 1496   83, 84, 97,
        187
    Hume 1497   83, 97
    Edinburgh c.1500   85
    1502   87
    1503   90, 187
    Greensward 1503   91, 187
    Midsummer 1504   93–4
    Leith 1505   94
    1505   90, 187
    1506   90, 187
    Stirling 1506   86
    Wild Knight and Black Lady 1507
        63, 83, 91, 94, 95–6, 187
    Wild Knight and Black Lady 1508
        28, 53–4, 63, 83, 94, 96–7, 109,
        162, 176, 187
    Holyrood 1527   99
    Stirling 1529   99
    Holyrood 1530   99
    Stirling 1531   99
    1532   99
    1533   99
    Stirling 1534   99
    1535   100
    Paris 1537   100–1
    St Andrews 1538   101
    Falkland 1539   102
    1539   102
    Edinburgh 1540   102
    1541   102
    1542   102
Tournelles   100
tourneying societies   69
Tours, Anne de la   81
Towers, George, burgess of Edinburgh
    30 n.84
Towers, John, of Dalry   105
Travels of Sir John Mandeville   113
treason   11, 22, 38, 64–5, 70, 81
Treyton, John of   93
Treyton, Lord   93
trial by arms *see* duels
Troyes, Chrétien de, *Lancelot*   67
truce with England   31, 37, 55, 141
Tudor, Margaret, wife of James IV   32
    n.99, 53–4, 91–3, 95, 97, 187, 188
Tullibardine   122
Turnbull, John   35 n.115, 59

227

Umfraville, Ingram 153
unicorns 78, 129, 120, 183
Upsettlington 51
Usana, Bertrand 70

Verneuil 50 n.40
Vernon, Laurence 35 n.115, 59
Vinea, Peter de, Frederick II's chancellor 8
violence 12, 39–40, 84, 144, 145, 150, 151, 152–3, 154, 157
visitors to Scotland 23, 26, 47, 49–50, 52–3, 72–6, 85–6, 91

The Wallace see Blind Harry
Wallace, Andrew, elder brother of William Wallace 14
Wallace, Malcolm, father of William Wallace 14–15
Wallace, William 14–15, 150–1, 167
Wallace, William, of Craigie 183
Waltheof, abbot of Melrose 176–7
wapinschawings 20–1, 175
war 5, 7, 8, 11, 17, 20–1, 34, 39, 45, 56, 138–9, 144–5, 154, 158, 179, 184, 186–7
  against England 20, 21, 24–5, 26, 27, 28–9, 31, 32–4, 60, 107, 143, 150, 151, 157, 184, 186, 190
  desertion 174–5
  England and France at 71
  Italian wars 28
  mustering for battle 23
  payment of labourers 24

Warbeck, Perkin 32, 34, 83, 84, 187
Wardlaw, John, of Riccarton 116
Wardlaw, Henry, bishop of St Andrews 44, 115
Wardlaw, Walter 104
Wark Castle 29, 183
Wawane, Adam 73
weapons 19, 20
Webiton, John 167
Wedderburn 184
weddings, royal 52, 54
Wells, Lord 139
Wemyss, Sir John, of Kincaldrum 135
Whithorn 95, 118
Wild Knight and the Black Lady *see* tournaments
Windsor Castle 170
Wood, Andrew, of Largo 18-19, 30–2, 33 n.105, 51, 118, 184
Worcester, earl of 75
Wyntoun, Alan 110
Wyntoun, Andrew (d.1426) 14, 44
  Original Chronicle 135–9, 166–7
Wyntoun, Ingram, squire 138

Yellow Carvel 31
Yester 121
York 37
York, archbishop of 93